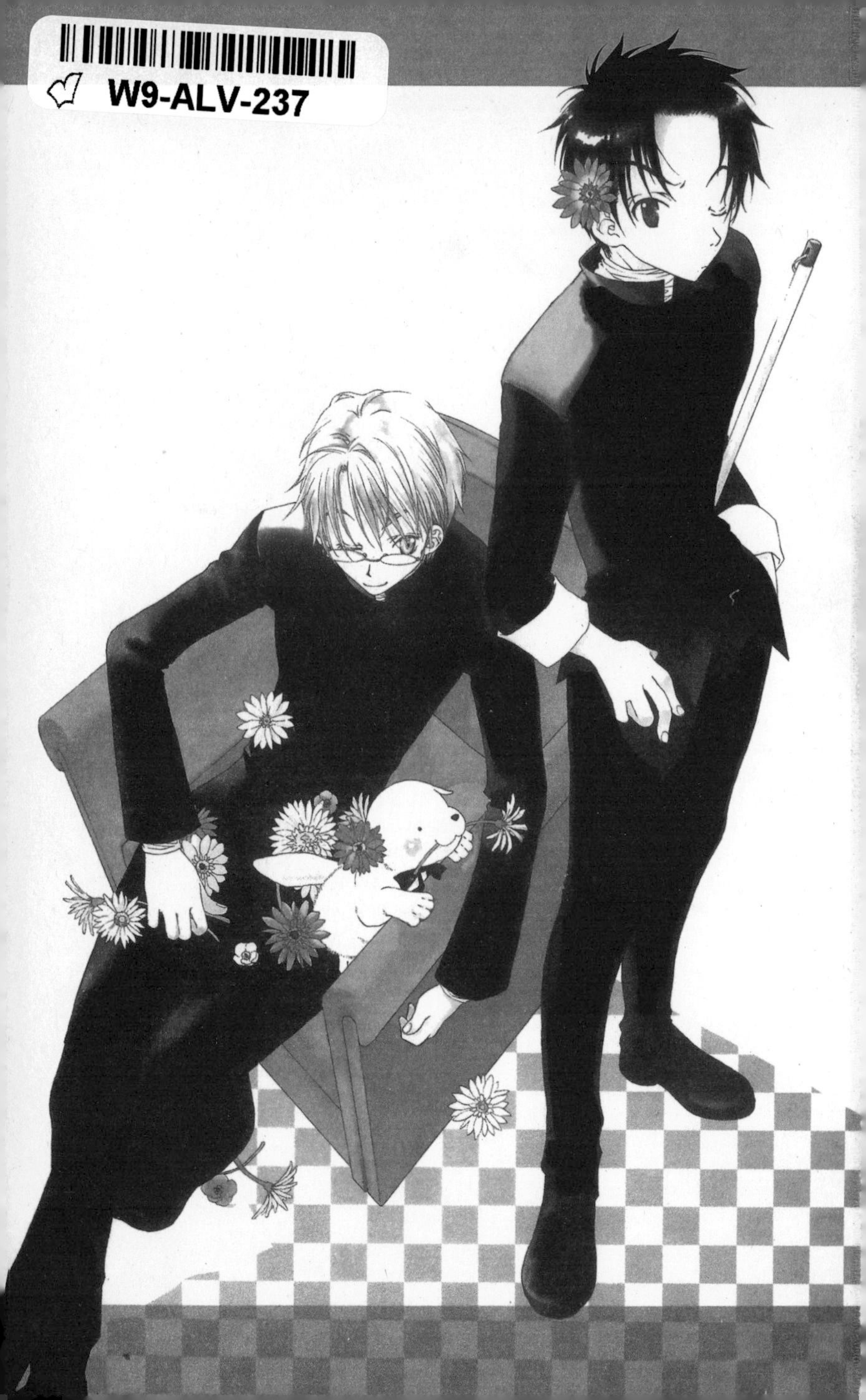

Translation – Christine Schilling
Adaptation – Mallory Reaves
Lettering – Jihye Hong
Production Manager – James Dashiell
Editor – Brynne Chandler

A Go! Comi manga

Published by Go! Media Entertainment, LLC

Black Sun Silver Moon Volume 2
© 2003 TOMO MAEDA
All rights reserved.
First published in Japan in 2003 by SHINSHOKAN Co., Ltd. Tokyo
English Version published by Go! Media Entertainment, LLC under license
from SHINSHOKAN Co., Ltd.

English Text © 2007 Go! Media Entertainment, LLC. All rights reserved.

Visit us online at www.gocomi.com
e-mail: info@gocomi.com

T 251322

ISBN 978-1-933617-21-3

First printed in July 2007

1   2   3   4   5   6   7   8   9

Manufactured in the United States of America

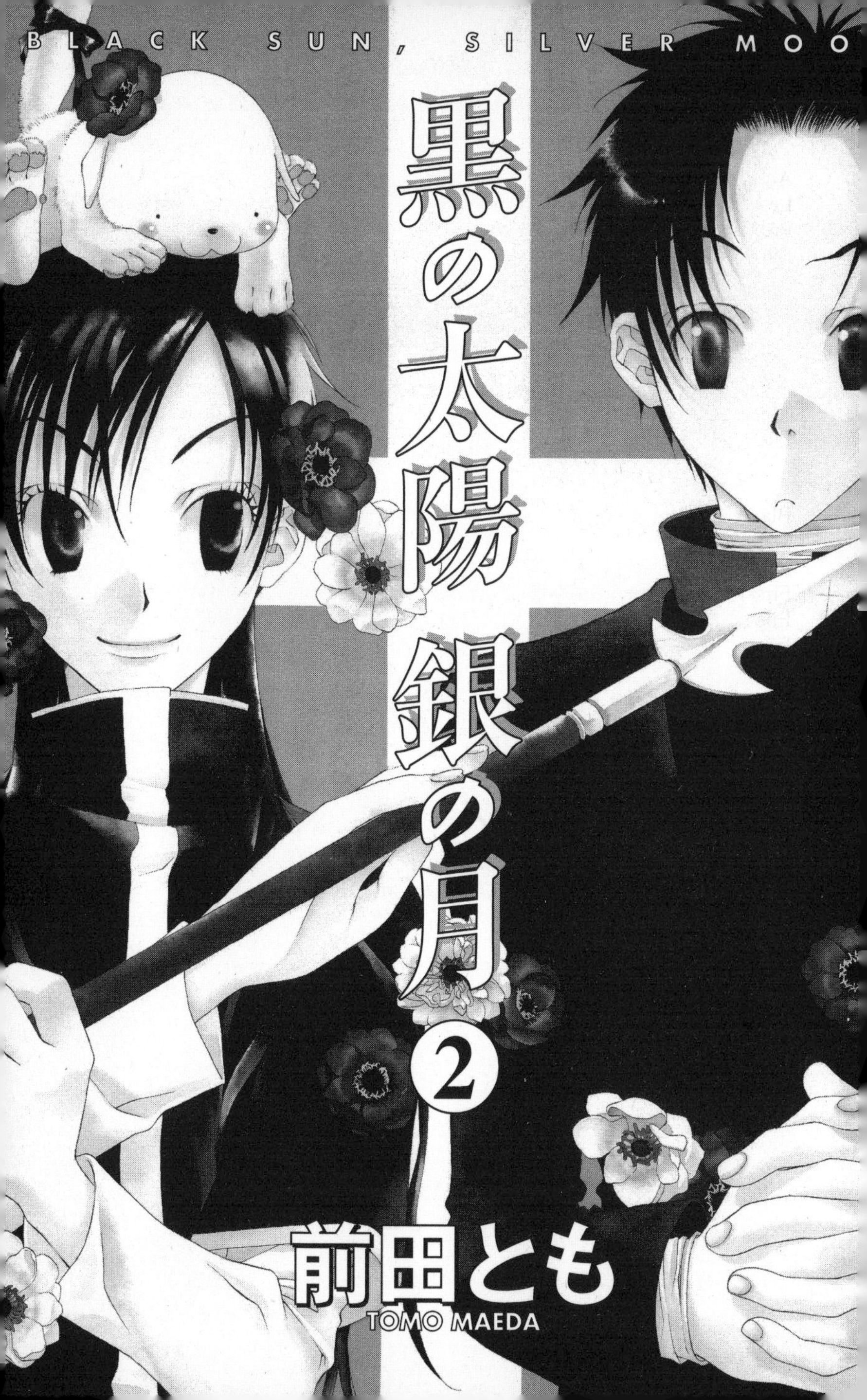
BLACK SUN, SILVER MOO
黒の太陽銀の月
2
前田とも
TOMO MAEDA

CONTENTS

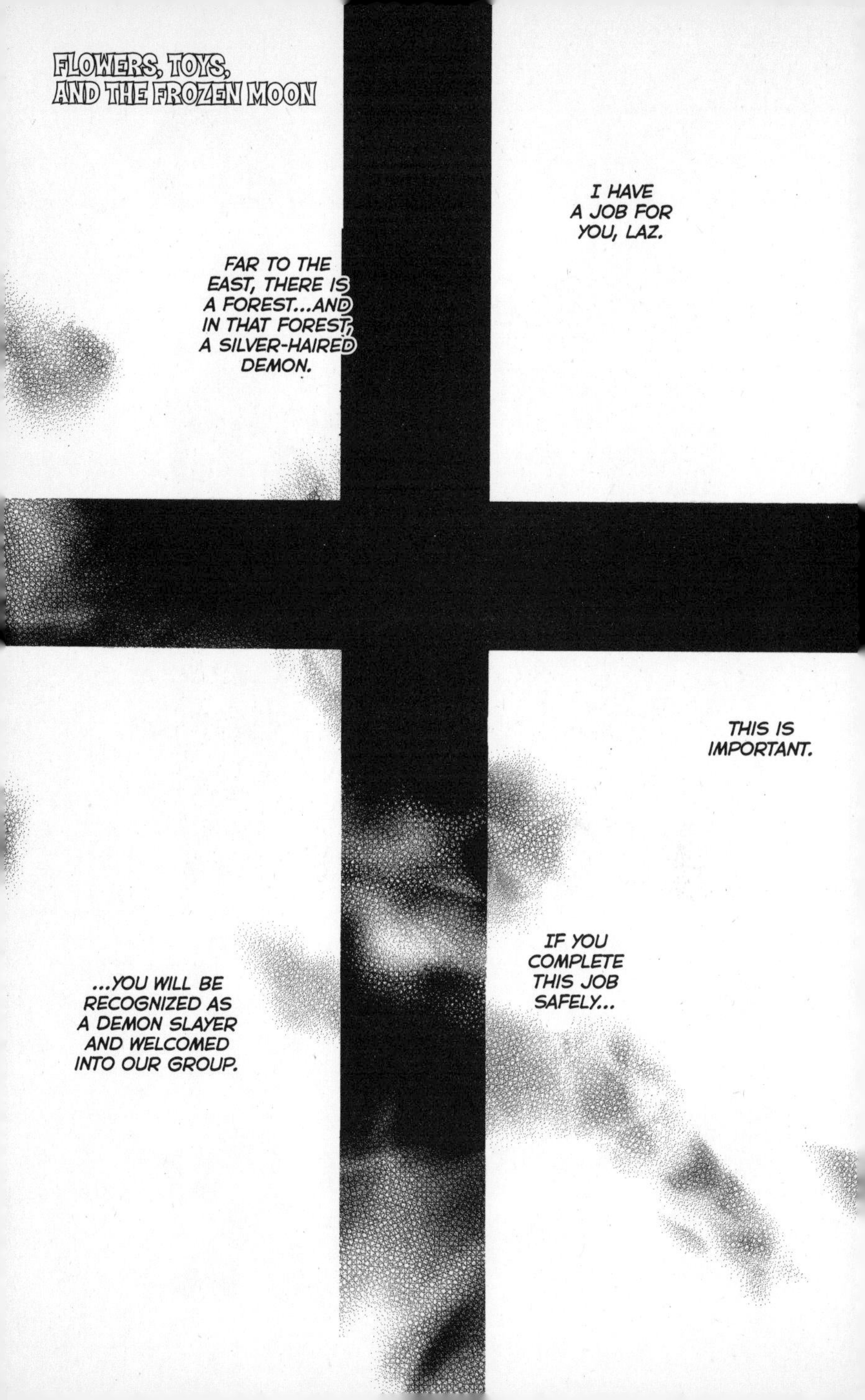
FLOWERS, TOYS, AND THE FROZEN MOON
I HAVE A JOB FOR YOU, LAZ.
FAR TO THE EAST, THERE IS A FOREST...AND IN THAT FOREST, A SILVER-HAIRED DEMON.
THIS IS IMPORTANT.
IF YOU COMPLETE THIS JOB SAFELY...
...YOU WILL BE RECOGNIZED AS A DEMON SLAYER AND WELCOMED INTO OUR GROUP.

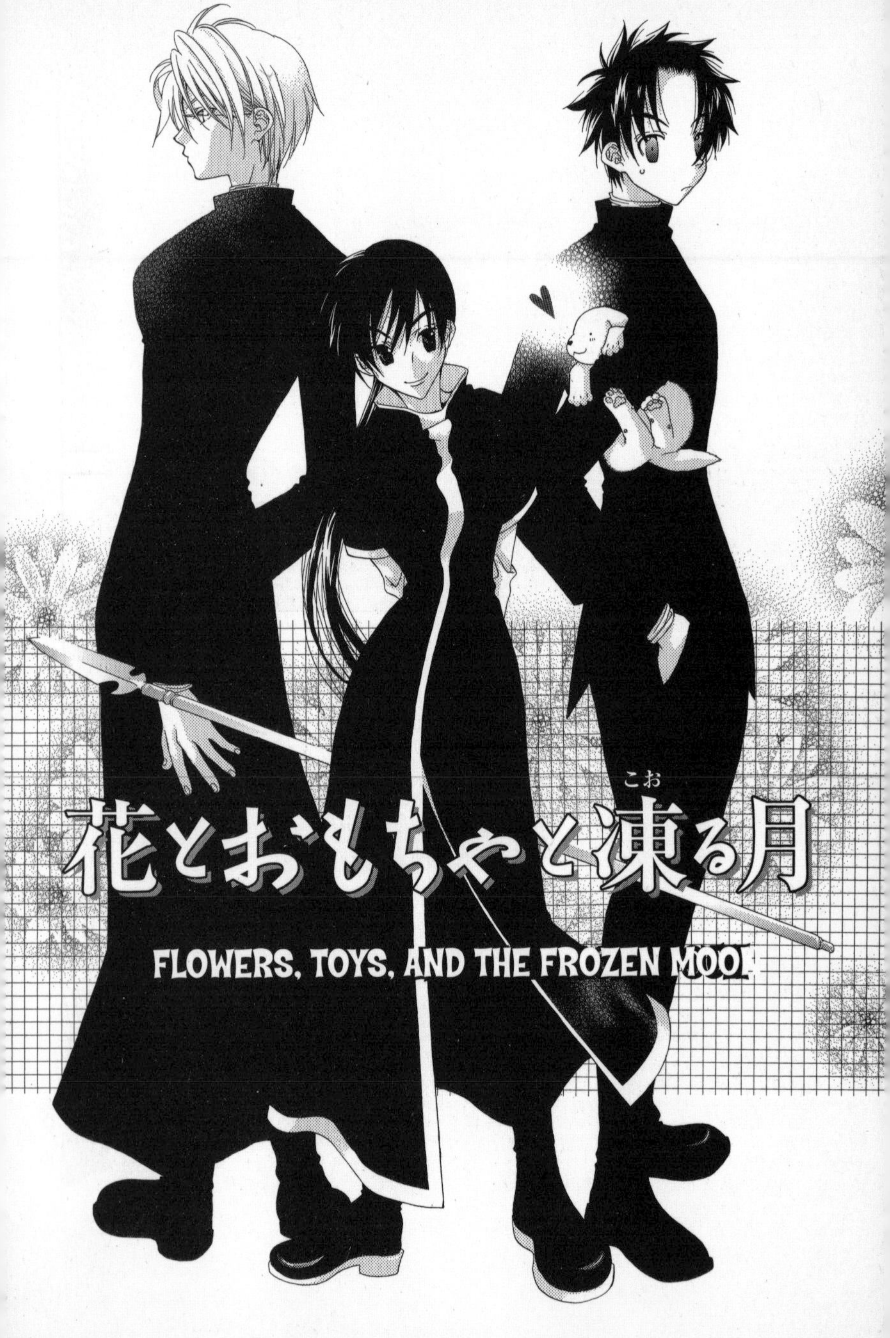
花とおもちゃと凍る月
FLOWERS, TOYS, AND THE FROZEN MOON

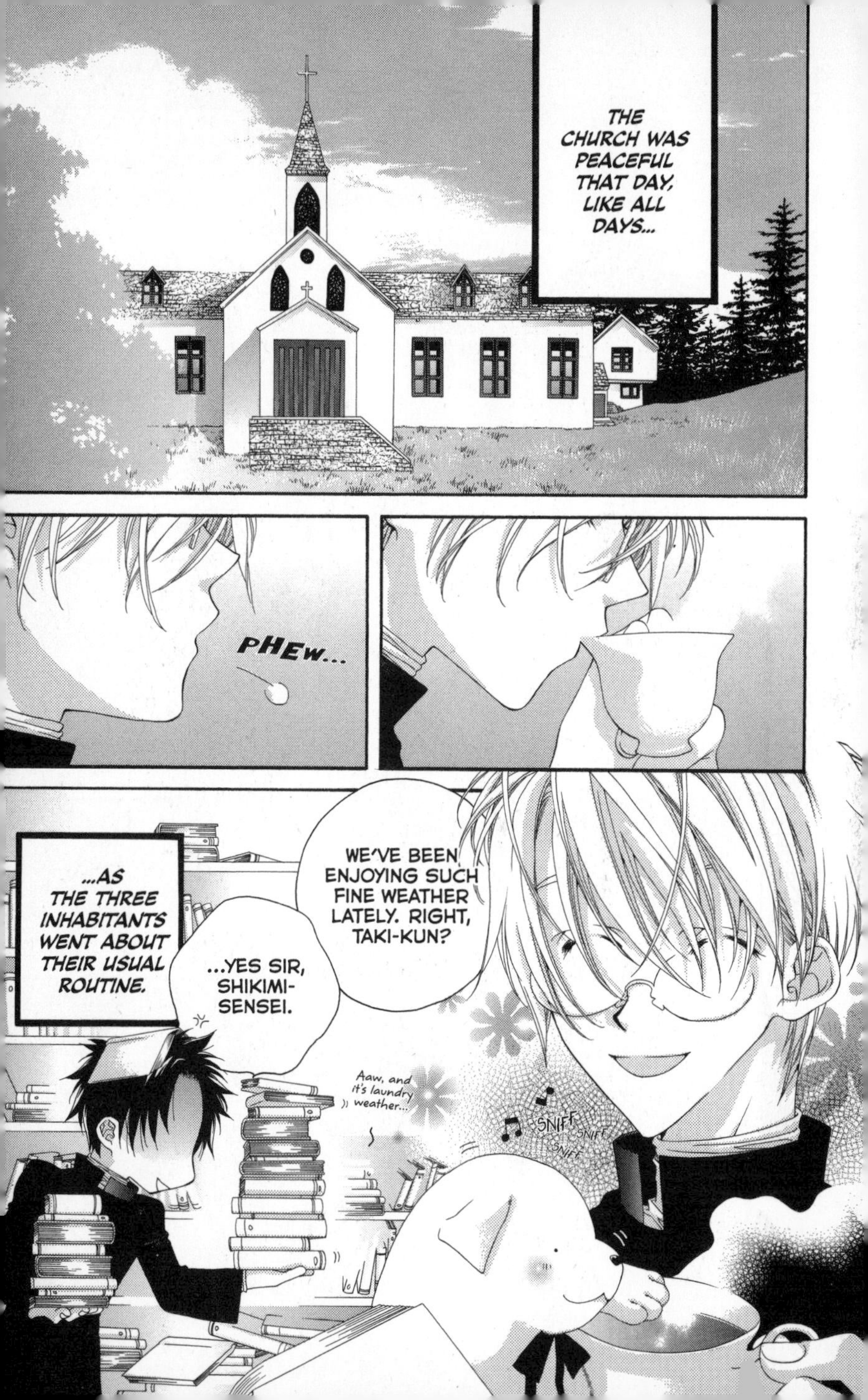
THE CHURCH WAS PEACEFUL THAT DAY, LIKE ALL DAYS...
PHEW...
WE'VE BEEN ENJOYING SUCH FINE WEATHER LATELY. RIGHT, TAKI-KUN?
...AS THE THREE INHABITANTS WENT ABOUT THEIR USUAL ROUTINE.
...YES SIR, SHIKIMI-SENSEI.
Aaw, and it's laundry weather...
SNIFF SNIFF SNIFF

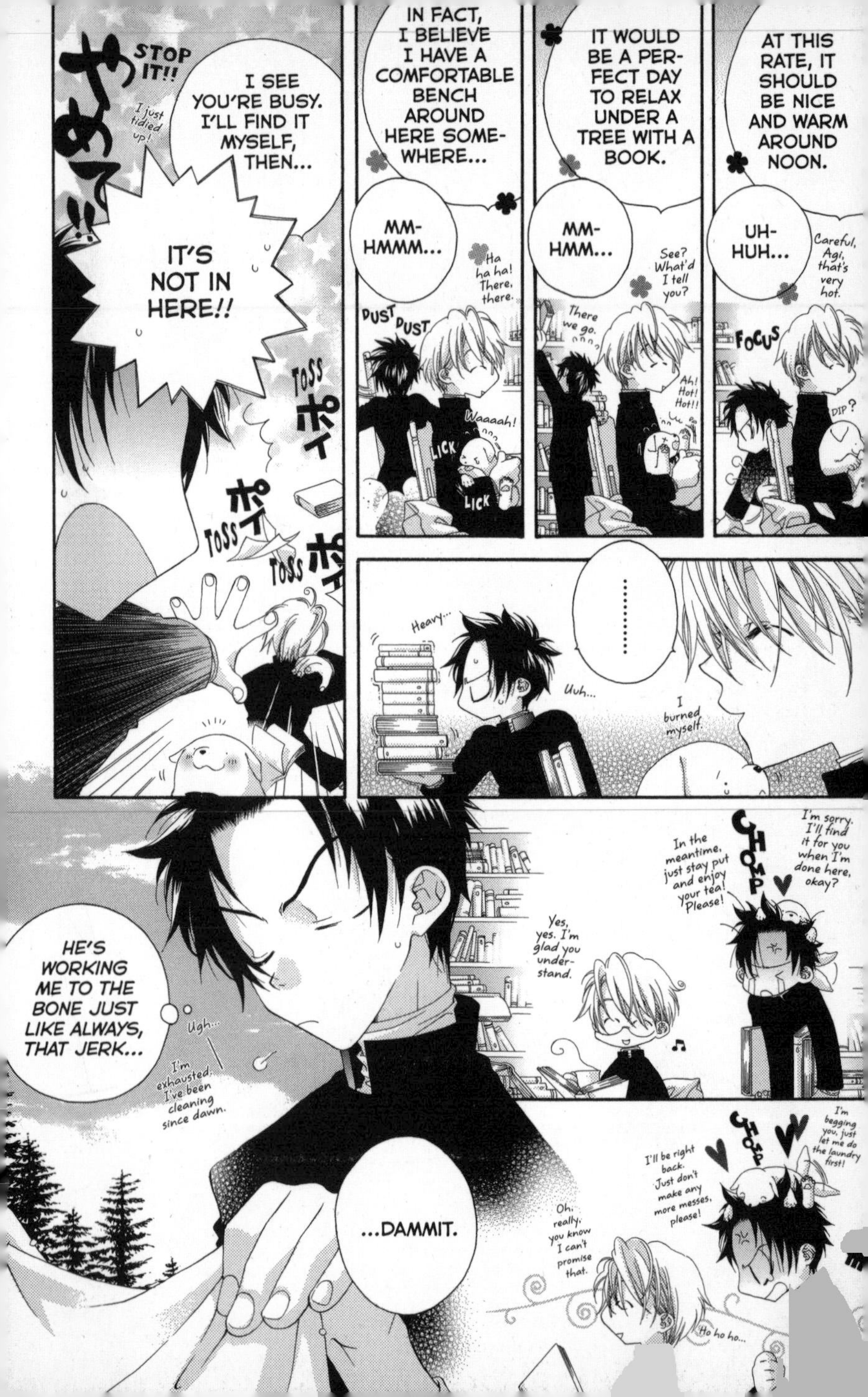
AT THIS RATE, IT SHOULD BE NICE AND WARM AROUND NOON.
Careful, Agi, that's very hot.
UH-HUH...
FOCUS
DIP?
IT WOULD BE A PERFECT DAY TO RELAX UNDER A TREE WITH A BOOK.
See? What'd I tell you?
MM-HMM...
Ah! Hot! Hot!!
There we go.
IN FACT, I BELIEVE I HAVE A COMFORTABLE BENCH AROUND HERE SOMEWHERE...
Ha ha ha! There, there.
MM-HMMM...
Waaaah!
DUST DUST
LICK
LICK
......
I burned myself.
Uuh...
Heavy...
I SEE YOU'RE BUSY. I'LL FIND IT MYSELF, THEN...
STOP IT!!
やめて!!
I just tidied up!
IT'S NOT IN HERE!!
TOSS ポイ
TOSS ポイ
TOSS ポイ
I'm sorry. I'll find it for you when I'm done here, okay?
CHOMP
In the meantime, just stay put and enjoy your tea! Please!
Yes, yes. I'm glad you understand.
I'm begging you, just let me do the laundry first!
CHOMP
I'll be right back. Just don't make any more messes, please!
Oh, really, you know I can't promise that.
Ho ho ho...
Ugh...
HE'S WORKING ME TO THE BONE JUST LIKE ALWAYS, THAT JERK...
I'm exhausted. I've been cleaning since dawn.
...DAMMIT.

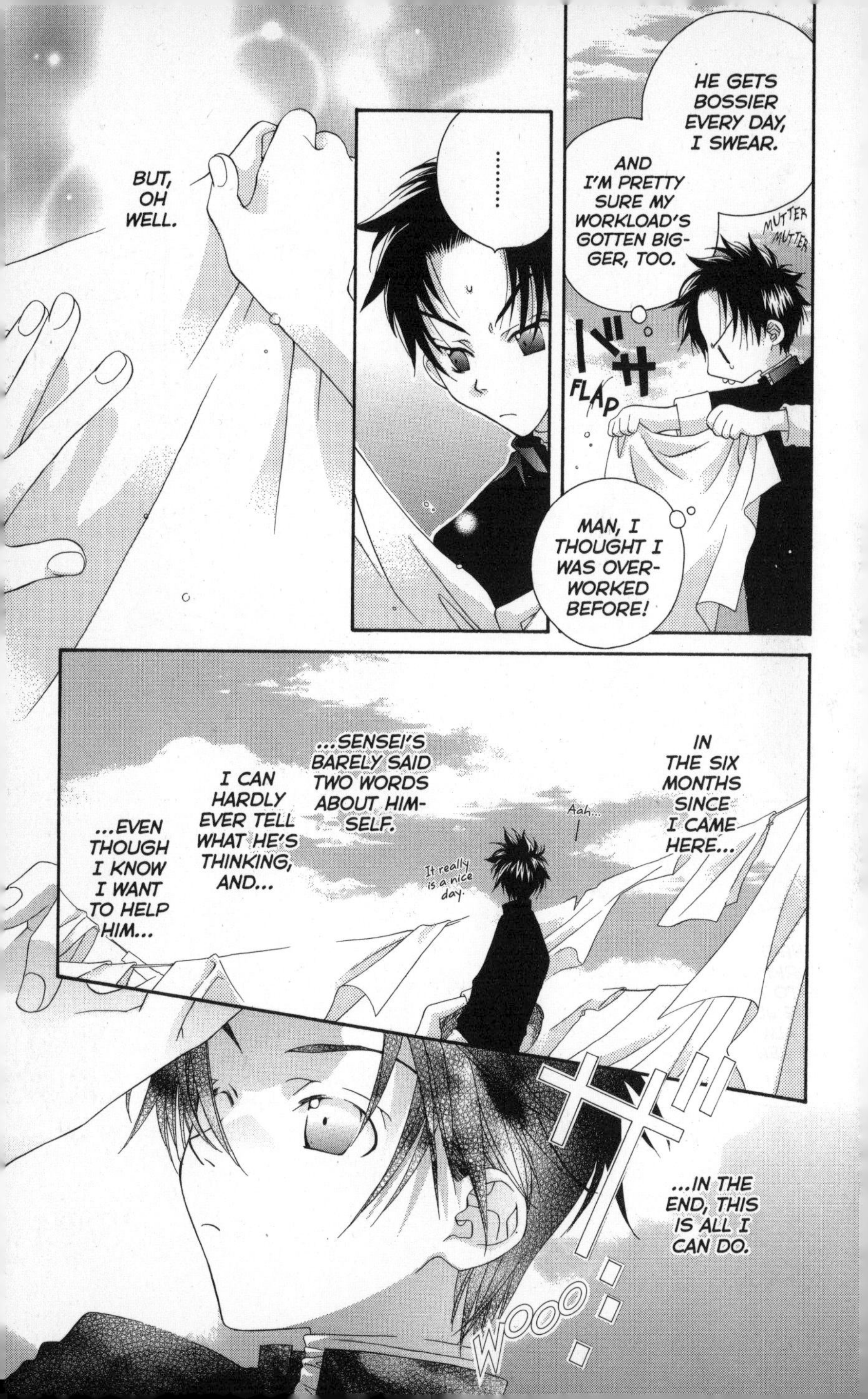
HE GETS BOSSIER EVERY DAY, I SWEAR.
AND I'M PRETTY SURE MY WORKLOAD'S GOTTEN BIGGER, TOO.
MUTTER MUTTER
FLAP
MAN, I THOUGHT I WAS OVERWORKED BEFORE!
......
BUT, OH WELL.
IN THE SIX MONTHS SINCE I CAME HERE...
Aah...
It really is a nice day.
...SENSEI'S BARELY SAID TWO WORDS ABOUT HIMSELF.
I CAN HARDLY EVER TELL WHAT HE'S THINKING, AND...
...EVEN THOUGH I KNOW I WANT TO HELP HIM...
...IN THE END, THIS IS ALL I CAN DO.
WOOO...

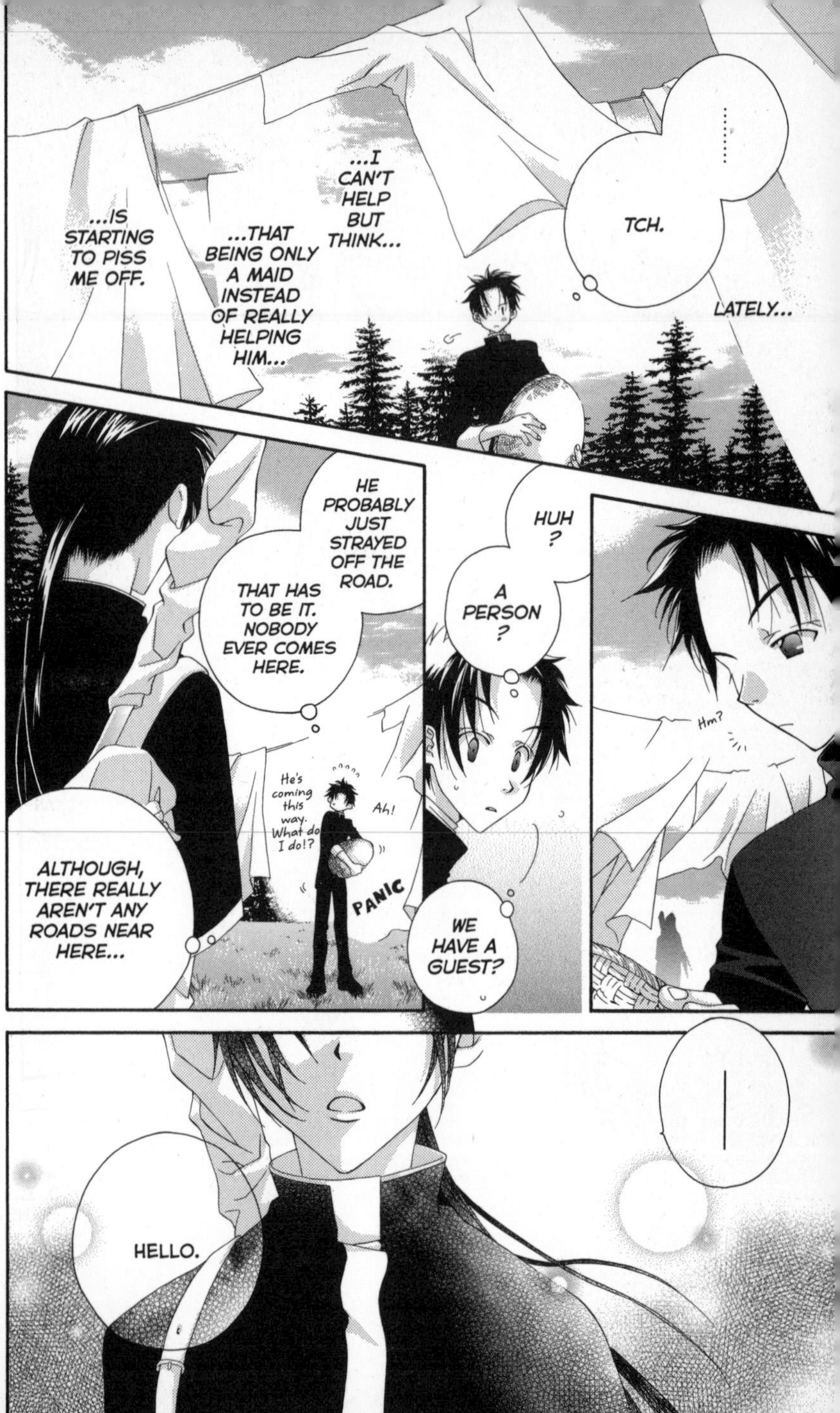
......
TCH.
LATELY...
...I CAN'T HELP BUT THINK...
...THAT BEING ONLY A MAID INSTEAD OF REALLY HELPING HIM...
...IS STARTING TO PISS ME OFF.
Hm?
HUH?
A PERSON?
WE HAVE A GUEST?
HE PROBABLY JUST STRAYED OFF THE ROAD.
THAT HAS TO BE IT. NOBODY EVER COMES HERE.
He's coming this way. What do I do!?
Ah!
PANIC
ALTHOUGH, THERE REALLY AREN'T ANY ROADS NEAR HERE...
—
HELLO.

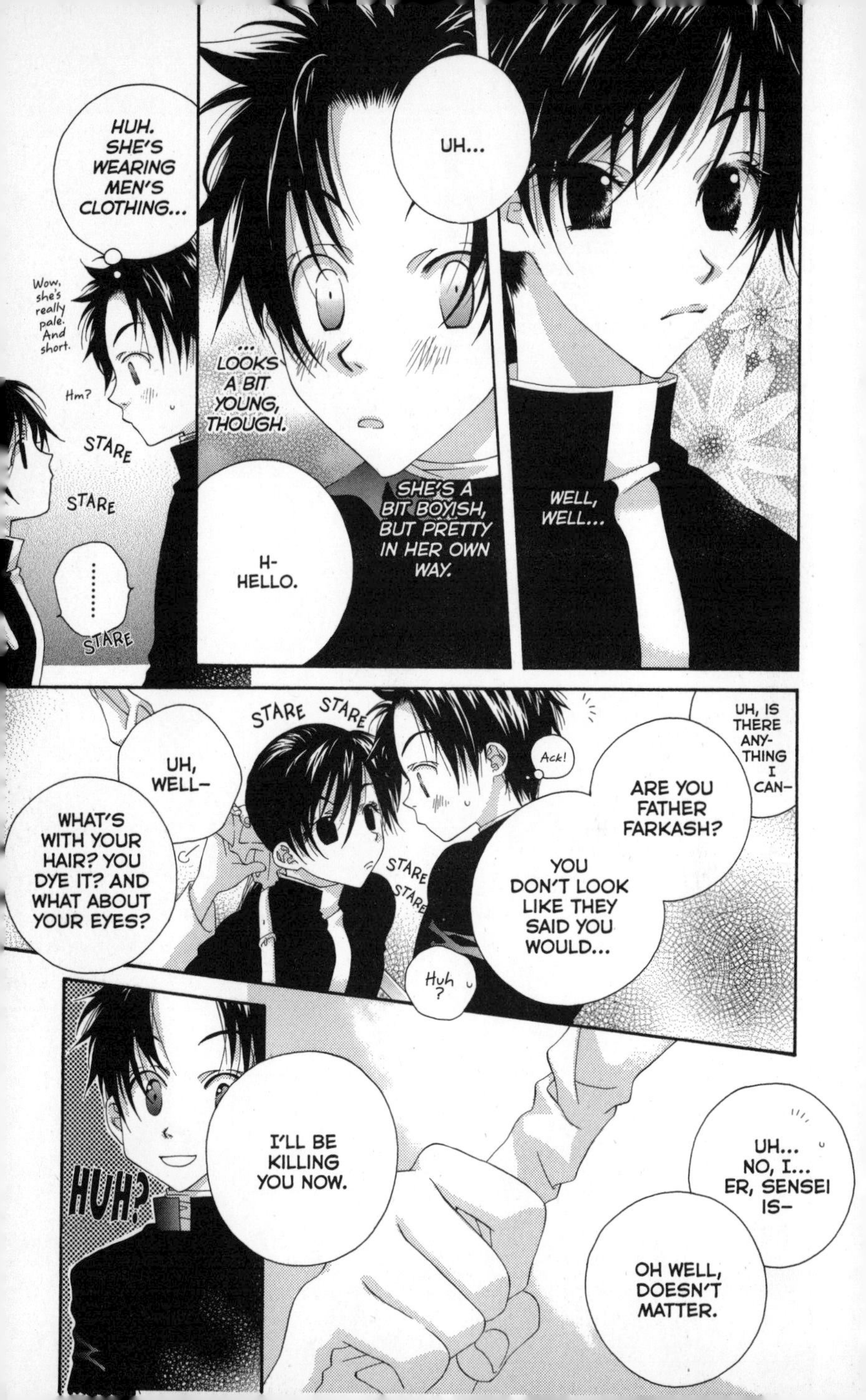
UH...
WELL, WELL...
... LOOKS A BIT YOUNG, THOUGH.
SHE'S A BIT BOYISH, BUT PRETTY IN HER OWN WAY.
H- HELLO.
HUH. SHE'S WEARING MEN'S CLOTHING...
Wow, she's really pale. And short.
Hm?
STARE
STARE
......
STARE
UH, IS THERE ANYTHING I CAN-
Ack!
ARE YOU FATHER FARKASH?
YOU DON'T LOOK LIKE THEY SAID YOU WOULD...
STARE STARE
UH, WELL-
WHAT'S WITH YOUR HAIR? YOU DYE IT? AND WHAT ABOUT YOUR EYES?
STARE STARE
Huh?
UH... NO, I... ER, SENSEI IS-
OH WELL, DOESN'T MATTER.
I'LL BE KILLING YOU NOW.
HUH?

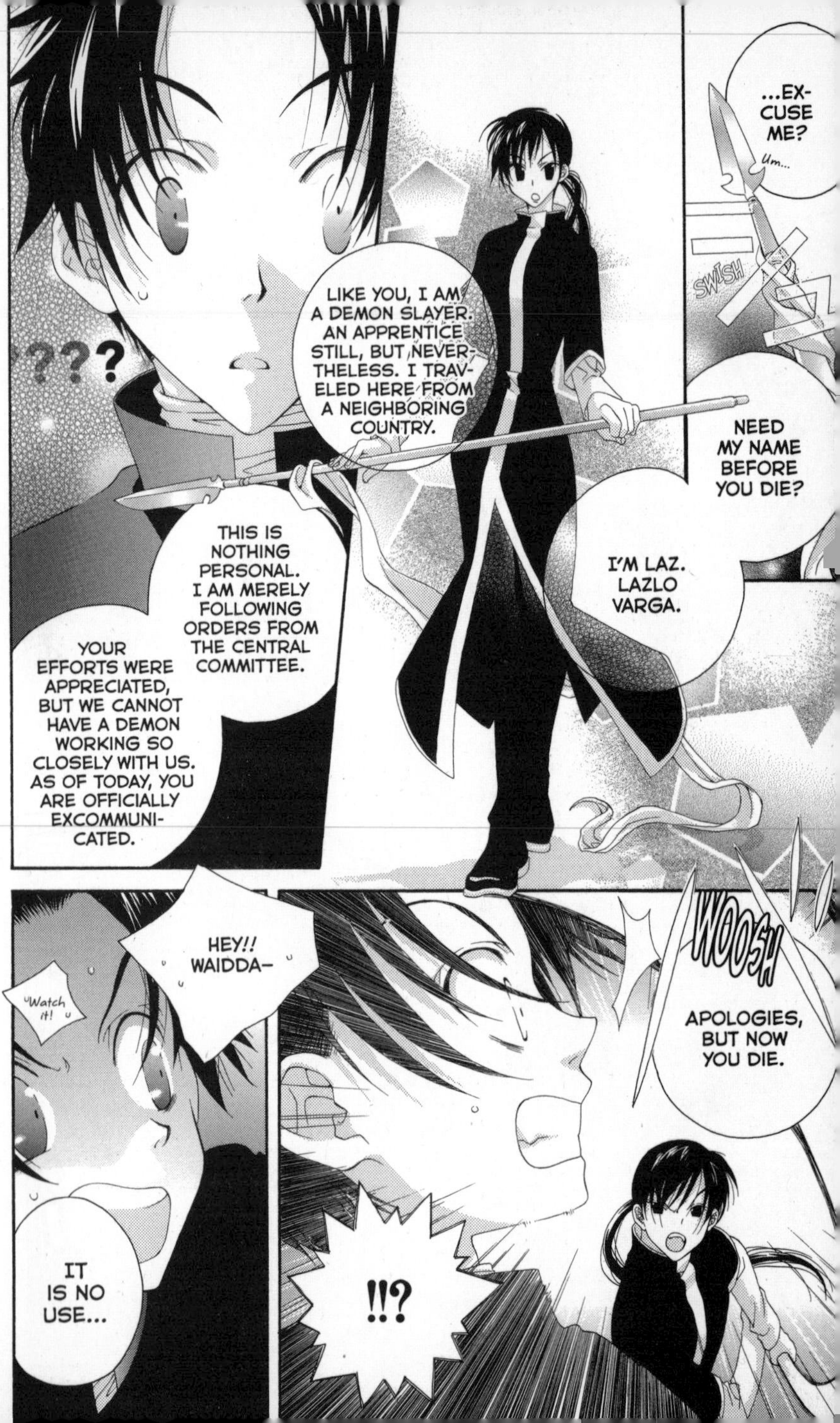
...EX-CUSE ME?
Um...
SWISH
NEED MY NAME BEFORE YOU DIE?
I'M LAZ. LAZLO VARGA.
LIKE YOU, I AM A DEMON SLAYER. AN APPRENTICE STILL, BUT NEVERTHELESS. I TRAVELED HERE FROM A NEIGHBORING COUNTRY.
???
THIS IS NOTHING PERSONAL. I AM MERELY FOLLOWING ORDERS FROM THE CENTRAL COMMITTEE.
YOUR EFFORTS WERE APPRECIATED, BUT WE CANNOT HAVE A DEMON WORKING SO CLOSELY WITH US. AS OF TODAY, YOU ARE OFFICIALLY EXCOMMUNICATED.
WOOSH
APOLOGIES, BUT NOW YOU DIE.
!!?
HEY!! WAIDDA-
Watch it!
IT IS NO USE...

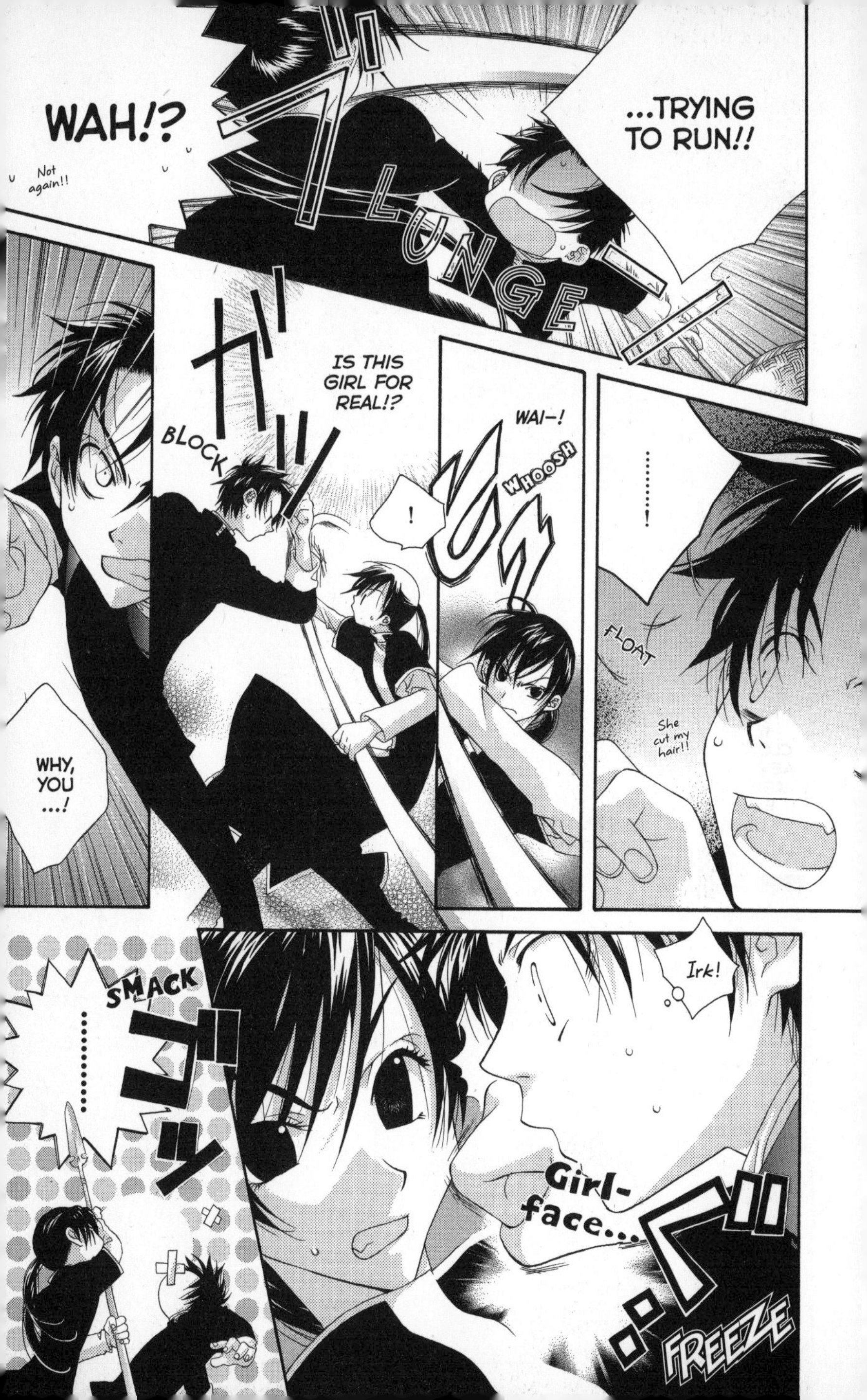
...TRYING TO RUN!!
LUNGE
WAH!?
Not again!!
......!
FLOAT
She cut my hair!!
WAI-!
WHOOSH
!
IS THIS GIRL FOR REAL!?
BLOCK
WHY, YOU ...!
Irk!
Girl-face...
FREEZE
SMACK
......

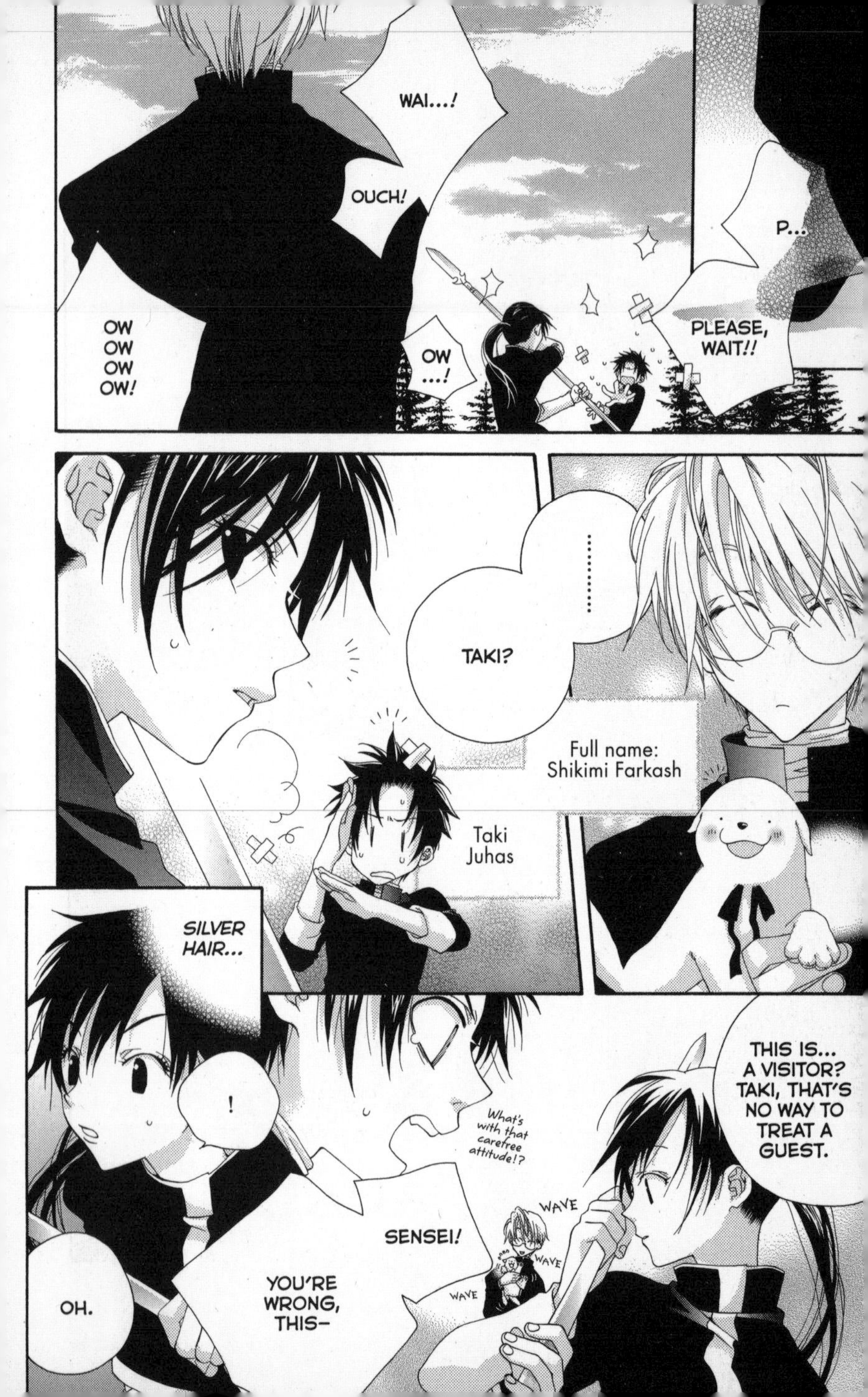
P...
PLEASE, WAIT!!
WAI...!
OUCH!
OW ...!
OW OW OW OW!
......
TAKI?
Full name: Shikimi Farkash
Taki Juhas
SILVER HAIR...
THIS IS... A VISITOR? TAKI, THAT'S NO WAY TO TREAT A GUEST.
WAVE
WAVE
WAVE
What's with that carefree attitude!?
SENSEI!
YOU'RE WRONG, THIS–
!
OH.

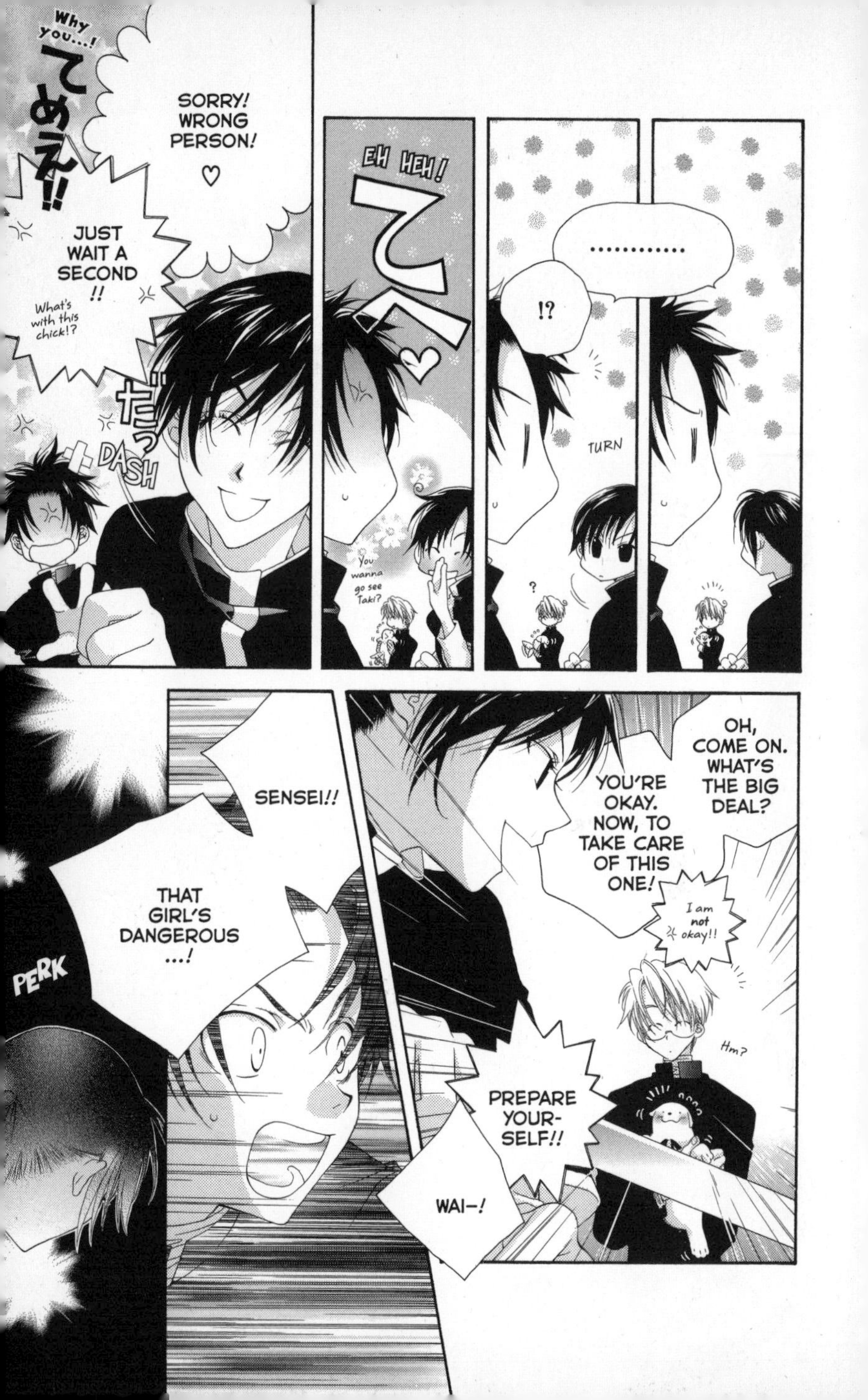

....
!?
TURN
?
EH HEH!
てへ
You wanna go see Taki?
SORRY! WRONG PERSON!
Why you...!
てめえ!!
JUST WAIT A SECOND!!
What's with this chick!?
だっ
DASH
OH, COME ON. WHAT'S THE BIG DEAL?
YOU'RE OKAY. NOW, TO TAKE CARE OF THIS ONE!
I am not okay!!
Hm?
PREPARE YOURSELF!!
WAI-!
SENSEI!!
THAT GIRL'S DANGEROUS...!
PERK

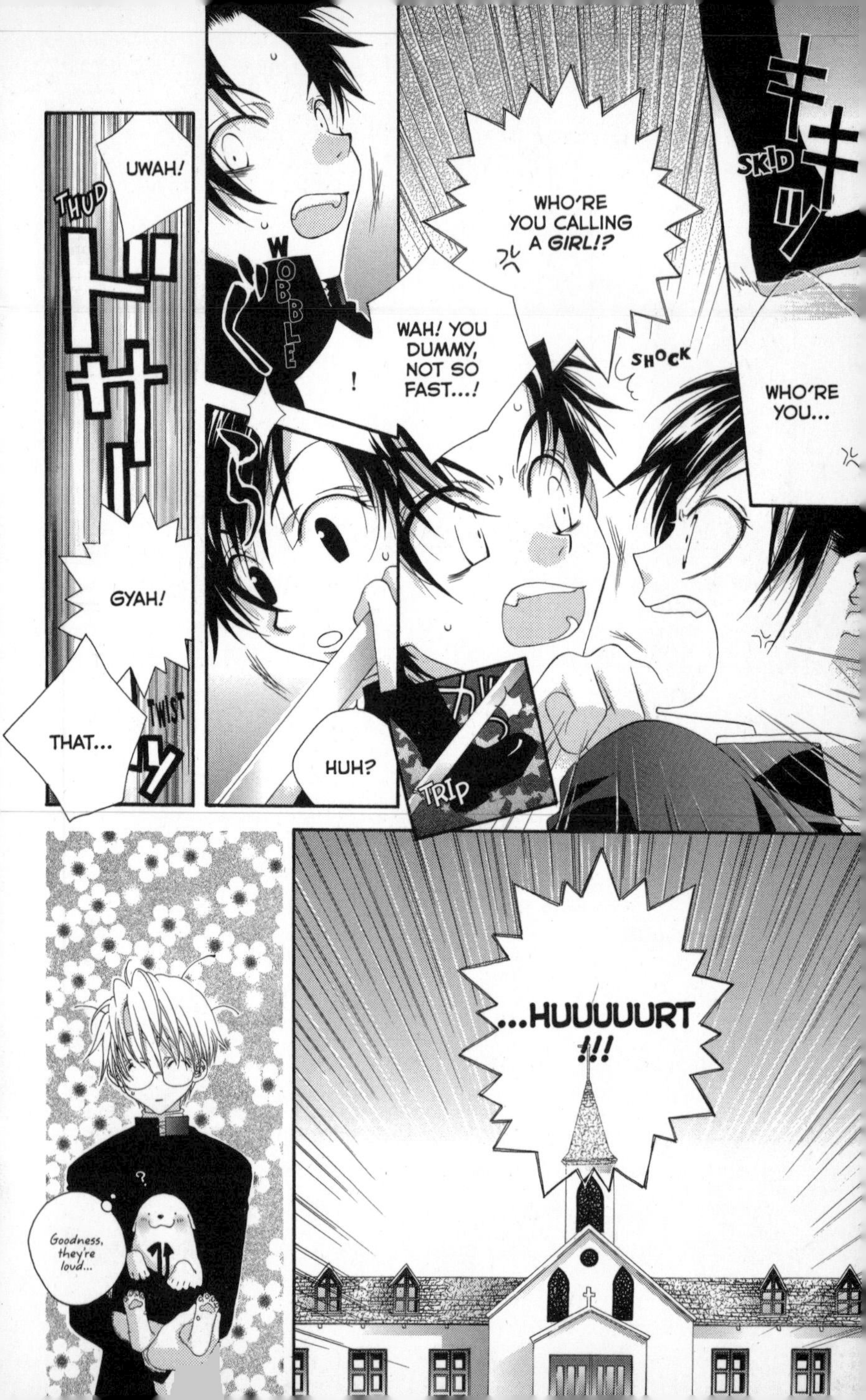
SKID
WHO'RE YOU...
WHO'RE YOU CALLING A GIRL!?
SHOCK
WAH! YOU DUMMY, NOT SO FAST...!
TRIP
WOBBLE
!
HUH?
UWAH!
THUD
GYAH!
TWIST
THAT...
...HUUUUURT !!!
Goodness, they're loud...

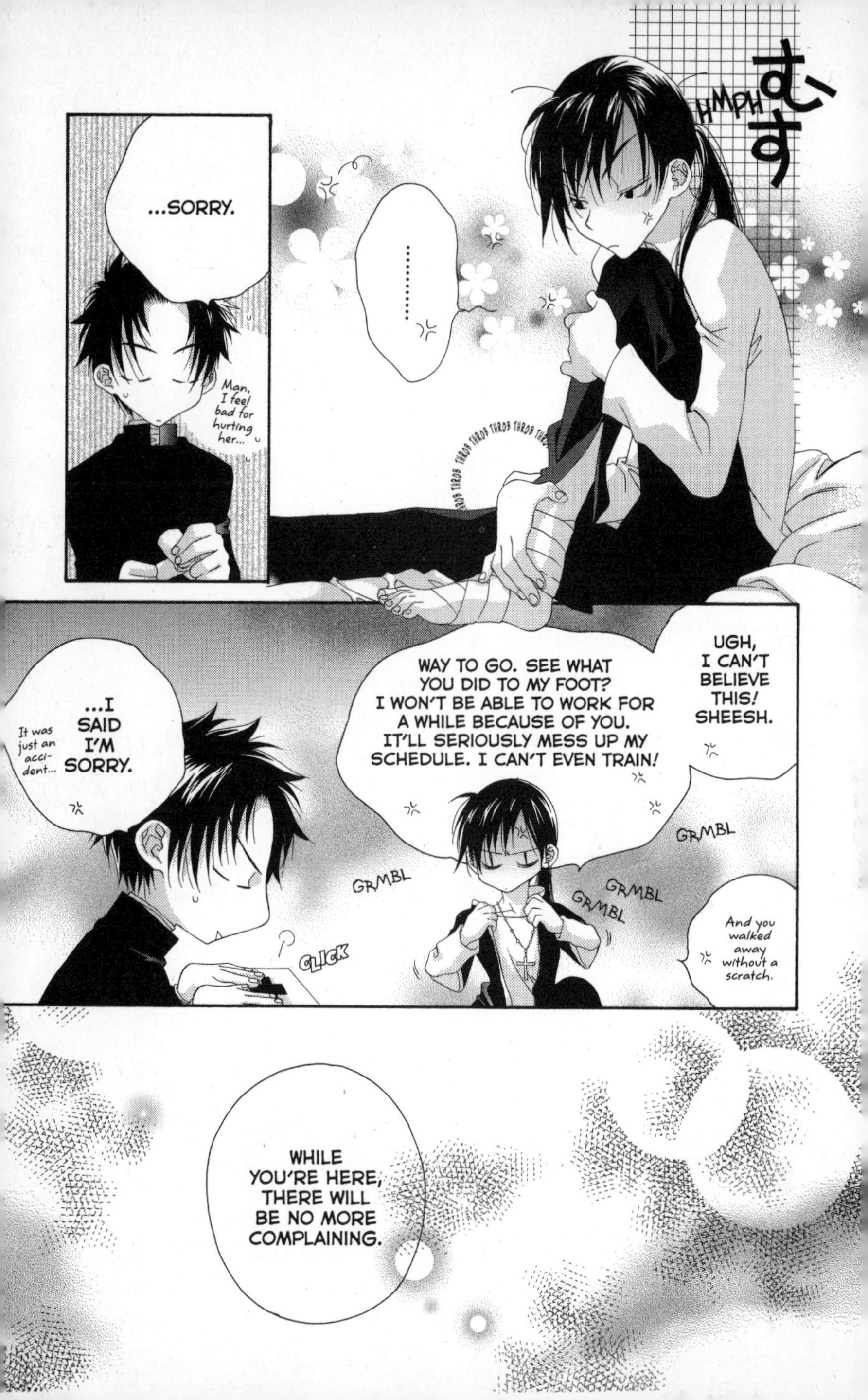
むす
HMPH
......
THROB THROB THROB THROB
...SORRY.
Man, I feel bad for hurting her...
UGH, I CAN'T BELIEVE THIS! SHEESH.
WAY TO GO. SEE WHAT YOU DID TO MY FOOT? I WON'T BE ABLE TO WORK FOR A WHILE BECAUSE OF YOU. IT'LL SERIOUSLY MESS UP MY SCHEDULE. I CAN'T EVEN TRAIN!
GRMBL
And you walked away without a scratch.
GRMBL
GRMBL
GRMBL
...I SAID I'M SORRY.
It was just an accident...
CLICK
WHILE YOU'RE HERE, THERE WILL BE NO MORE COMPLAINING.

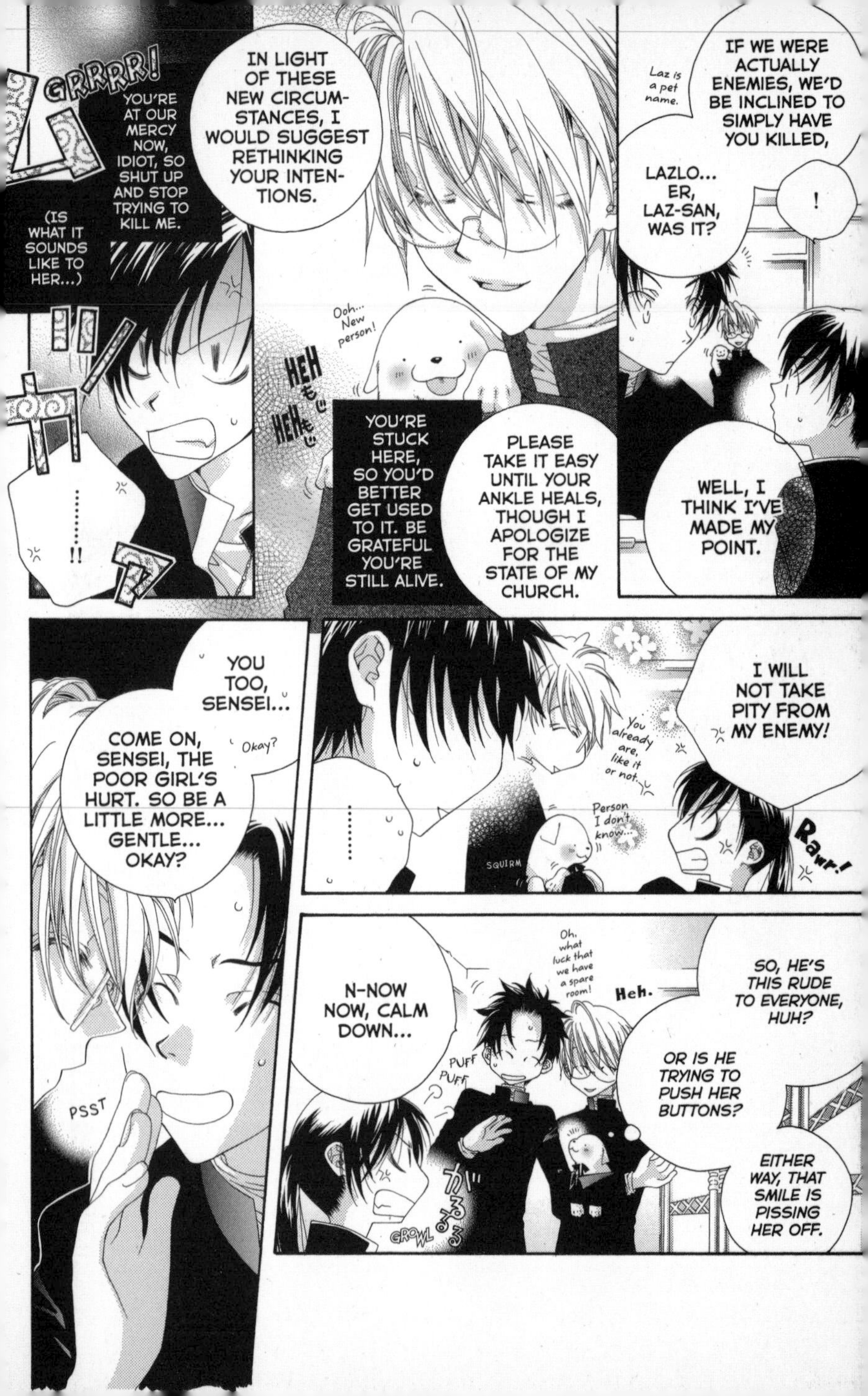
IF WE WERE ACTUALLY ENEMIES, WE'D BE INCLINED TO SIMPLY HAVE YOU KILLED,
Laz is a pet name.
LAZLO... ER, LAZ-SAN, WAS IT?
!
WELL, I THINK I'VE MADE MY POINT.
IN LIGHT OF THESE NEW CIRCUM-STANCES, I WOULD SUGGEST RETHINKING YOUR INTEN-TIONS.
Ooh... New person!
HEH HEH
PLEASE TAKE IT EASY UNTIL YOUR ANKLE HEALS, THOUGH I APOLOGIZE FOR THE STATE OF MY CHURCH.
YOU'RE STUCK HERE, SO YOU'D BETTER GET USED TO IT. BE GRATEFUL YOU'RE STILL ALIVE.
GRRRR!
YOU'RE AT OUR MERCY NOW, IDIOT, SO SHUT UP AND STOP TRYING TO KILL ME.
(IS WHAT IT SOUNDS LIKE TO HER...)
......!!
I WILL NOT TAKE PITY FROM MY ENEMY!
You already are, like it or not.
Rawr!
Person I don't know...
SQUIRM
......
SO, HE'S THIS RUDE TO EVERYONE, HUH?
OR IS HE TRYING TO PUSH HER BUTTONS?
EITHER WAY, THAT SMILE IS PISSING HER OFF.
Heh.
Oh, what luck that we have a spare room!
N-NOW NOW, CALM DOWN...
PUFF PUFF
GROWL
YOU TOO, SENSEI...
Okay?
COME ON, SENSEI, THE POOR GIRL'S HURT. SO BE A LITTLE MORE... GENTLE... OKAY?
PSST

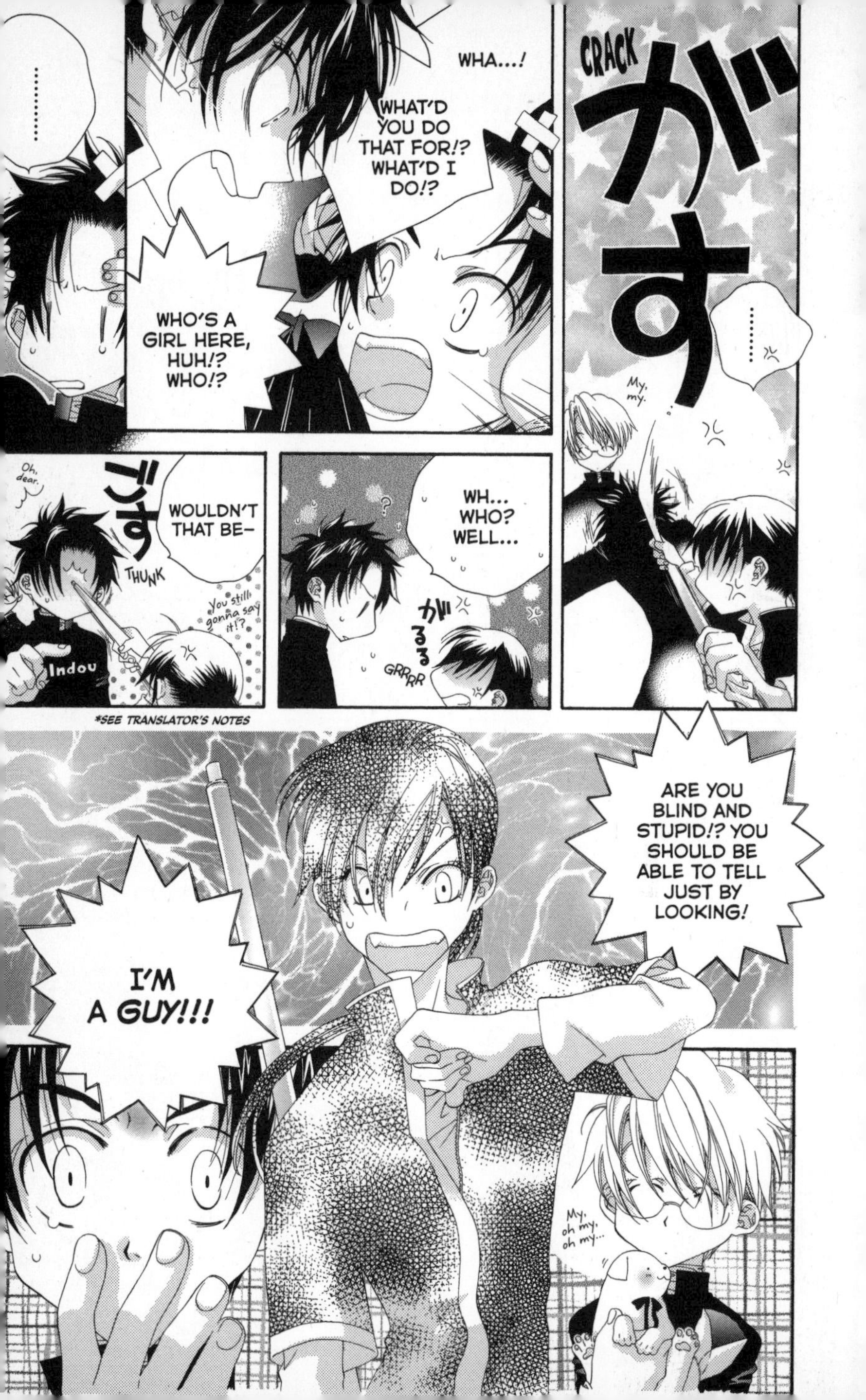
CRACK
がす
......
My, my.
WHA...!
WHAT'D YOU DO THAT FOR!? WHAT'D I DO!?
WHO'S A GIRL HERE, HUH!? WHO!?
......
WH... WHO? WELL...
がるる
GRRRR
Oh, dear.
ごす
THUNK
WOULDN'T THAT BE–
You still gonna say it!?
Indou
*SEE TRANSLATOR'S NOTES
ARE YOU BLIND AND STUPID!? YOU SHOULD BE ABLE TO TELL JUST BY LOOKING!
I'M A GUY!!!
My, oh my, oh my...

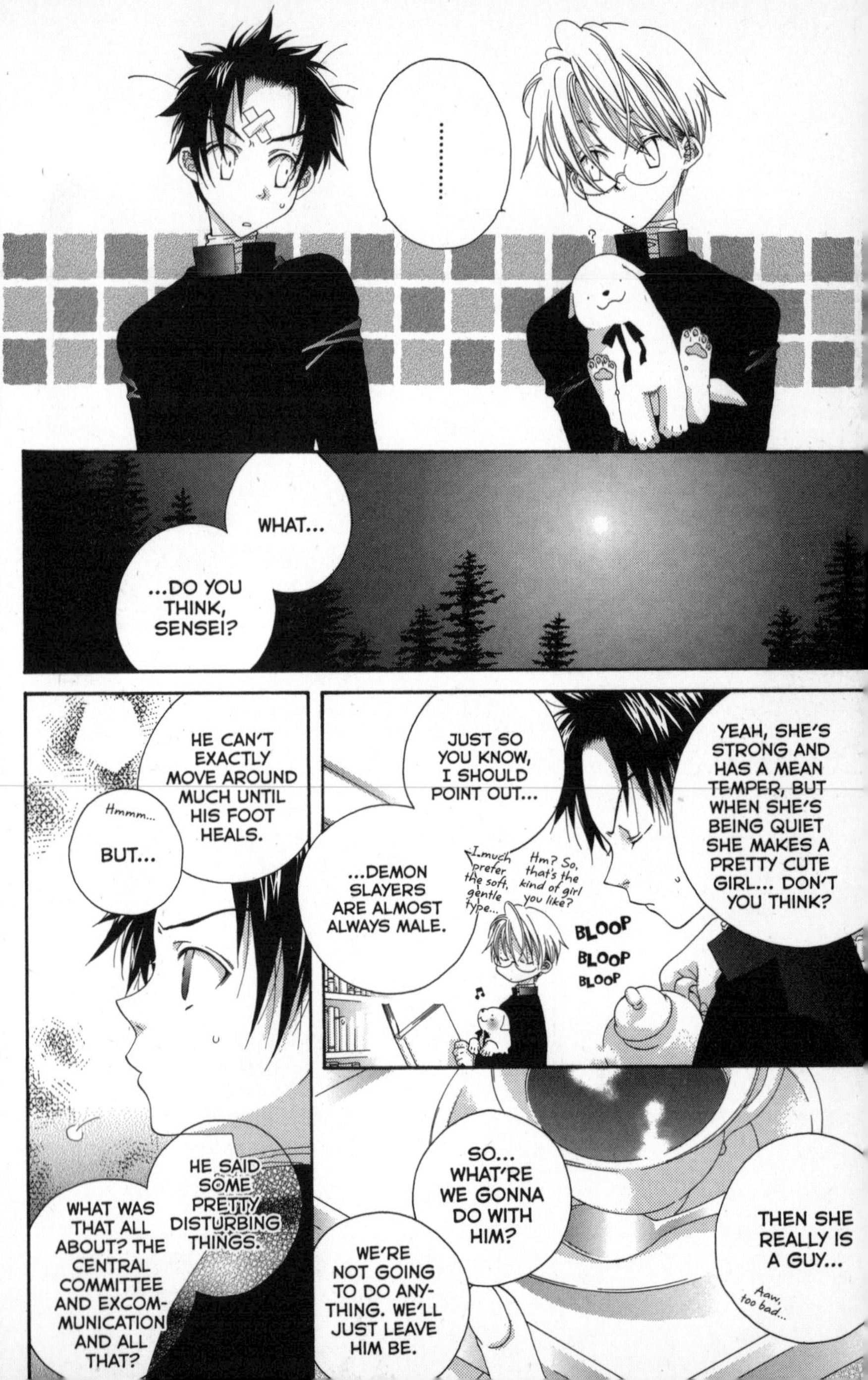
......
WHAT...
...DO YOU THINK, SENSEI?
YEAH, SHE'S STRONG AND HAS A MEAN TEMPER, BUT WHEN SHE'S BEING QUIET SHE MAKES A PRETTY CUTE GIRL... DON'T YOU THINK?
JUST SO YOU KNOW, I SHOULD POINT OUT...
Hm? So, that's the kind of girl you like?
I much prefer the soft, gentle type...
BLOOP
BLOOP
BLOOP
...DEMON SLAYERS ARE ALMOST ALWAYS MALE.
THEN SHE REALLY IS A GUY...
Aaw, too bad...
SO... WHAT'RE WE GONNA DO WITH HIM?
WE'RE NOT GOING TO DO ANY-THING. WE'LL JUST LEAVE HIM BE.
HE CAN'T EXACTLY MOVE AROUND MUCH UNTIL HIS FOOT HEALS.
Hmmm...
BUT...
HE SAID SOME PRETTY DISTURBING THINGS.
WHAT WAS THAT ALL ABOUT? THE CENTRAL COMMITTEE AND EXCOM-MUNICATION AND ALL THAT?

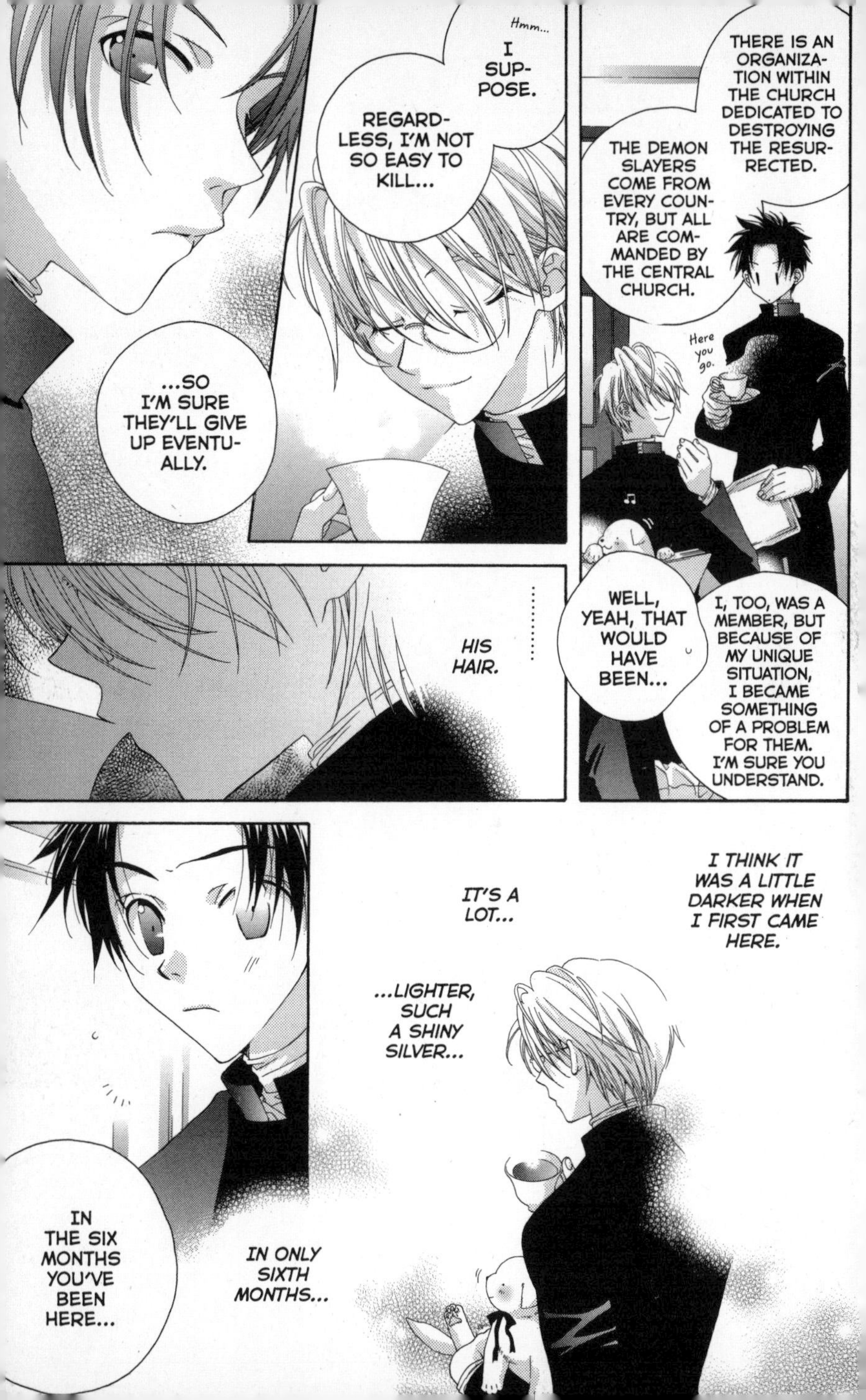
THERE IS AN ORGANIZA- TION WITHIN THE CHURCH DEDICATED TO DESTROYING THE RESUR- RECTED.
THE DEMON SLAYERS COME FROM EVERY COUN- TRY, BUT ALL ARE COM- MANDED BY THE CENTRAL CHURCH.
Here you go.
I, TOO, WAS A MEMBER, BUT BECAUSE OF MY UNIQUE SITUATION, I BECAME SOMETHING OF A PROBLEM FOR THEM. I'M SURE YOU UNDERSTAND.
WELL, YEAH, THAT WOULD HAVE BEEN...
Hmm...
I SUP- POSE.
REGARD- LESS, I'M NOT SO EASY TO KILL...
...SO I'M SURE THEY'LL GIVE UP EVENTU- ALLY.
....
HIS HAIR.
I THINK IT WAS A LITTLE DARKER WHEN I FIRST CAME HERE.
IT'S A LOT...
...LIGHTER, SUCH A SHINY SILVER...
IN ONLY SIXTH MONTHS...
IN THE SIX MONTHS YOU'VE BEEN HERE...

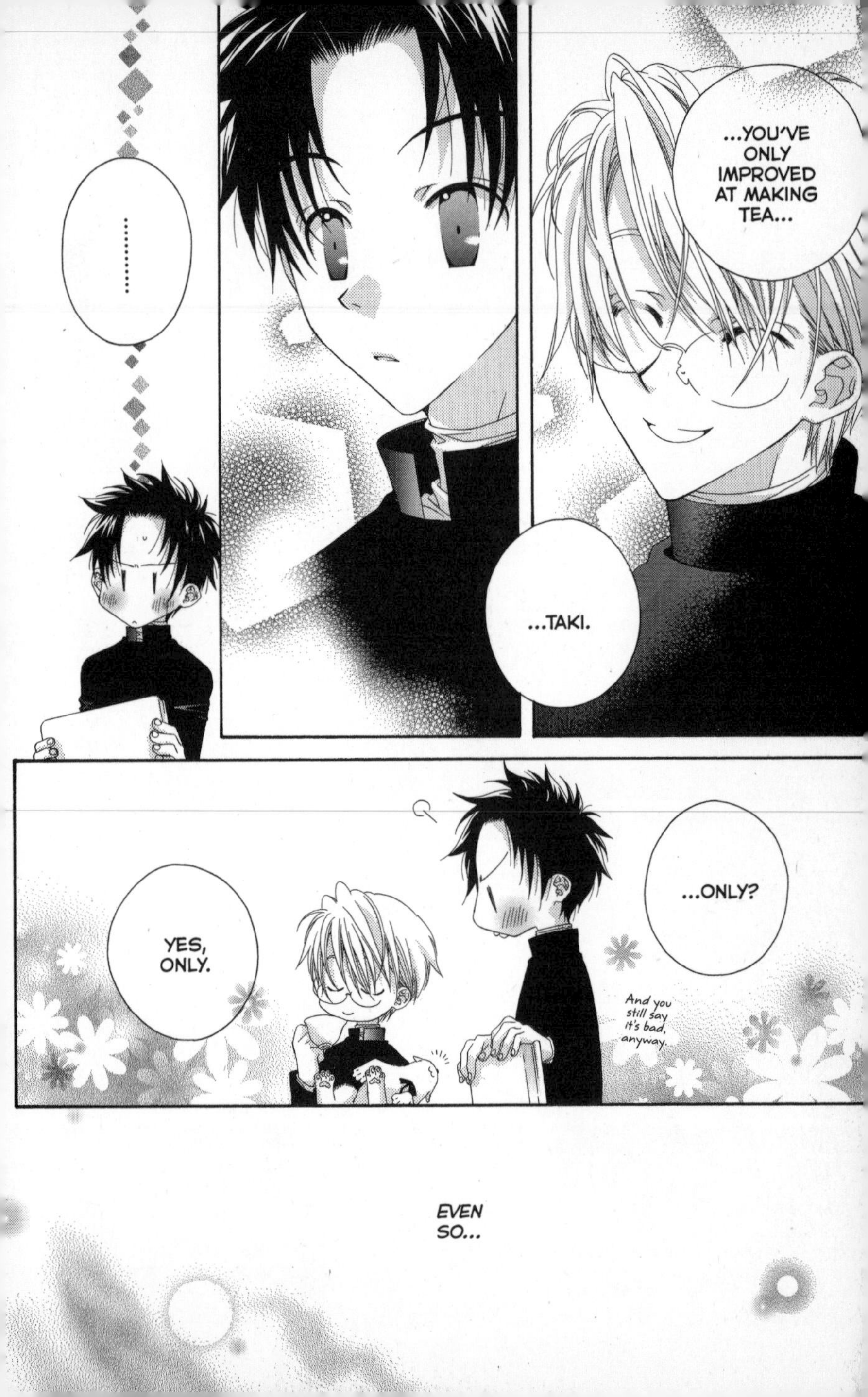
...YOU'VE ONLY IMPROVED AT MAKING TEA...
...TAKI.
......
...ONLY?
And you still say it's bad, anyway.
YES, ONLY.
EVEN SO...

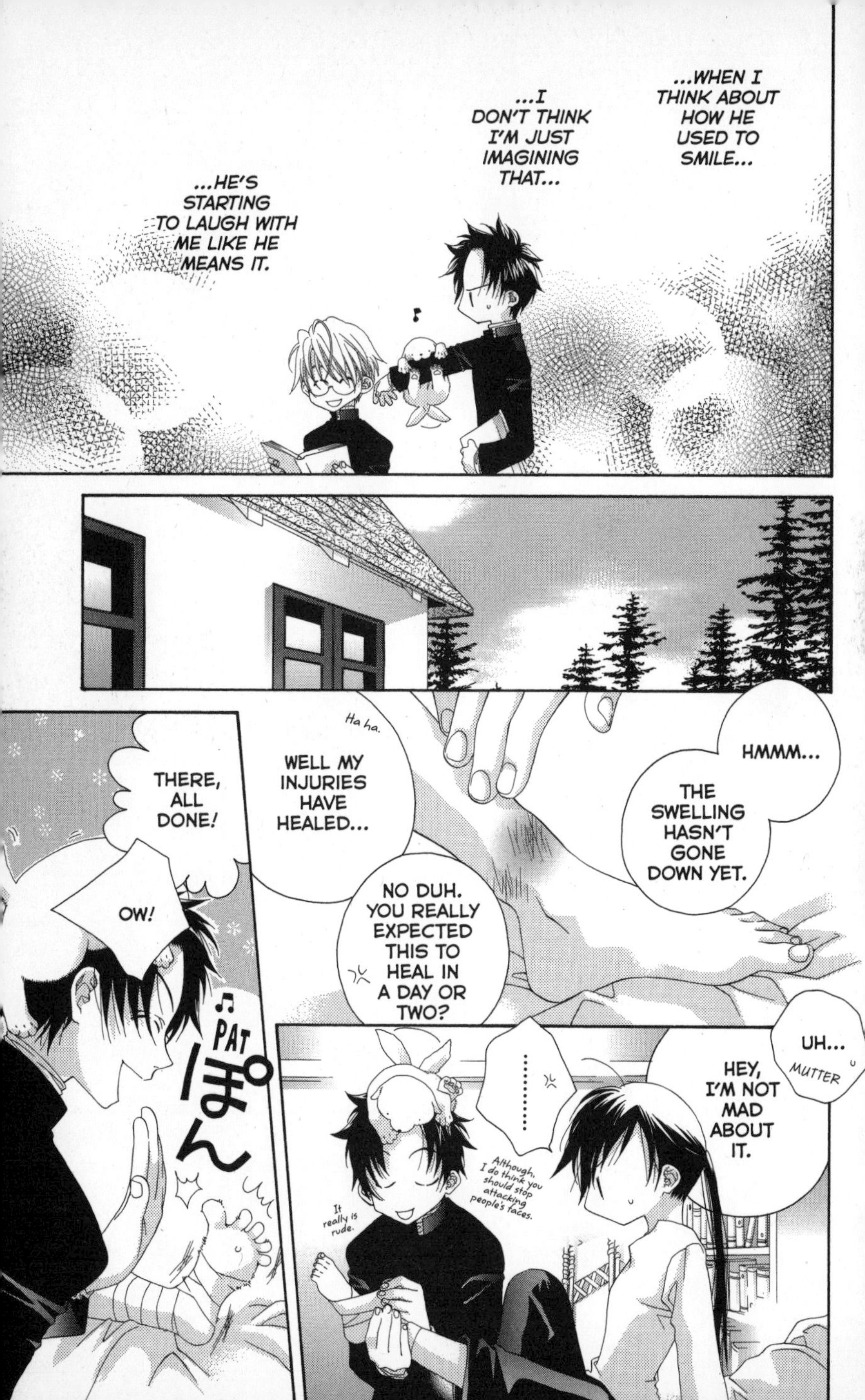
...WHEN I THINK ABOUT HOW HE USED TO SMILE...
...I DON'T THINK I'M JUST IMAGINING THAT...
...HE'S STARTING TO LAUGH WITH ME LIKE HE MEANS IT.
HMMM...
THE SWELLING HASN'T GONE DOWN YET.
Ha ha.
WELL MY INJURIES HAVE HEALED...
NO DUH. YOU REALLY EXPECTED THIS TO HEAL IN A DAY OR TWO?
UH...
MUTTER
HEY, I'M NOT MAD ABOUT IT.
....
Although, I do think you should stop attacking people's faces.
It really is rude.
THERE, ALL DONE!
OW!
PAT
ぽん

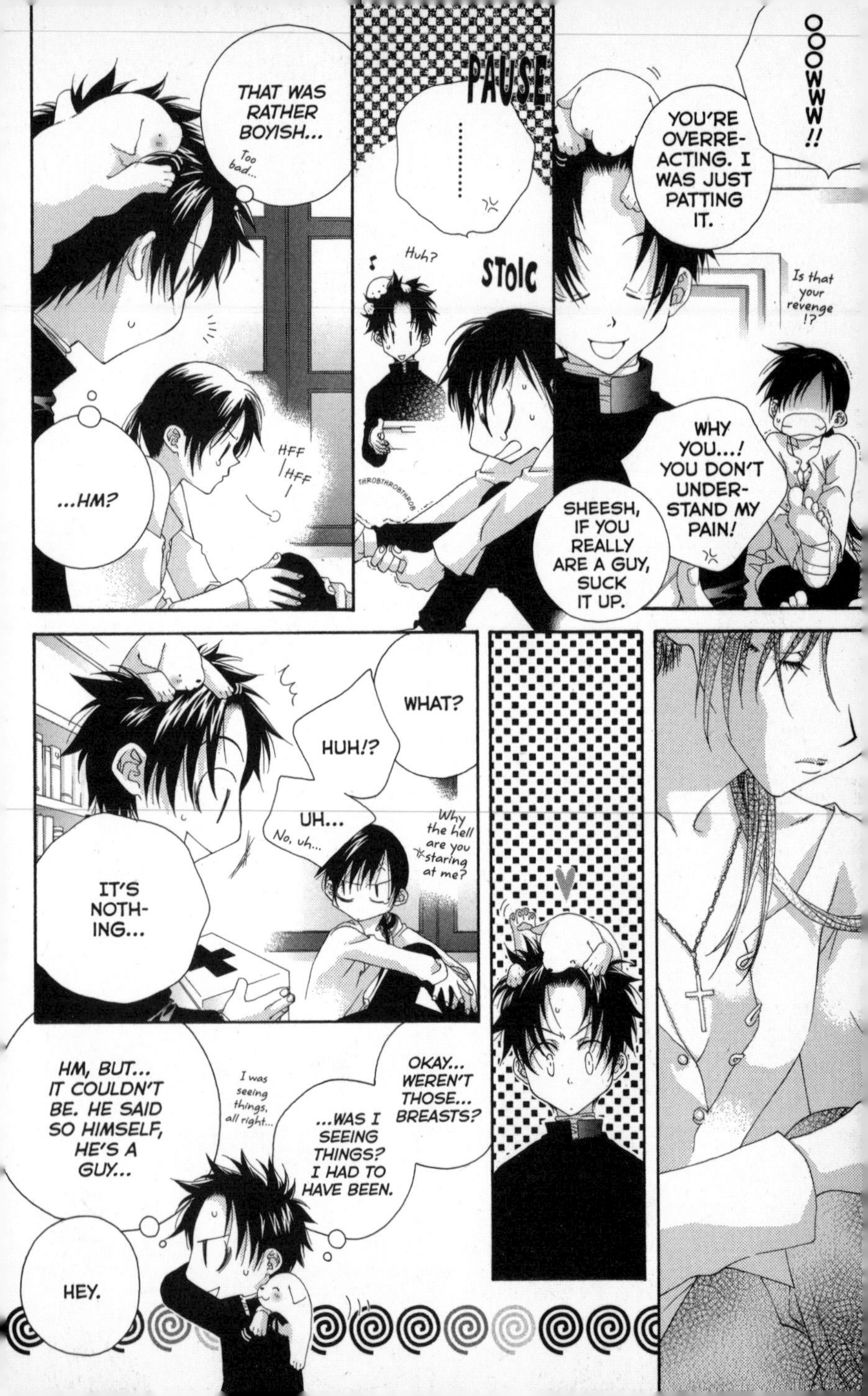
OOOWWW!!
YOU'RE OVERRE-ACTING. I WAS JUST PATTING IT.
Is that your revenge!?
WHY YOU...! YOU DON'T UNDER-STAND MY PAIN!
SHEESH, IF YOU REALLY ARE A GUY, SUCK IT UP.
PAUSE
......
Huh?
STOIC
THROBTHROBTHROB
THAT WAS RATHER BOYISH...
Too bad...
...HM?
HFF HFF
WHAT?
HUH!?
UH...
No, uh...
Why the hell are you staring at me?
IT'S NOTH-ING...
OKAY... WEREN'T THOSE... BREASTS?
...WAS I SEEING THINGS? I HAD TO HAVE BEEN.
I was seeing things, all right...
HM, BUT... IT COULDN'T BE. HE SAID SO HIMSELF, HE'S A GUY...
HEY.

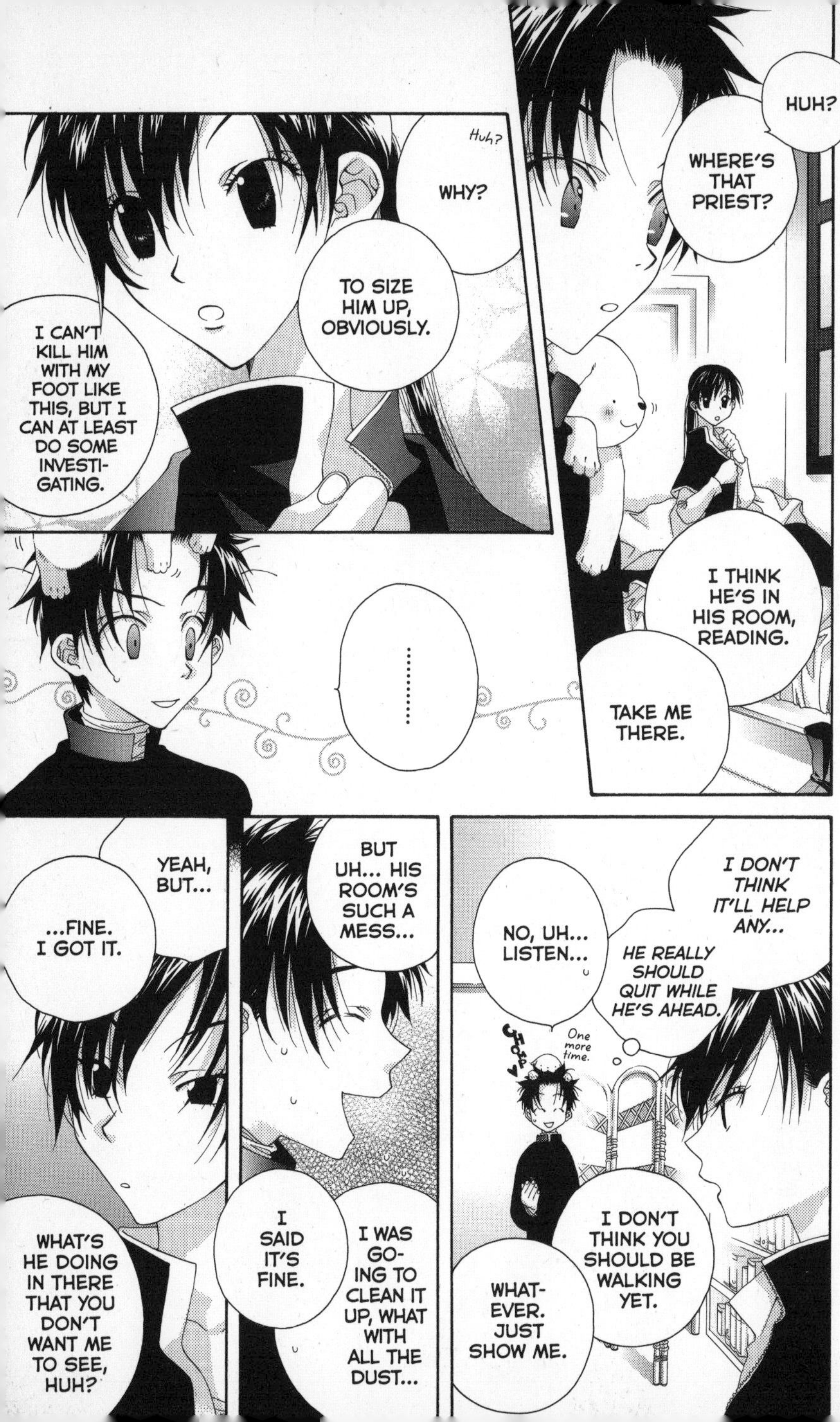
HUH?
WHERE'S THAT PRIEST?
I THINK HE'S IN HIS ROOM, READING.
TAKE ME THERE.
Huh?
WHY?
TO SIZE HIM UP, OBVIOUSLY.
I CAN'T KILL HIM WITH MY FOOT LIKE THIS, BUT I CAN AT LEAST DO SOME INVESTI-GATING.
....
I DON'T THINK IT'LL HELP ANY...
HE REALLY SHOULD QUIT WHILE HE'S AHEAD.
NO, UH... LISTEN...
One more time.
CHOMP
I DON'T THINK YOU SHOULD BE WALKING YET.
WHAT-EVER. JUST SHOW ME.
BUT UH... HIS ROOM'S SUCH A MESS...
I WAS GO-ING TO CLEAN IT UP, WHAT WITH ALL THE DUST...
I SAID IT'S FINE.
YEAH, BUT...
...FINE. I GOT IT.
WHAT'S HE DOING IN THERE THAT YOU DON'T WANT ME TO SEE, HUH?

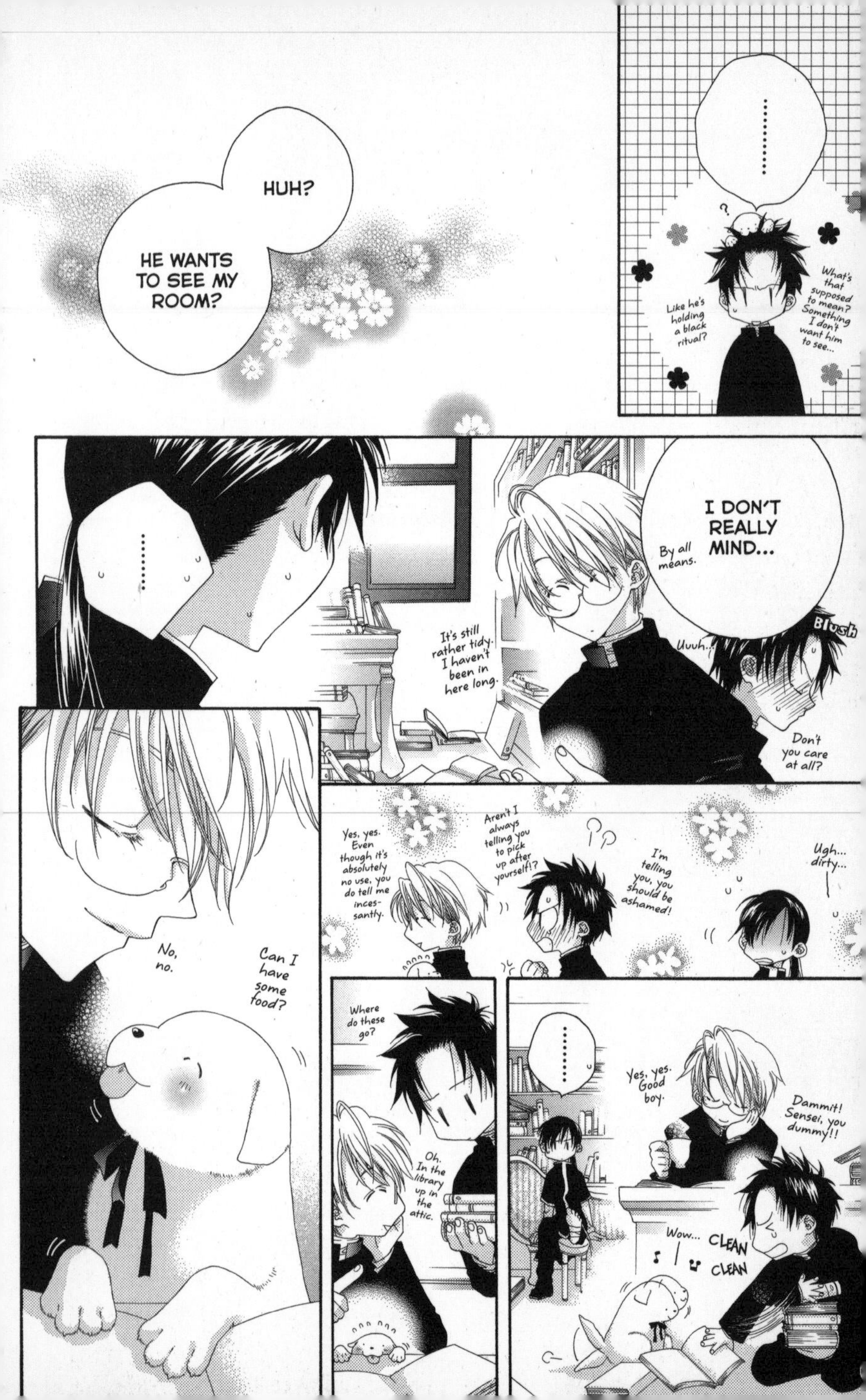
……
?
What's that supposed to mean? Something I don't want him to see...
Like he's holding a black ritual?
HUH?
HE WANTS TO SEE MY ROOM?
I DON'T REALLY MIND...
By all means.
Blush
Uuuh...
Don't you care at all?
It's still rather tidy. I haven't been in here long.
……
Ugh... dirty...
I'm telling you, you should be ashamed!
Aren't I always telling you to pick up after yourself!?
Yes, yes. Even though it's absolutely no use, you do tell me incessantly.
Dammit! Sensei, you dummy!!
Yes, yes. Good boy.
……
Wow... CLEAN CLEAN
Where do these go?
Oh. In the library up in the attic.
Can I have some food?
No, no.

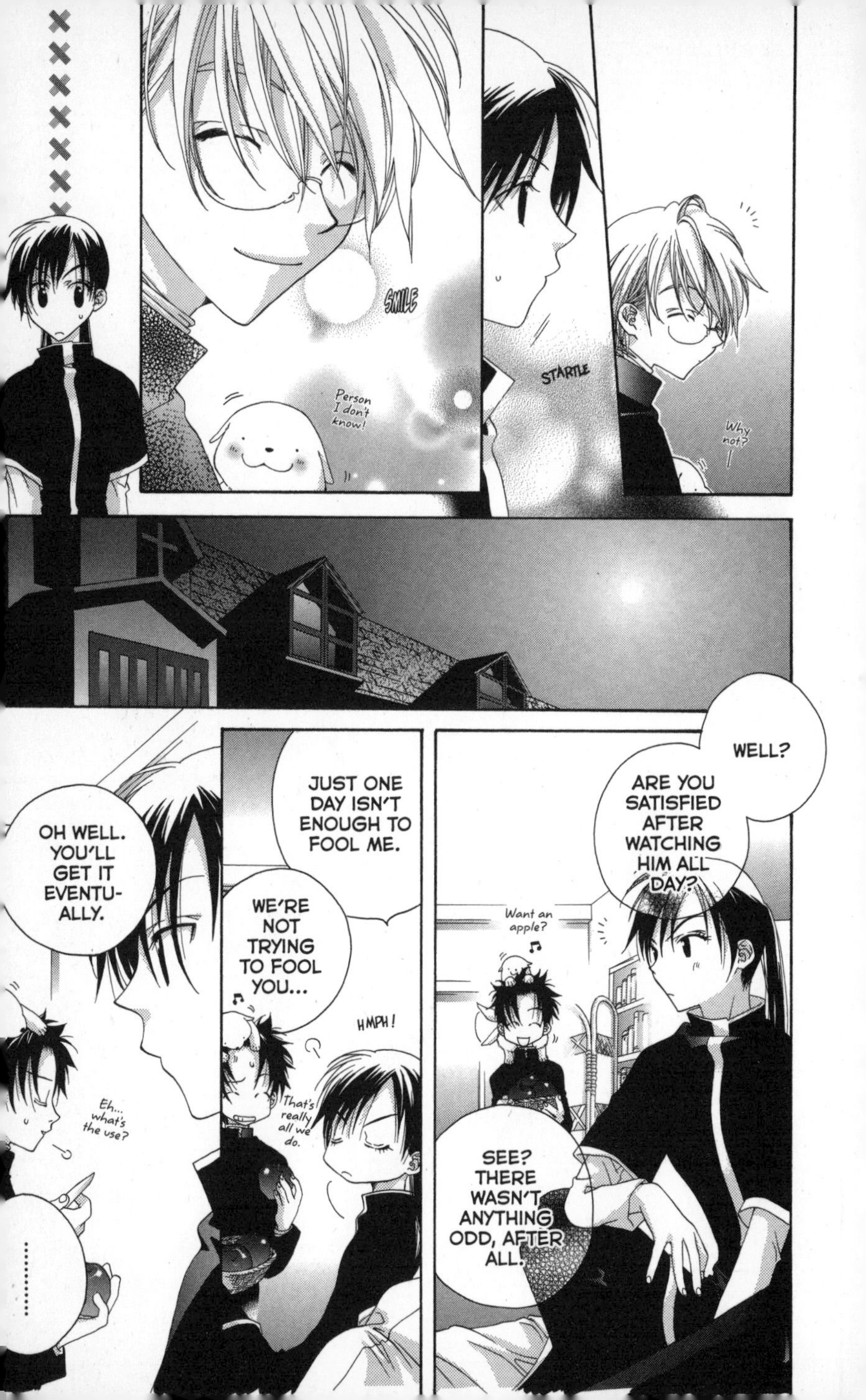
Why not?
STARTLE
SMILE
Person I don't know!
WELL?
ARE YOU SATISFIED AFTER WATCHING HIM ALL DAY?
Want an apple?
SEE? THERE WASN'T ANYTHING ODD, AFTER ALL.
JUST ONE DAY ISN'T ENOUGH TO FOOL ME.
HMPH!
WE'RE NOT TRYING TO FOOL YOU...
That's really all we do.
OH WELL. YOU'LL GET IT EVENTU-ALLY.
Eh... what's the use?
....

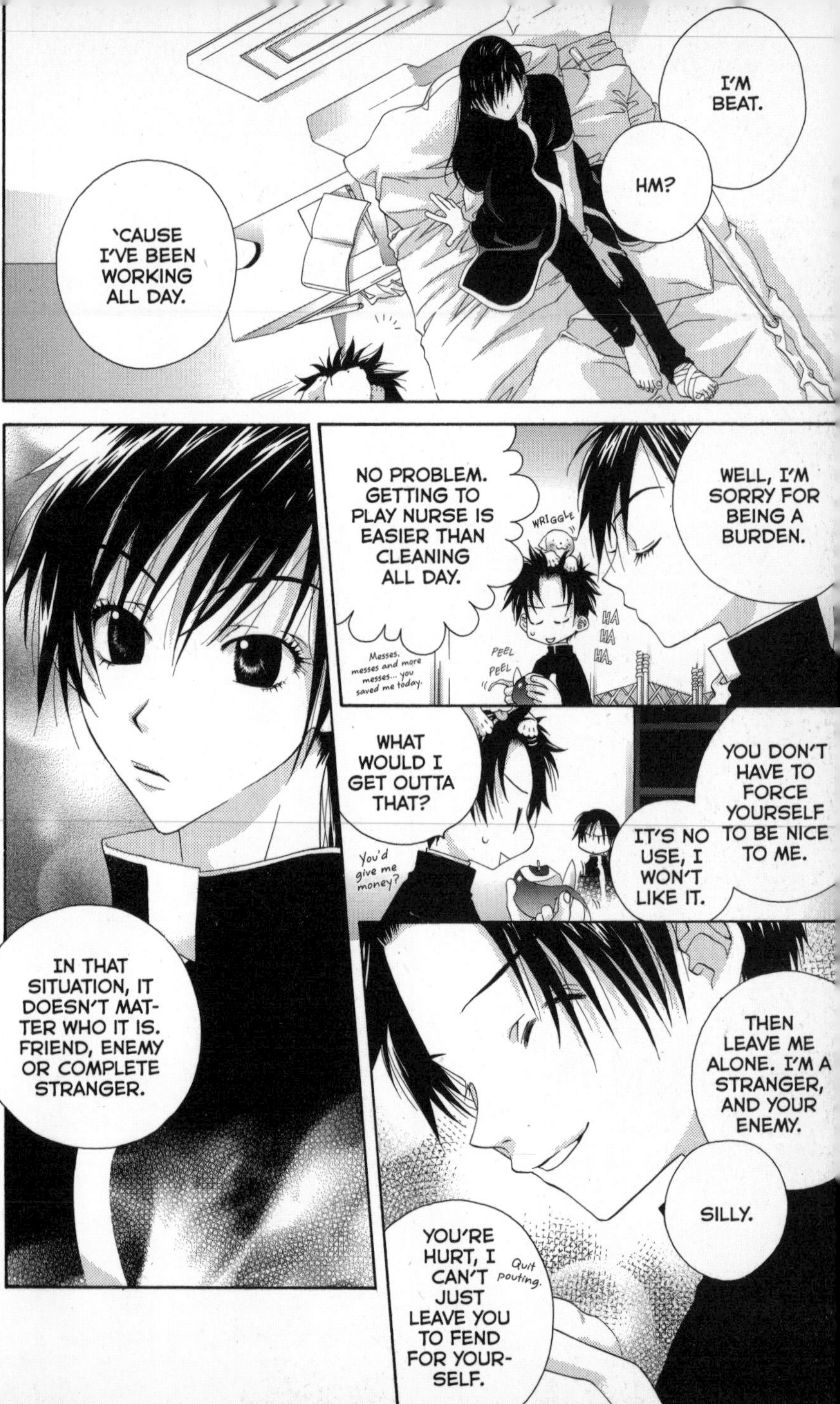
I'M BEAT.
HM?
'CAUSE I'VE BEEN WORKING ALL DAY.
WELL, I'M SORRY FOR BEING A BURDEN.
HA HA HA.
NO PROBLEM. GETTING TO PLAY NURSE IS EASIER THAN CLEANING ALL DAY.
WRIGGLE
Messes, messes and more messes... you saved me today.
PEEL PEEL
YOU DON'T HAVE TO FORCE YOURSELF TO BE NICE TO ME.
IT'S NO USE, I WON'T LIKE IT.
WHAT WOULD I GET OUTTA THAT?
You'd give me money?
THEN LEAVE ME ALONE. I'M A STRANGER, AND YOUR ENEMY.
SILLY.
Quit pouting.
YOU'RE HURT, I CAN'T JUST LEAVE YOU TO FEND FOR YOURSELF.
IN THAT SITUATION, IT DOESN'T MATTER WHO IT IS. FRIEND, ENEMY OR COMPLETE STRANGER.

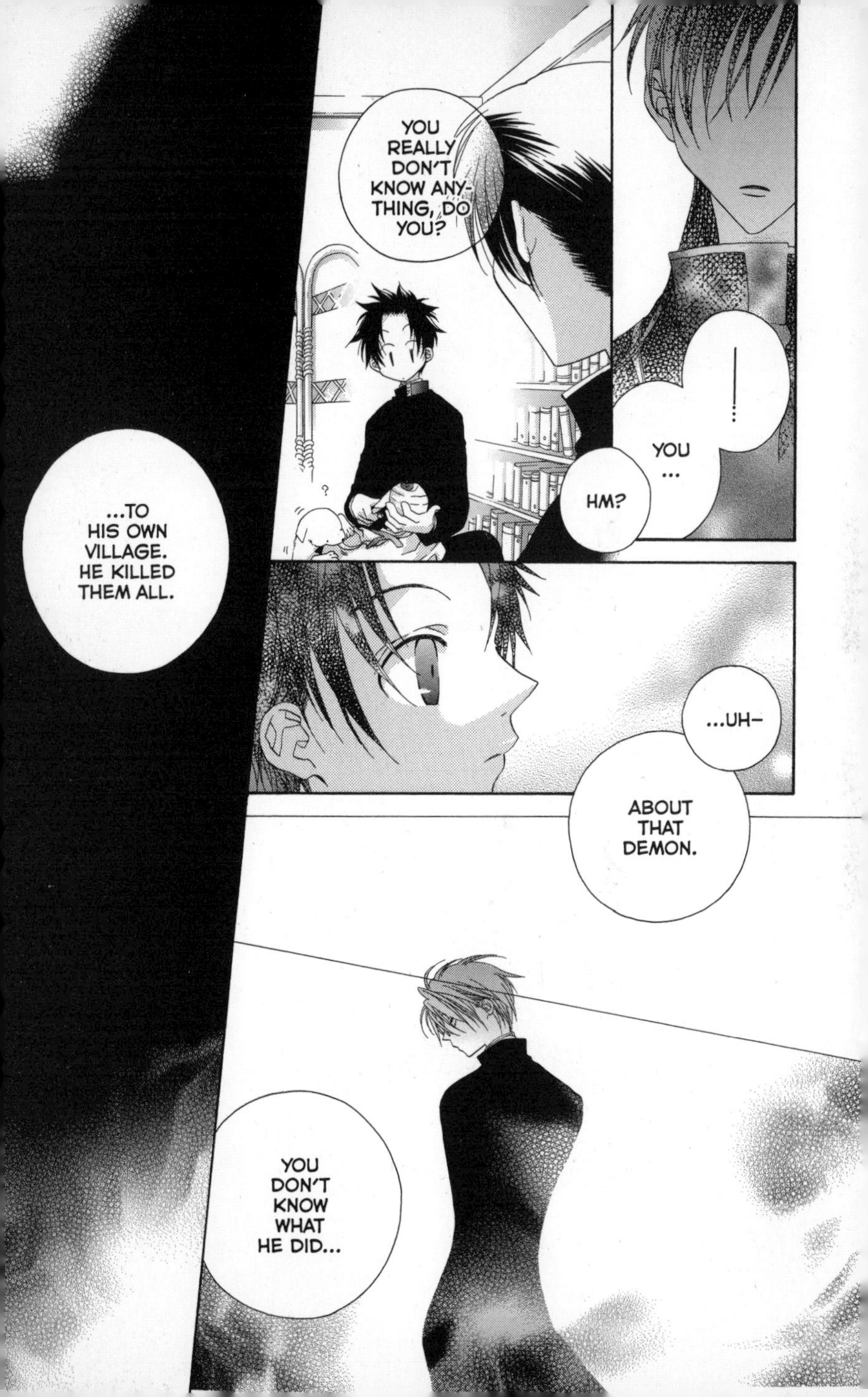

...!
YOU ...
YOU REALLY DON'T KNOW ANY-THING, DO YOU?
HM?
...UH–
ABOUT THAT DEMON.
YOU DON'T KNOW WHAT HE DID...
...TO HIS OWN VILLAGE. HE KILLED THEM ALL.

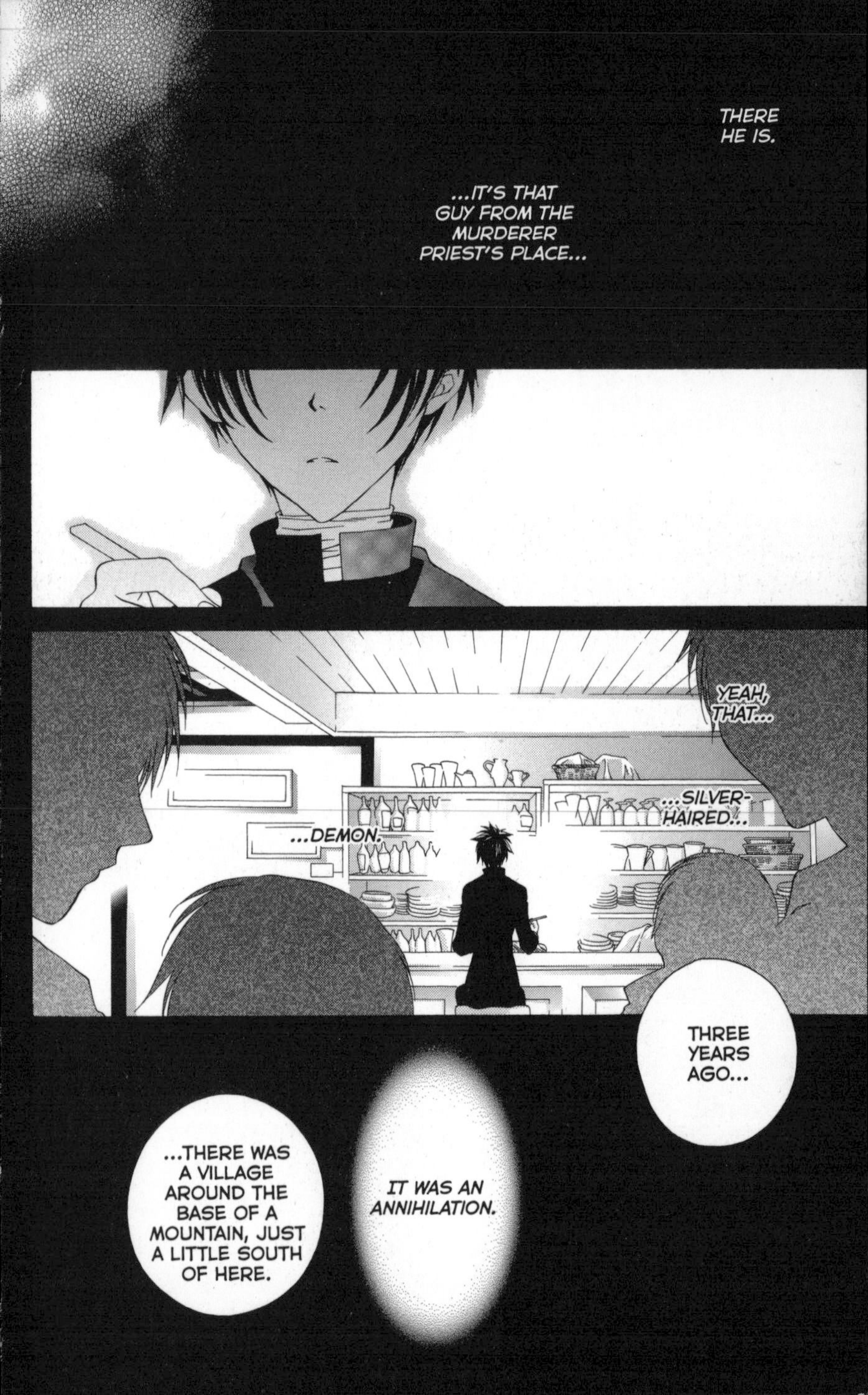
THERE HE IS.
...IT'S THAT GUY FROM THE MURDERER PRIEST'S PLACE...
YEAH, THAT...
...SILVER-HAIRED...
...DEMON.
THREE YEARS AGO...
IT WAS AN ANNIHILATION.
...THERE WAS A VILLAGE AROUND THE BASE OF A MOUNTAIN, JUST A LITTLE SOUTH OF HERE.

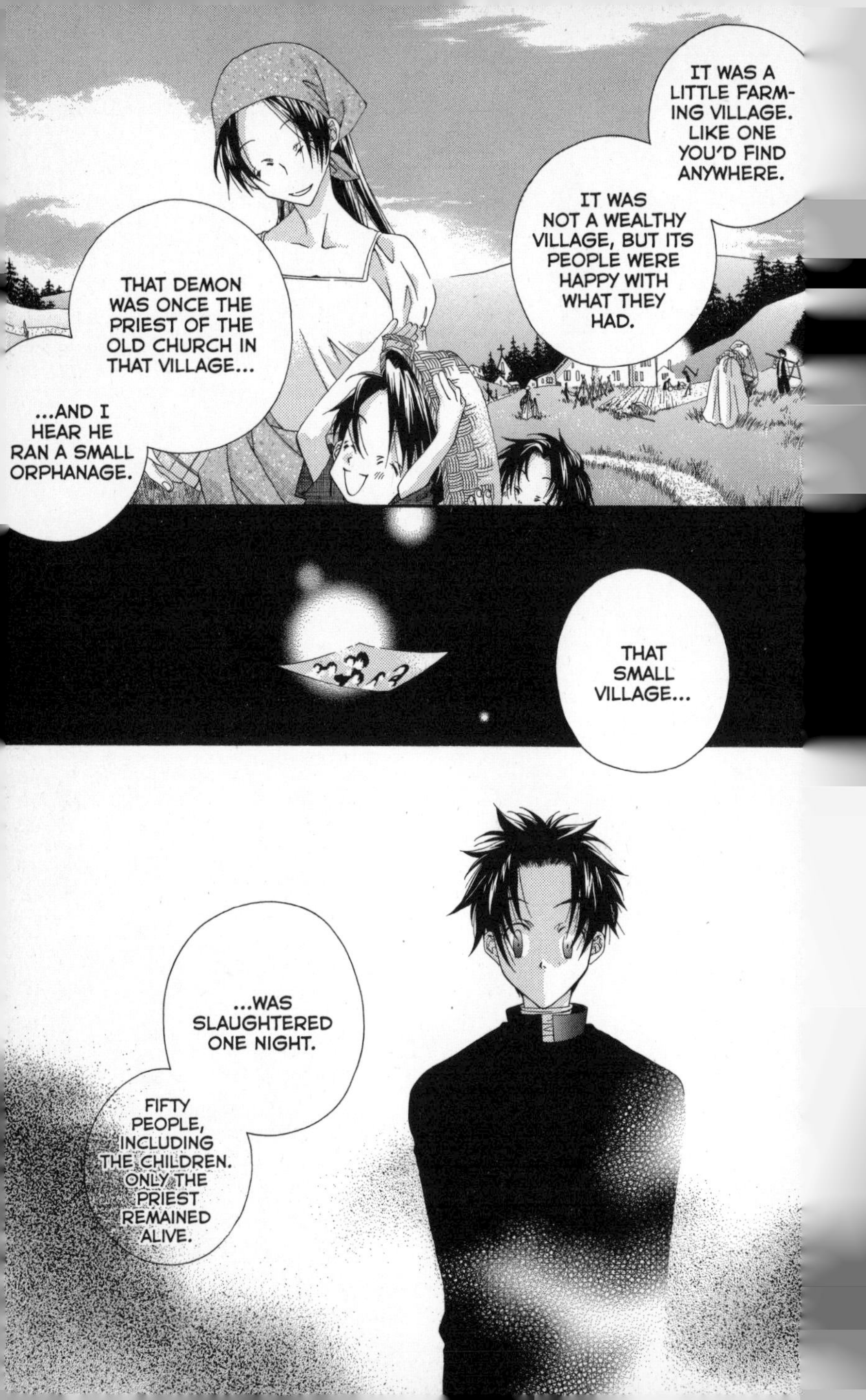
IT WAS A LITTLE FARMING VILLAGE. LIKE ONE YOU'D FIND ANYWHERE.
IT WAS NOT A WEALTHY VILLAGE, BUT ITS PEOPLE WERE HAPPY WITH WHAT THEY HAD.
THAT DEMON WAS ONCE THE PRIEST OF THE OLD CHURCH IN THAT VILLAGE...
...AND I HEAR HE RAN A SMALL ORPHANAGE.
THAT SMALL VILLAGE...
...WAS SLAUGHTERED ONE NIGHT.
FIFTY PEOPLE, INCLUDING THE CHILDREN. ONLY THE PRIEST REMAINED ALIVE.

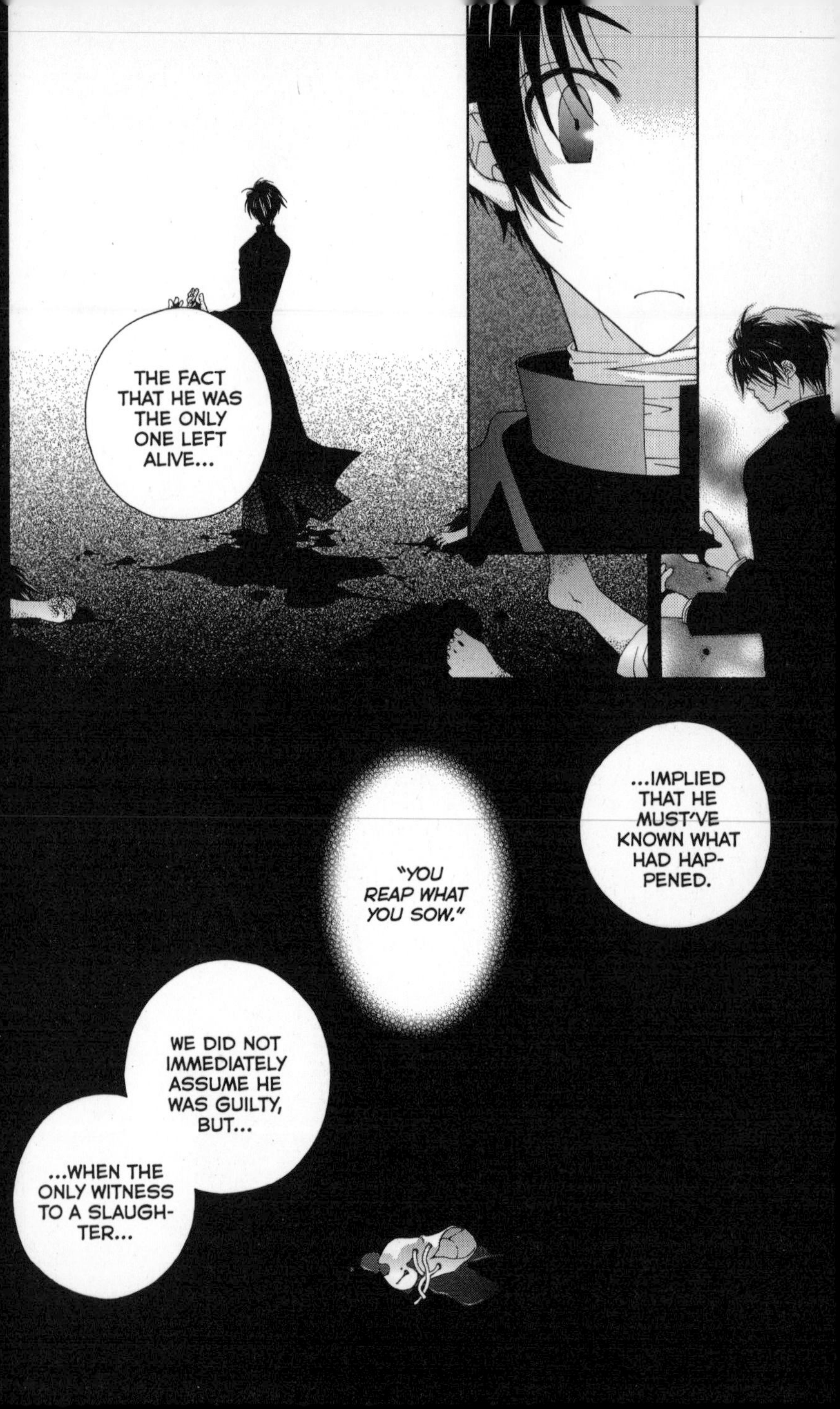
THE FACT THAT HE WAS THE ONLY ONE LEFT ALIVE...
...IMPLIED THAT HE MUST'VE KNOWN WHAT HAD HAP-PENED.
"YOU REAP WHAT YOU SOW."
WE DID NOT IMMEDIATELY ASSUME HE WAS GUILTY, BUT...
...WHEN THE ONLY WITNESS TO A SLAUGH-TER...

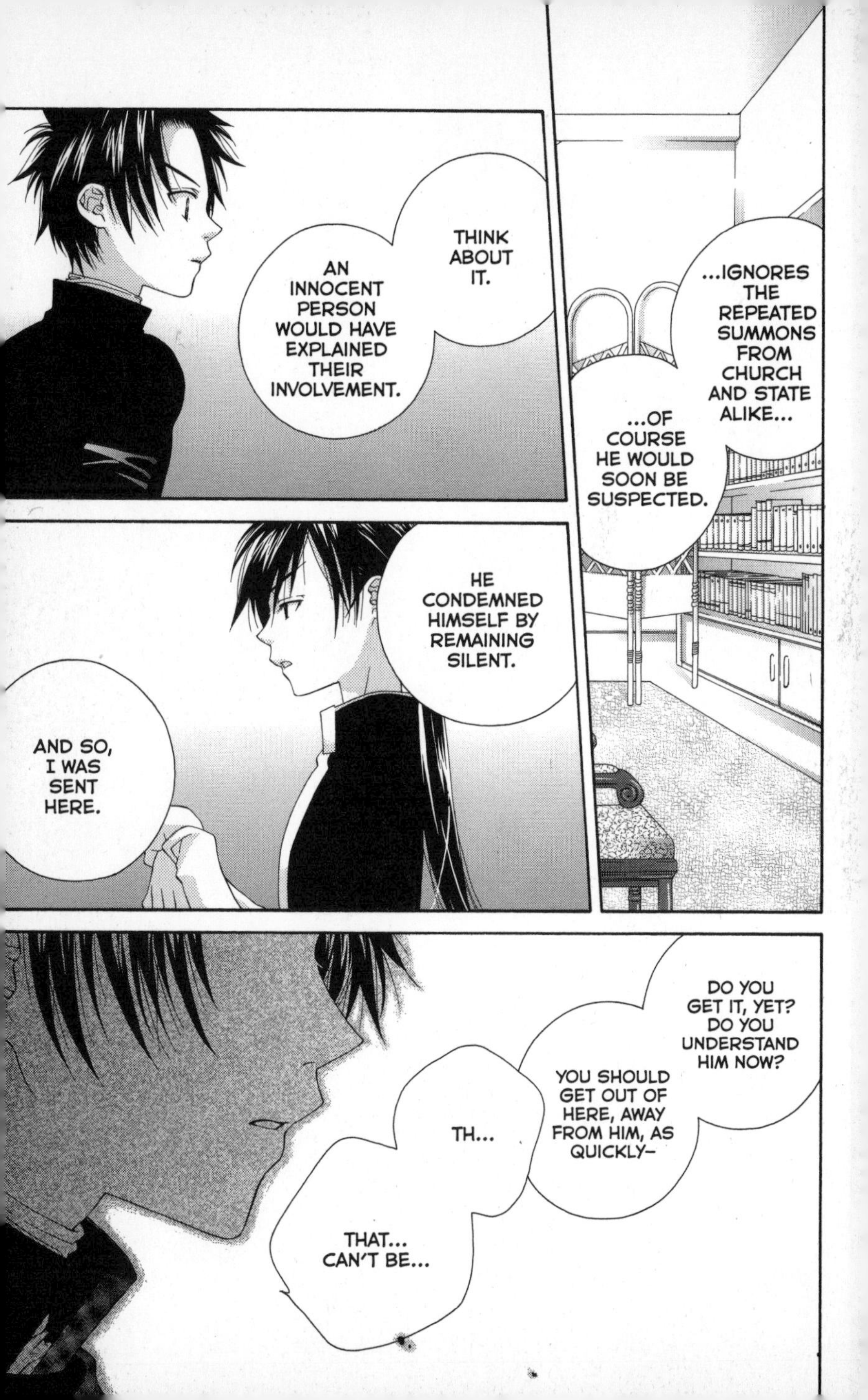
...IGNORES THE REPEATED SUMMONS FROM CHURCH AND STATE ALIKE...
...OF COURSE HE WOULD SOON BE SUSPECTED.
THINK ABOUT IT.
AN INNOCENT PERSON WOULD HAVE EXPLAINED THEIR INVOLVEMENT.
HE CONDEMNED HIMSELF BY REMAINING SILENT.
AND SO, I WAS SENT HERE.
DO YOU GET IT, YET? DO YOU UNDERSTAND HIM NOW?
YOU SHOULD GET OUT OF HERE, AWAY FROM HIM, AS QUICKLY–
TH...
THAT... CAN'T BE...

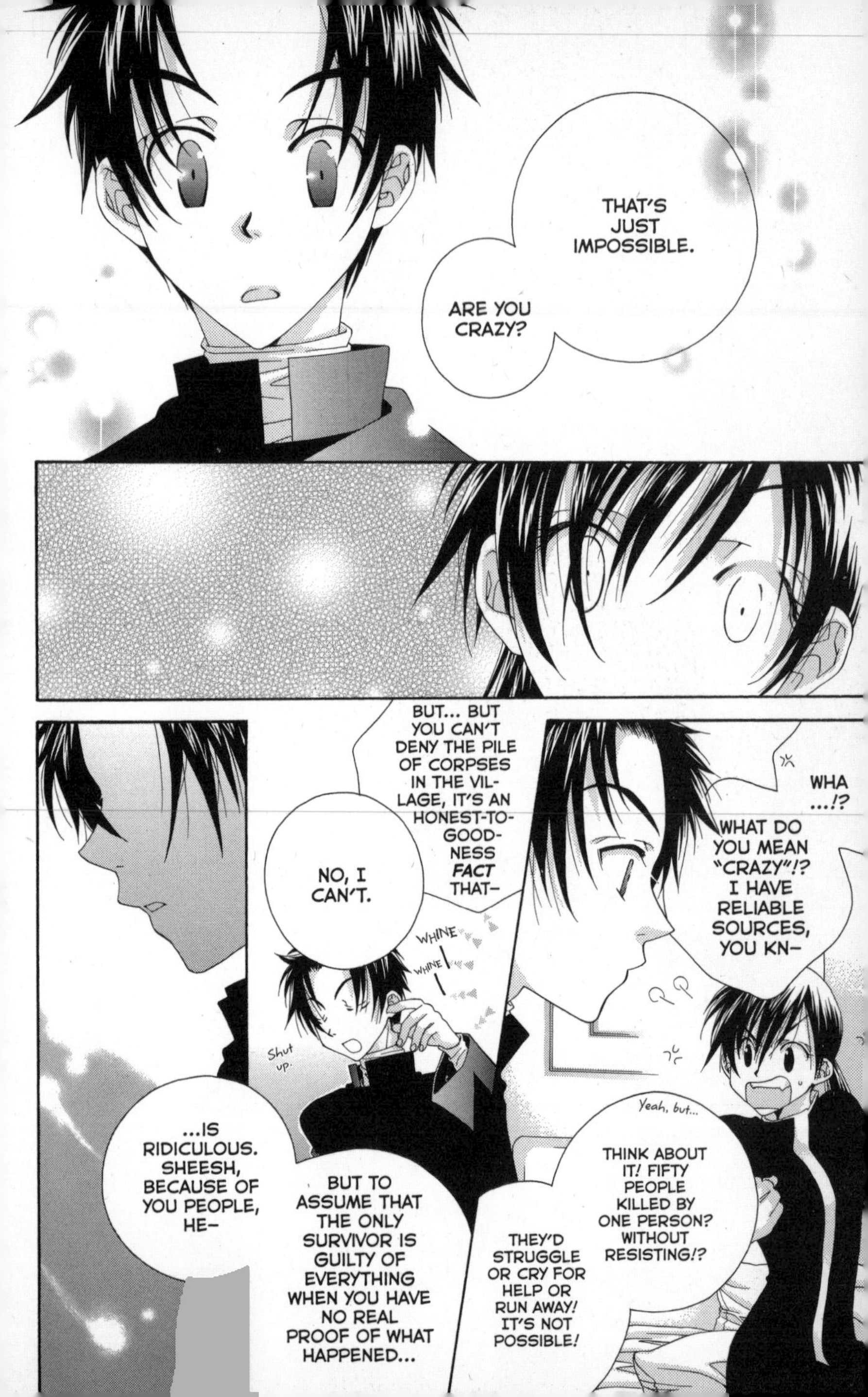
THAT'S JUST IMPOSSIBLE.
ARE YOU CRAZY?
WHA ...!?
WHAT DO YOU MEAN "CRAZY"!? I HAVE RELIABLE SOURCES, YOU KN–
Yeah, but...
THINK ABOUT IT! FIFTY PEOPLE KILLED BY ONE PERSON? WITHOUT RESISTING!?
THEY'D STRUGGLE OR CRY FOR HELP OR RUN AWAY! IT'S NOT POSSIBLE!
BUT... BUT YOU CAN'T DENY THE PILE OF CORPSES IN THE VIL- LAGE, IT'S AN HONEST-TO- GOOD- NESS *FACT* THAT–
NO, I CAN'T.
WHINE
WHINE
Shut up.
BUT TO ASSUME THAT THE ONLY SURVIVOR IS GUILTY OF EVERYTHING WHEN YOU HAVE NO REAL PROOF OF WHAT HAPPENED...
...IS RIDICULOUS. SHEESH, BECAUSE OF YOU PEOPLE, HE–

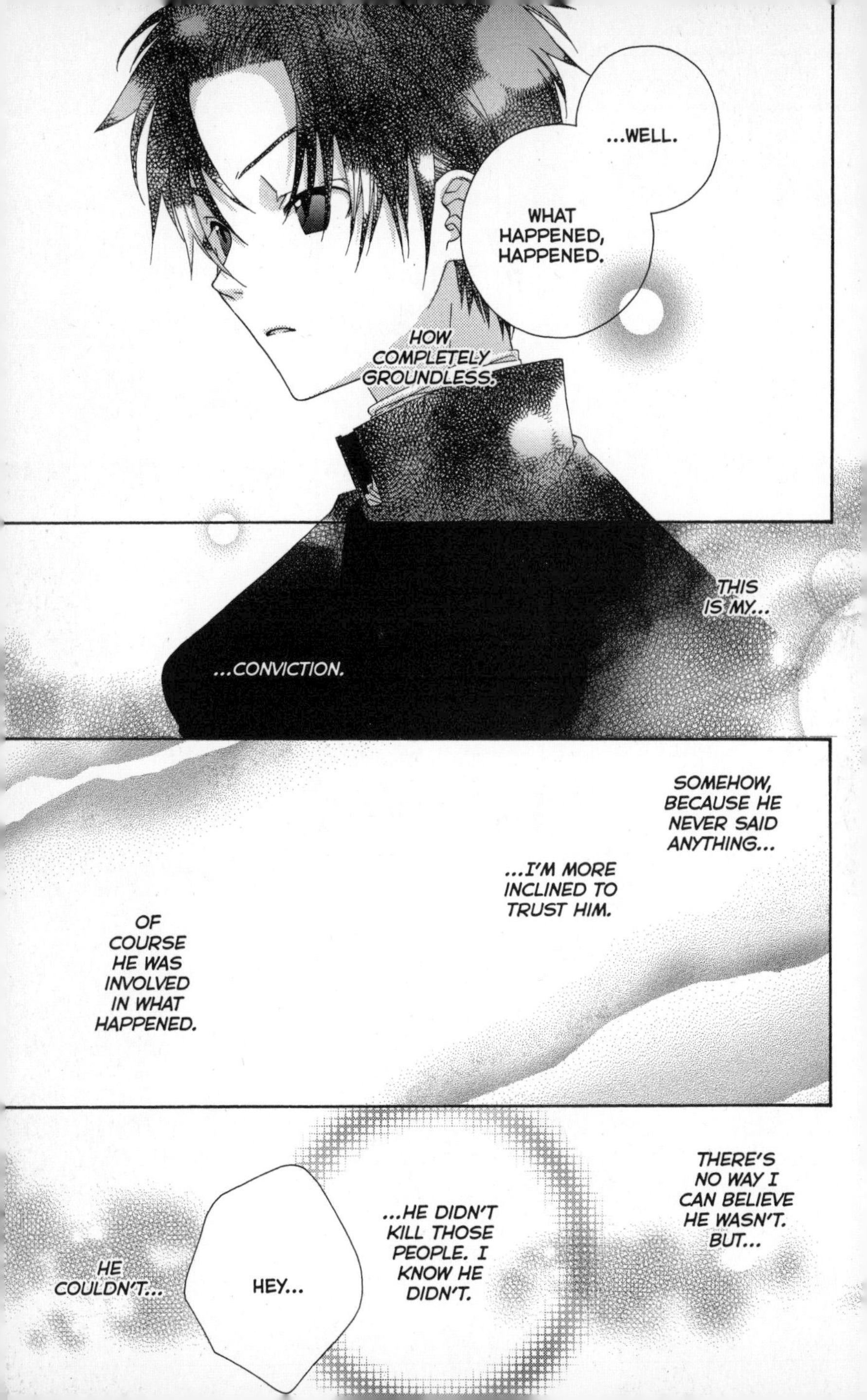

...WELL.
WHAT HAPPENED, HAPPENED.
HOW COMPLETELY GROUNDLESS.
THIS IS MY...
...CONVICTION.
SOMEHOW, BECAUSE HE NEVER SAID ANYTHING...
...I'M MORE INCLINED TO TRUST HIM.
OF COURSE HE WAS INVOLVED IN WHAT HAPPENED.
THERE'S NO WAY I CAN BELIEVE HE WASN'T. BUT...
...HE DIDN'T KILL THOSE PEOPLE. I KNOW HE DIDN'T.
HEY...
HE COULDN'T...

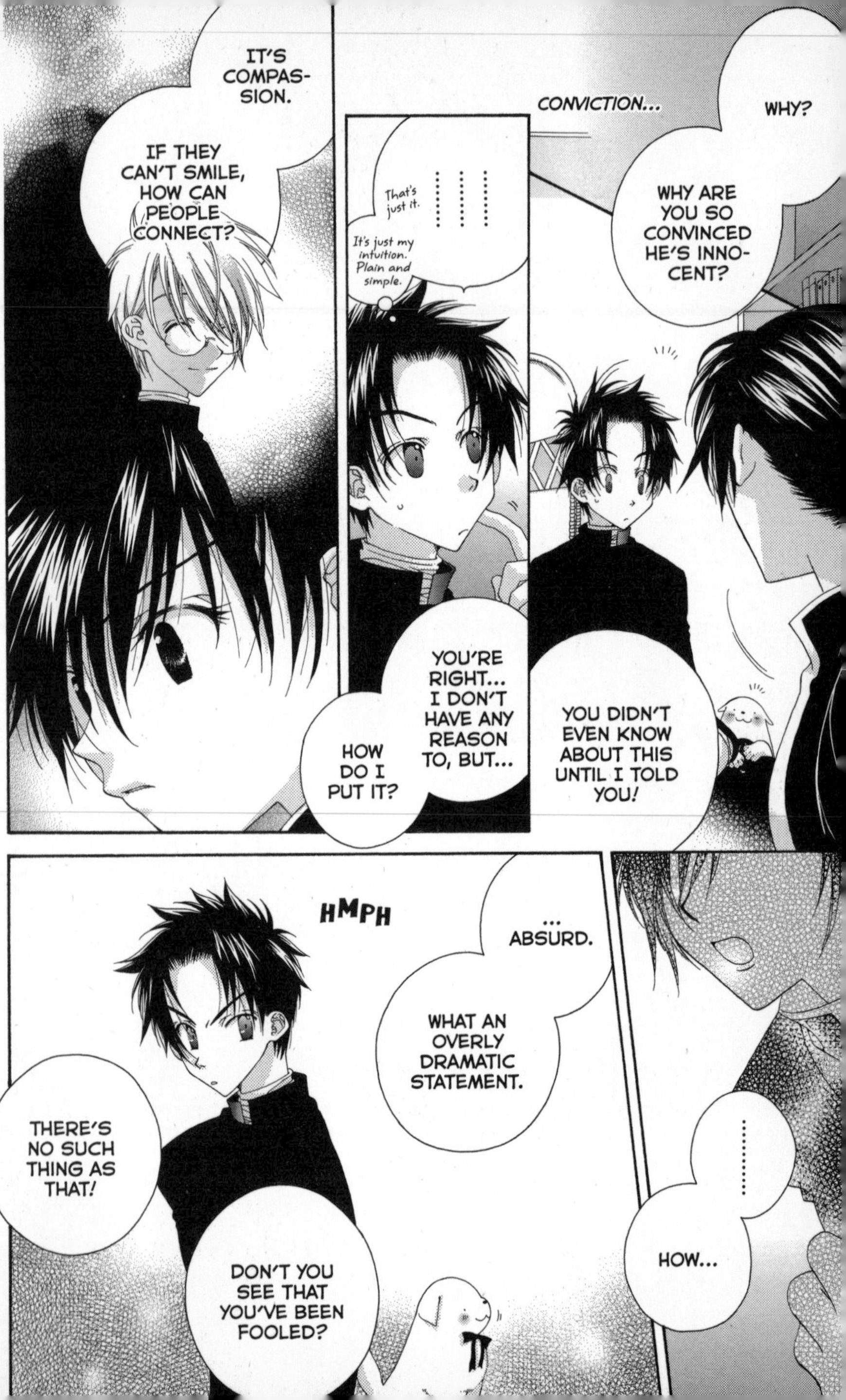
WHY?
CONVICTION...
WHY ARE YOU SO CONVINCED HE'S INNOCENT?
YOU DIDN'T EVEN KNOW ABOUT THIS UNTIL I TOLD YOU!
......
That's just it.
It's just my intuition. Plain and simple.
YOU'RE RIGHT... I DON'T HAVE ANY REASON TO, BUT...
HOW DO I PUT IT?
IT'S COMPASSION.
IF THEY CAN'T SMILE, HOW CAN PEOPLE CONNECT?
......
HOW...
... ABSURD.
HMPH
WHAT AN OVERLY DRAMATIC STATEMENT.
THERE'S NO SUCH THING AS THAT!
DON'T YOU SEE THAT YOU'VE BEEN FOOLED?

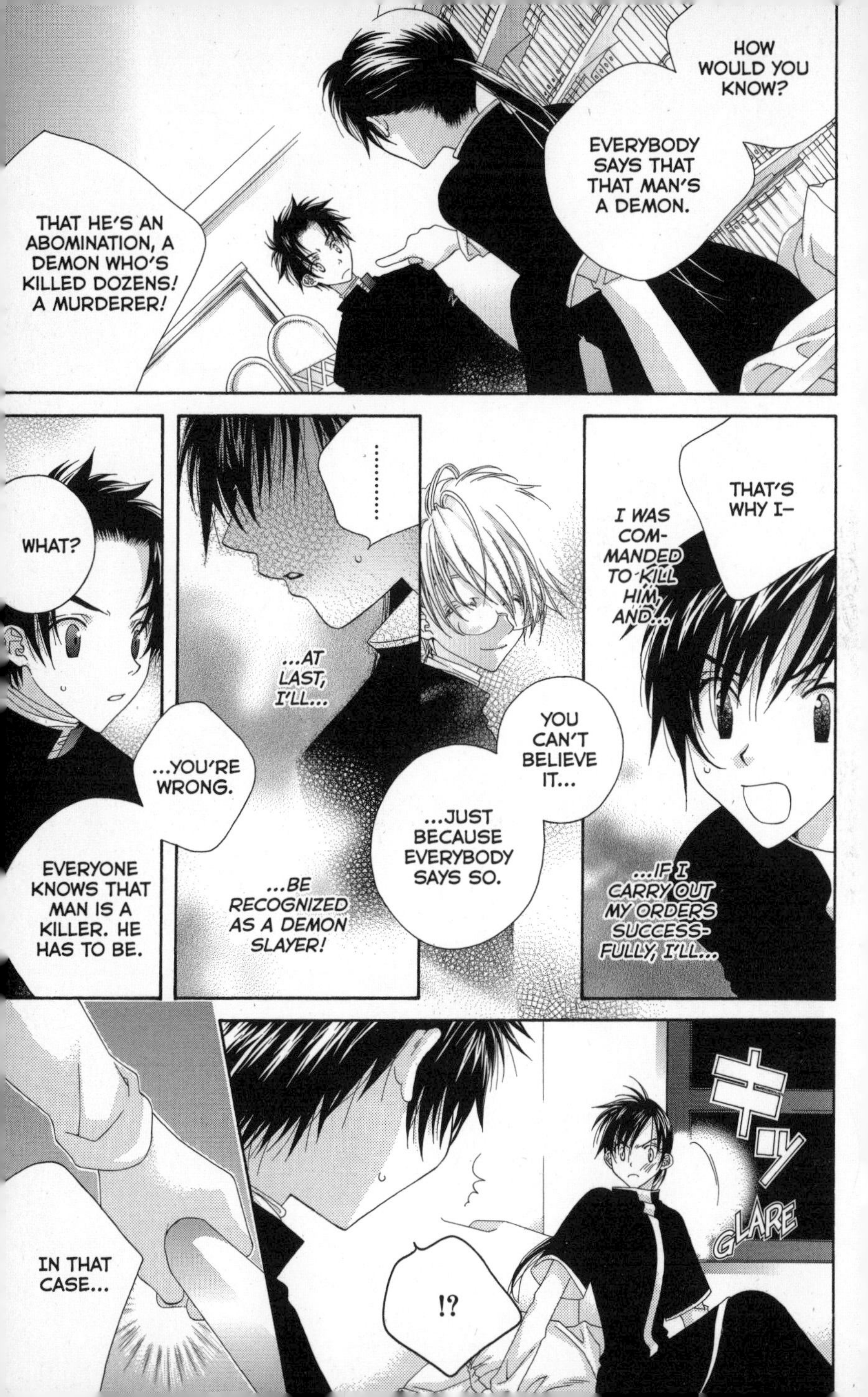
HOW WOULD YOU KNOW?
EVERYBODY SAYS THAT THAT MAN'S A DEMON.
THAT HE'S AN ABOMINATION, A DEMON WHO'S KILLED DOZENS! A MURDERER!
THAT'S WHY I—
I WAS COMMANDED TO KILL HIM, AND...
...IF I CARRY OUT MY ORDERS SUCCESSFULLY, I'LL...
......
...AT LAST, I'LL...
YOU CAN'T BELIEVE IT...
...JUST BECAUSE EVERYBODY SAYS SO.
...BE RECOGNIZED AS A DEMON SLAYER!
WHAT?
...YOU'RE WRONG.
EVERYONE KNOWS THAT MAN IS A KILLER. HE HAS TO BE.
キッ
GLARE
!?
IN THAT CASE...

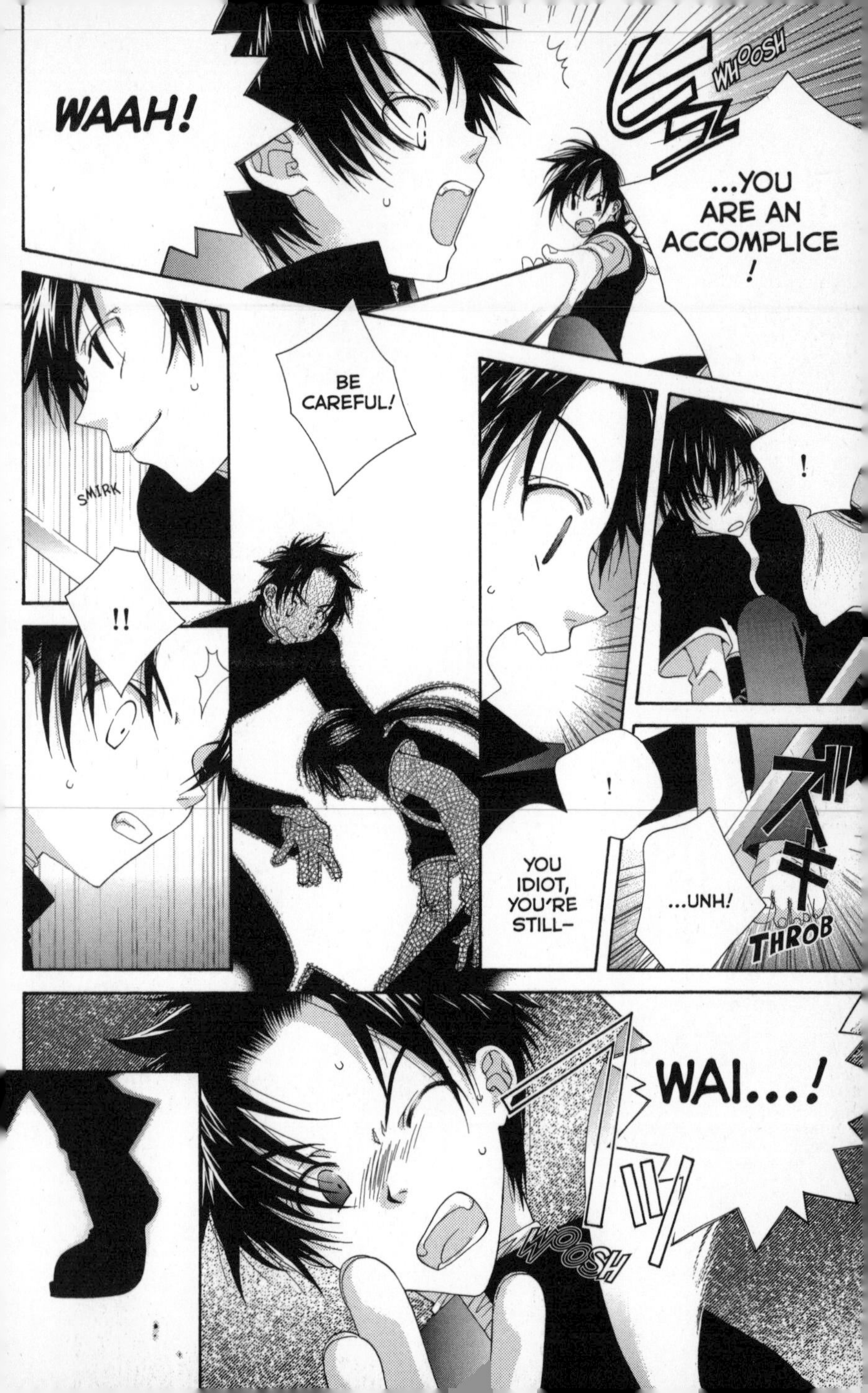
WHOOSH
...YOU ARE AN ACCOMPLICE!
WAAH!
!
...UNH!
THROB
!
YOU IDIOT, YOU'RE STILL—
BE CAREFUL!
SMIRK
!!
WAI...!
WOOSH

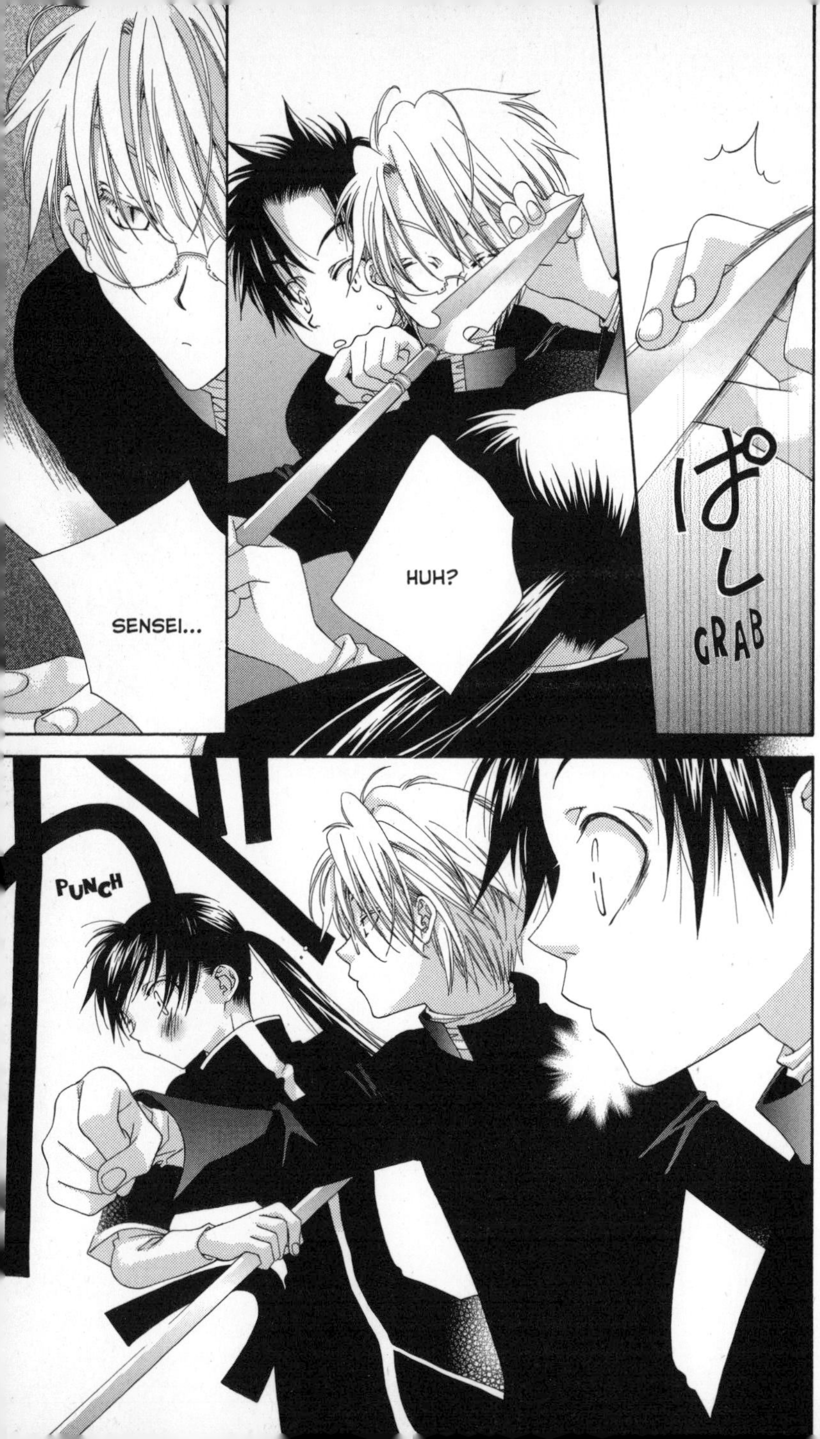
ぱし
GRAB
HUH?
SENSEI...
PUNCH

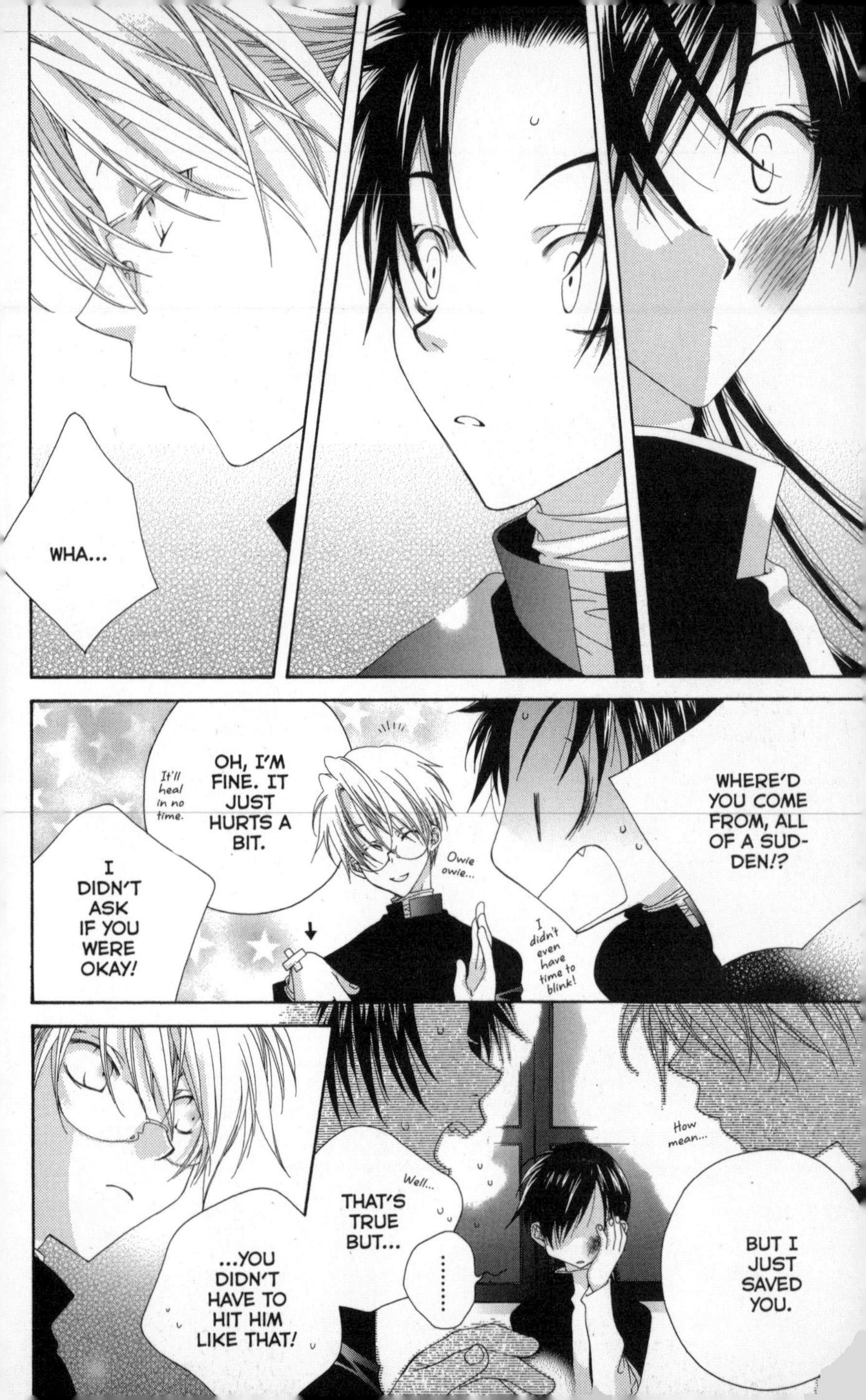
WHA...
WHERE'D YOU COME FROM, ALL OF A SUD-DEN!?
I didn't even have time to blink!
Owie owie...
OH, I'M FINE. IT JUST HURTS A BIT.
It'll heal in no time.
I DIDN'T ASK IF YOU WERE OKAY!
How mean...
BUT I JUST SAVED YOU.
Well...
THAT'S TRUE BUT...
....
...YOU DIDN'T HAVE TO HIT HIM LIKE THAT!

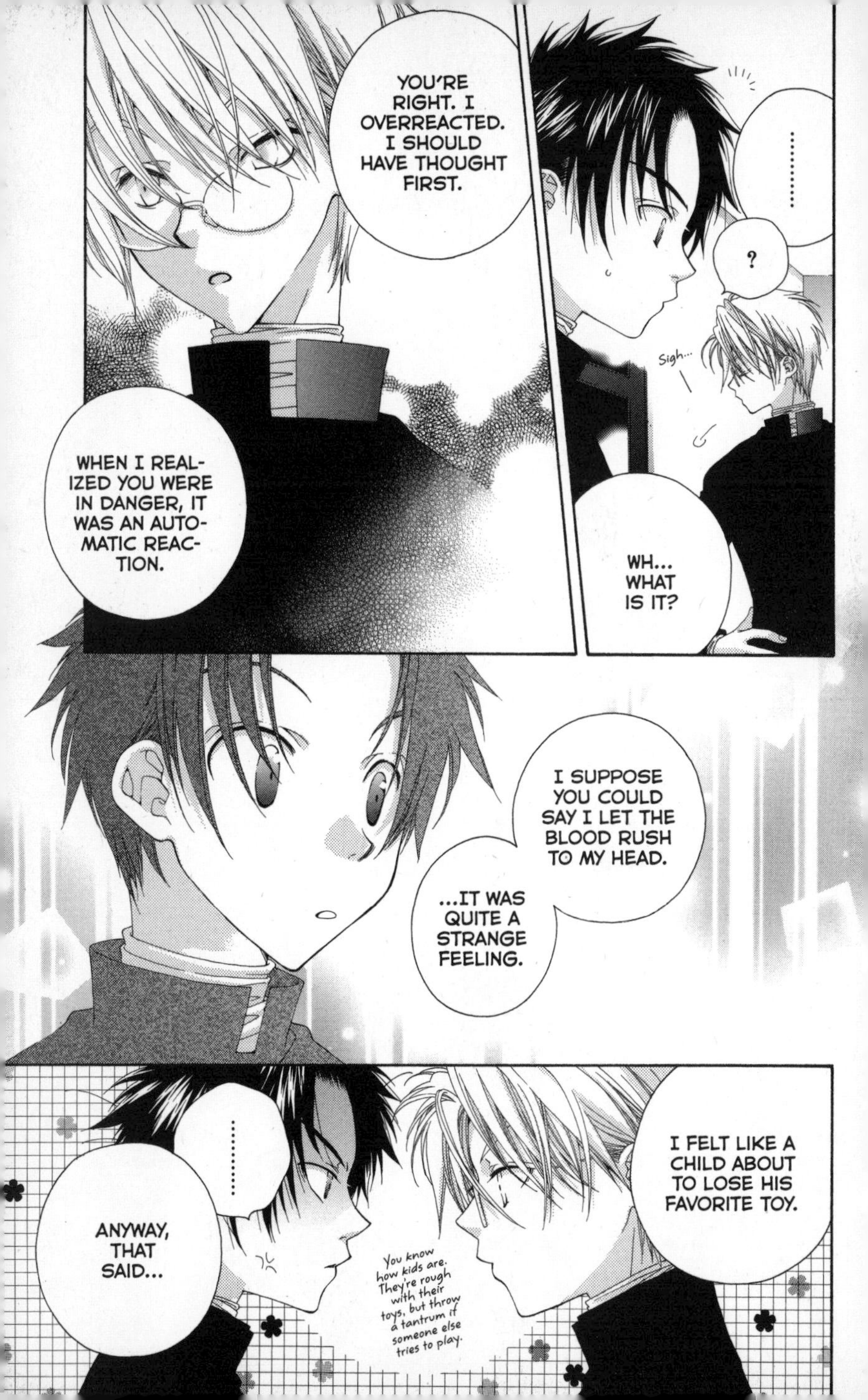
......
?
Sigh...
WH... WHAT IS IT?
YOU'RE RIGHT. I OVERREACTED. I SHOULD HAVE THOUGHT FIRST.
WHEN I REAL-IZED YOU WERE IN DANGER, IT WAS AN AUTO-MATIC REAC-TION.
I SUPPOSE YOU COULD SAY I LET THE BLOOD RUSH TO MY HEAD.
...IT WAS QUITE A STRANGE FEELING.
I FELT LIKE A CHILD ABOUT TO LOSE HIS FAVORITE TOY.
You know how kids are. They're rough with their toys, but throw a tantrum if someone else tries to play.
......
ANYWAY, THAT SAID...

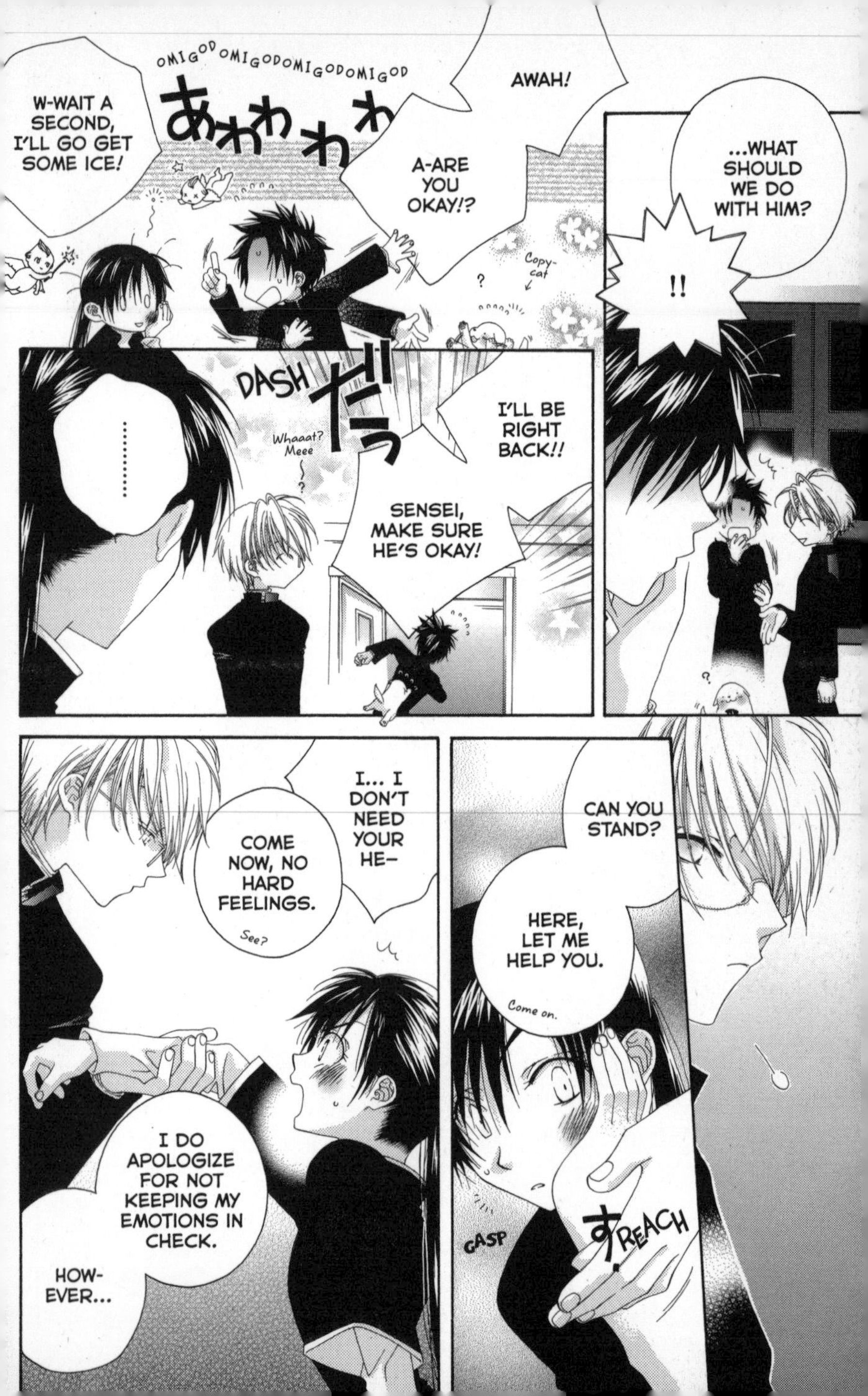
AWAH!
A-ARE YOU OKAY!?
OMIGOD OMIGODOMIGODOMIGOD
あわわわわ
W-WAIT A SECOND, I'LL GO GET SOME ICE!
Copy-cat
?
...WHAT SHOULD WE DO WITH HIM?
!!
?
I'LL BE RIGHT BACK!!
SENSEI, MAKE SURE HE'S OKAY!
DASH
だっ
Whaaat? Meee
?
......
CAN YOU STAND?
HERE, LET ME HELP YOU.
Come on.
すっ REACH
GASP
I... I DON'T NEED YOUR HE—
COME NOW, NO HARD FEELINGS.
See?
I DO APOLOGIZE FOR NOT KEEPING MY EMOTIONS IN CHECK.
HOW-EVER...

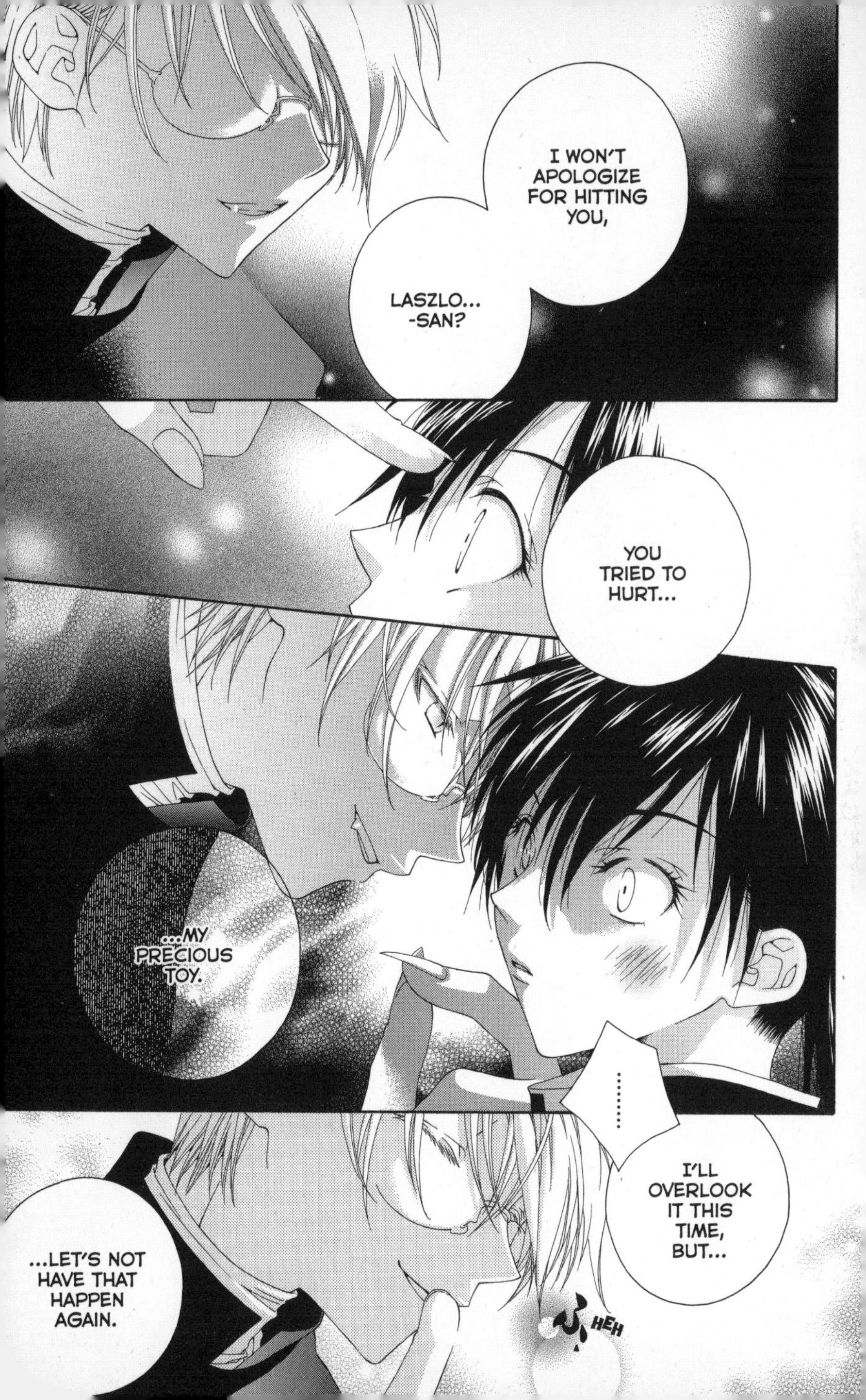
I WON'T APOLOGIZE FOR HITTING YOU,
LASZLO... -SAN?
YOU TRIED TO HURT...
...MY PRECIOUS TOY.
......
I'LL OVERLOOK IT THIS TIME, BUT...
ふ HEH
...LET'S NOT HAVE THAT HAPPEN AGAIN.

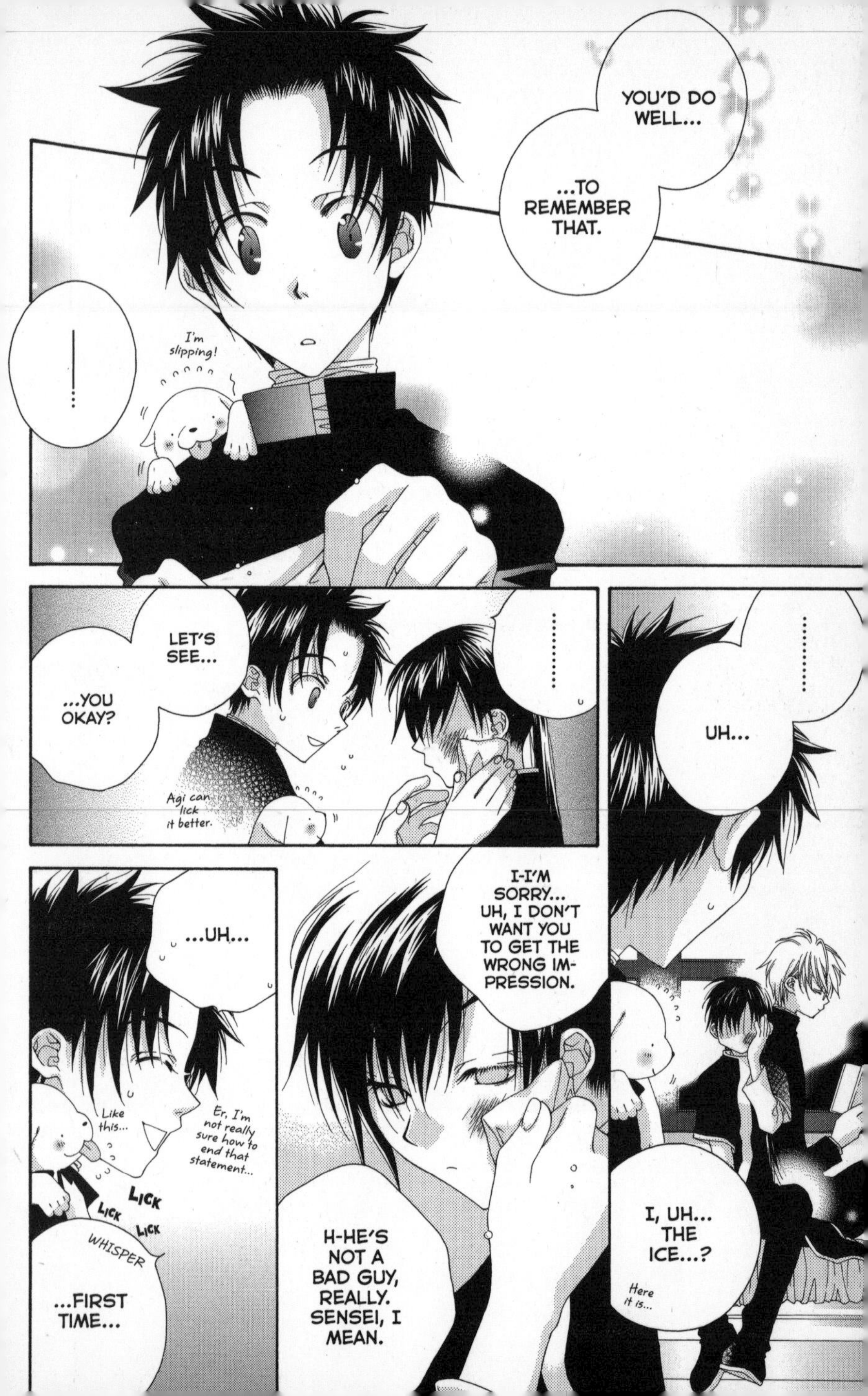
YOU'D DO WELL...
...TO REMEMBER THAT.
I'm slipping!
—......
....
UH...
I, UH... THE ICE...?
Here it is...
....
LET'S SEE...
...YOU OKAY?
Agi can lick it better.
I-I'M SORRY... UH, I DON'T WANT YOU TO GET THE WRONG IM-PRESSION.
H-HE'S NOT A BAD GUY, REALLY. SENSEI, I MEAN.
...UH...
Er, I'm not really sure how to end that statement...
Like this...
LICK
LICK
LICK
WHISPER
...FIRST TIME...

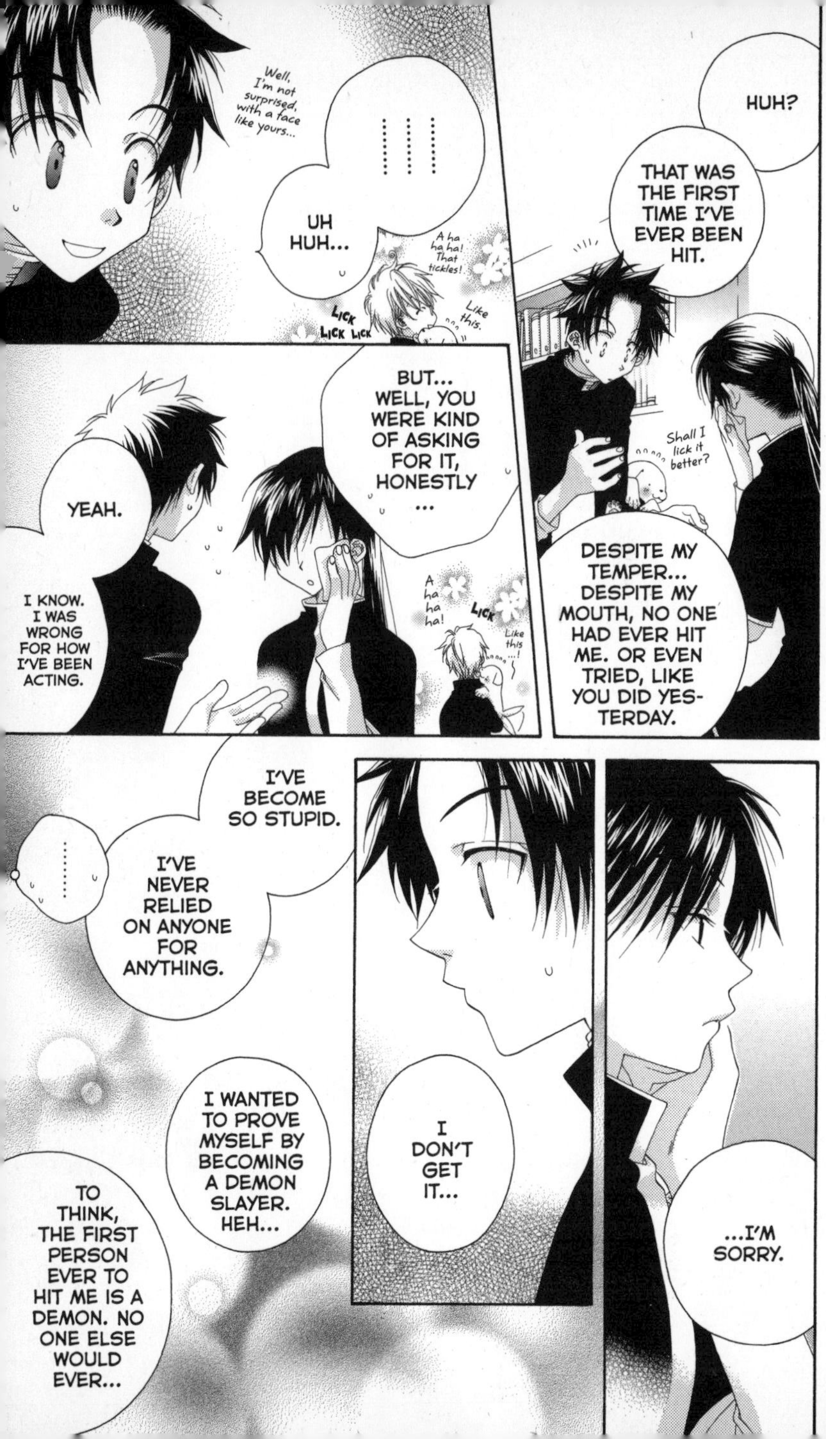
HUH?
THAT WAS THE FIRST TIME I'VE EVER BEEN HIT.
Shall I lick it better?
DESPITE MY TEMPER... DESPITE MY MOUTH, NO ONE HAD EVER HIT ME. OR EVEN TRIED, LIKE YOU DID YESTERDAY.
......
Well, I'm not surprised, with a face like yours...
UH HUH...
A ha ha ha! That tickles!
Like this.
LICK LICK LICK
BUT... WELL, YOU WERE KIND OF ASKING FOR IT, HONESTLY ...
A ha ha ha!
LICK
Like this...!
YEAH.
I KNOW. I WAS WRONG FOR HOW I'VE BEEN ACTING.
...I'M SORRY.
I DON'T GET IT...
I'VE BECOME SO STUPID.
......
I'VE NEVER RELIED ON ANYONE FOR ANYTHING.
I WANTED TO PROVE MYSELF BY BECOMING A DEMON SLAYER. HEH...
TO THINK, THE FIRST PERSON EVER TO HIT ME IS A DEMON. NO ONE ELSE WOULD EVER...

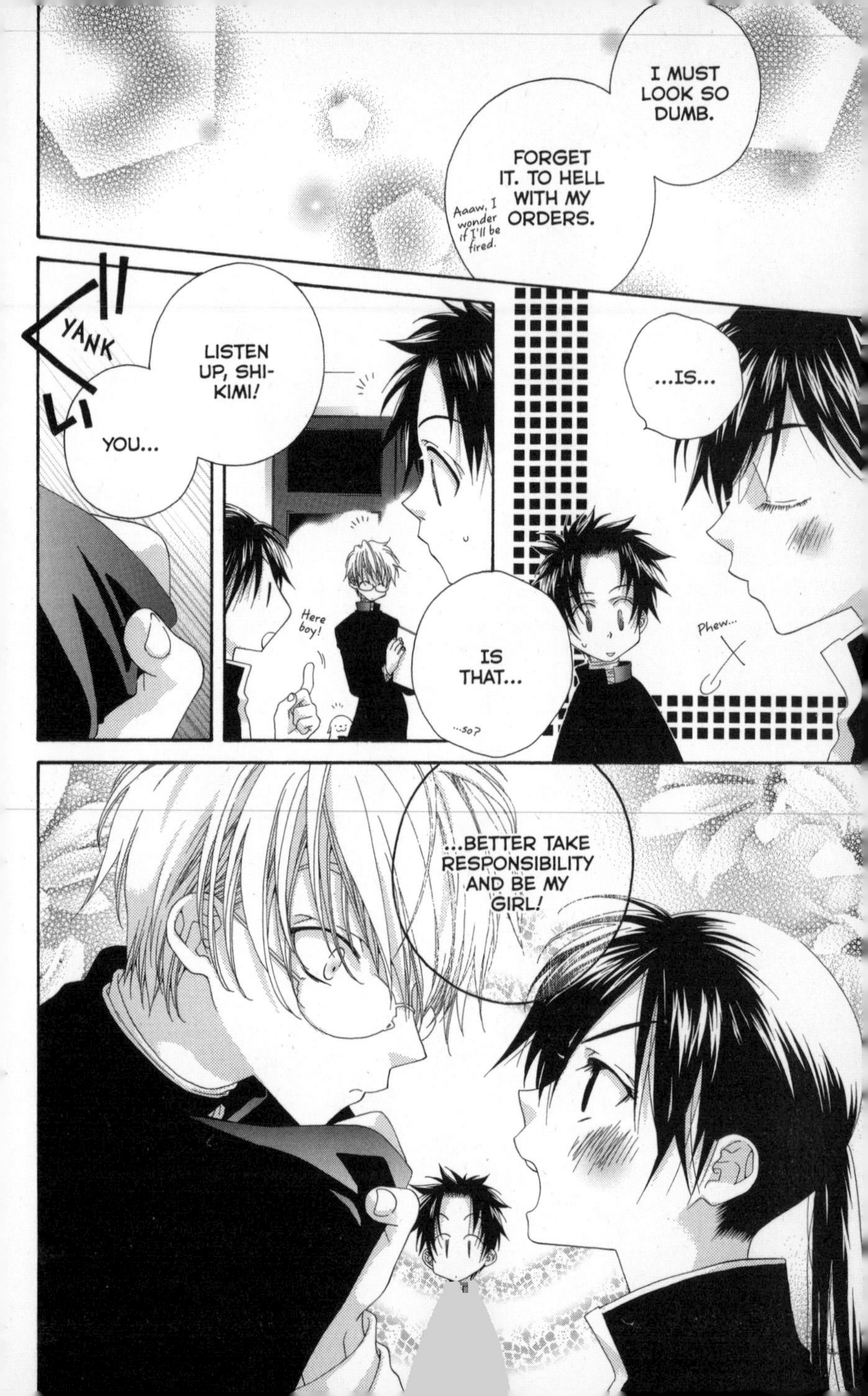
I MUST LOOK SO DUMB.
FORGET IT. TO HELL WITH MY ORDERS.
Aaaw, I wonder if I'll be fired.
...IS...
Phew...
IS THAT...
...so?
Here boy!
LISTEN UP, SHI-KIMI!
YANK
YOU...
...BETTER TAKE RESPONSIBILITY AND BE MY GIRL!

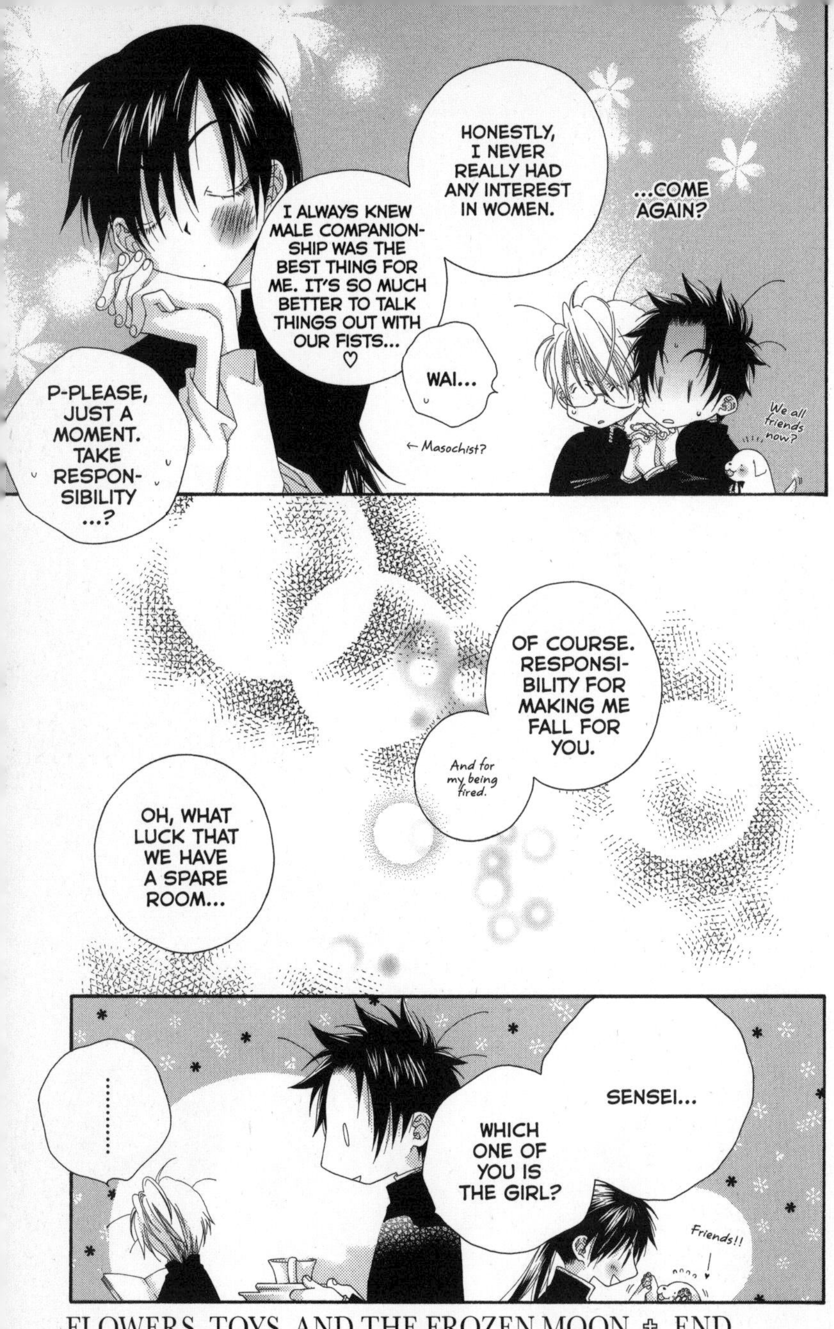
...COME AGAIN?
HONESTLY, I NEVER REALLY HAD ANY INTEREST IN WOMEN.
I ALWAYS KNEW MALE COMPANIONSHIP WAS THE BEST THING FOR ME. IT'S SO MUCH BETTER TO TALK THINGS OUT WITH OUR FISTS... ♡
We all friends now?
WAI...
← Masochist?
P-PLEASE, JUST A MOMENT. TAKE RESPONSIBILITY ...?
OF COURSE. RESPONSIBILITY FOR MAKING ME FALL FOR YOU.
And for my being fired.
OH, WHAT LUCK THAT WE HAVE A SPARE ROOM...
SENSEI...
WHICH ONE OF YOU IS THE GIRL?
Friends!!
....

FLOWERS, TOYS, AND THE FROZEN MOON ✝ END

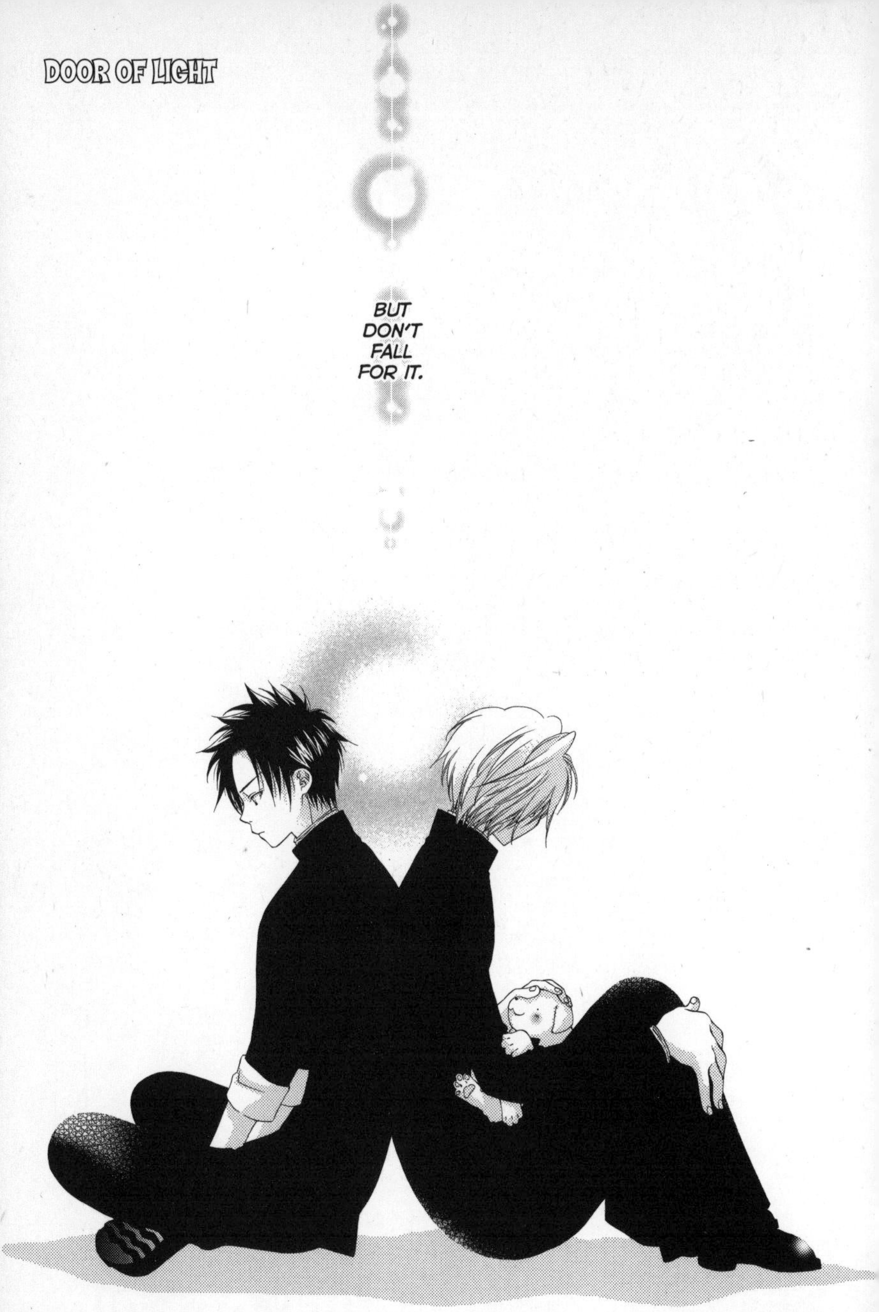
BUT DON'T FALL FOR IT.

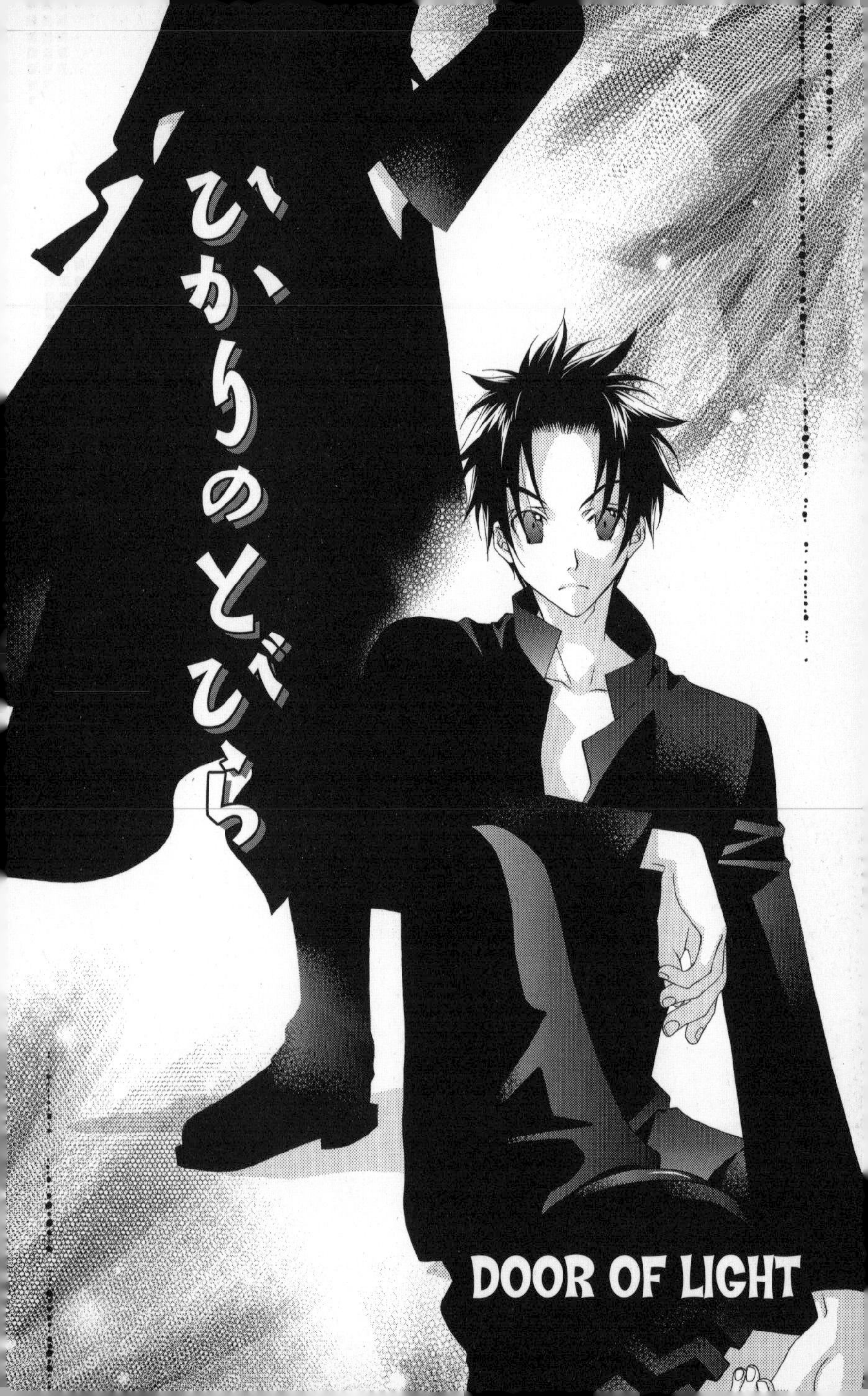
ひかりのとびら
DOOR OF LIGHT

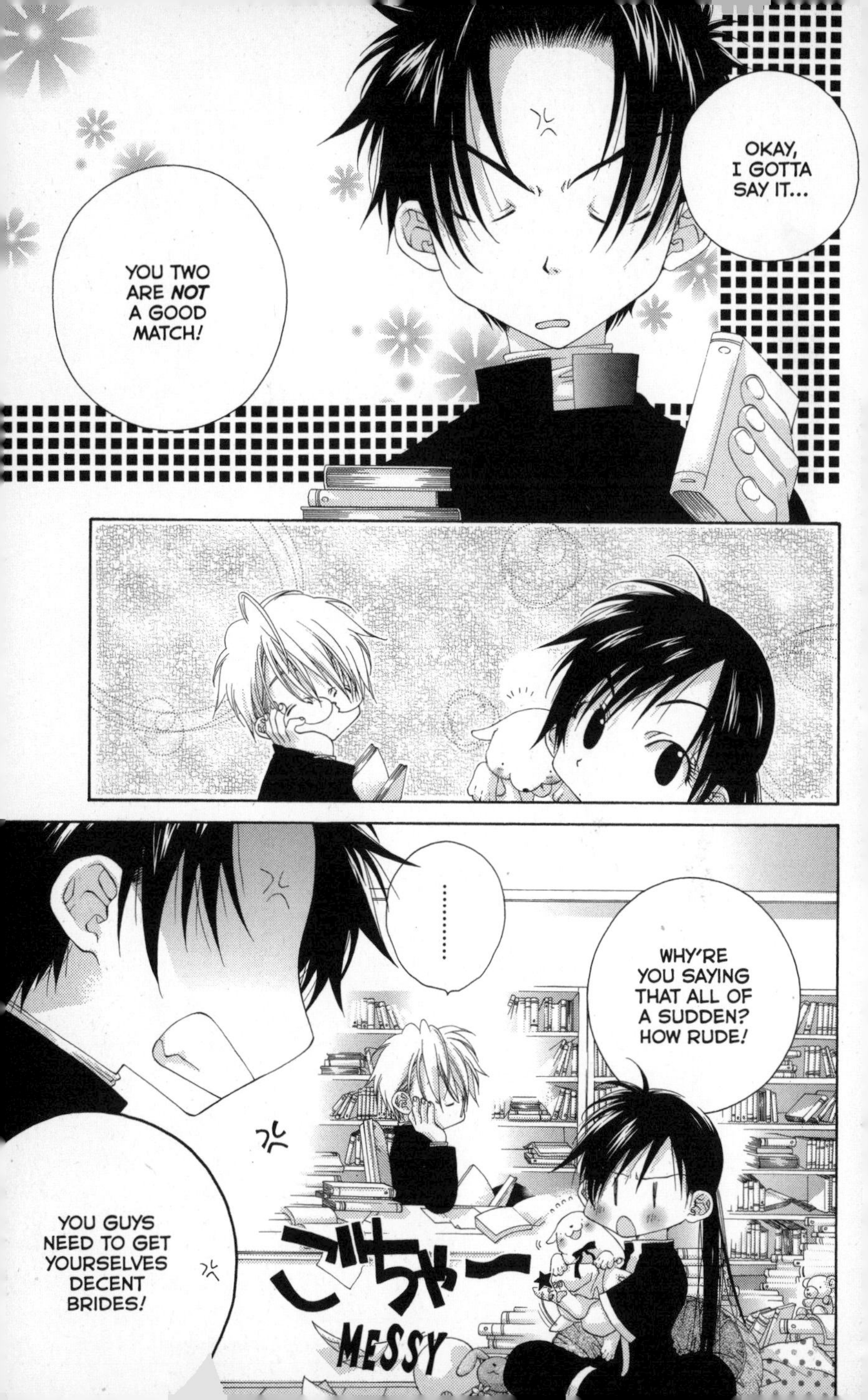

OKAY, I GOTTA SAY IT...
YOU TWO ARE *NOT* A GOOD MATCH!
WHY'RE YOU SAYING THAT ALL OF A SUDDEN? HOW RUDE!
......
YOU GUYS NEED TO GET YOURSELVES DECENT BRIDES!
ごちゃー
MESSY

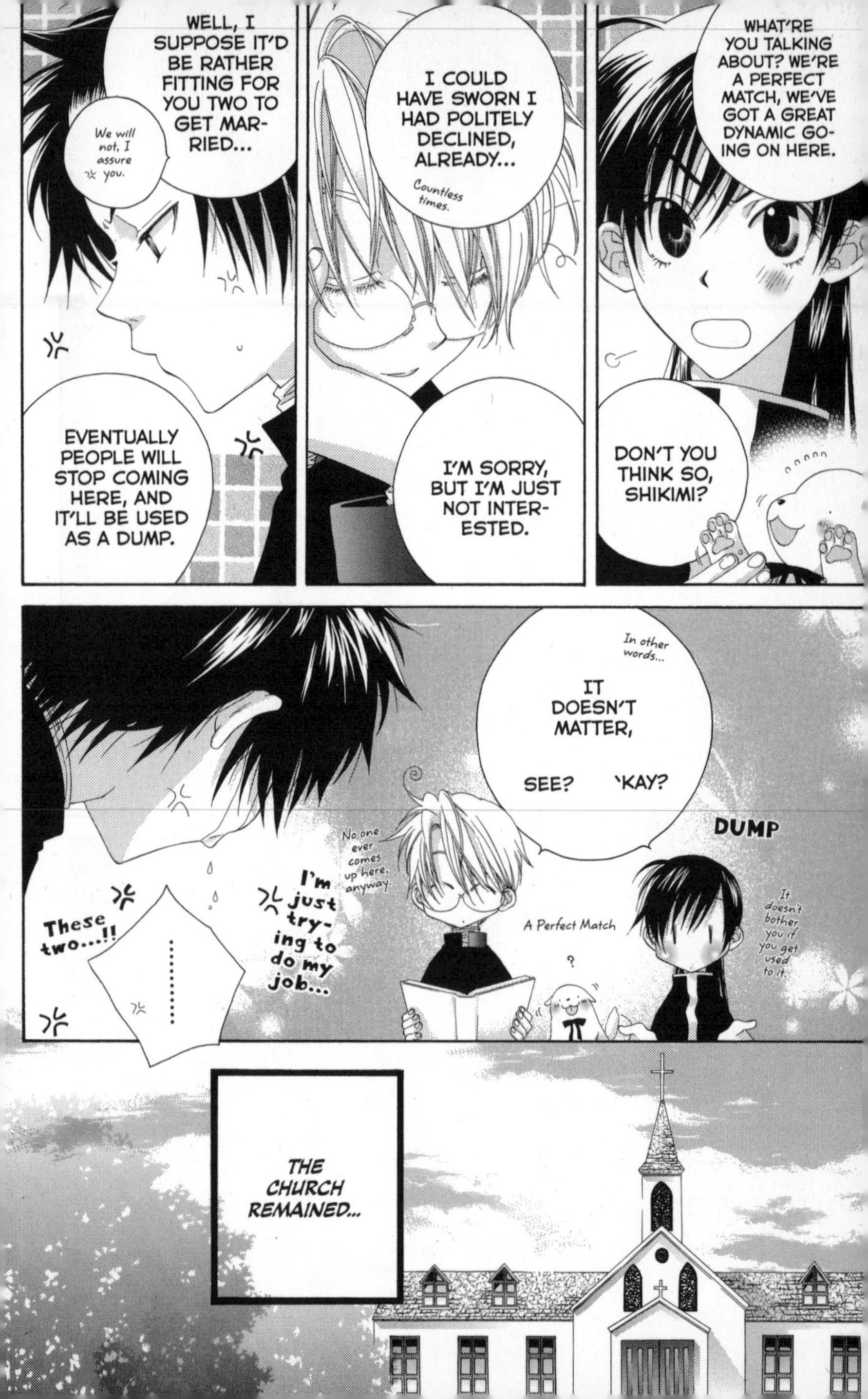
WHAT'RE YOU TALKING ABOUT? WE'RE A PERFECT MATCH, WE'VE GOT A GREAT DYNAMIC GO-ING ON HERE.
DON'T YOU THINK SO, SHIKIMI?
I COULD HAVE SWORN I HAD POLITELY DECLINED, ALREADY...
Countless times.
I'M SORRY, BUT I'M JUST NOT INTER-ESTED.
WELL, I SUPPOSE IT'D BE RATHER FITTING FOR YOU TWO TO GET MAR-RIED...
We will not, I assure you.
EVENTUALLY PEOPLE WILL STOP COMING HERE, AND IT'LL BE USED AS A DUMP.
It doesn't bother you if you get used to it.
DUMP
In other words...
IT DOESN'T MATTER,
SEE? 'KAY?
A Perfect Match
?
No one ever comes up here, anyway.
I'm just try-ing to do my job...
These two...!!
....
THE CHURCH REMAINED...

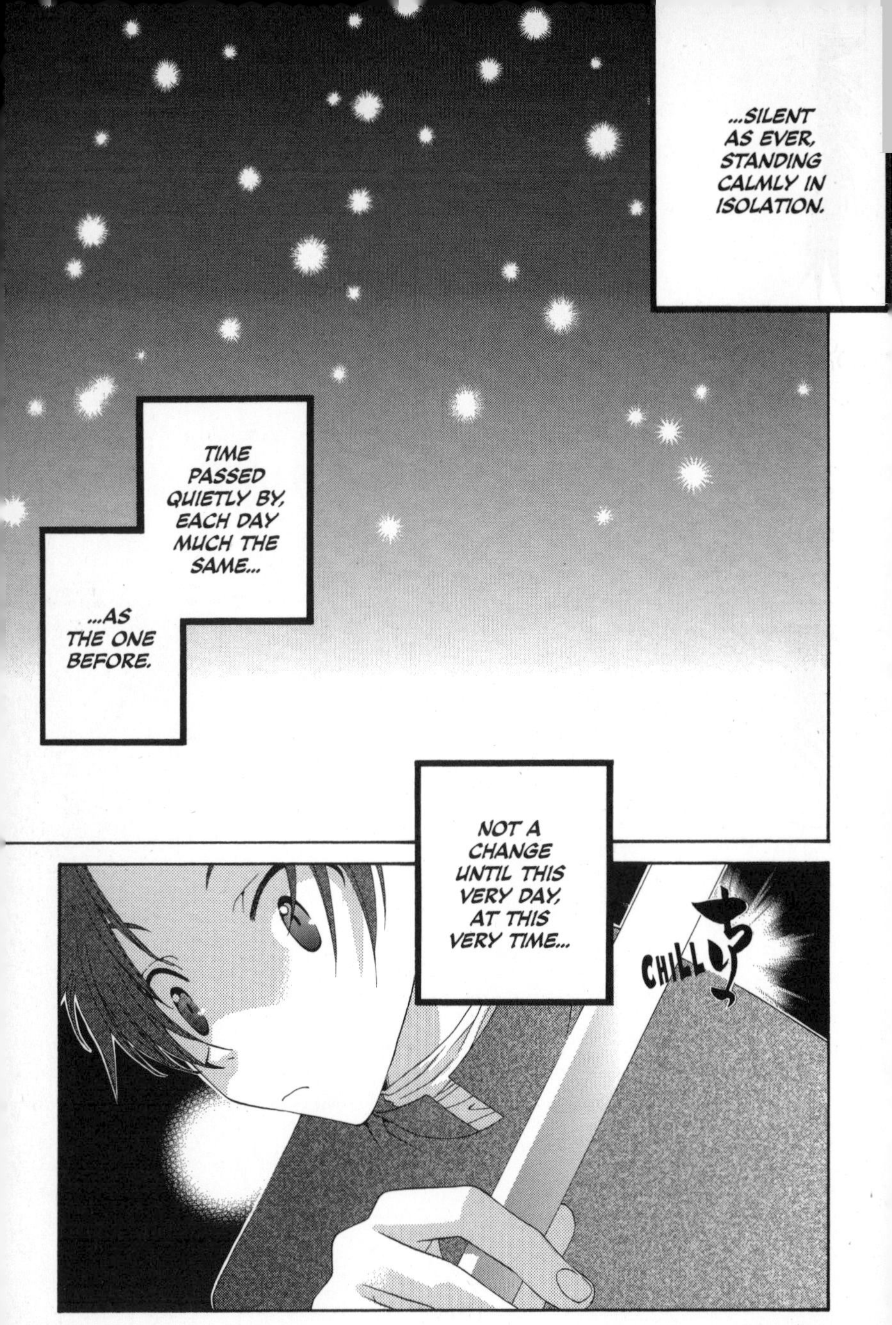
...SILENT AS EVER, STANDING CALMLY IN ISOLATION.
TIME PASSED QUIETLY BY, EACH DAY MUCH THE SAME...
...AS THE ONE BEFORE.
NOT A CHANGE UNTIL THIS VERY DAY, AT THIS VERY TIME...
CHILL

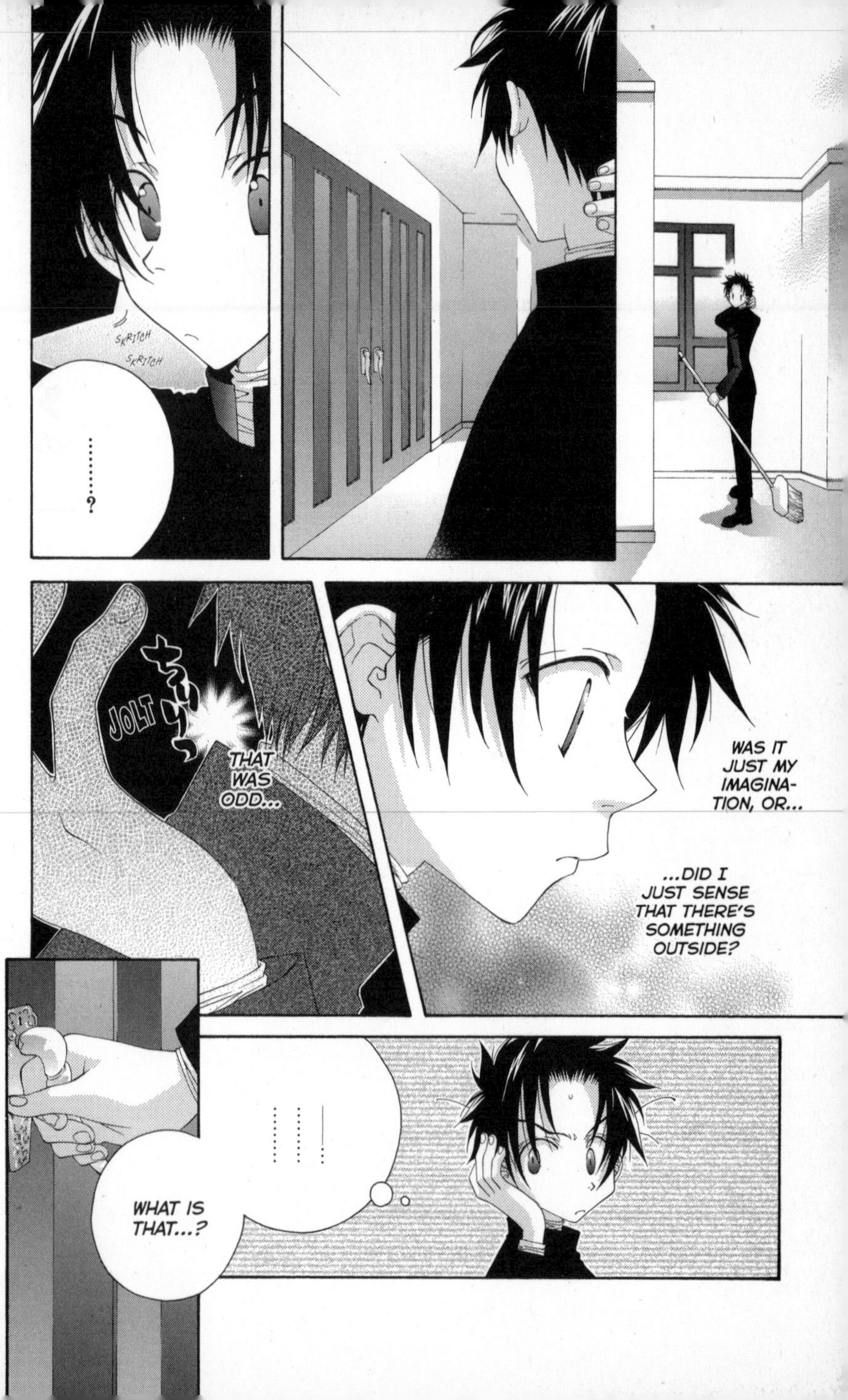
SKRITCH
SKRITCH
......?
WAS IT JUST MY IMAGINATION, OR...
...DID I JUST SENSE THAT THERE'S SOMETHING OUTSIDE?
JOLT
THAT WAS ODD...
......
......!
WHAT IS THAT...?

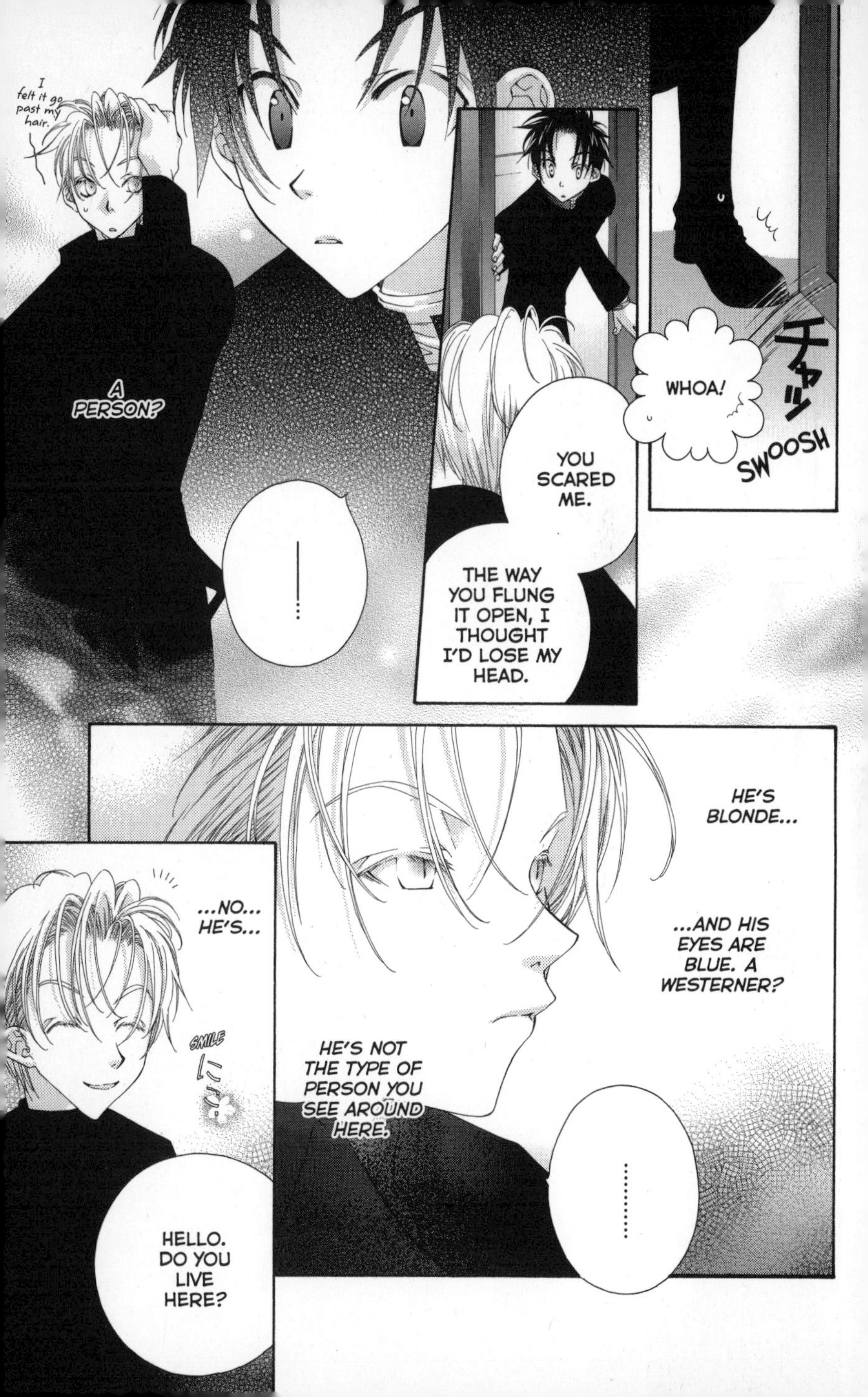
WHOA!
SWOOSH
YOU SCARED ME.
THE WAY YOU FLUNG IT OPEN, I THOUGHT I'D LOSE MY HEAD.
I felt it go past my hair.
A PERSON?
——…
HE'S BLONDE...
...AND HIS EYES ARE BLUE. A WESTERNER?
……
HE'S NOT THE TYPE OF PERSON YOU SEE AROUND HERE.
...NO... HE'S...
SMILE
HELLO. DO YOU LIVE HERE?

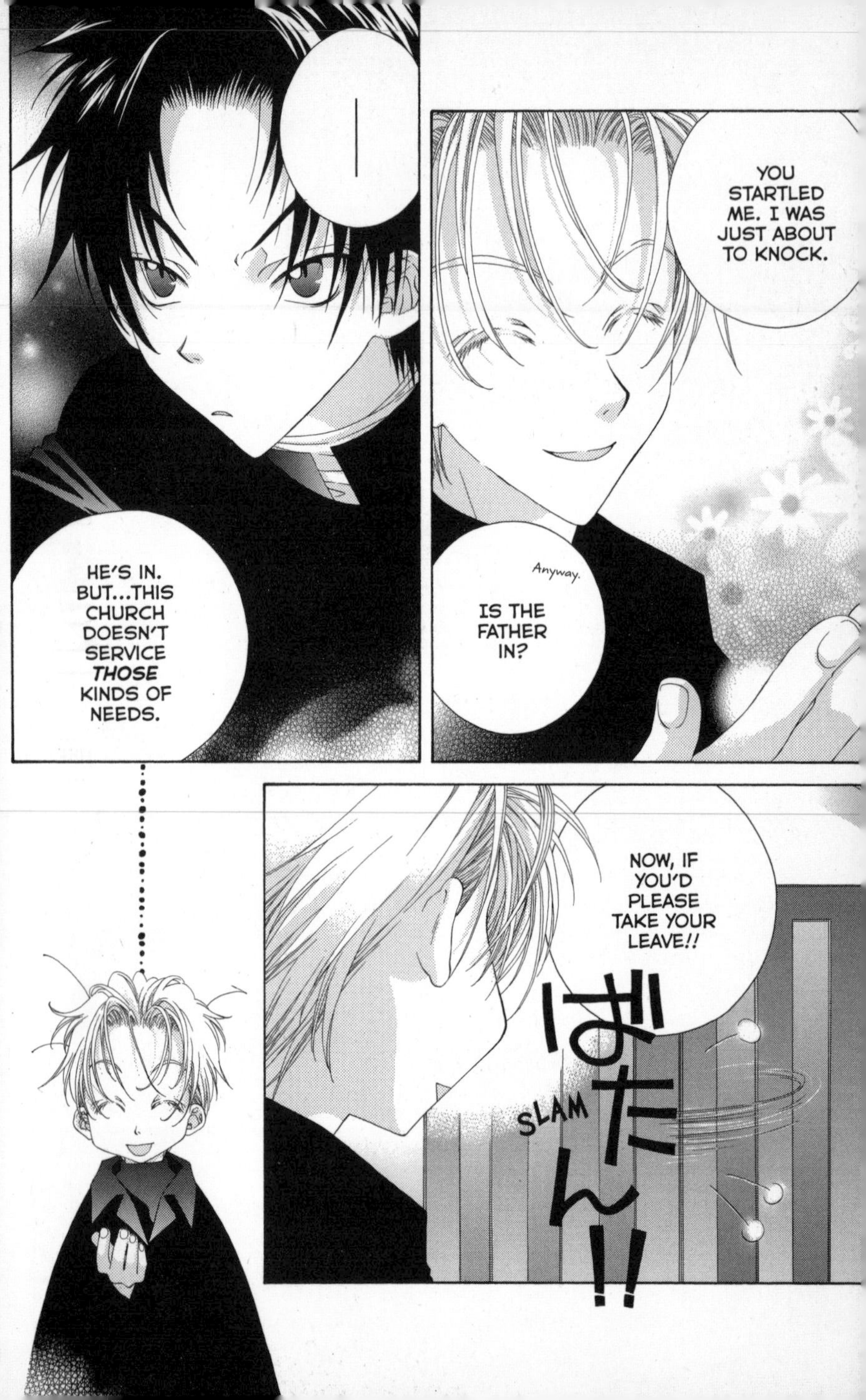
YOU STARTLED ME. I WAS JUST ABOUT TO KNOCK.
Anyway.
IS THE FATHER IN?
—
HE'S IN. BUT...THIS CHURCH DOESN'T SERVICE *THOSE* KINDS OF NEEDS.
NOW, IF YOU'D PLEASE TAKE YOUR LEAVE!!
ばたん!!
SLAM

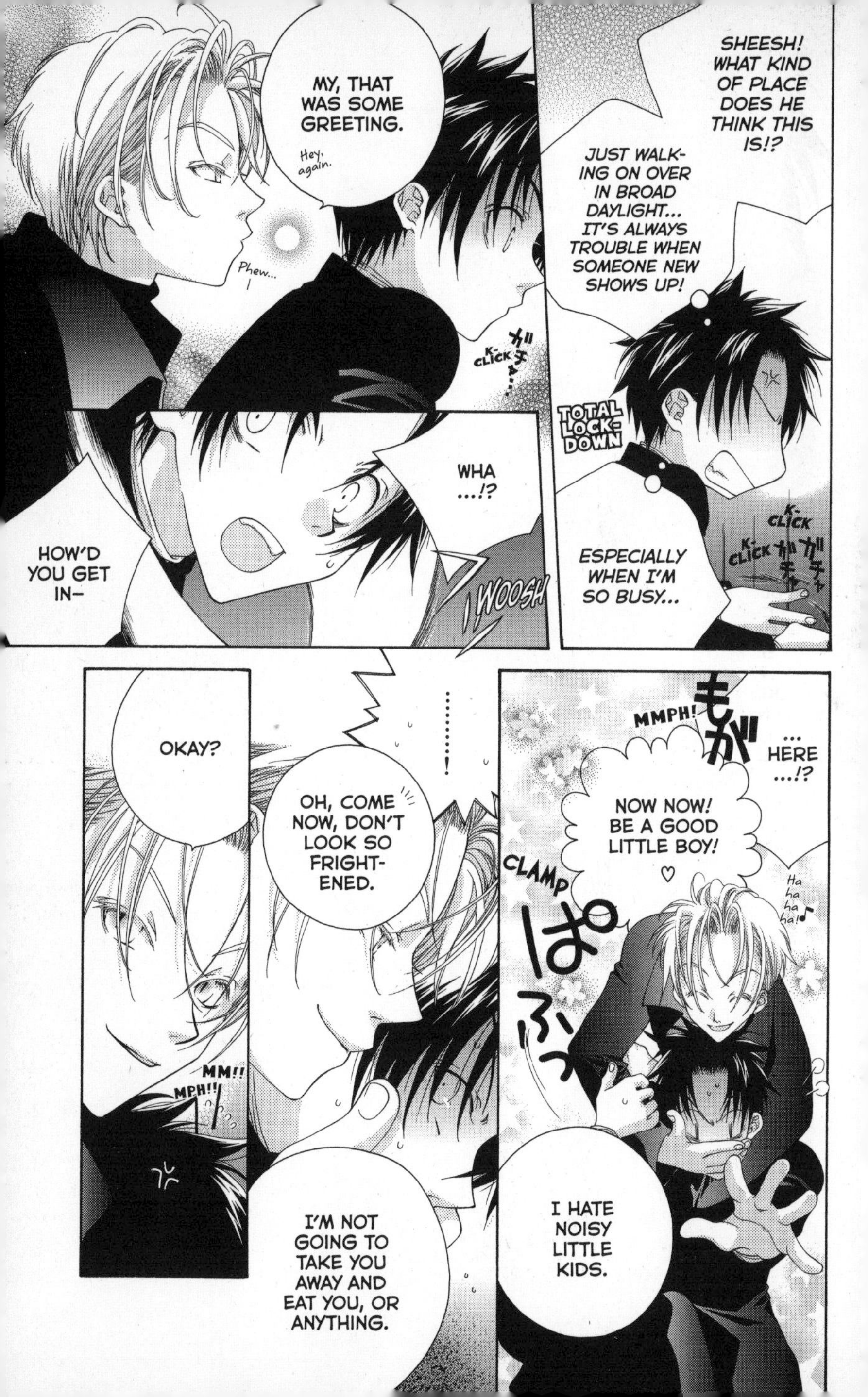
SHEESH! WHAT KIND OF PLACE DOES HE THINK THIS IS!?
JUST WALKING ON OVER IN BROAD DAYLIGHT... IT'S ALWAYS TROUBLE WHEN SOMEONE NEW SHOWS UP!
TOTAL LOCKDOWN
ESPECIALLY WHEN I'M SO BUSY...
K-CLICK
K-CLICK
ガチャ
MY, THAT WAS SOME GREETING.
Hey, again.
Phew...!
K-CLICK
WHA ...!?
WOOSH
HOW'D YOU GET IN–
... HERE ...!?
MMPH!
もが
NOW NOW! BE A GOOD LITTLE BOY!
Ha ha ha ha!
CLAMP
ぱふっ
I HATE NOISY LITTLE KIDS.
......!
OH, COME NOW, DON'T LOOK SO FRIGHTENED.
I'M NOT GOING TO TAKE YOU AWAY AND EAT YOU, OR ANYTHING.
OKAY?
MM!!
MPH!!

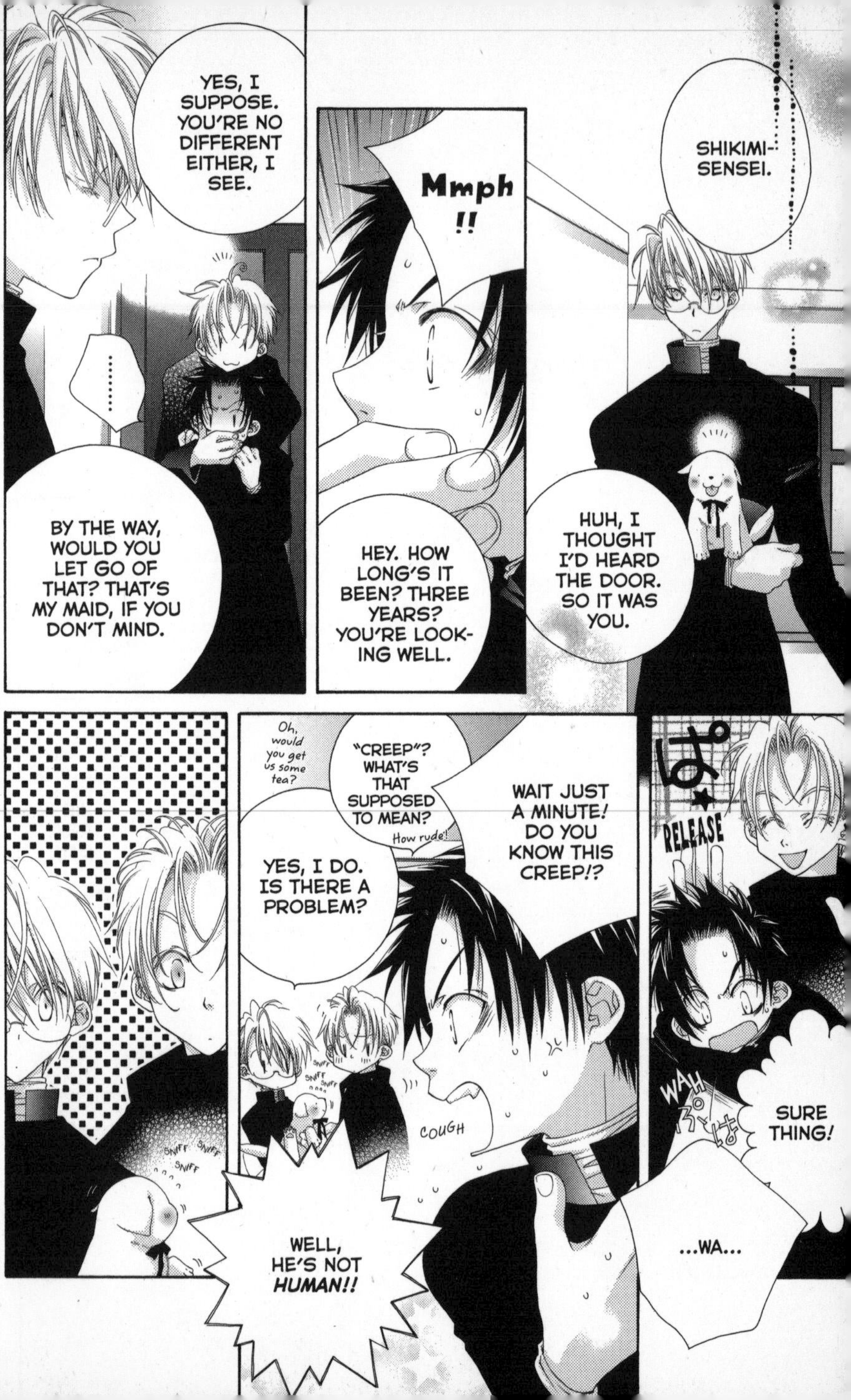
SHIKIMI-SENSEI.
HUH, I THOUGHT I'D HEARD THE DOOR. SO IT WAS YOU.
Mmph !!
HEY. HOW LONG'S IT BEEN? THREE YEARS? YOU'RE LOOKING WELL.
YES, I SUPPOSE. YOU'RE NO DIFFERENT EITHER, I SEE.
......
BY THE WAY, WOULD YOU LET GO OF THAT? THAT'S MY MAID, IF YOU DON'T MIND.
ぱ
RELEASE
SURE THING!
WAH
...WA...
WAIT JUST A MINUTE! DO YOU KNOW THIS CREEP!?
"CREEP"? WHAT'S THAT SUPPOSED TO MEAN?
How rude!
YES, I DO. IS THERE A PROBLEM?
Oh, would you get us some tea?
SNIFF SNIFF SNIFF
COUGH
SNIFF SNIFF SNIFF
WELL, HE'S NOT HUMAN!!

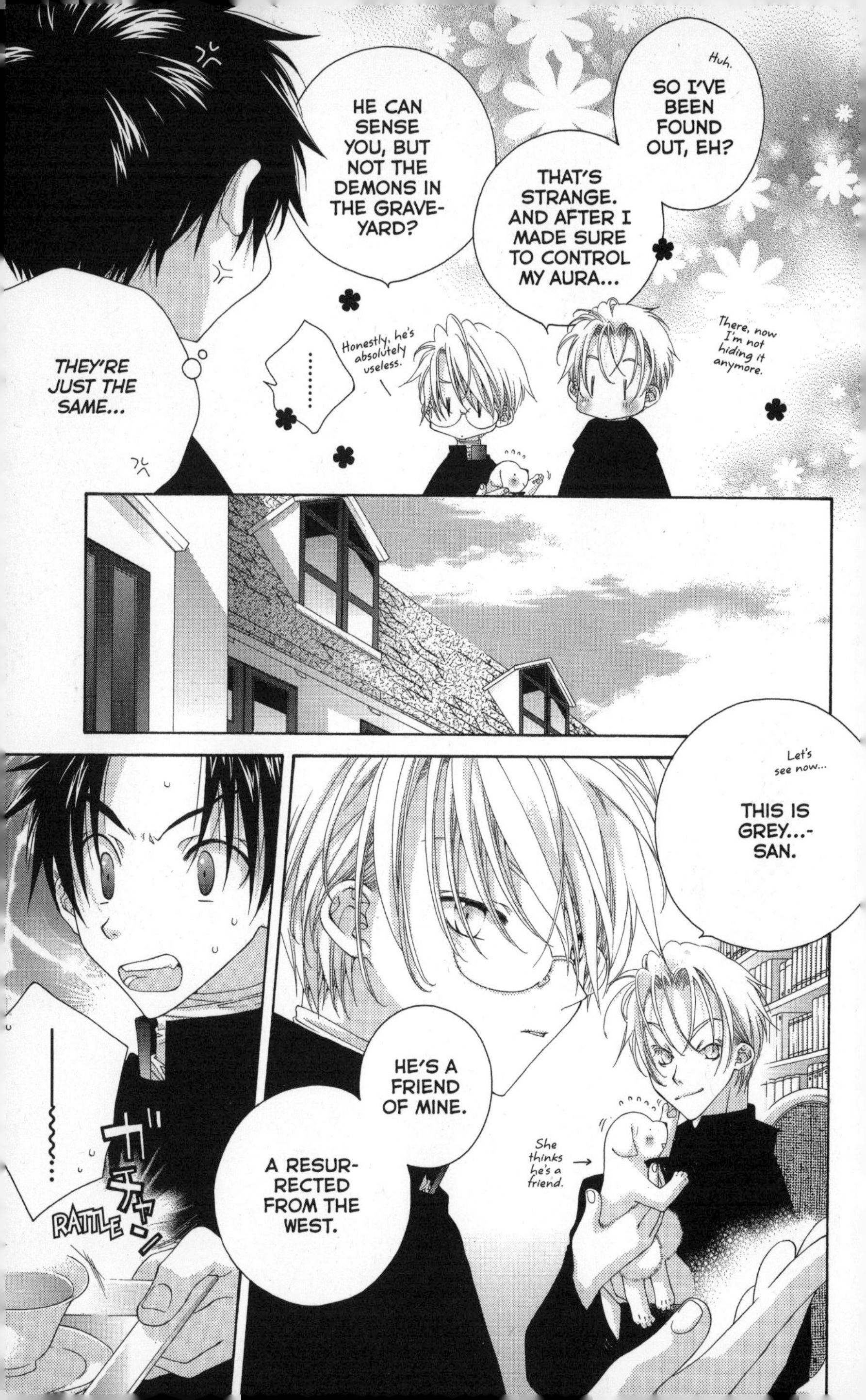
Huh.
SO I'VE BEEN FOUND OUT, EH?
THAT'S STRANGE. AND AFTER I MADE SURE TO CONTROL MY AURA...
There, now I'm not hiding it anymore.
HE CAN SENSE YOU, BUT NOT THE DEMONS IN THE GRAVE-YARD?
Honestly, he's absolutely useless.
......
THEY'RE JUST THE SAME...
Let's see now...
THIS IS GREY...-SAN.
HE'S A FRIEND OF MINE.
A RESUR-RECTED FROM THE WEST.
She thinks he's a friend.
......
RATTLE

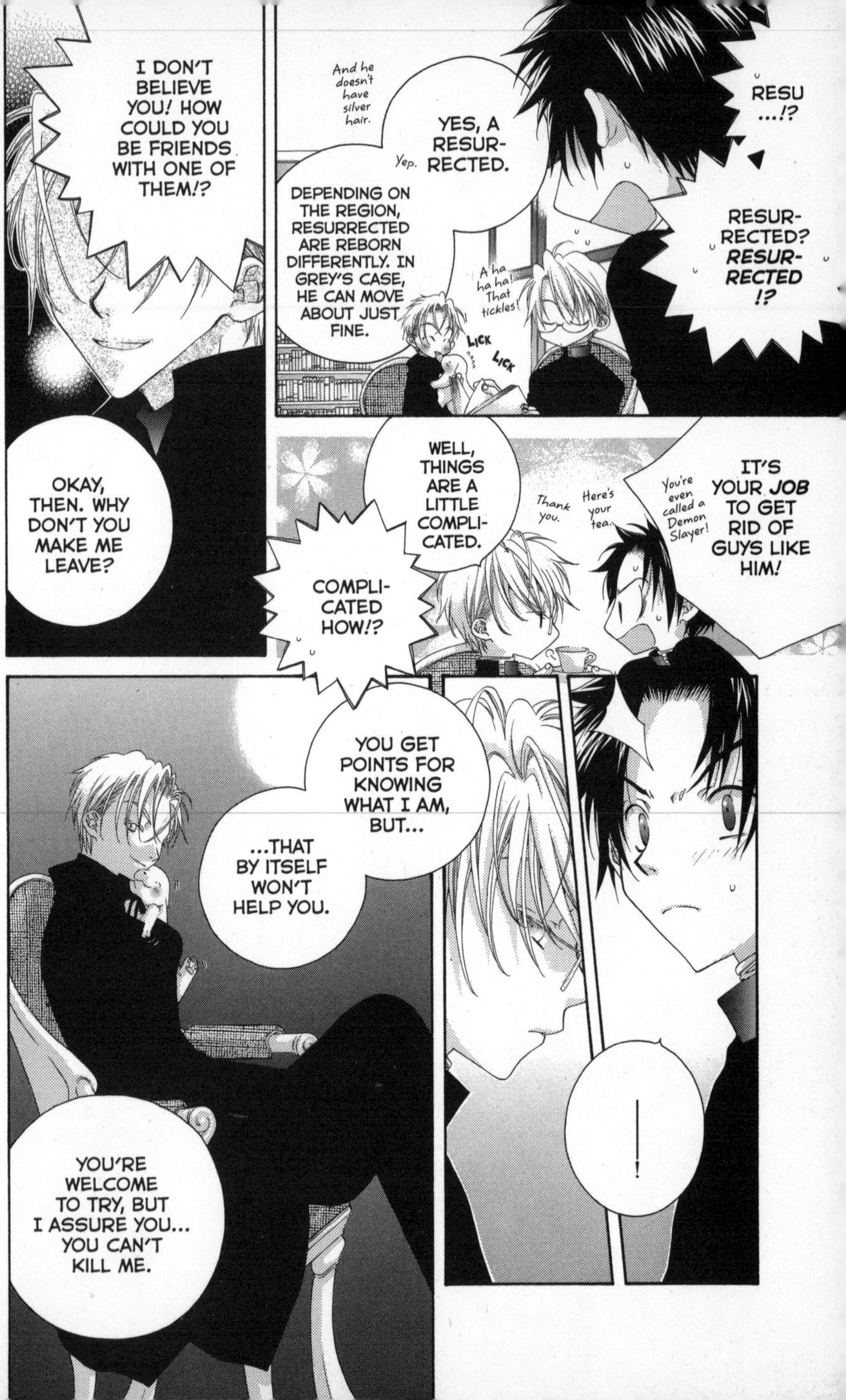
RESU ...!?
RESURRECTED? RESURRECTED!?
YES, A RESURRECTED.
Yep.
And he doesn't have silver hair.
DEPENDING ON THE REGION, RESURRECTED ARE REBORN DIFFERENTLY. IN GREY'S CASE, HE CAN MOVE ABOUT JUST FINE.
A ha ha ha! That tickles!
LICK
LICK
IT'S YOUR JOB TO GET RID OF GUYS LIKE HIM!
You're even called a Demon Slayer!
Here's your tea.
Thank you.
WELL, THINGS ARE A LITTLE COMPLICATED.
COMPLICATED HOW!?
I DON'T BELIEVE YOU! HOW COULD YOU BE FRIENDS WITH ONE OF THEM!?
OKAY, THEN. WHY DON'T YOU MAKE ME LEAVE?
!
YOU GET POINTS FOR KNOWING WHAT I AM, BUT...
...THAT BY ITSELF WON'T HELP YOU.
YOU'RE WELCOME TO TRY, BUT I ASSURE YOU... YOU CAN'T KILL ME.

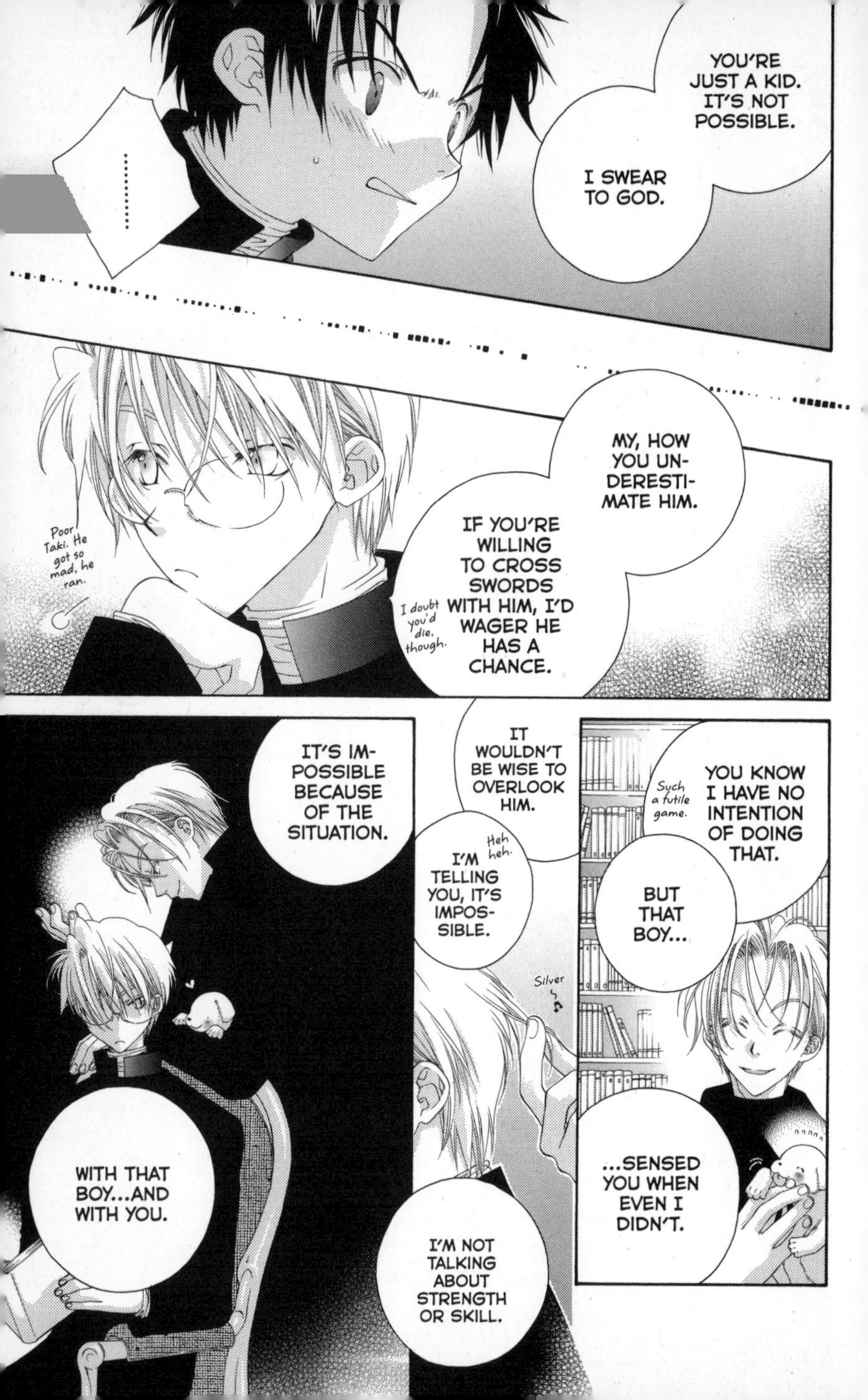
YOU'RE JUST A KID. IT'S NOT POSSIBLE.
I SWEAR TO GOD.
......
MY, HOW YOU UN-DERESTI-MATE HIM.
IF YOU'RE WILLING TO CROSS SWORDS WITH HIM, I'D WAGER HE HAS A CHANCE.
I doubt you'd die, though.
Poor Taki. He got so mad, he ran.
YOU KNOW I HAVE NO INTENTION OF DOING THAT.
Such a futile game.
IT WOULDN'T BE WISE TO OVERLOOK HIM.
BUT THAT BOY...
Heh heh.
I'M TELLING YOU, IT'S IMPOS-SIBLE.
Silver
...SENSED YOU WHEN EVEN I DIDN'T.
I'M NOT TALKING ABOUT STRENGTH OR SKILL.
IT'S IM-POSSIBLE BECAUSE OF THE SITUATION.
WITH THAT BOY...AND WITH YOU.

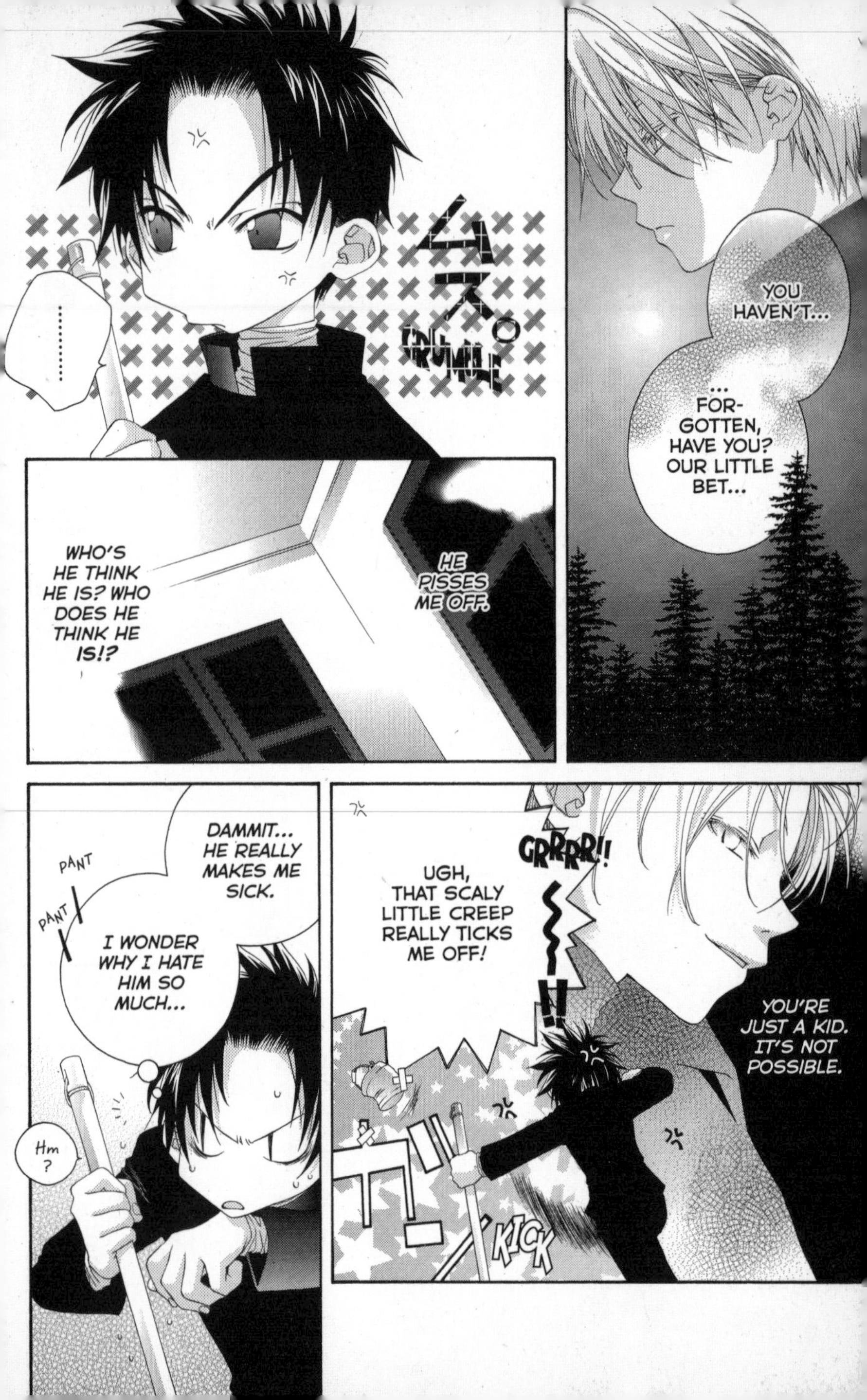
YOU HAVEN'T...
... FOR-GOTTEN, HAVE YOU? OUR LITTLE BET...
......
ムス。
GRUMBLE
HE PISSES ME OFF.
WHO'S HE THINK HE IS? WHO DOES HE THINK HE IS!?
GRRRR!!
UGH, THAT SCALY LITTLE CREEP REALLY TICKS ME OFF!
YOU'RE JUST A KID. IT'S NOT POSSIBLE.
KICK
DAMMIT... HE REALLY MAKES ME SICK.
PANT
PANT
I WONDER WHY I HATE HIM SO MUCH...
Hm?

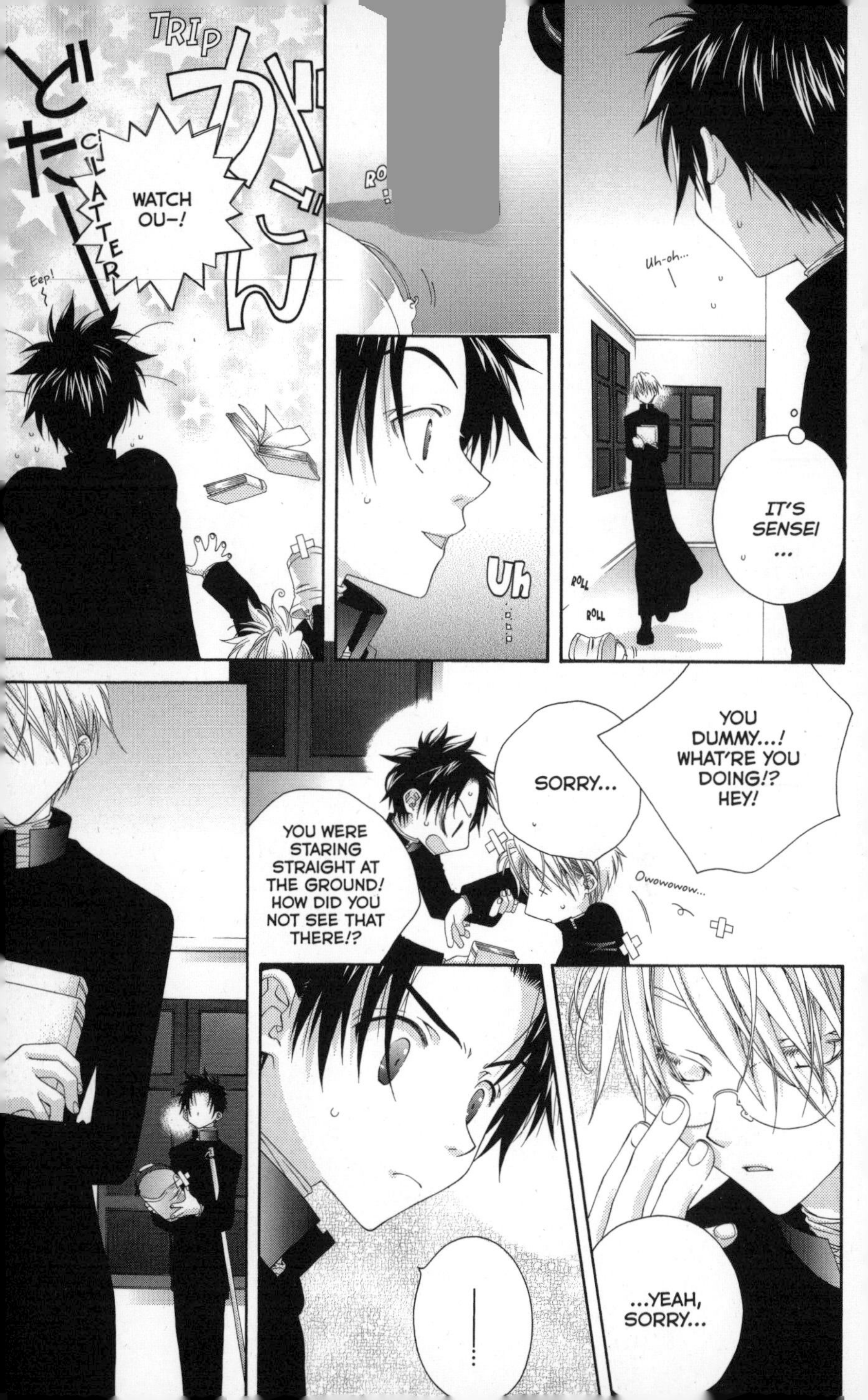
Uh-oh...
IT'S SENSEI ...
ROLL
ROLL
Uh...
TRIP
CLATTER
WATCH OU–!
どたー
Eep!
YOU DUMMY...! WHAT'RE YOU DOING!? HEY!
SORRY...
YOU WERE STARING STRAIGHT AT THE GROUND! HOW DID YOU NOT SEE THAT THERE!?
Owowowow...
...YEAH, SORRY...
—...

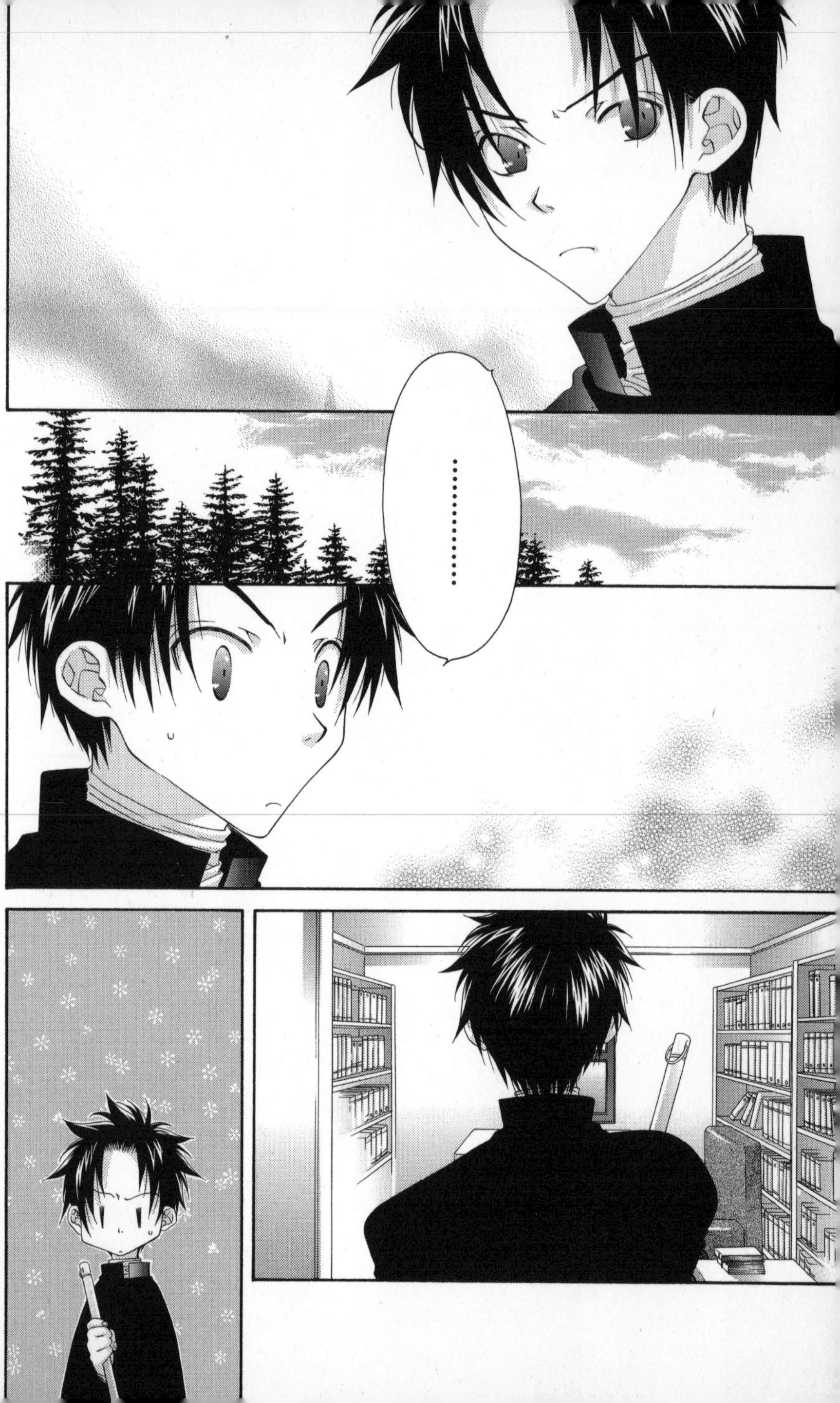
……

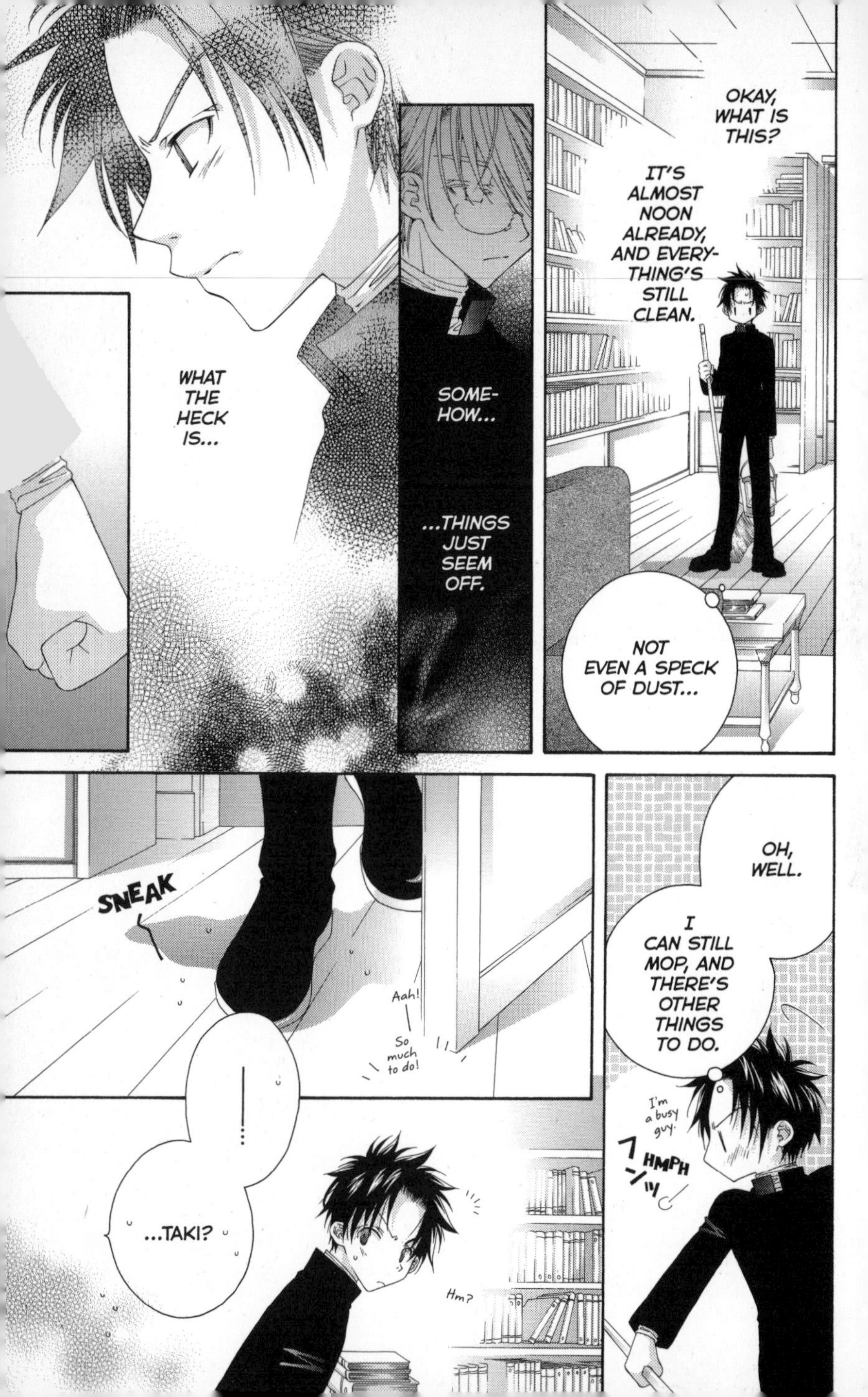
OKAY, WHAT IS THIS?
IT'S ALMOST NOON ALREADY, AND EVERY-THING'S STILL CLEAN.
NOT EVEN A SPECK OF DUST...
SOME-HOW...
...THINGS JUST SEEM OFF.
WHAT THE HECK IS...
OH, WELL.
I CAN STILL MOP, AND THERE'S OTHER THINGS TO DO.
I'm a busy guy.
HMPH
SNEAK
Aah!
So much to do!
......
...TAKI?
Hm?

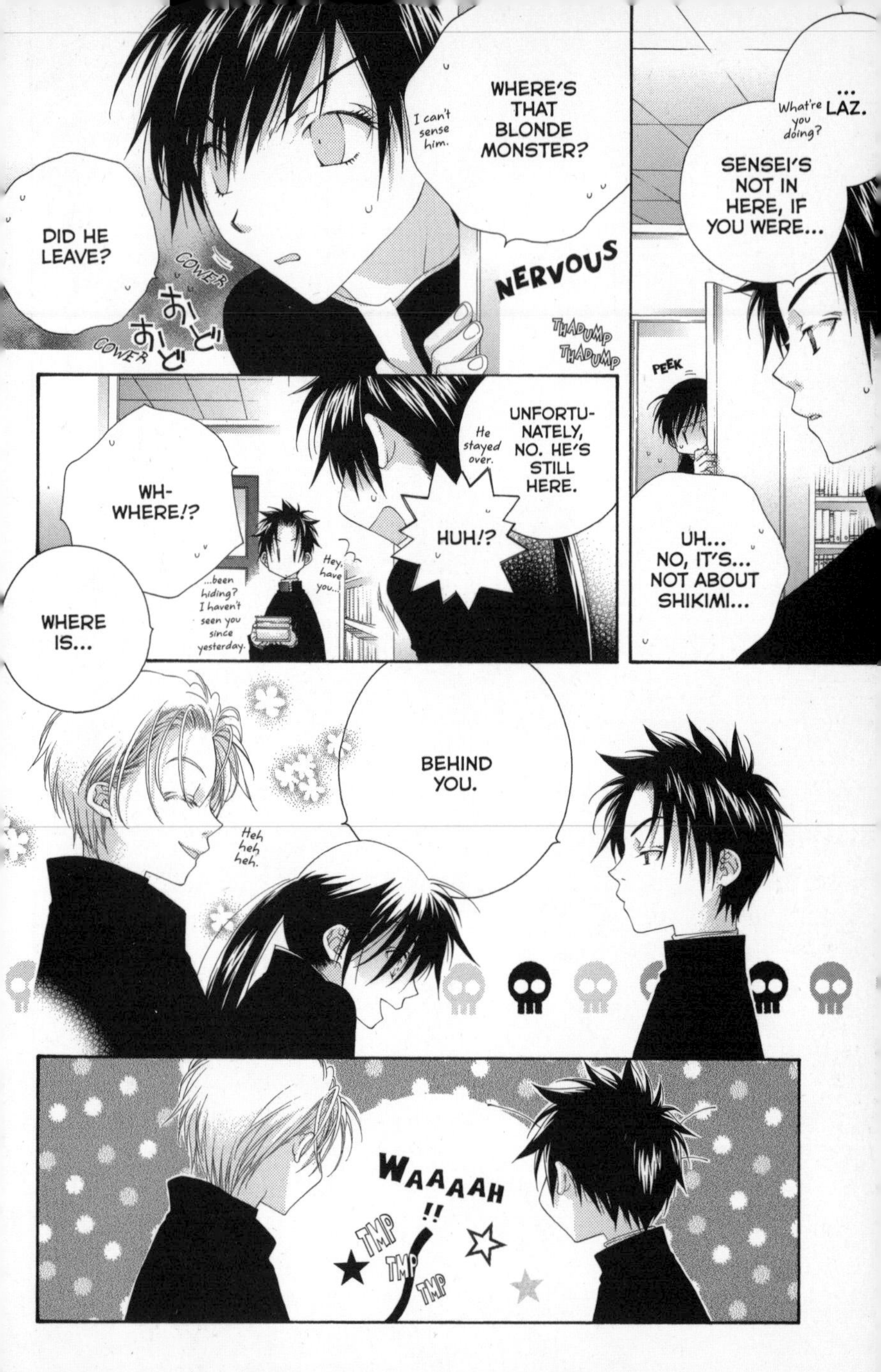

... LAZ.
What're you doing?
SENSEI'S NOT IN HERE, IF YOU WERE...
PEEK
UH... NO, IT'S... NOT ABOUT SHIKIMI...
WHERE'S THAT BLONDE MONSTER?
I can't sense him.
NERVOUS
THADUMP THADUMP
DID HE LEAVE?
おど おど
COWER COWER
UNFORTU-NATELY, NO. HE'S STILL HERE.
He stayed over.
HUH!?
Hey, have you...
...been hiding? I haven't seen you since yesterday.
WH- WHERE!?
WHERE IS...
BEHIND YOU.
Heh heh heh.
WAAAAH!!
TMP TMP TMP

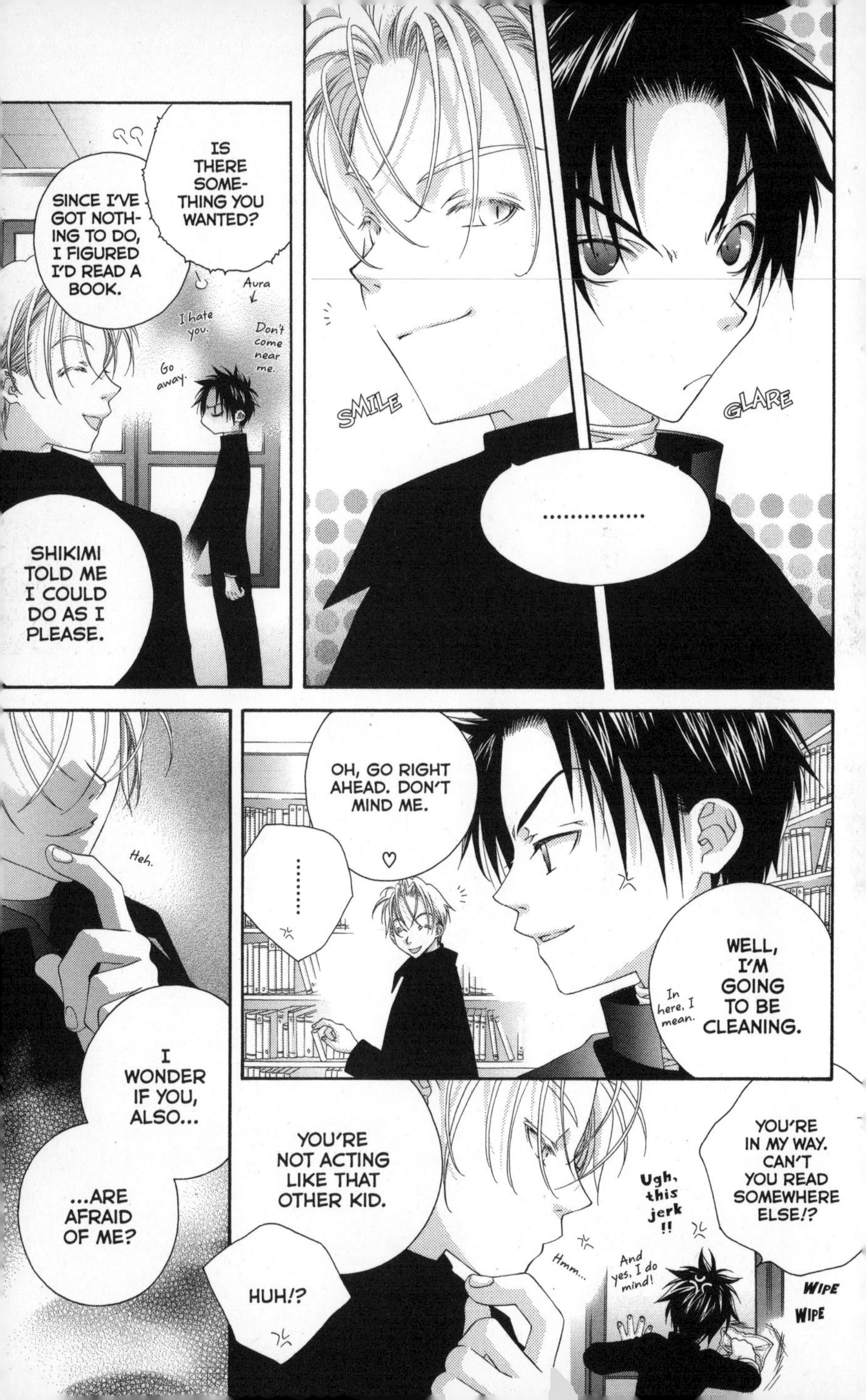
SMILE
GLARE
....
IS THERE SOMETHING YOU WANTED?
SINCE I'VE GOT NOTHING TO DO, I FIGURED I'D READ A BOOK.
Aura
I hate you.
Don't come near me.
Go away.
SHIKIMI TOLD ME I COULD DO AS I PLEASE.
WELL, I'M GOING TO BE CLEANING.
In here, I mean.
OH, GO RIGHT AHEAD. DON'T MIND ME.
....
YOU'RE IN MY WAY. CAN'T YOU READ SOMEWHERE ELSE!?
Ugh, this jerk!!
And yes, I do mind!
WIPE
WIPE
Hmm...
YOU'RE NOT ACTING LIKE THAT OTHER KID.
HUH!?
Heh.
I WONDER IF YOU, ALSO...
...ARE AFRAID OF ME?

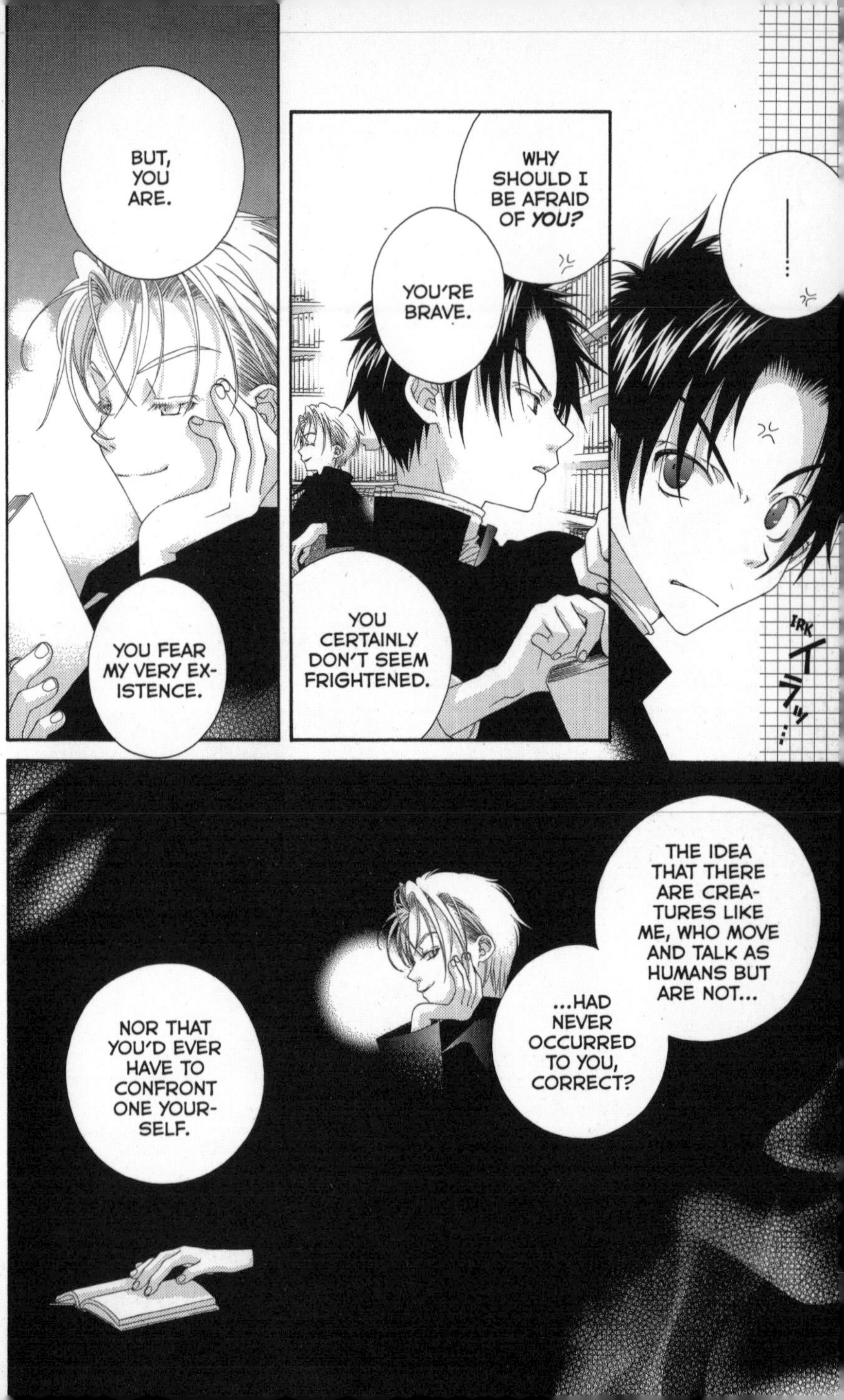
......
IRK
イラッ…
WHY SHOULD I BE AFRAID OF *YOU?*
YOU'RE BRAVE.
YOU CERTAINLY DON'T SEEM FRIGHTENED.
BUT, YOU ARE.
YOU FEAR MY VERY EX-ISTENCE.
THE IDEA THAT THERE ARE CREA-TURES LIKE ME, WHO MOVE AND TALK AS HUMANS BUT ARE NOT...
...HAD NEVER OCCURRED TO YOU, CORRECT?
NOR THAT YOU'D EVER HAVE TO CONFRONT ONE YOUR-SELF.

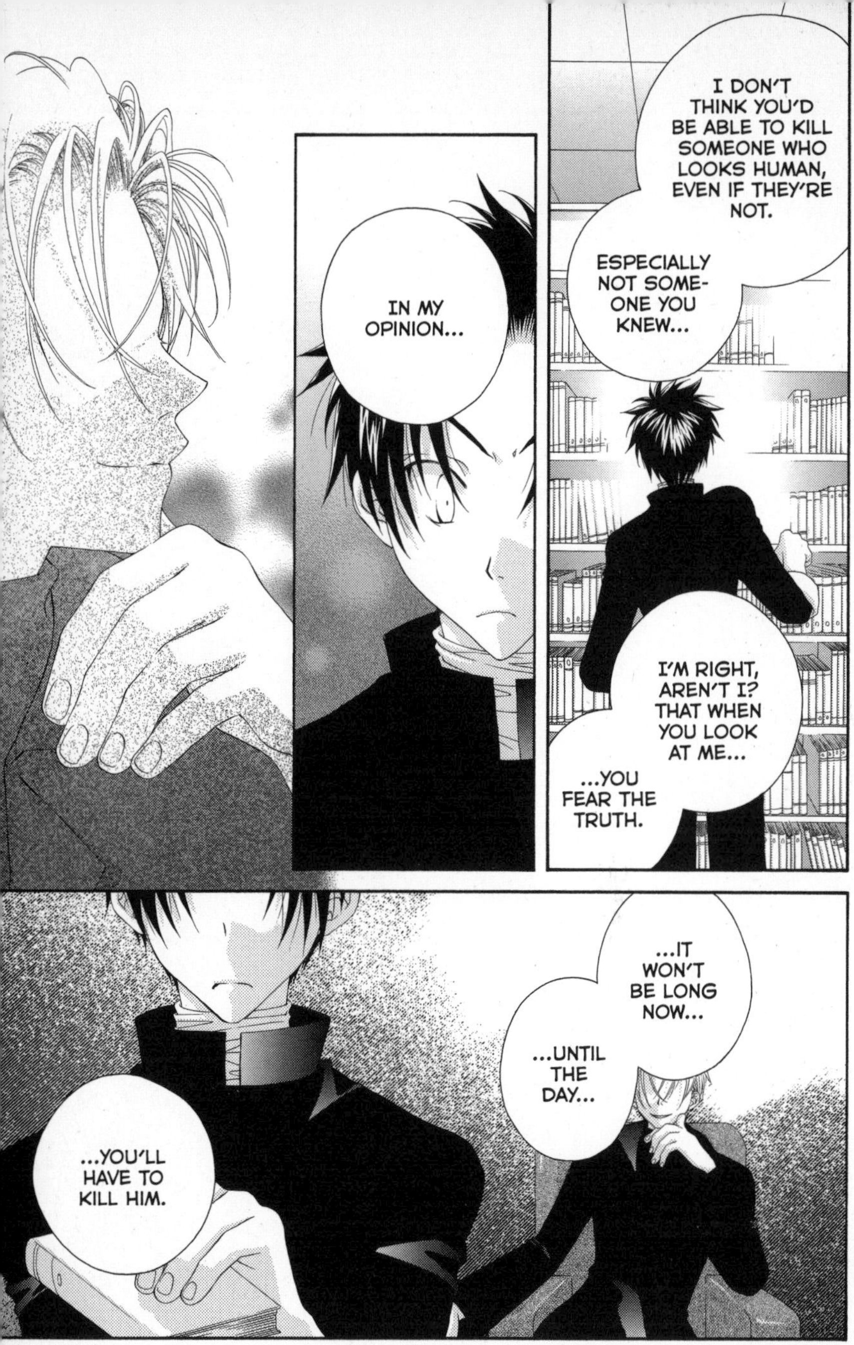
I DON'T THINK YOU'D BE ABLE TO KILL SOMEONE WHO LOOKS HUMAN, EVEN IF THEY'RE NOT.
ESPECIALLY NOT SOME-ONE YOU KNEW...
I'M RIGHT, AREN'T I? THAT WHEN YOU LOOK AT ME...
...YOU FEAR THE TRUTH.
IN MY OPINION...
...IT WON'T BE LONG NOW...
...UNTIL THE DAY...
...YOU'LL HAVE TO KILL HIM.

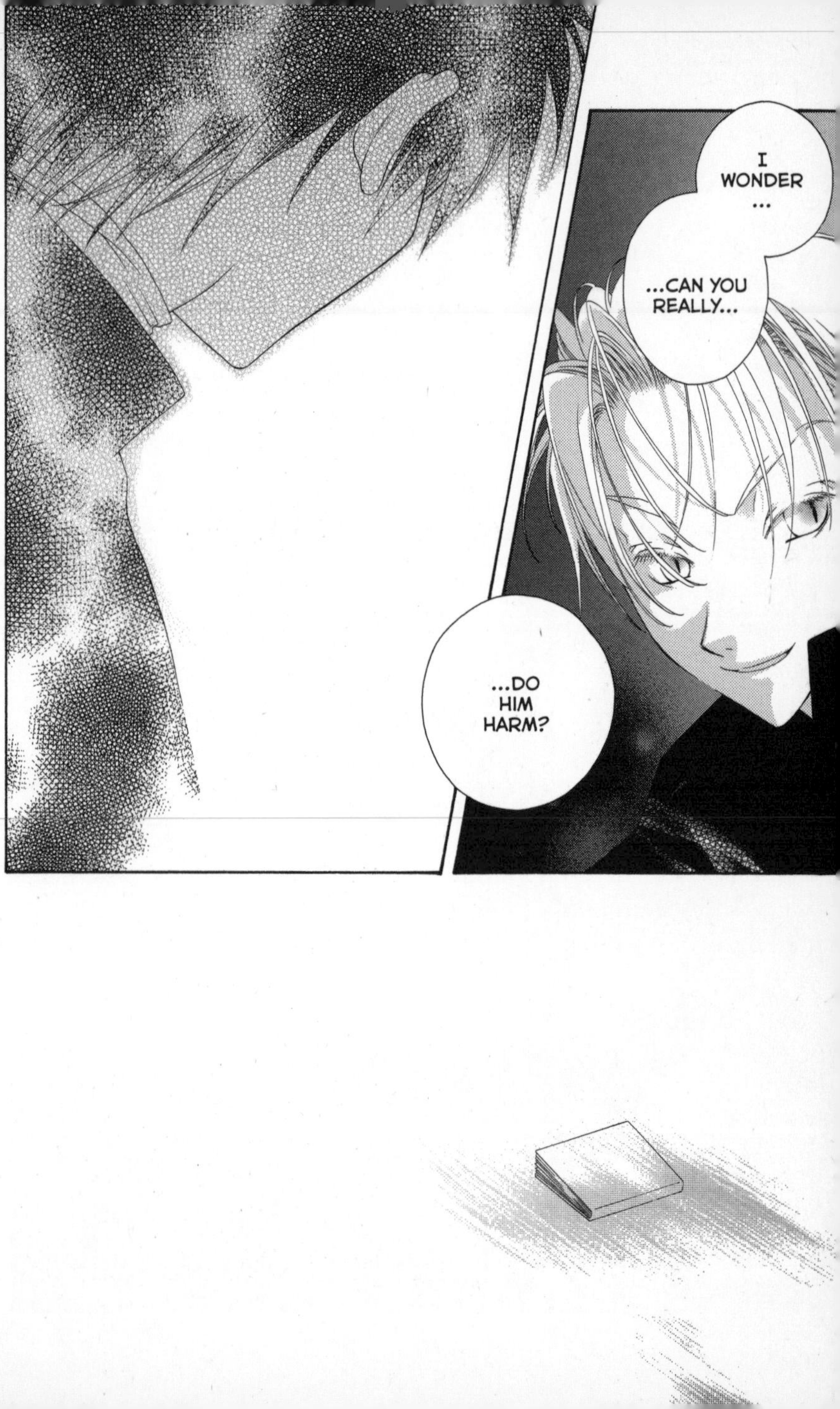
I WONDER ...
...CAN YOU REALLY...
...DO HIM HARM?

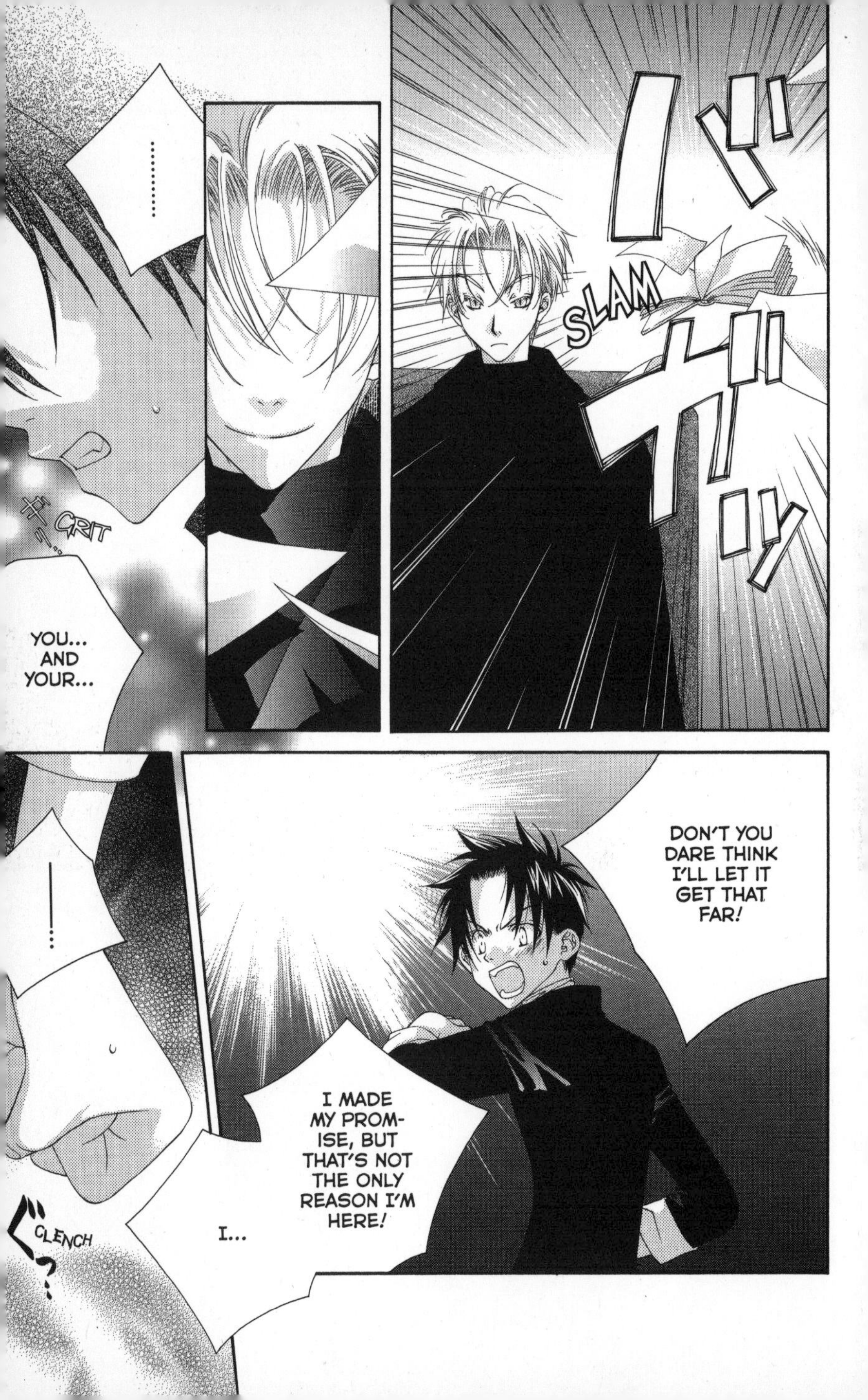
SLAM
......
GRIT
YOU... AND YOUR...
DON'T YOU DARE THINK I'LL LET IT GET THAT FAR!
I MADE MY PROMISE, BUT THAT'S NOT THE ONLY REASON I'M HERE!
I...
——......
CLENCH

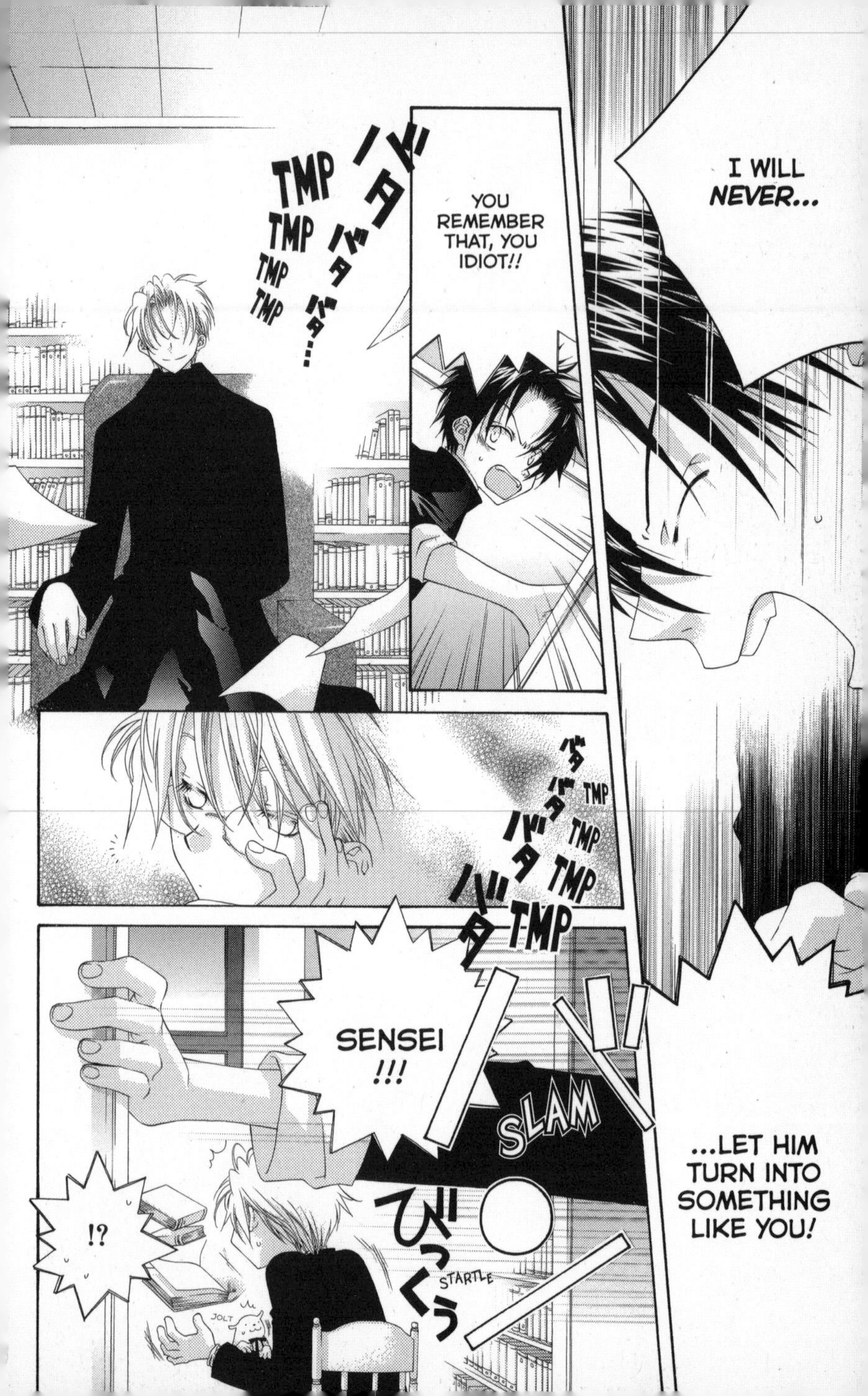
I WILL NEVER...
...LET HIM TURN INTO SOMETHING LIKE YOU!
YOU REMEMBER THAT, YOU IDIOT!!
バタバタバタ...
TMP TMP TMP TMP
バタバタ
バタバタ
TMP TMP TMP TMP
SENSEI !!!
SLAM
びっくう
STARTLE
!?
JOLT

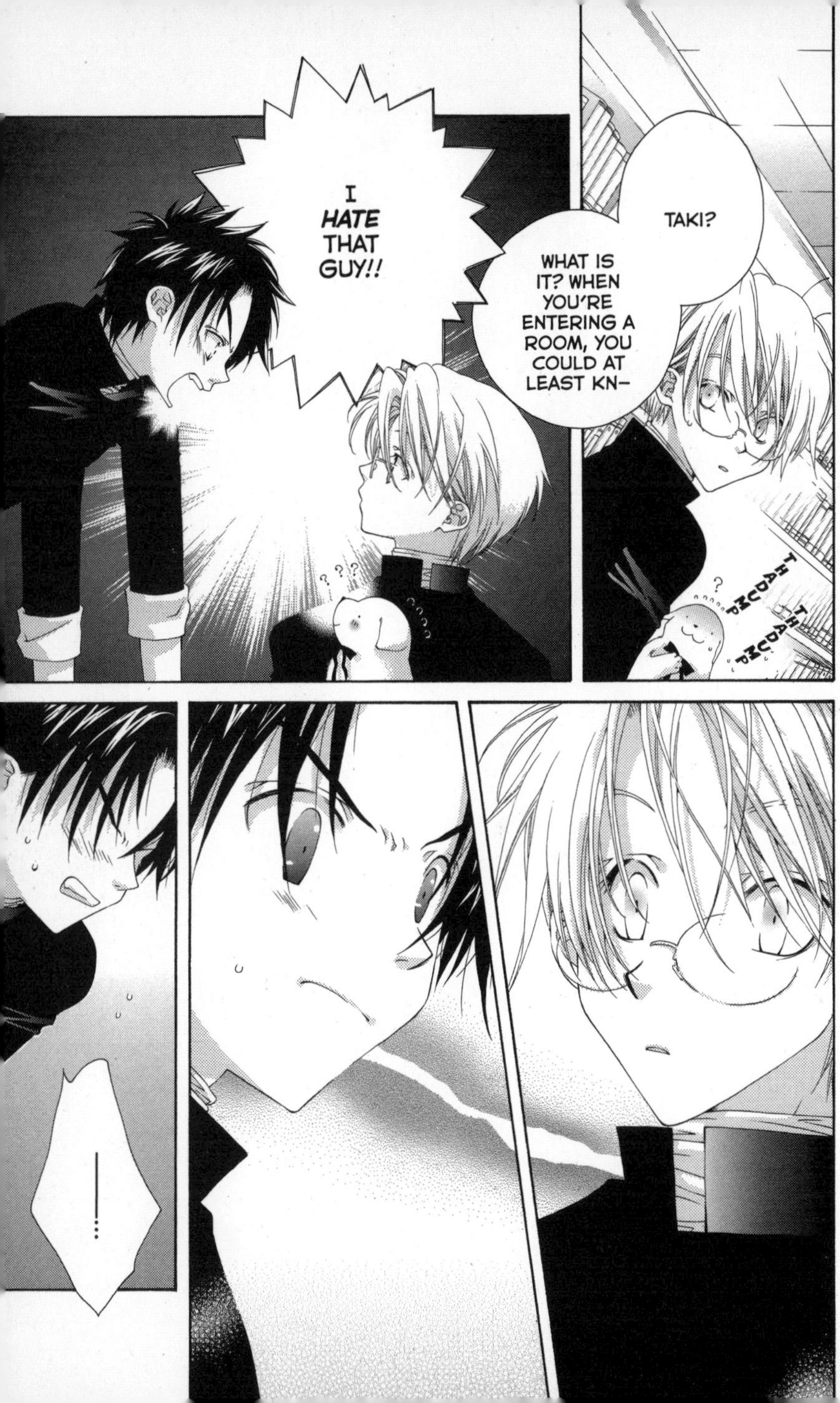
TAKI?
WHAT IS IT? WHEN YOU'RE ENTERING A ROOM, YOU COULD AT LEAST KN—
THADUMP
THADUMP
I *HATE* THAT GUY!!
—...

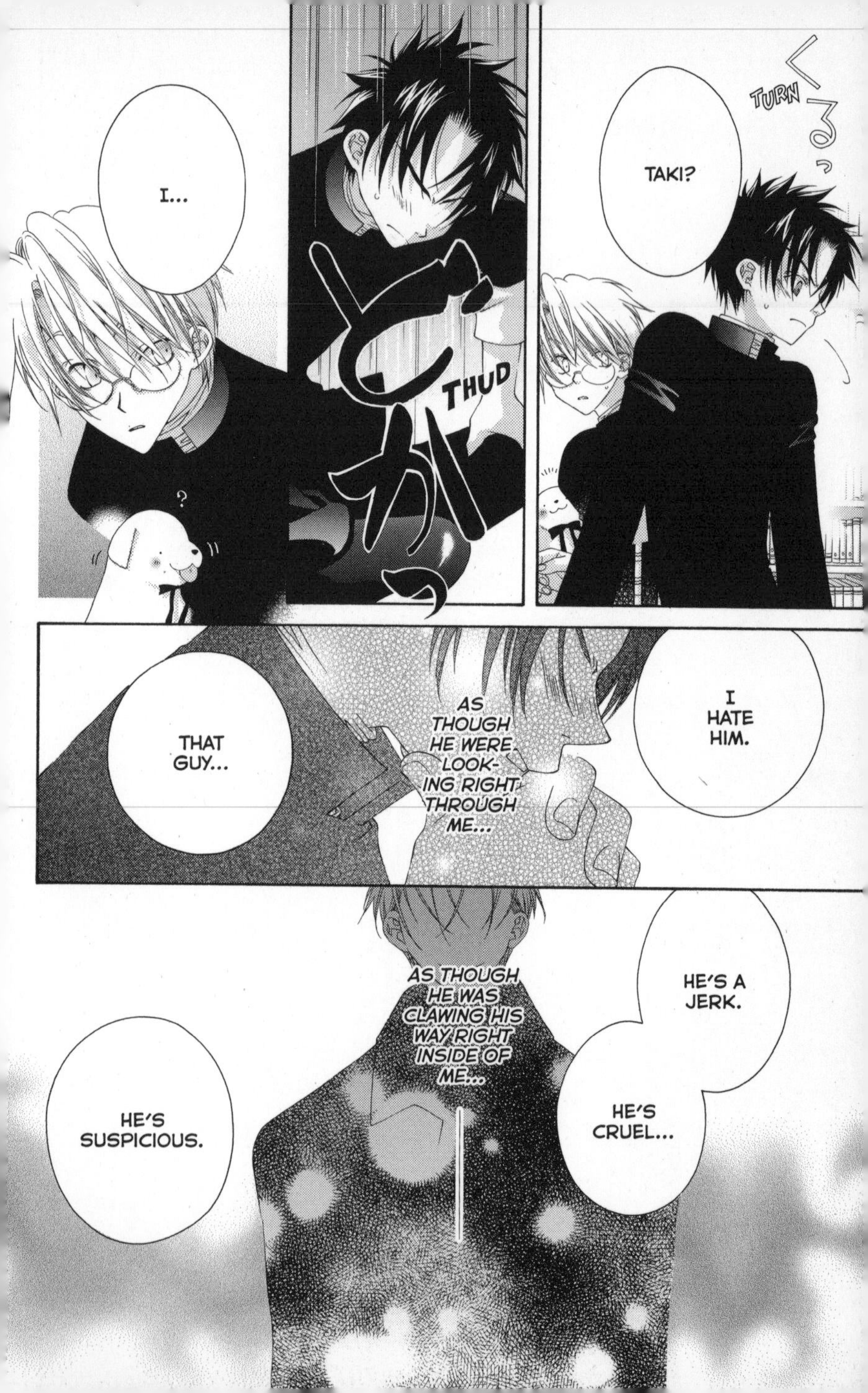
くるっ
TURN
TAKI?
どかっ
THUD
I...
I HATE HIM.
AS THOUGH HE WERE LOOK-ING RIGHT THROUGH ME...
THAT GUY...
HE'S A JERK.
HE'S CRUEL...
AS THOUGH HE WAS CLAWING HIS WAY RIGHT INSIDE OF ME...
HE'S SUSPICIOUS.

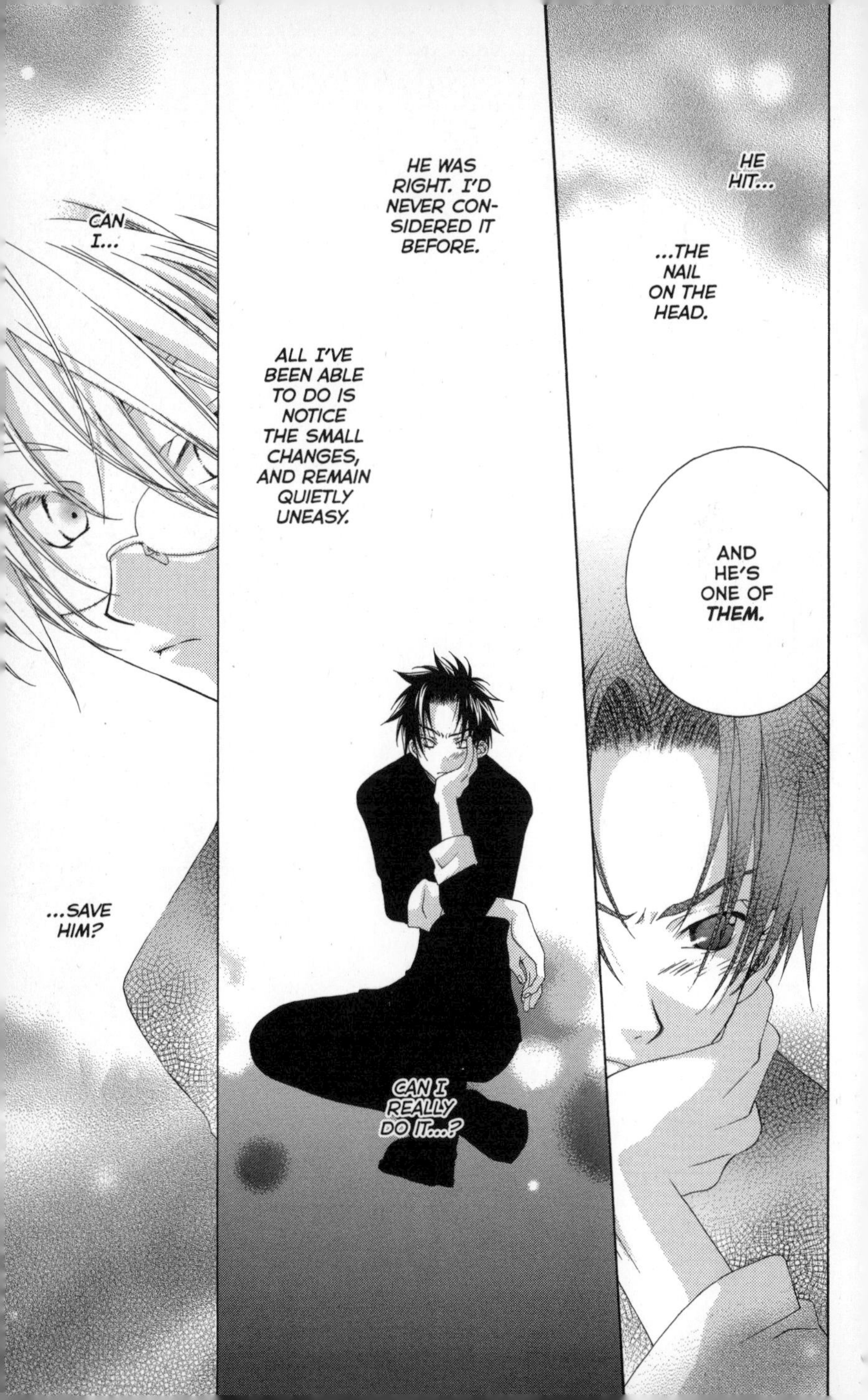
HE HIT...
...THE NAIL ON THE HEAD.
AND HE'S ONE OF *THEM.*
HE WAS RIGHT. I'D NEVER CON-SIDERED IT BEFORE.
ALL I'VE BEEN ABLE TO DO IS NOTICE THE SMALL CHANGES, AND REMAIN QUIETLY UNEASY.
CAN I REALLY DO IT...?
CAN I...
...SAVE HIM?

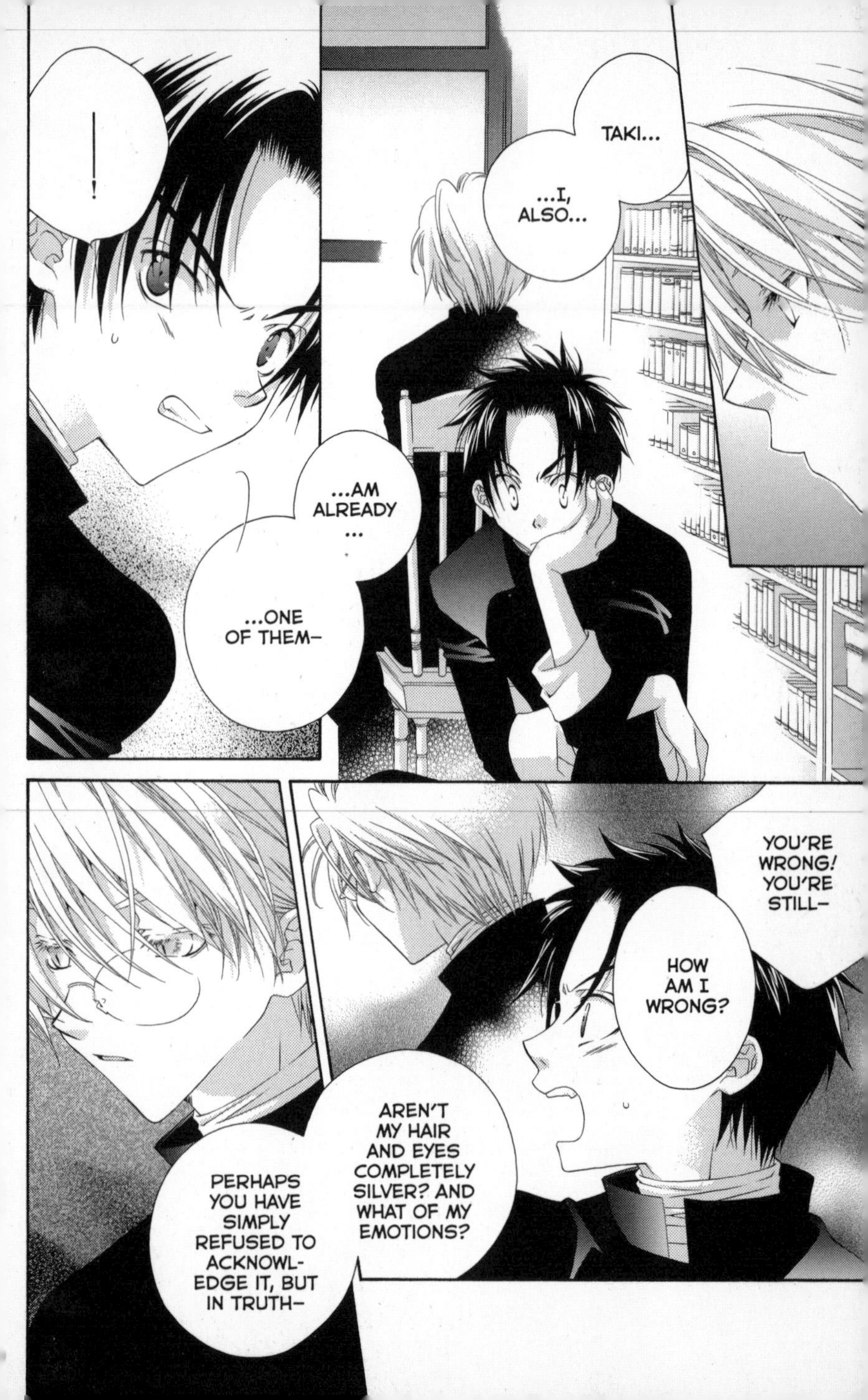
TAKI...
...I, ALSO...
...AM ALREADY...
...ONE OF THEM–
!
YOU'RE WRONG! YOU'RE STILL–
HOW AM I WRONG?
AREN'T MY HAIR AND EYES COMPLETELY SILVER? AND WHAT OF MY EMOTIONS?
PERHAPS YOU HAVE SIMPLY REFUSED TO ACKNOWL-EDGE IT, BUT IN TRUTH–

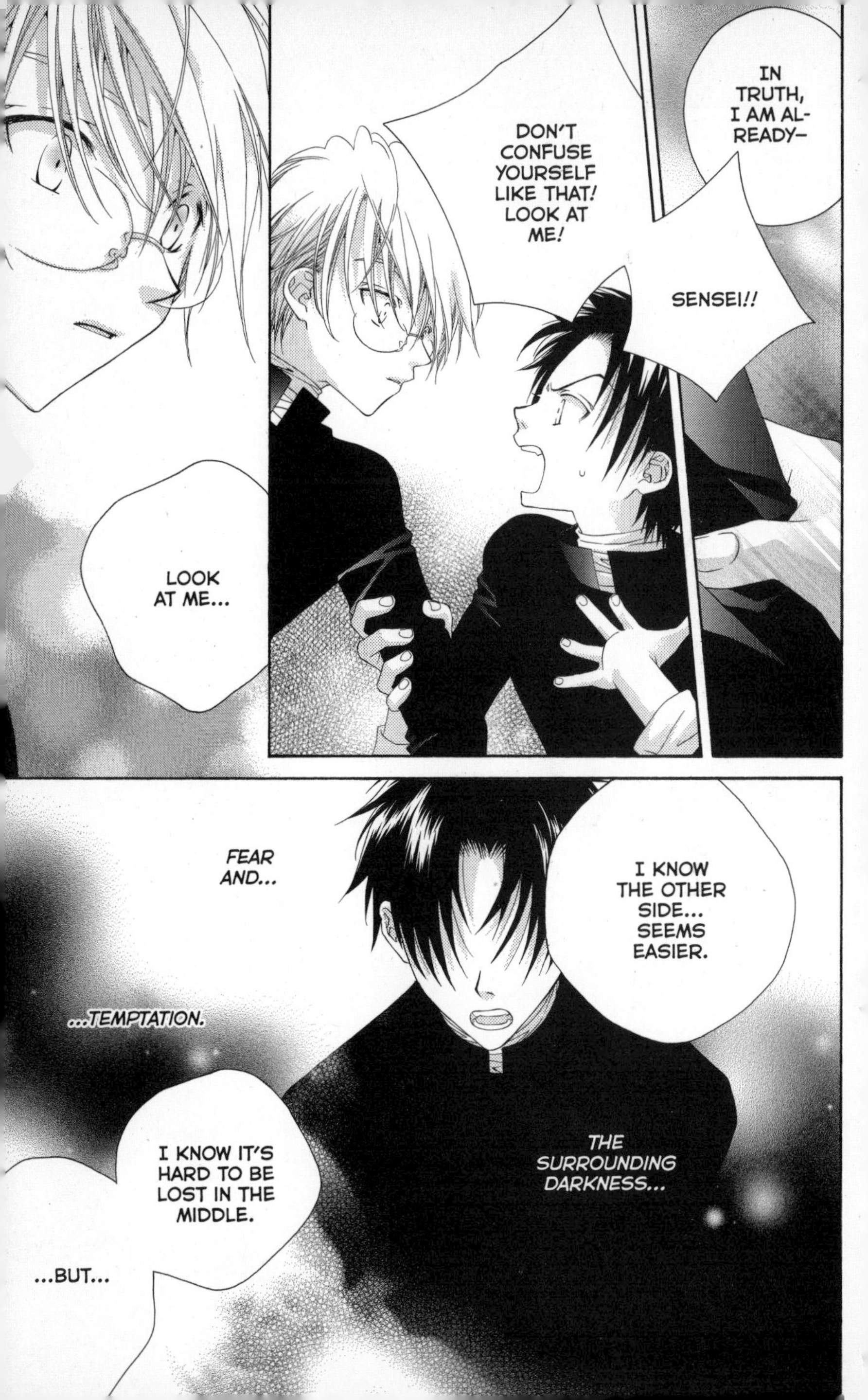
IN TRUTH, I AM AL-READY–
SENSEI!!
DON'T CONFUSE YOURSELF LIKE THAT! LOOK AT ME!
LOOK AT ME...
I KNOW THE OTHER SIDE... SEEMS EASIER.
FEAR AND...
...TEMPTATION.
THE SURROUNDING DARKNESS...
I KNOW IT'S HARD TO BE LOST IN THE MIDDLE.
...BUT...

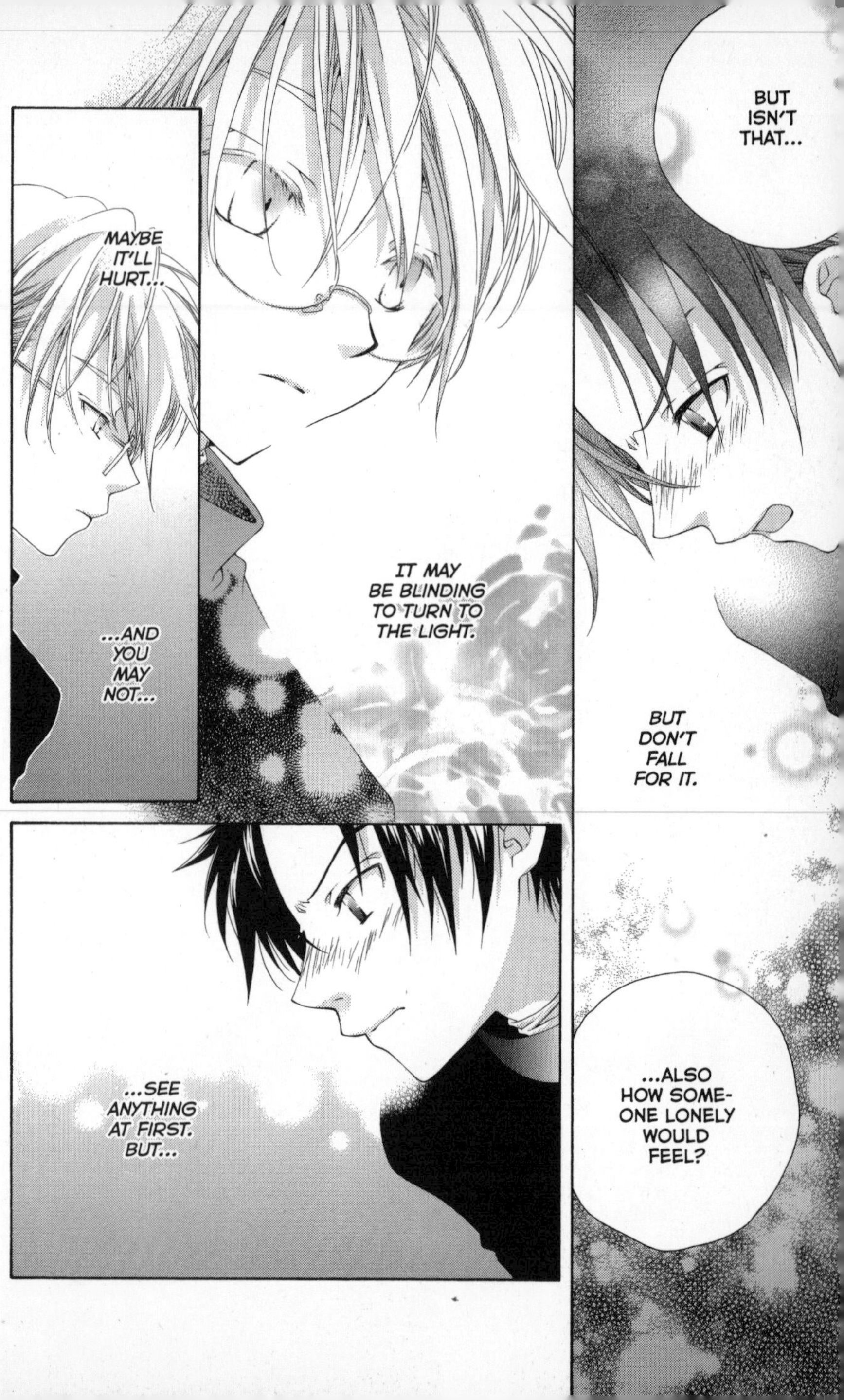
BUT ISN'T THAT...
BUT DON'T FALL FOR IT.
...ALSO HOW SOME-ONE LONELY WOULD FEEL?
IT MAY BE BLINDING TO TURN TO THE LIGHT.
MAYBE IT'LL HURT...
...AND YOU MAY NOT...
...SEE ANYTHING AT FIRST. BUT...

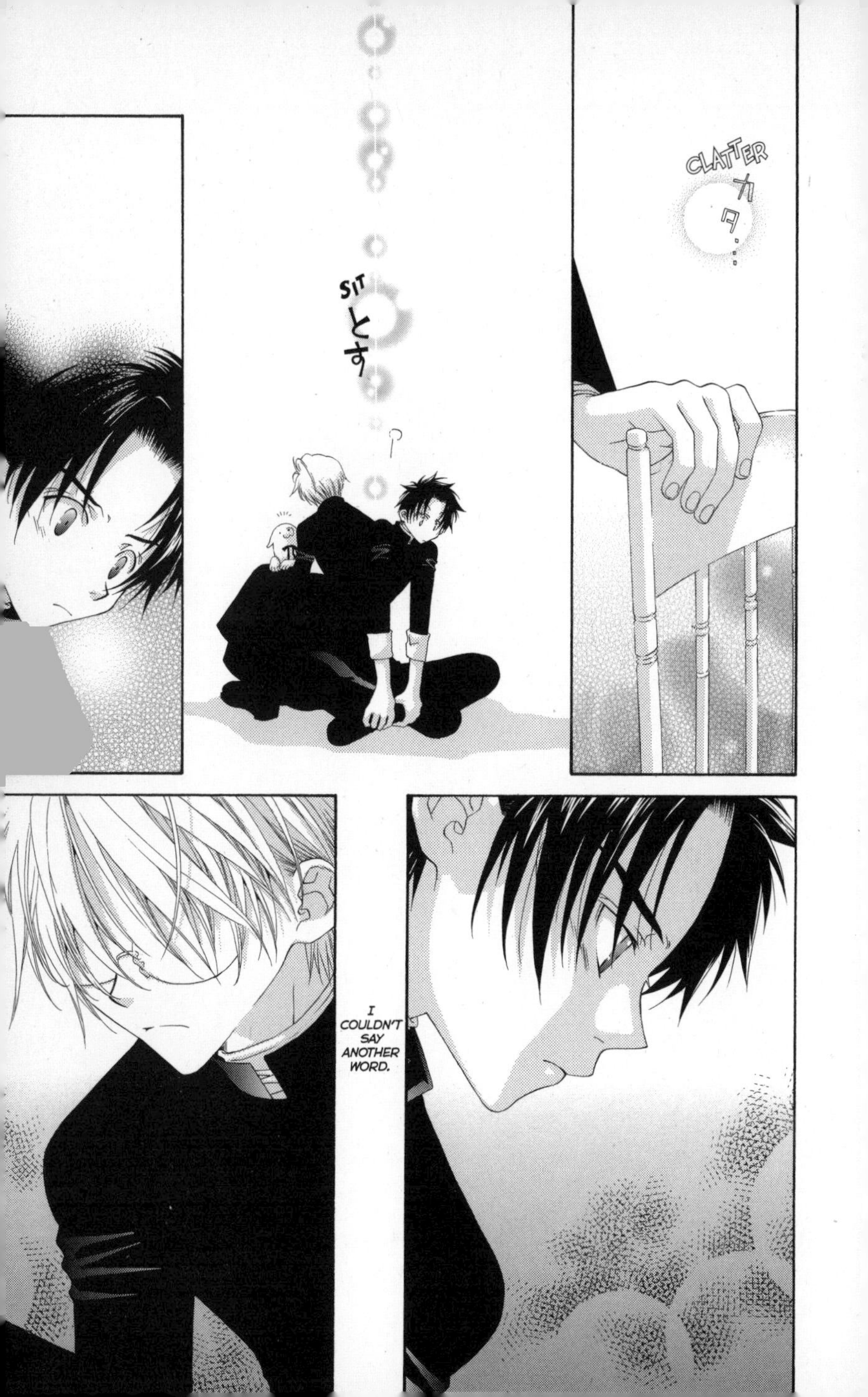
CLATTER
カタ…
SIT
とす
I COULDN'T SAY ANOTHER WORD.

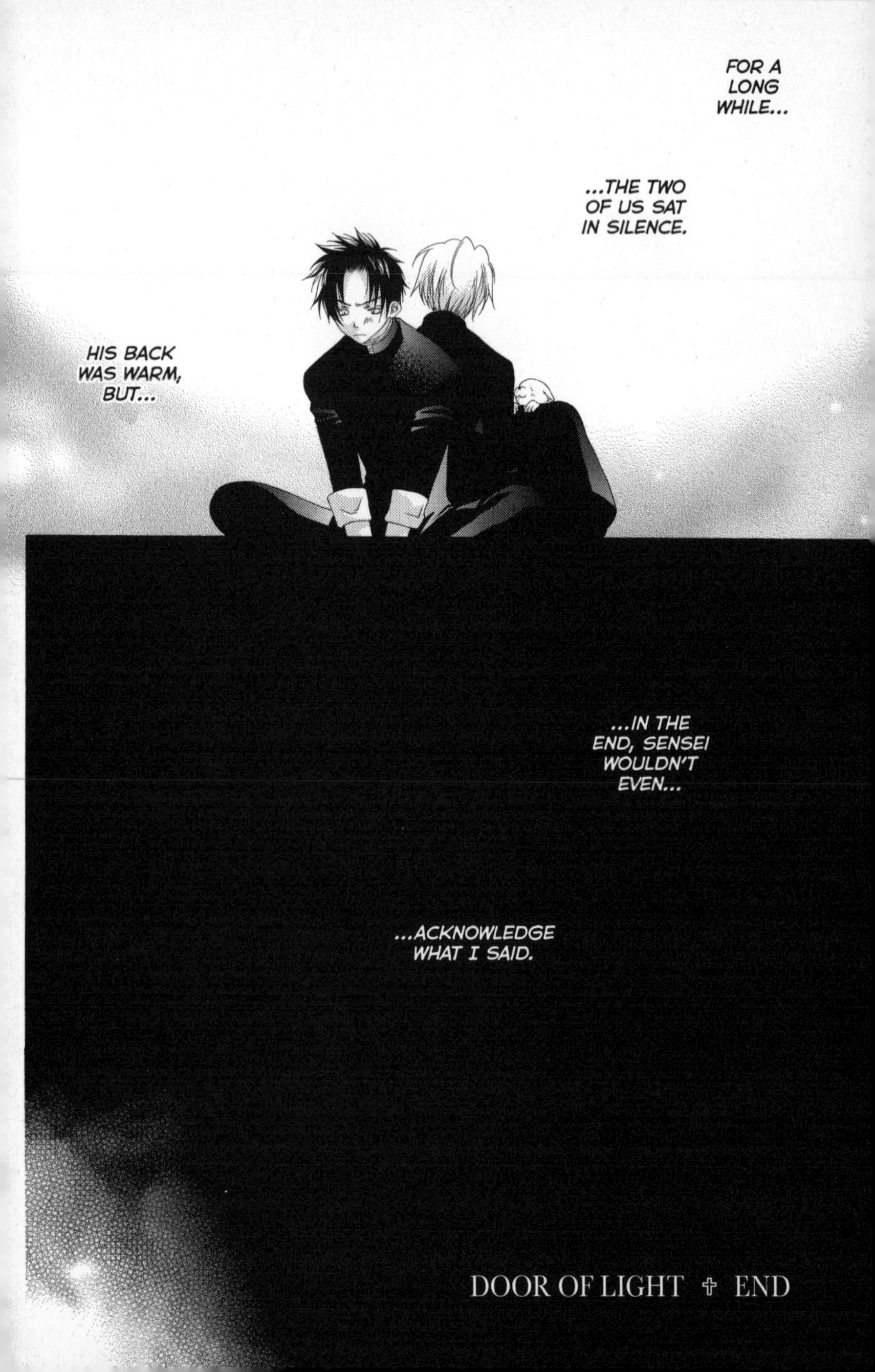
FOR A LONG WHILE...
...THE TWO OF US SAT IN SILENCE.
HIS BACK WAS WARM, BUT...
...IN THE END, SENSEI WOULDN'T EVEN...
...ACKNOWLEDGE WHAT I SAID.
DOOR OF LIGHT ✝ END

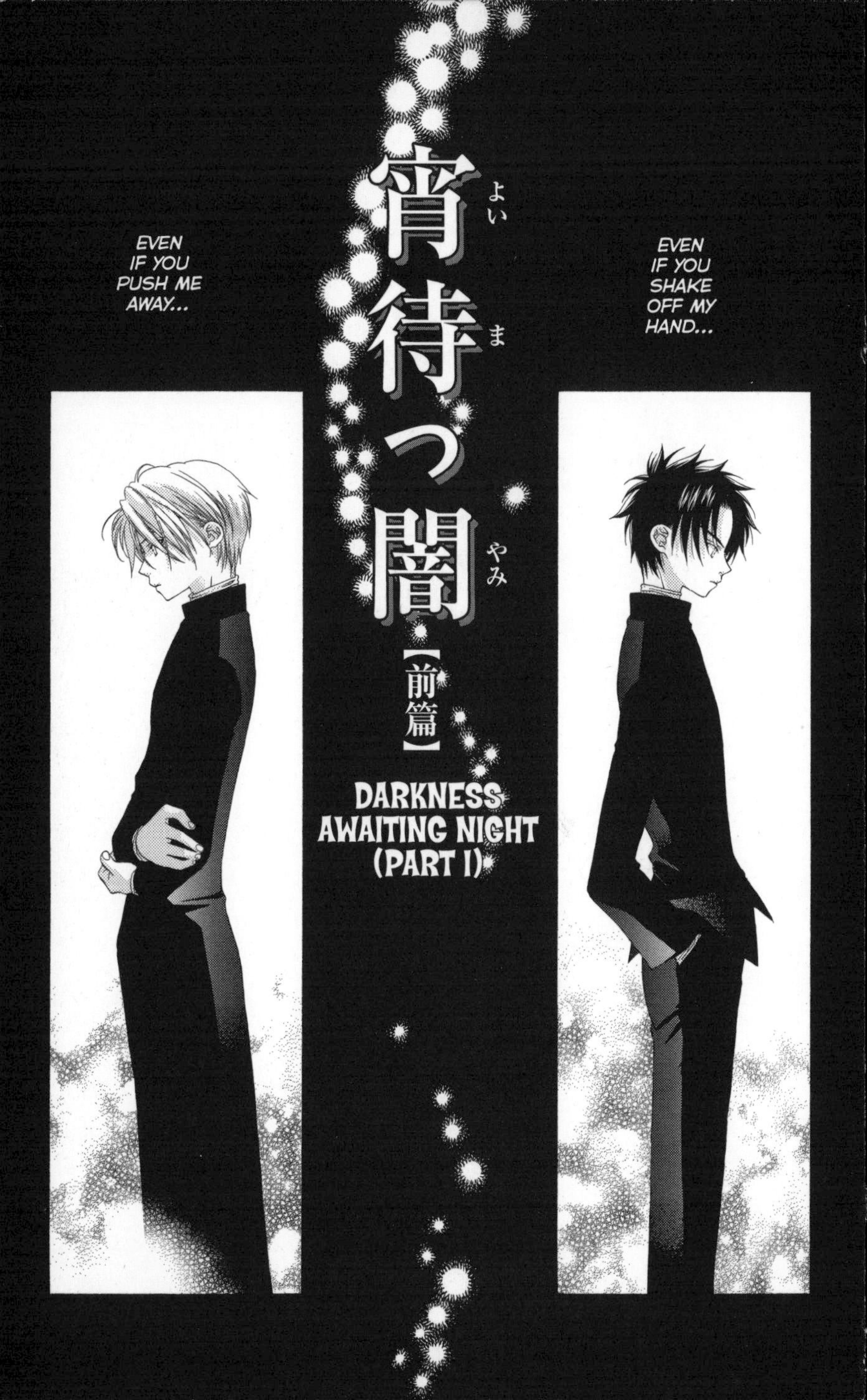
EVEN IF YOU SHAKE OFF MY HAND...
宵待つ闇
よい ま やみ
【前篇】
DARKNESS AWAITING NIGHT (PART I)
EVEN IF YOU PUSH ME AWAY...

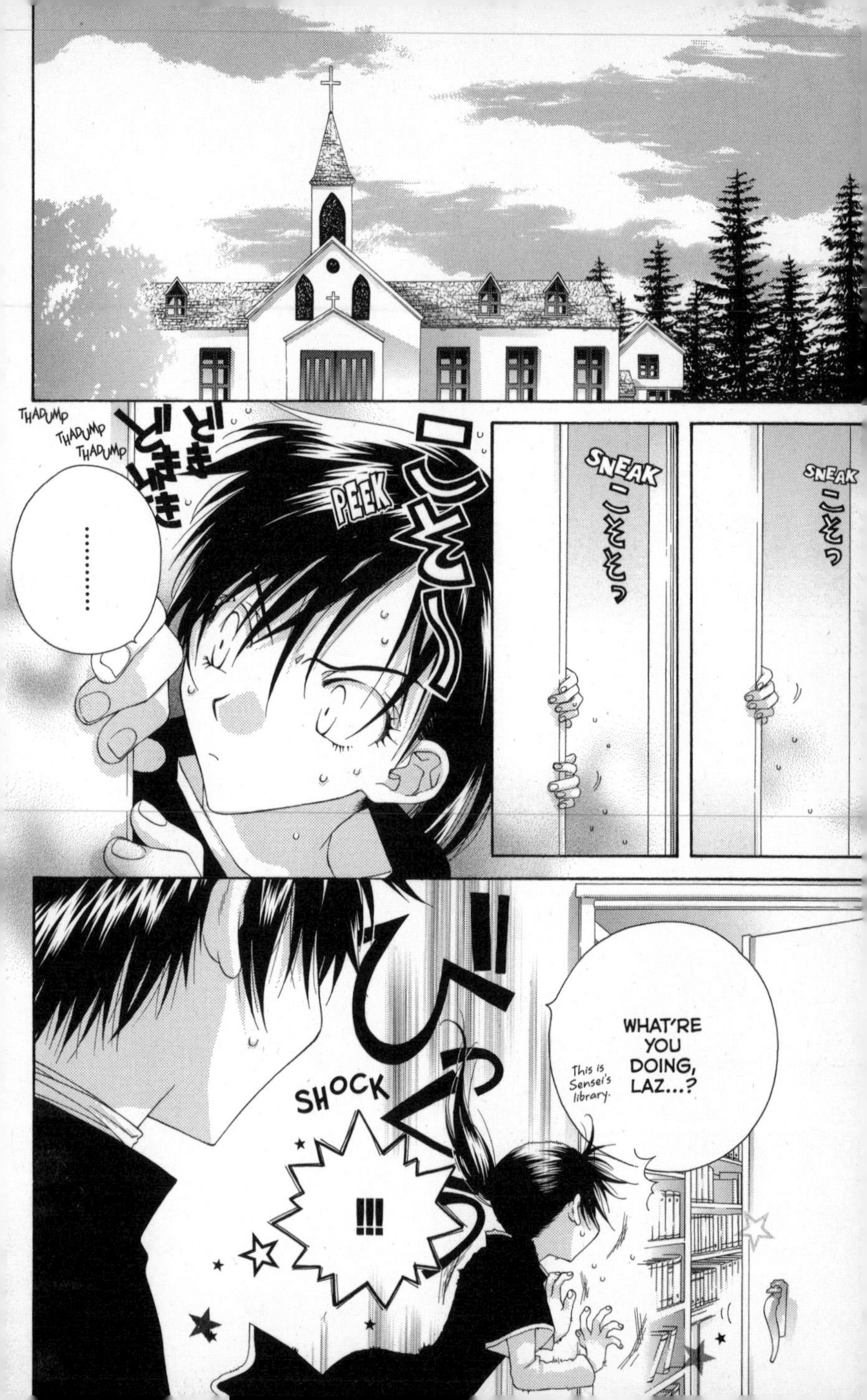
SNEAK
こそっ
SNEAK
こそっ
PEEK
THADUMP THADUMP THADUMP
どきどき
……
WHAT'RE YOU DOING, LAZ...?
This is Sensei's library.
SHOCK
!!!

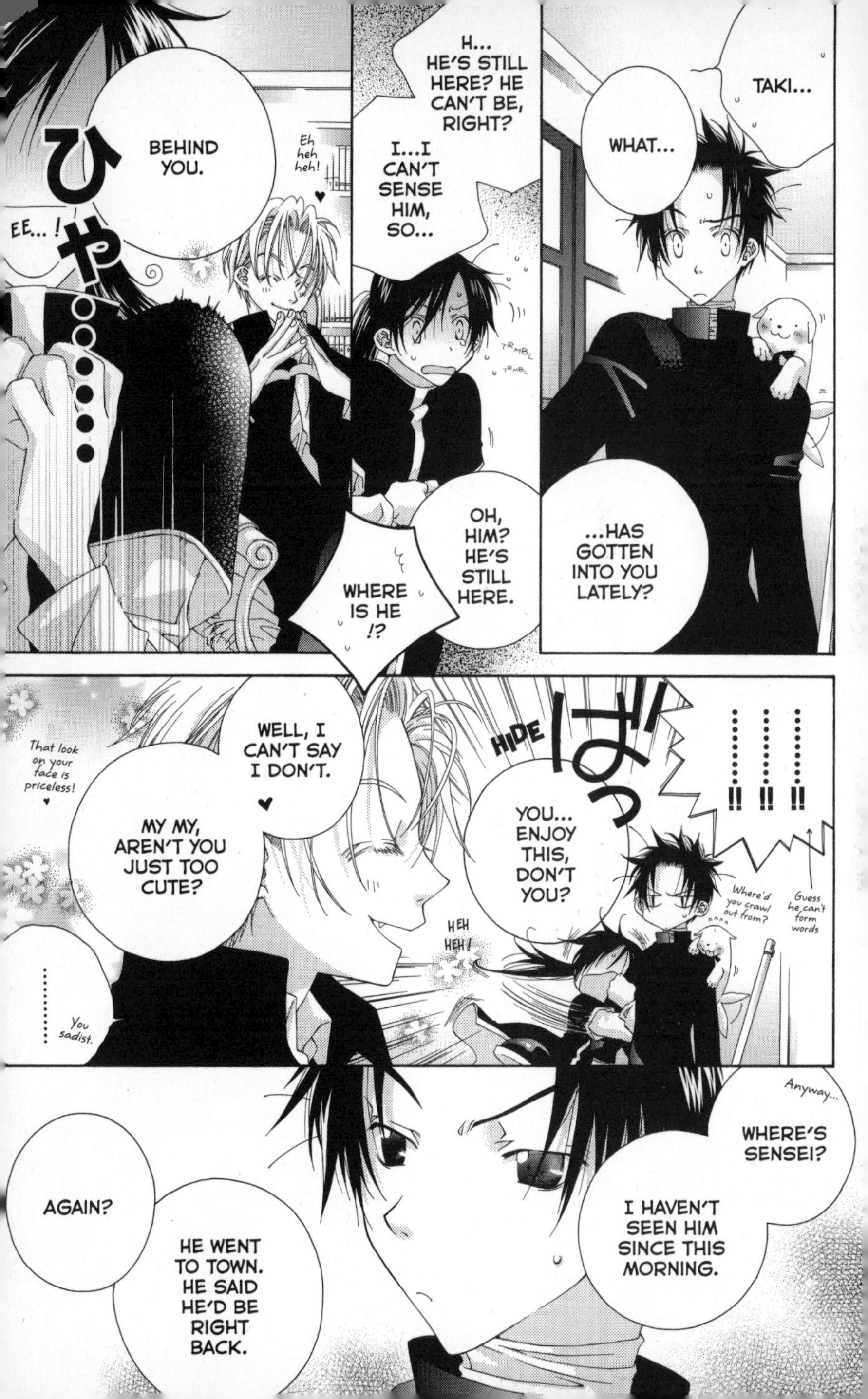
TAKI...
WHAT...
...HAS GOTTEN INTO YOU LATELY?
H... HE'S STILL HERE? HE CAN'T BE, RIGHT?
I...I CAN'T SENSE HIM, SO...
TRMBL TRMBL
OH, HIM? HE'S STILL HERE.
WHERE IS HE !?
BEHIND YOU.
Eh heh heh!
ひや
EE...!
......!! ......!! ......!!
HIDE
ぱっ
YOU... ENJOY THIS, DON'T YOU?
Where'd you crawl out from?
Guess he can't form words
HEH HEH!
WELL, I CAN'T SAY I DON'T.
MY MY, AREN'T YOU JUST TOO CUTE?
That look on your face is priceless!
......
You sadist.
Anyway...
WHERE'S SENSEI?
I HAVEN'T SEEN HIM SINCE THIS MORNING.
AGAIN?
HE WENT TO TOWN. HE SAID HE'D BE RIGHT BACK.

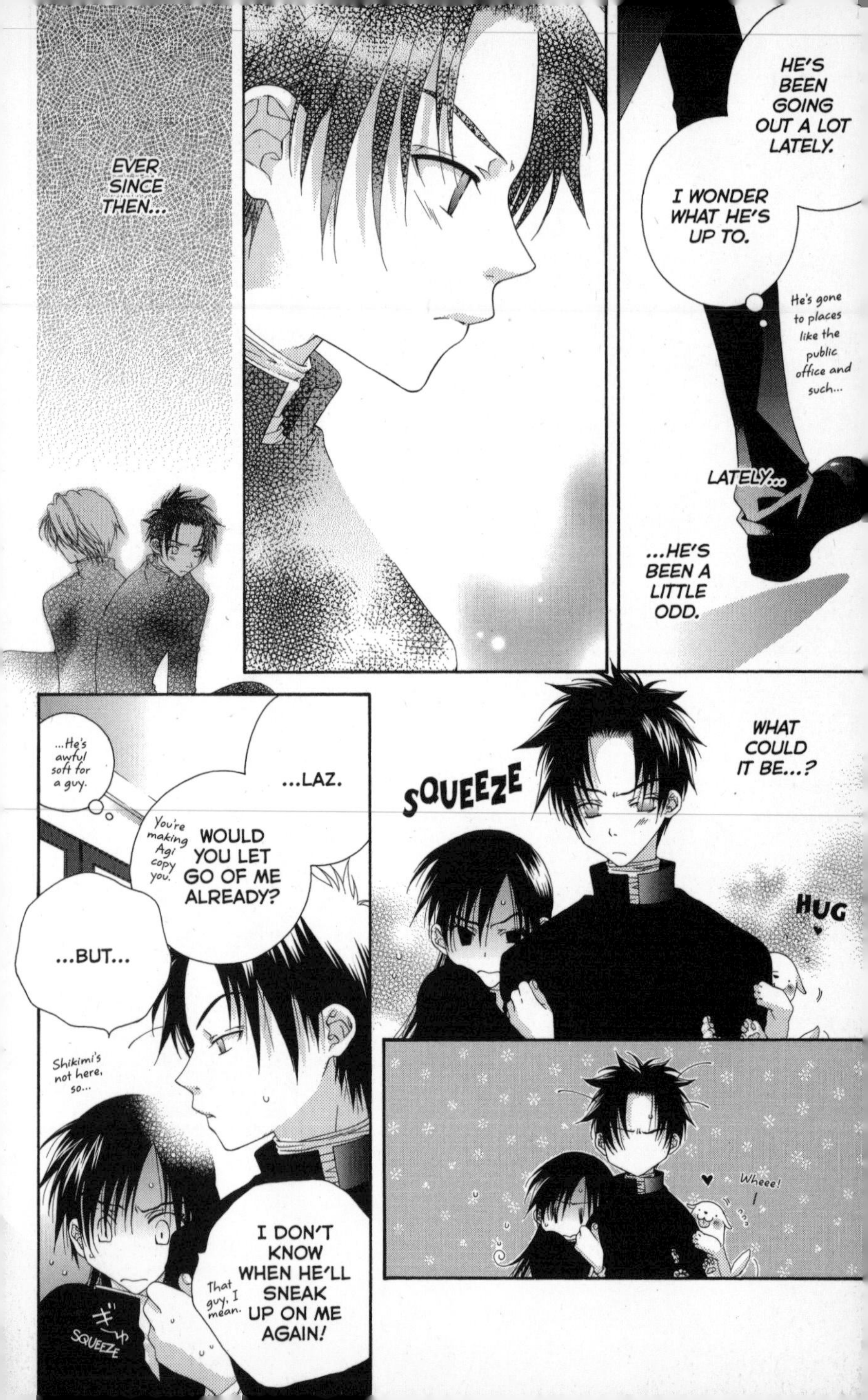
HE'S BEEN GOING OUT A LOT LATELY.
I WONDER WHAT HE'S UP TO.
He's gone to places like the public office and such...
LATELY...
...HE'S BEEN A LITTLE ODD.
EVER SINCE THEN...
WHAT COULD IT BE...?
SQUEEZE
HUG
Wheee!
...LAZ.
WOULD YOU LET GO OF ME ALREADY?
You're making Agi copy you.
...He's awful soft for a guy.
...BUT...
Shikimi's not here, so...
I DON'T KNOW WHEN HE'LL SNEAK UP ON ME AGAIN!
That guy, I mean.
ギュ
SQUEEZE

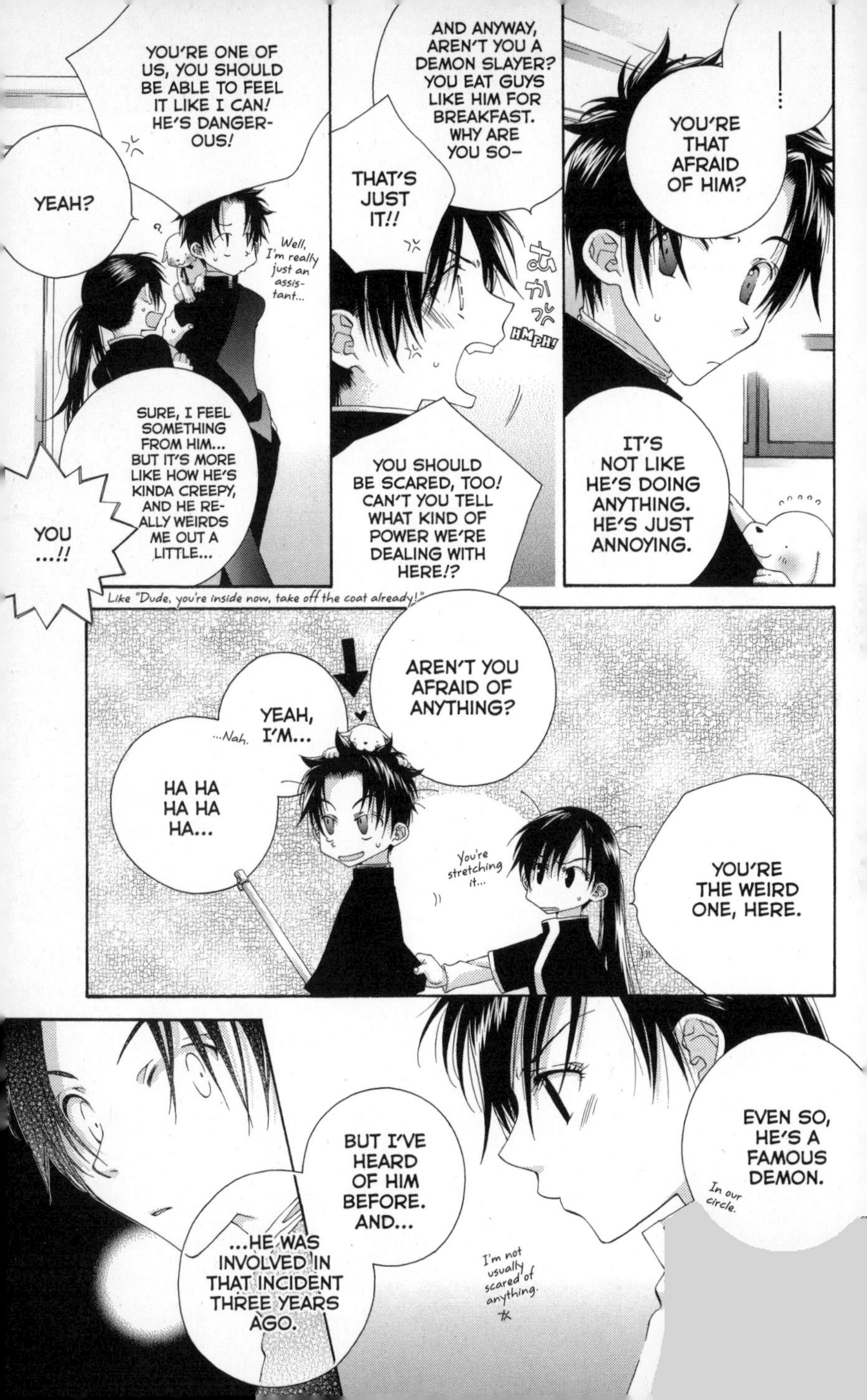
......
YOU'RE THAT AFRAID OF HIM?
IT'S NOT LIKE HE'S DOING ANYTHING. HE'S JUST ANNOYING.
AND ANYWAY, AREN'T YOU A DEMON SLAYER? YOU EAT GUYS LIKE HIM FOR BREAKFAST. WHY ARE YOU SO–
THAT'S JUST IT!!
HMPH!
YOU SHOULD BE SCARED, TOO! CAN'T YOU TELL WHAT KIND OF POWER WE'RE DEALING WITH HERE!?
YOU'RE ONE OF US, YOU SHOULD BE ABLE TO FEEL IT LIKE I CAN! HE'S DANGER-OUS!
YEAH?
Well, I'm really just an assis-tant...
SURE, I FEEL SOMETHING FROM HIM... BUT IT'S MORE LIKE HOW HE'S KINDA CREEPY, AND HE RE-ALLY WEIRDS ME OUT A LITTLE...
YOU ...!!
Like "Dude, you're inside now, take off the coat already!"
AREN'T YOU AFRAID OF ANYTHING?
YEAH, I'M...
...Nah.
HA HA HA HA HA...
YOU'RE THE WEIRD ONE, HERE.
You're stretching it...
EVEN SO, HE'S A FAMOUS DEMON.
In our circle.
I'm not usually scared of anything.
BUT I'VE HEARD OF HIM BEFORE. AND...
...HE WAS INVOLVED IN THAT INCIDENT THREE YEARS AGO.

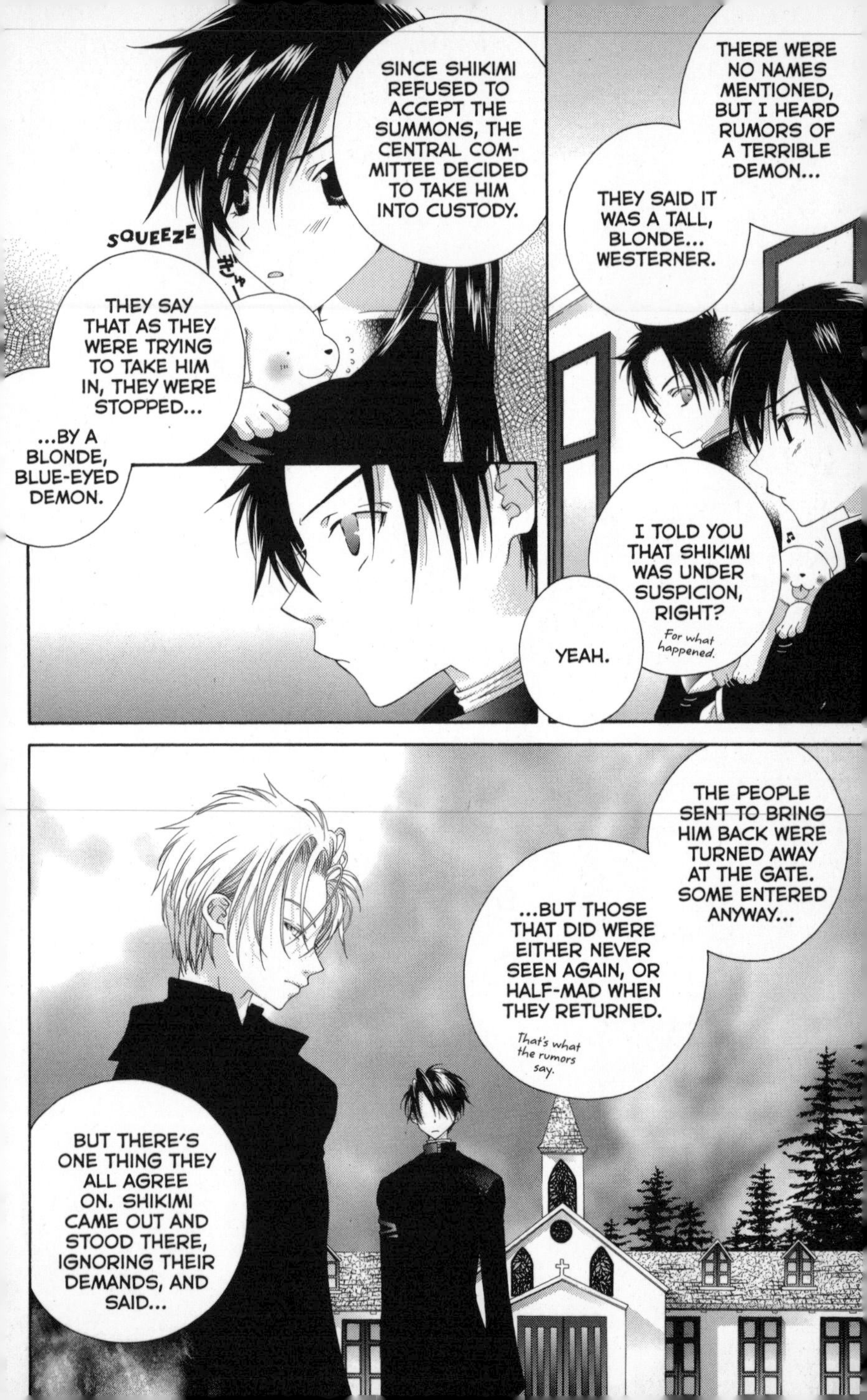
I TOLD YOU THAT SHIKIMI WAS UNDER SUSPICION, RIGHT?
For what happened.
YEAH.
SINCE SHIKIMI REFUSED TO ACCEPT THE SUMMONS, THE CENTRAL COM-MITTEE DECIDED TO TAKE HIM INTO CUSTODY.
SQUEEZE
THEY SAY THAT AS THEY WERE TRYING TO TAKE HIM IN, THEY WERE STOPPED...
...BY A BLONDE, BLUE-EYED DEMON.
THERE WERE NO NAMES MENTIONED, BUT I HEARD RUMORS OF A TERRIBLE DEMON...
THEY SAID IT WAS A TALL, BLONDE... WESTERNER.
THE PEOPLE SENT TO BRING HIM BACK WERE TURNED AWAY AT THE GATE. SOME ENTERED ANYWAY...
...BUT THOSE THAT DID WERE EITHER NEVER SEEN AGAIN, OR HALF-MAD WHEN THEY RETURNED.
That's what the rumors say.
BUT THERE'S ONE THING THEY ALL AGREE ON. SHIKIMI CAME OUT AND STOOD THERE, IGNORING THEIR DEMANDS, AND SAID...

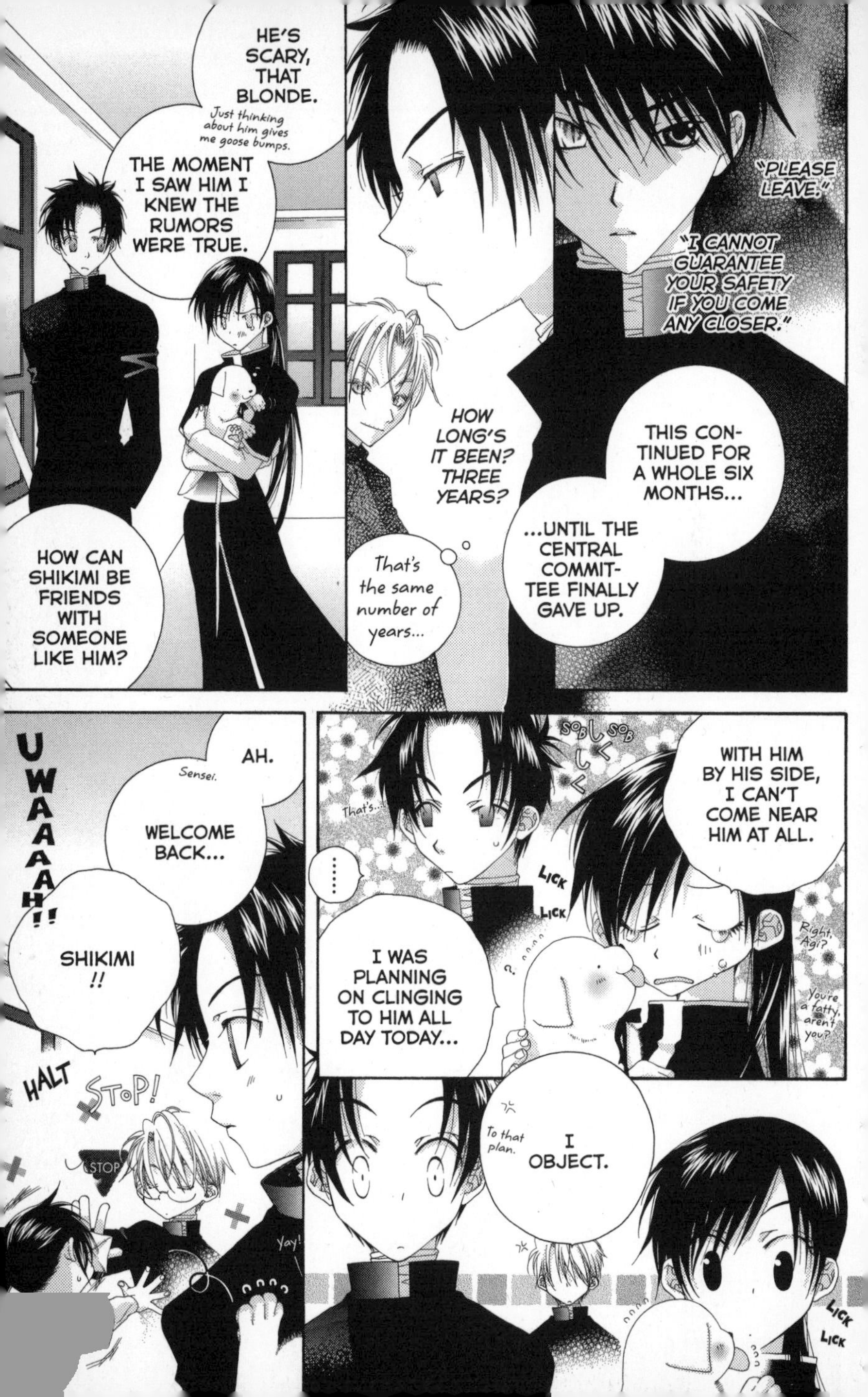
"PLEASE LEAVE."
"I CANNOT GUARANTEE YOUR SAFETY IF YOU COME ANY CLOSER."
THIS CONTINUED FOR A WHOLE SIX MONTHS...
...UNTIL THE CENTRAL COMMITTEE FINALLY GAVE UP.
HOW LONG'S IT BEEN? THREE YEARS?
That's the same number of years...
HE'S SCARY, THAT BLONDE.
Just thinking about him gives me goose bumps.
THE MOMENT I SAW HIM I KNEW THE RUMORS WERE TRUE.
HOW CAN SHIKIMI BE FRIENDS WITH SOMEONE LIKE HIM?
WITH HIM BY HIS SIDE, I CAN'T COME NEAR HIM AT ALL.
SOB SOB
That's...
......
LICK
LICK
Right, Agi?
You're a fatty, aren't you?
I WAS PLANNING ON CLINGING TO HIM ALL DAY TODAY...
I OBJECT.
To that plan.
LICK
LICK
AH.
Sensei.
WELCOME BACK...
UWAAAAAH!!
SHIKIMI !!
HALT
STOP!
STOP
Yay!

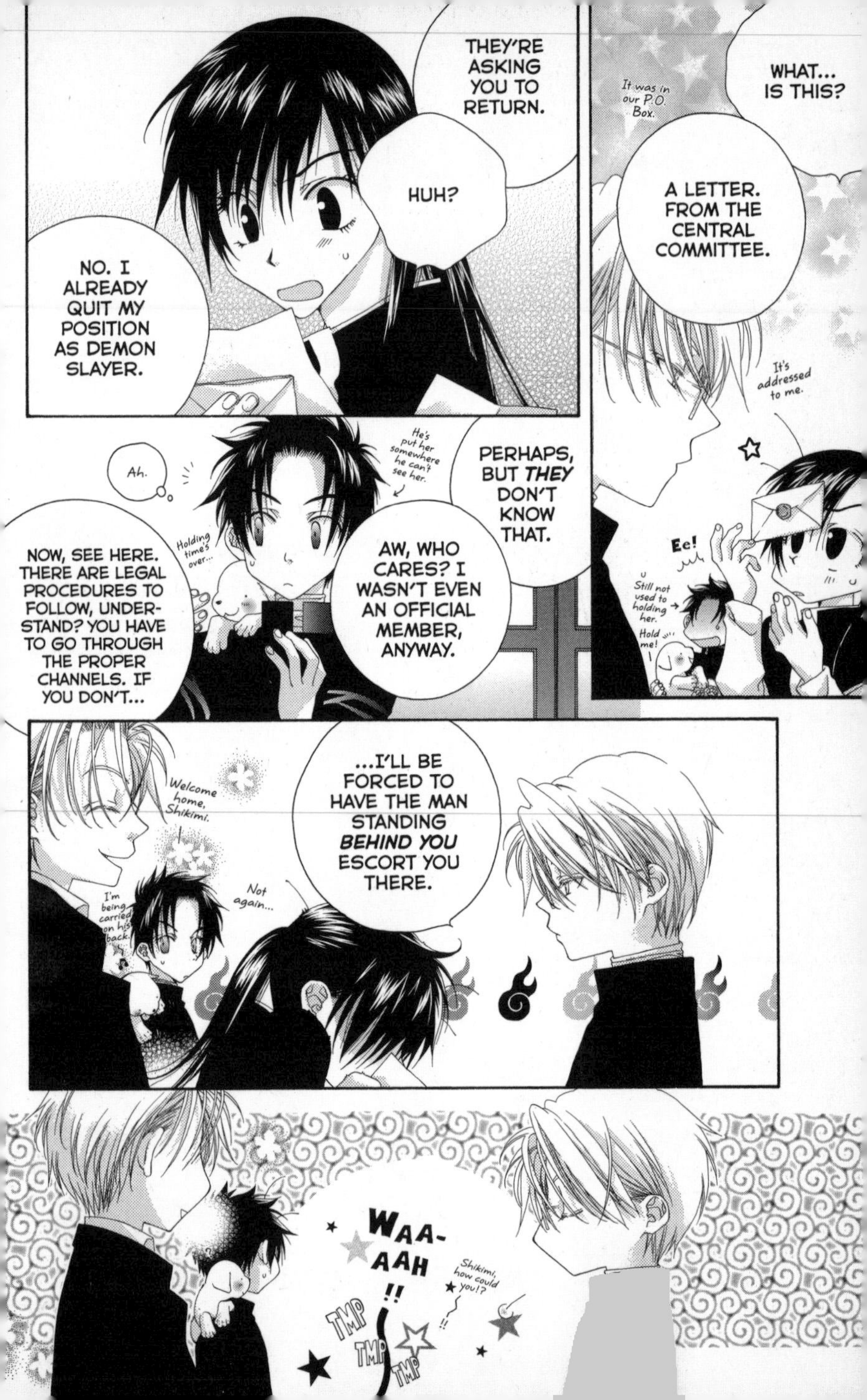
WHAT... IS THIS?
It was in our P.O. Box.
A LETTER. FROM THE CENTRAL COMMITTEE.
It's addressed to me.
Ee!
Still not used to holding her.
Hold me!
THEY'RE ASKING YOU TO RETURN.
HUH?
NO. I ALREADY QUIT MY POSITION AS DEMON SLAYER.
PERHAPS, BUT *THEY* DON'T KNOW THAT.
He's put her somewhere he can't see her.
AW, WHO CARES? I WASN'T EVEN AN OFFICIAL MEMBER, ANYWAY.
Ah.
Holding time's over...
NOW, SEE HERE. THERE ARE LEGAL PROCEDURES TO FOLLOW, UNDERSTAND? YOU HAVE TO GO THROUGH THE PROPER CHANNELS. IF YOU DON'T...
...I'LL BE FORCED TO HAVE THE MAN STANDING *BEHIND YOU* ESCORT YOU THERE.
Not again...
Welcome home, Shikimi.
I'm being carried on his back.
Shikimi, how could you!?
WAA-AAH!!
TMP
TMP
TMP

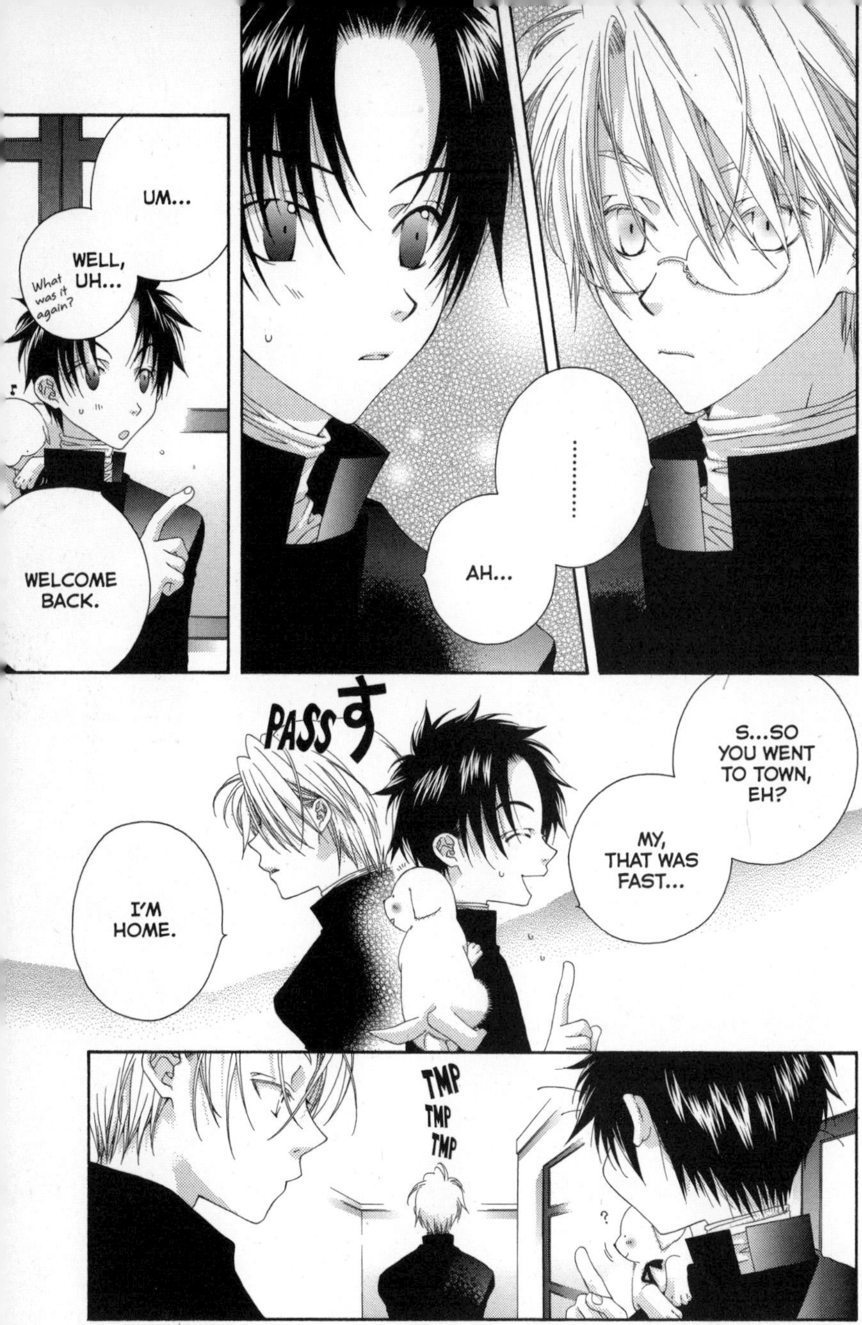
......
AH...
UM...
WELL, UH...
What was it again?
WELCOME BACK.
S...SO YOU WENT TO TOWN, EH?
MY, THAT WAS FAST...
PASS す
I'M HOME.
TMP TMP TMP

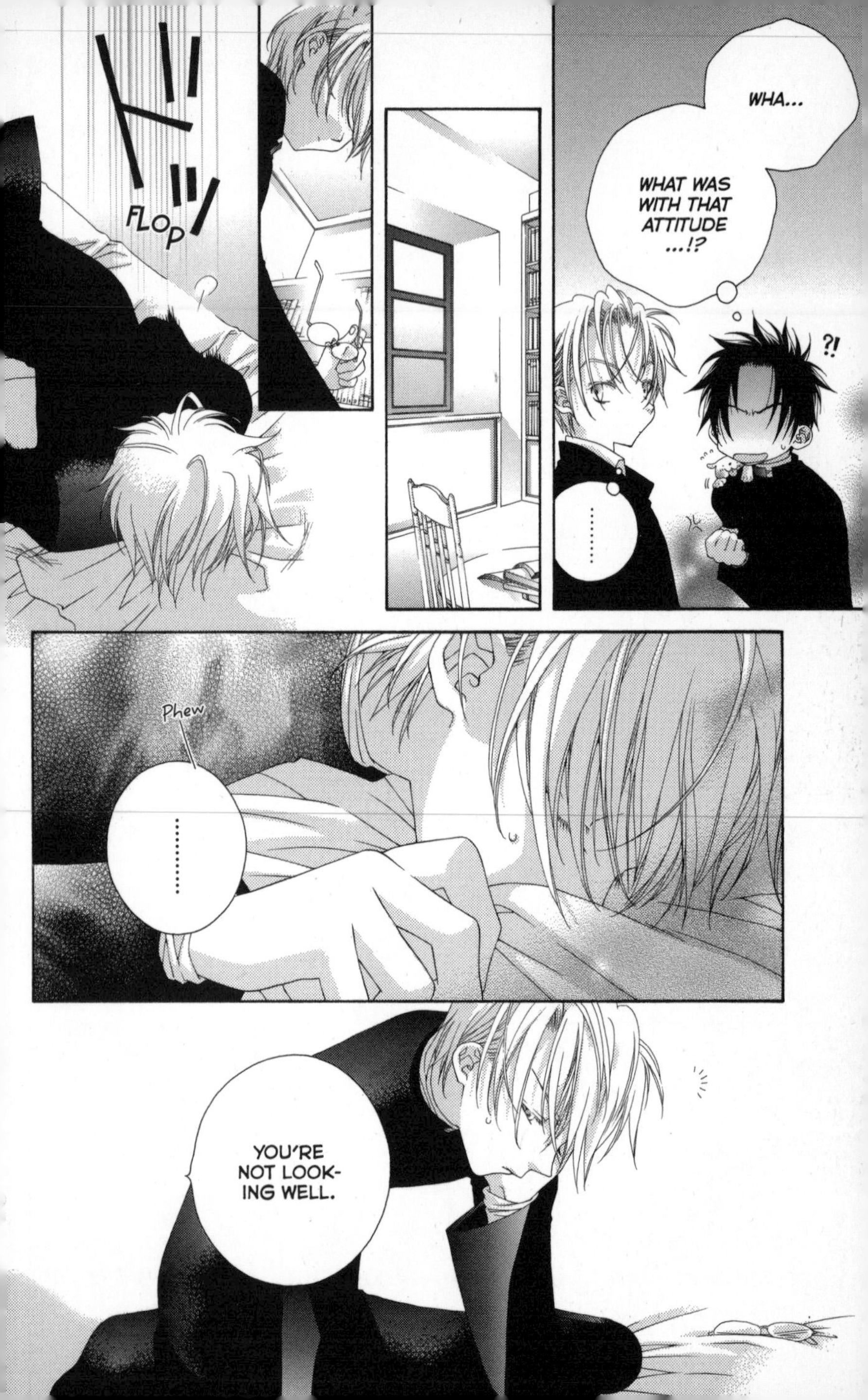
WHA...
WHAT WAS WITH THAT ATTITUDE ...!?
?!
......
FLOP
Phew
....
YOU'RE NOT LOOK-ING WELL.

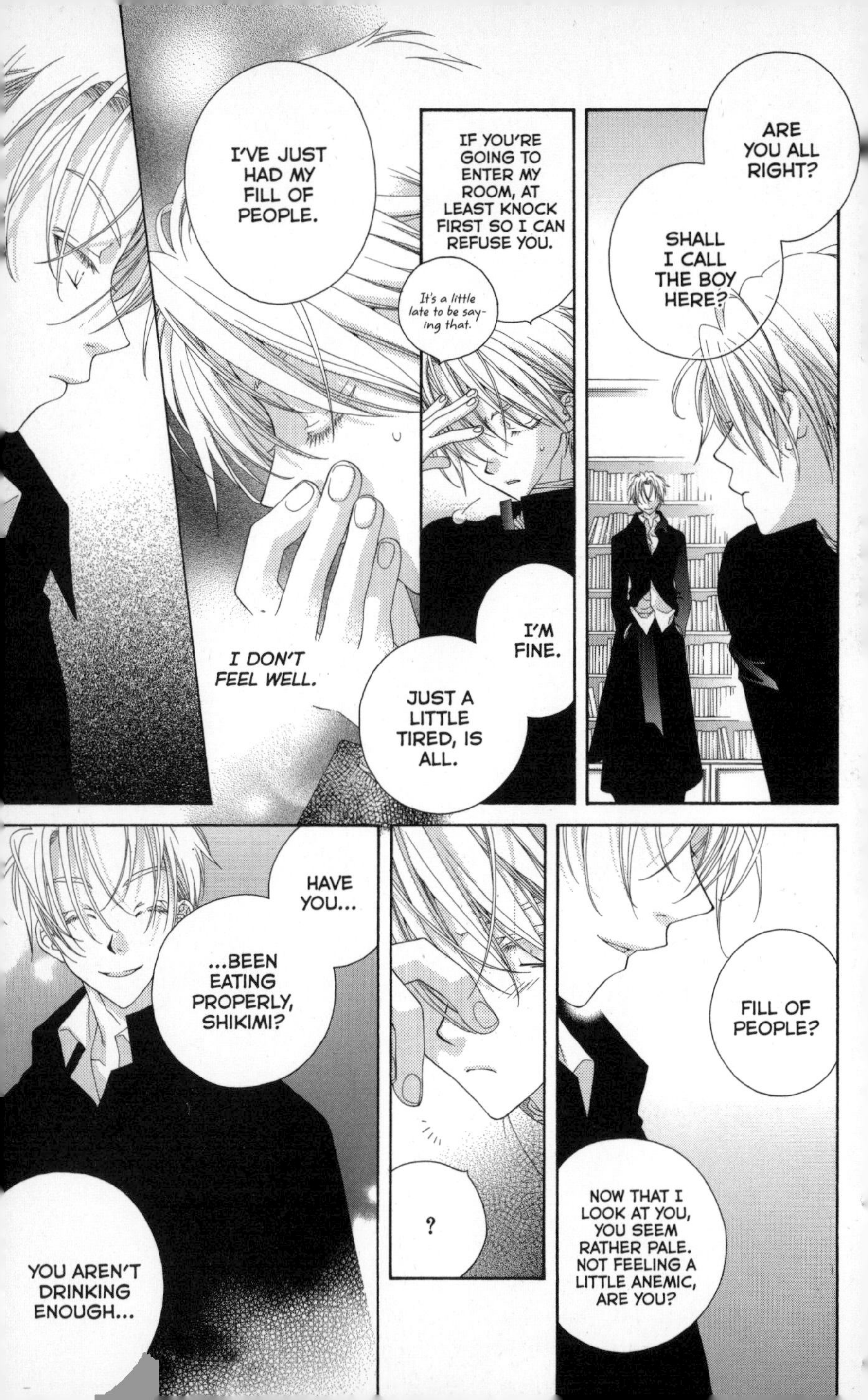
ARE YOU ALL RIGHT?
SHALL I CALL THE BOY HERE?
IF YOU'RE GOING TO ENTER MY ROOM, AT LEAST KNOCK FIRST SO I CAN REFUSE YOU.
It's a little late to be saying that.
I'M FINE.
JUST A LITTLE TIRED, IS ALL.
I'VE JUST HAD MY FILL OF PEOPLE.
I DON'T FEEL WELL.
FILL OF PEOPLE?
NOW THAT I LOOK AT YOU, YOU SEEM RATHER PALE. NOT FEELING A LITTLE ANEMIC, ARE YOU?
?
HAVE YOU...
...BEEN EATING PROPERLY, SHIKIMI?
YOU AREN'T DRINKING ENOUGH...

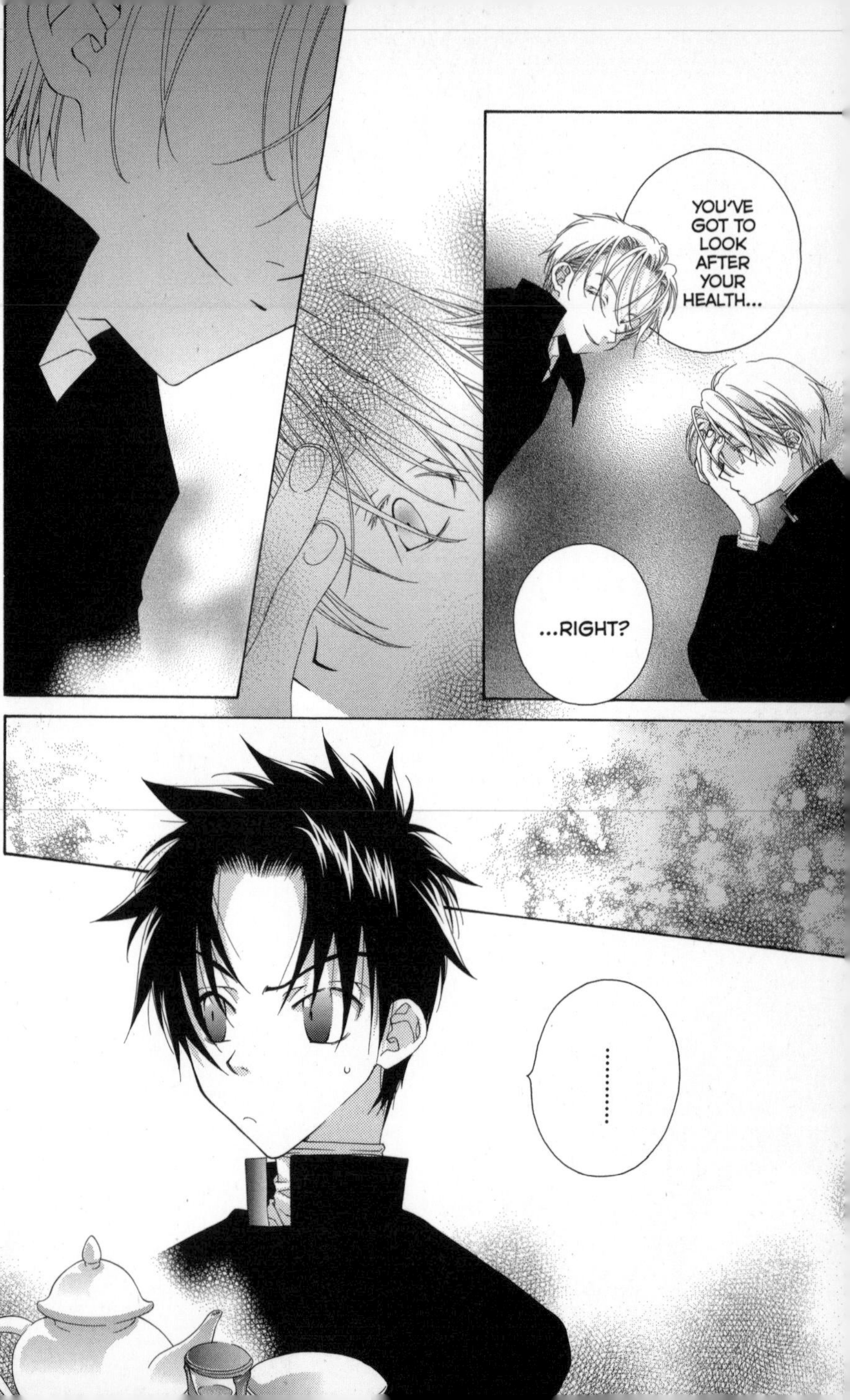
YOU'VE GOT TO LOOK AFTER YOUR HEALTH...
...RIGHT?
....

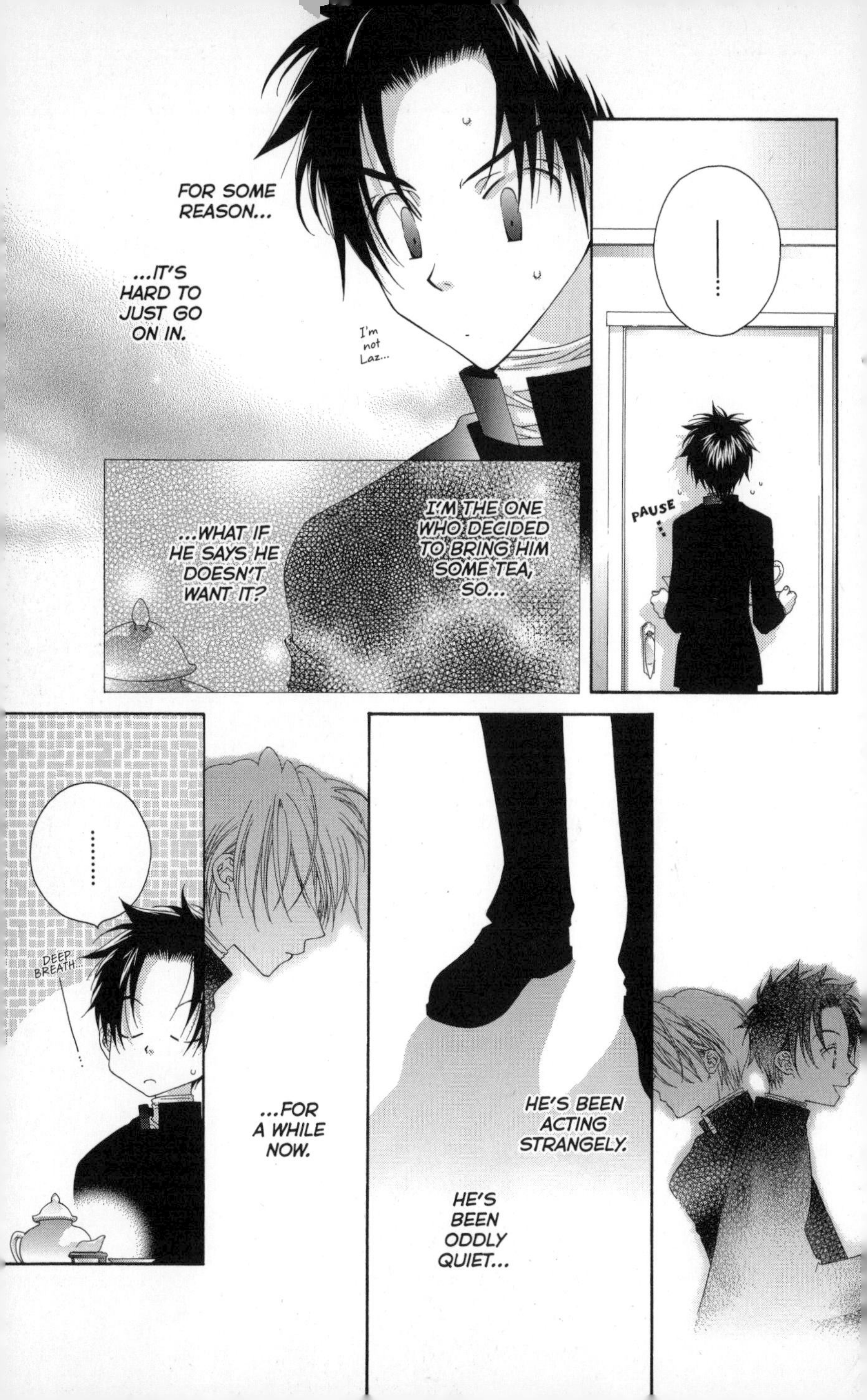

PAUSE
FOR SOME REASON...
...IT'S HARD TO JUST GO ON IN.
I'm not Laz...
I'M THE ONE WHO DECIDED TO BRING HIM SOME TEA, SO...
...WHAT IF HE SAYS HE DOESN'T WANT IT?
HE'S BEEN ACTING STRANGELY.
HE'S BEEN ODDLY QUIET...
...FOR A WHILE NOW.
......
DEEP BREATH...

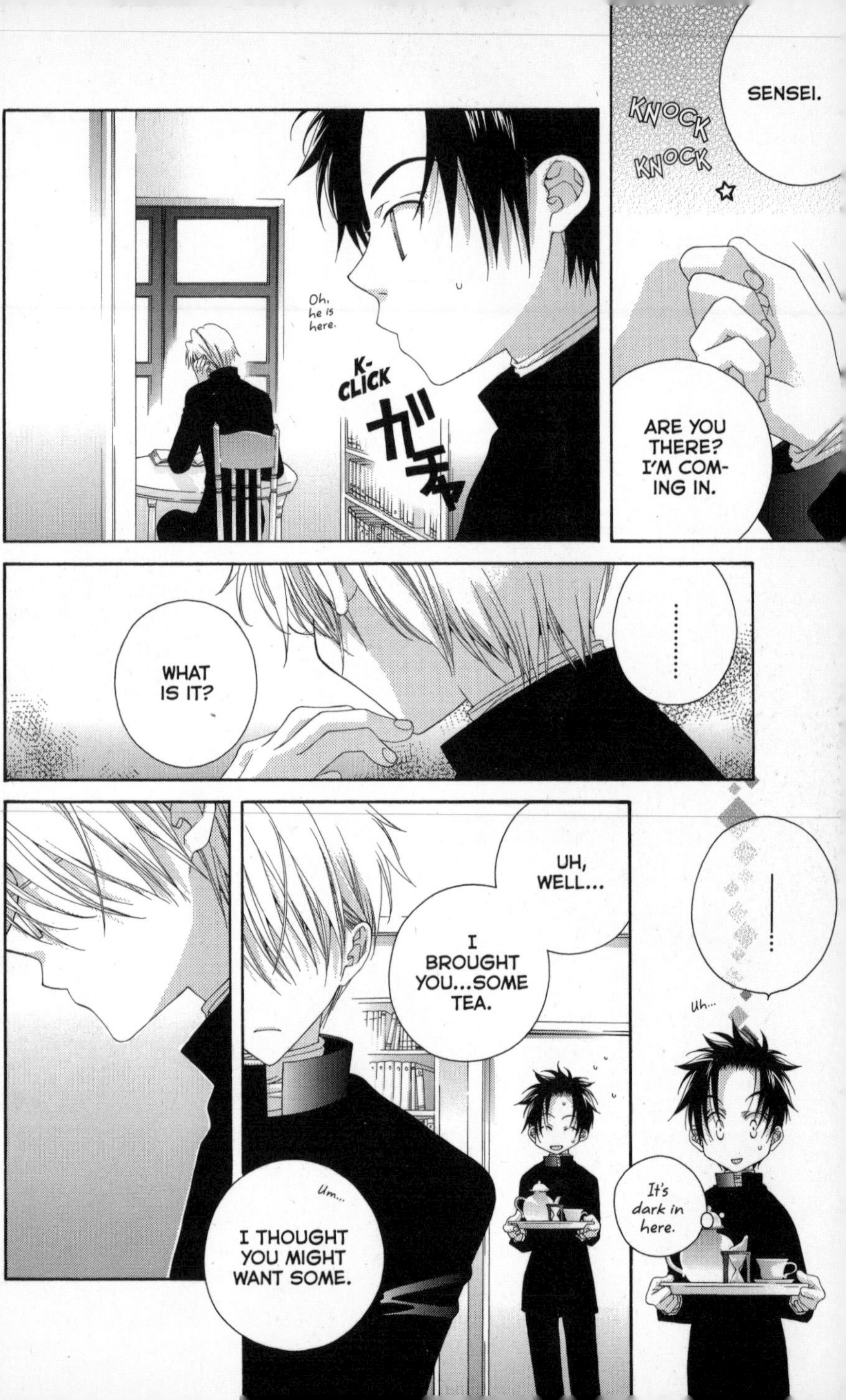
SENSEI.
KNOCK KNOCK ☆
ARE YOU THERE? I'M COMING IN.
K-CLICK
ガチャ
Oh, he is here.
......
WHAT IS IT?
......!
Uh...
It's dark in here.
UH, WELL...
I BROUGHT YOU...SOME TEA.
Um...
I THOUGHT YOU MIGHT WANT SOME.

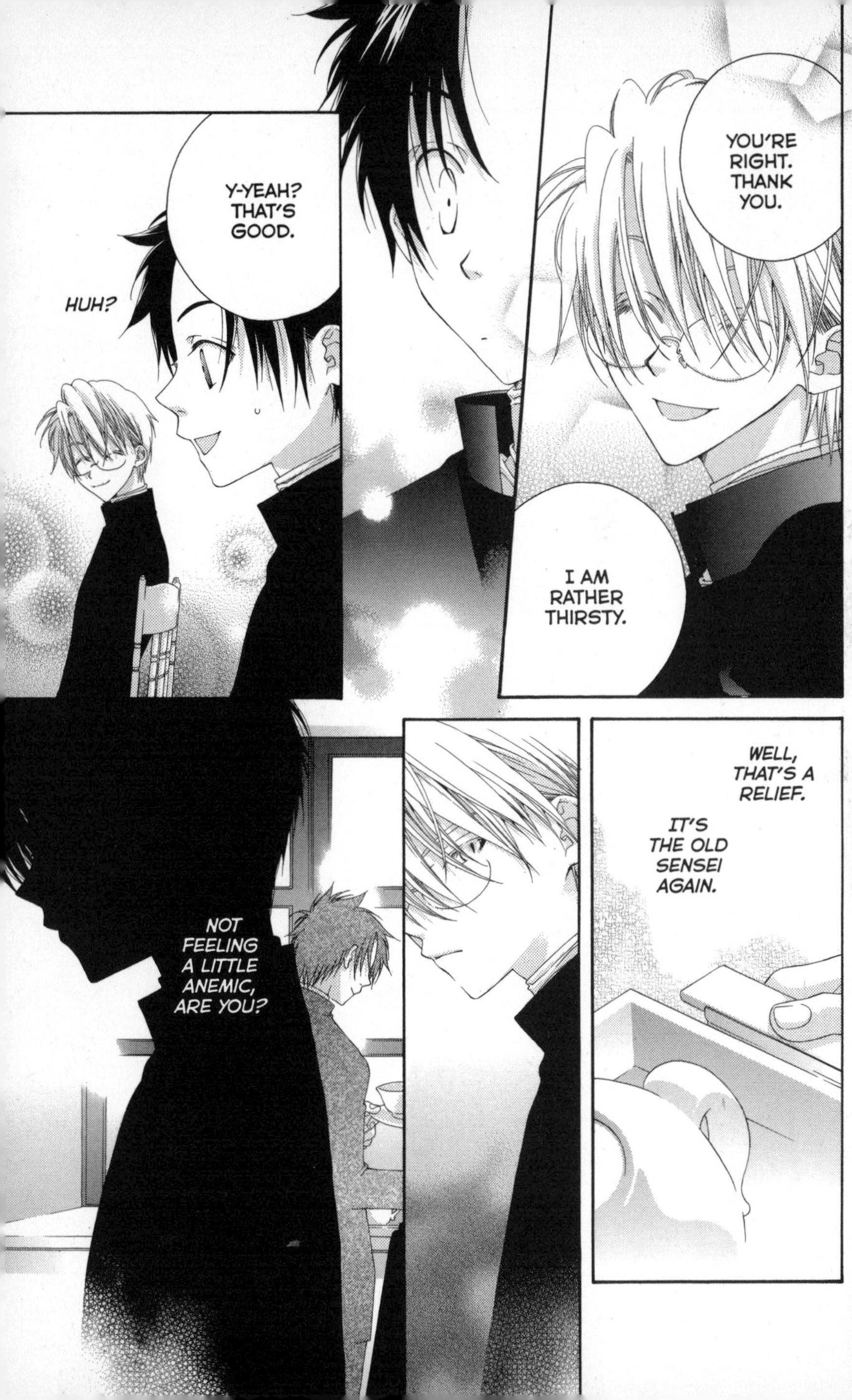
YOU'RE RIGHT. THANK YOU.
I AM RATHER THIRSTY.
Y-YEAH? THAT'S GOOD.
HUH?
WELL, THAT'S A RELIEF.
IT'S THE OLD SENSEI AGAIN.
NOT FEELING A LITTLE ANEMIC, ARE YOU?

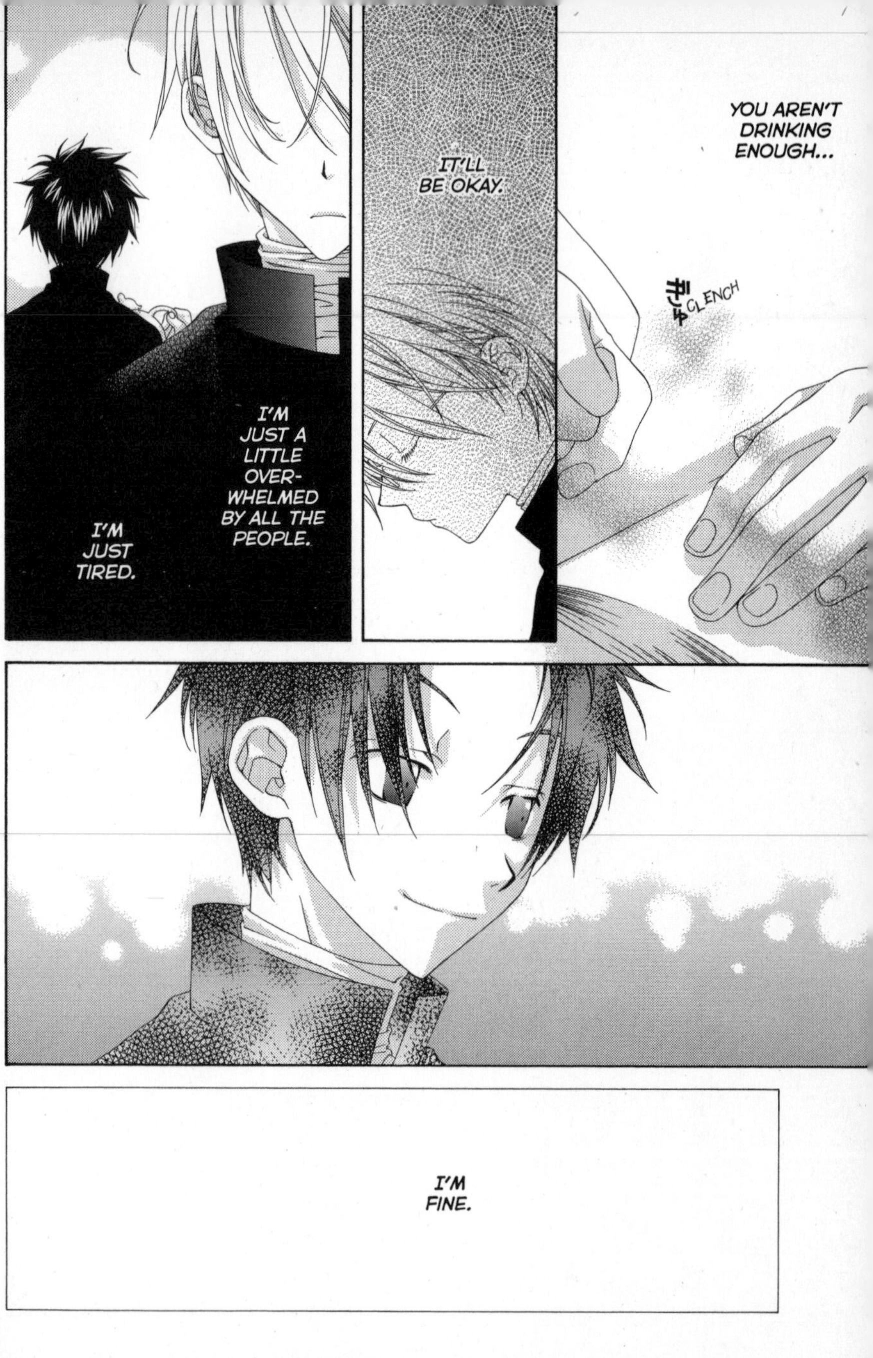
YOU AREN'T DRINKING ENOUGH...
CLENCH
IT'LL BE OKAY.
I'M JUST A LITTLE OVER-WHELMED BY ALL THE PEOPLE.
I'M JUST TIRED.
I'M FINE.

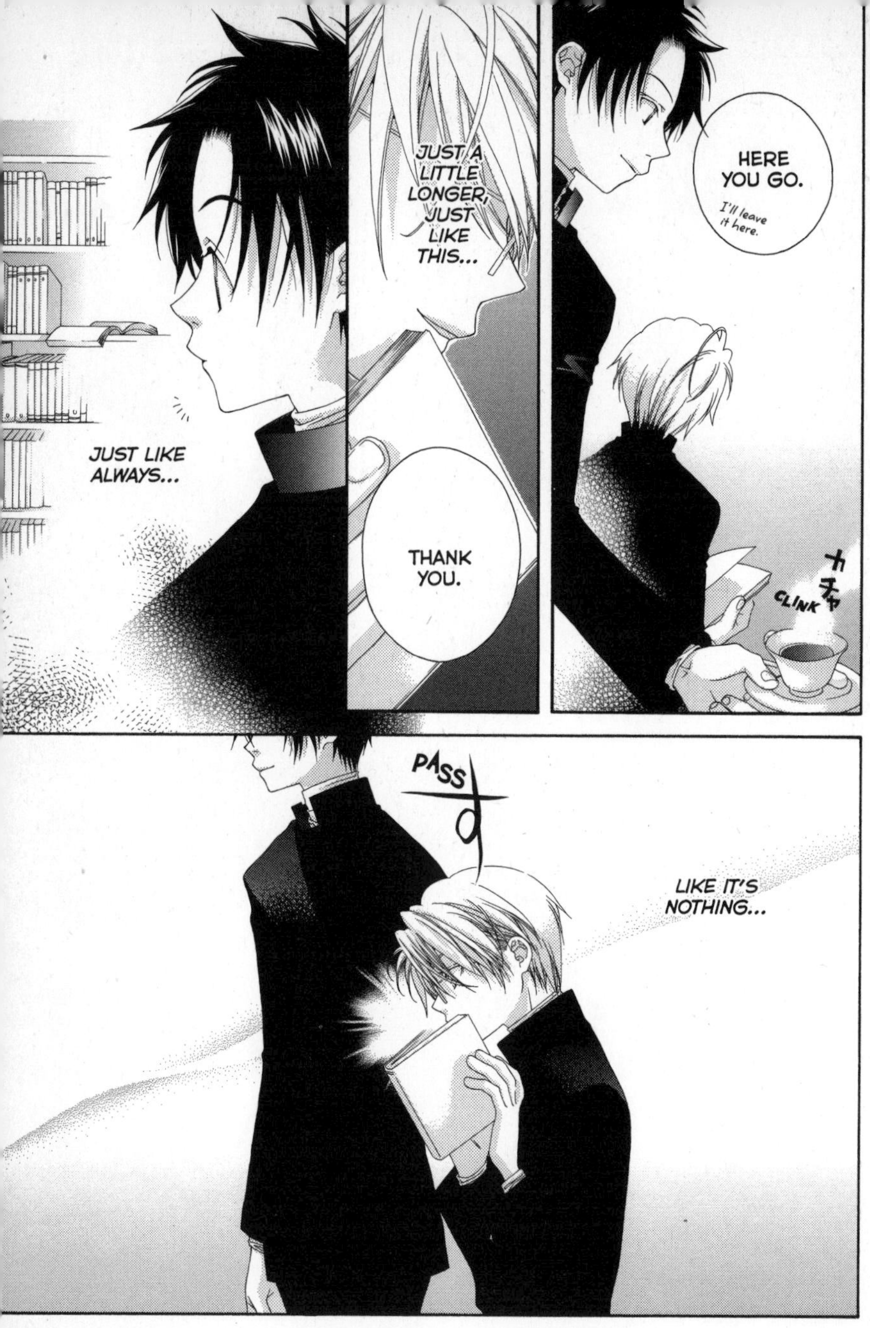
HERE YOU GO.
I'll leave it here.
カチャ
CLINK
JUST A LITTLE LONGER, JUST LIKE THIS...
THANK YOU.
JUST LIKE ALWAYS...
PASS
LIKE IT'S NOTHING...

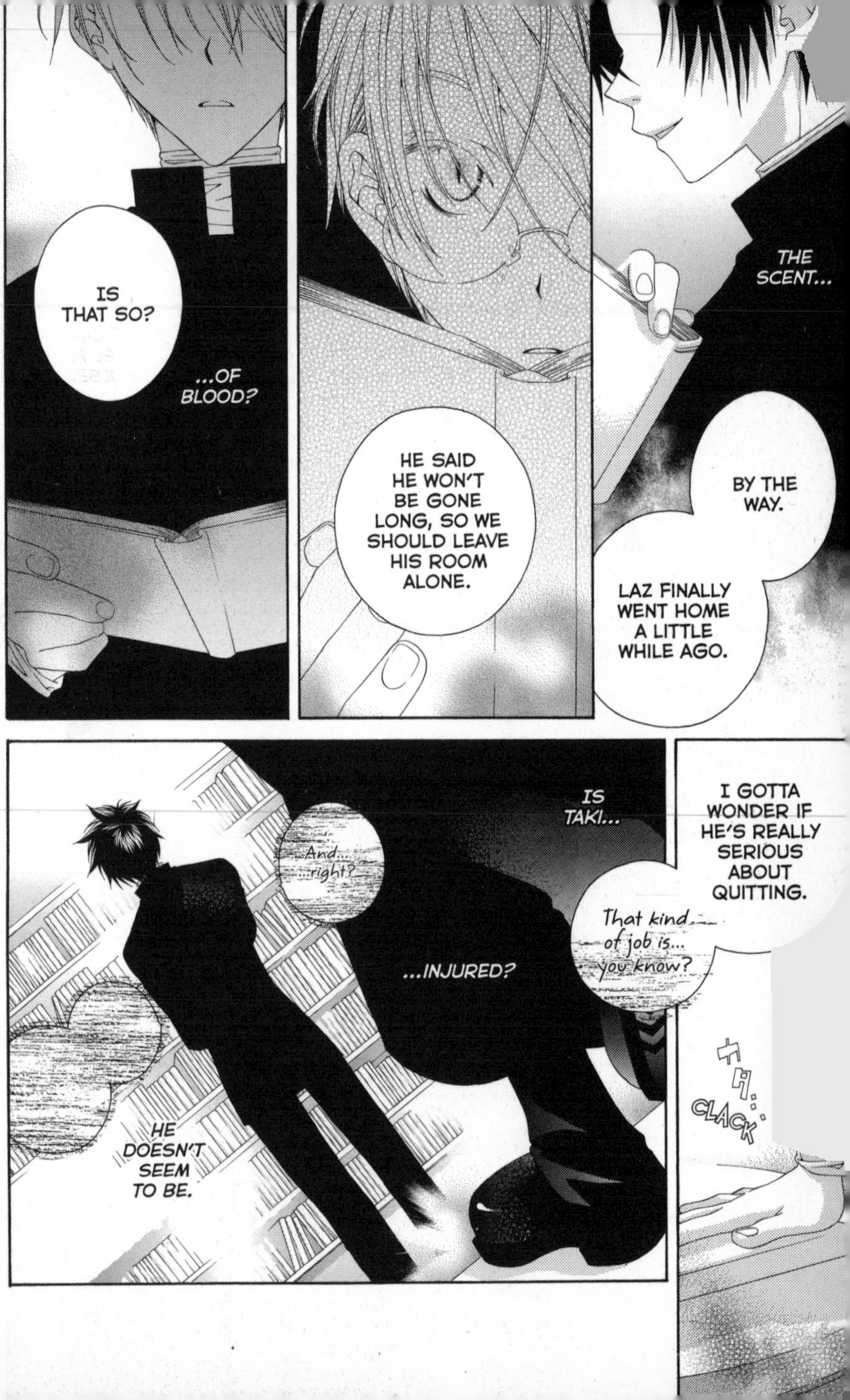
THE SCENT...
BY THE WAY.
LAZ FINALLY WENT HOME A LITTLE WHILE AGO.
HE SAID HE WON'T BE GONE LONG, SO WE SHOULD LEAVE HIS ROOM ALONE.
IS THAT SO?
...OF BLOOD?
I GOTTA WONDER IF HE'S REALLY SERIOUS ABOUT QUITTING.
That kind of job is... you know?
CLACK
IS TAKI...
And... ...right?
...INJURED?
HE DOESN'T SEEM TO BE.

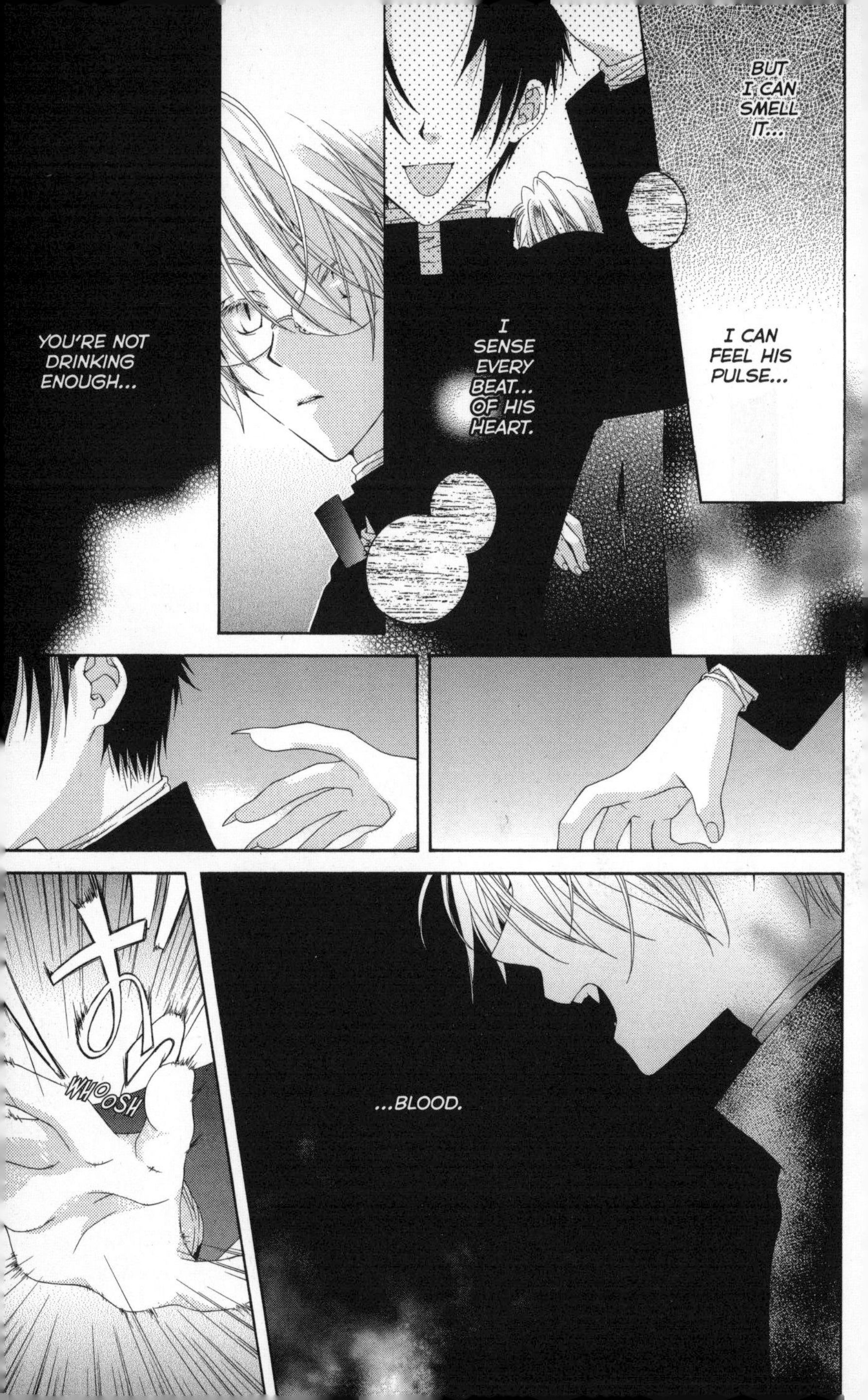

BUT I CAN SMELL IT...
I CAN FEEL HIS PULSE...
I SENSE EVERY BEAT... OF HIS HEART.
YOU'RE NOT DRINKING ENOUGH...
...BLOOD.
あ
WHOOSH

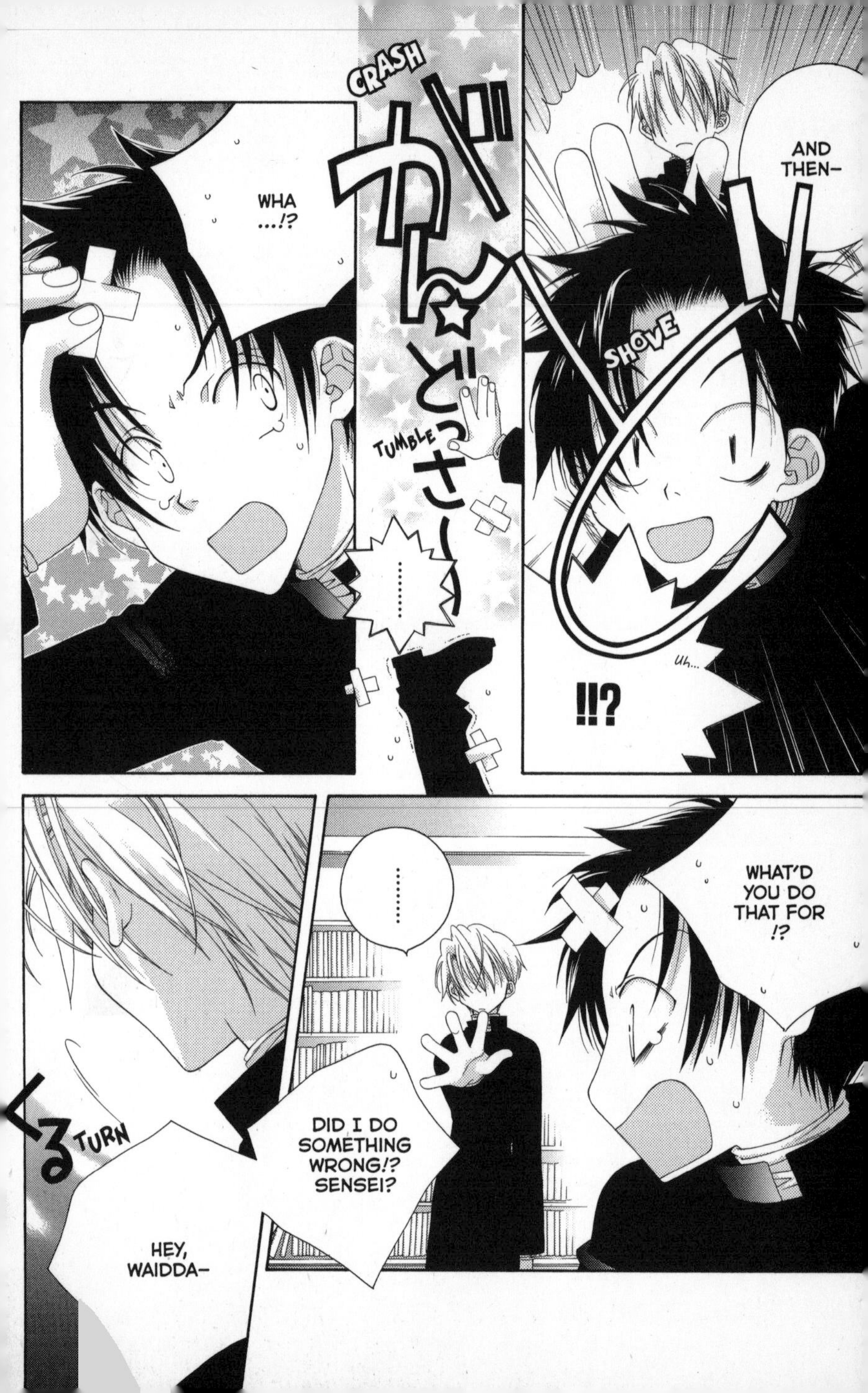
AND THEN-
SHOVE
Uh...
!!?
CRASH
ぱかん☆
TUMBLE
どっさー
......
WHA ...!?
WHAT'D YOU DO THAT FOR !?
....
DID I DO SOMETHING WRONG!? SENSEI?
くる
TURN
HEY, WAIDDA-

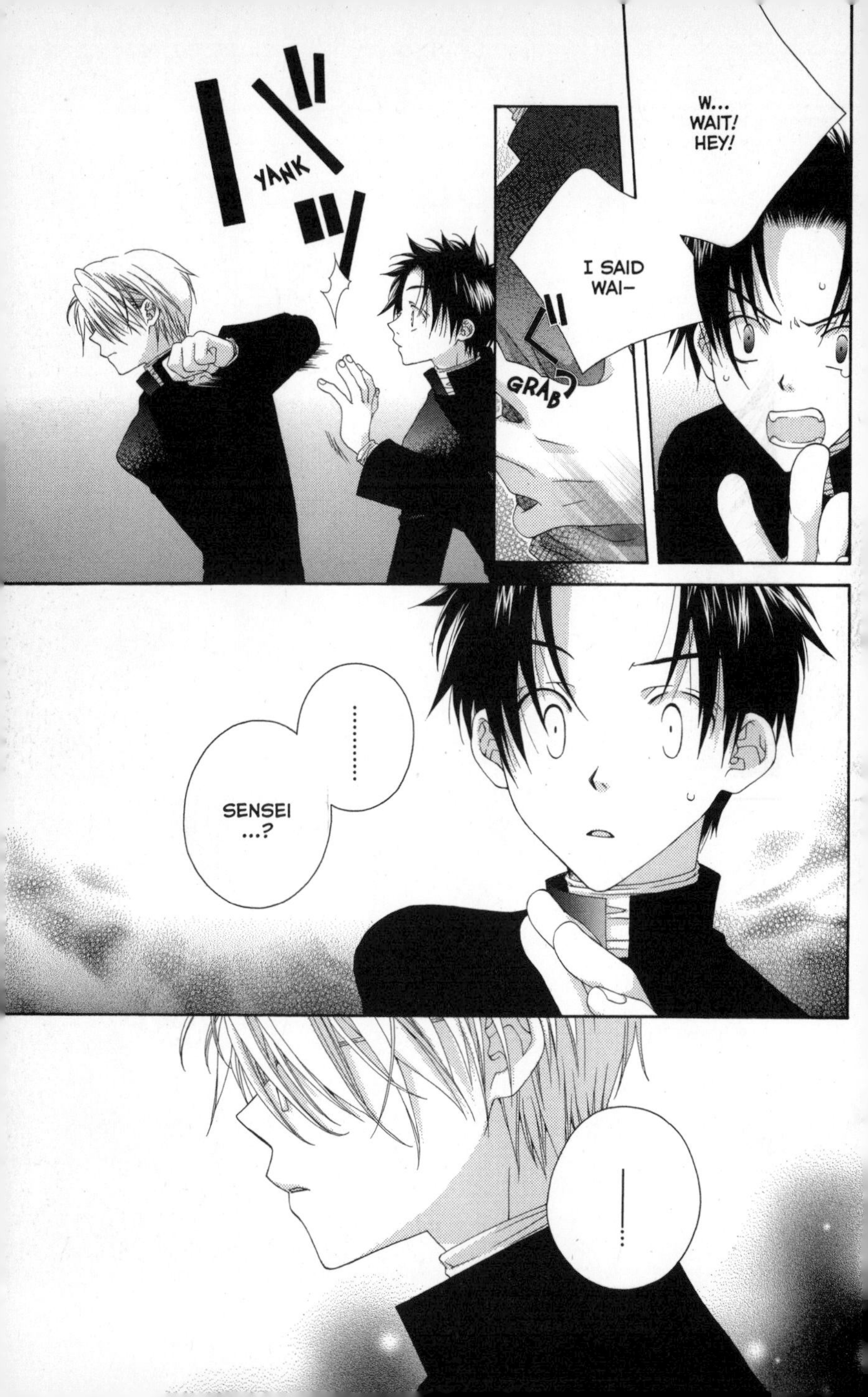
W...
WAIT!
HEY!
I SAID
WAI–
GRAB
YANK
....
SENSEI
...?
......

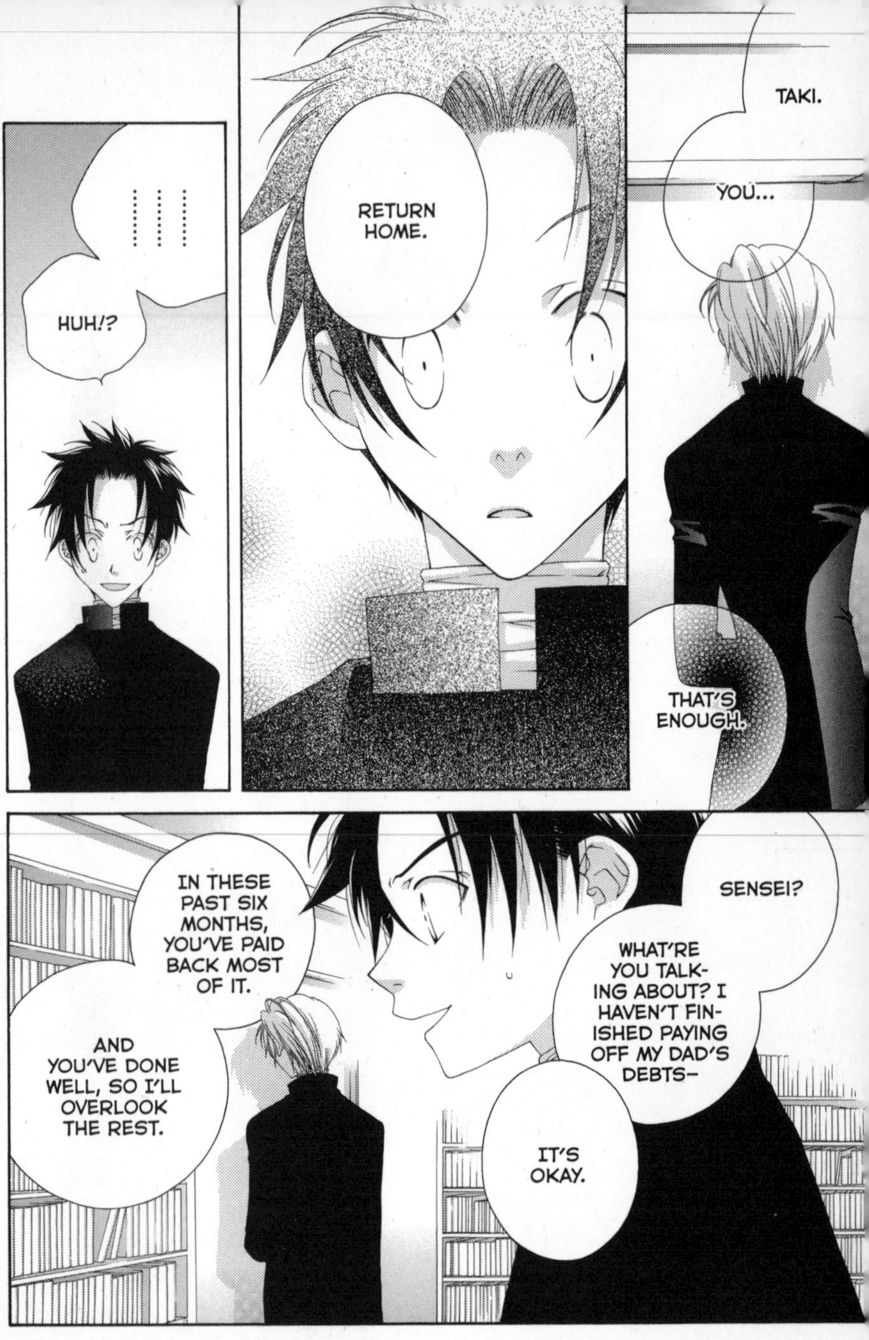
TAKI.
YOU...
THAT'S ENOUGH.
RETURN HOME.
......
HUH!?
SENSEI?
WHAT'RE YOU TALKING ABOUT? I HAVEN'T FINISHED PAYING OFF MY DAD'S DEBTS–
IT'S OKAY.
IN THESE PAST SIX MONTHS, YOU'VE PAID BACK MOST OF IT.
AND YOU'VE DONE WELL, SO I'LL OVERLOOK THE REST.

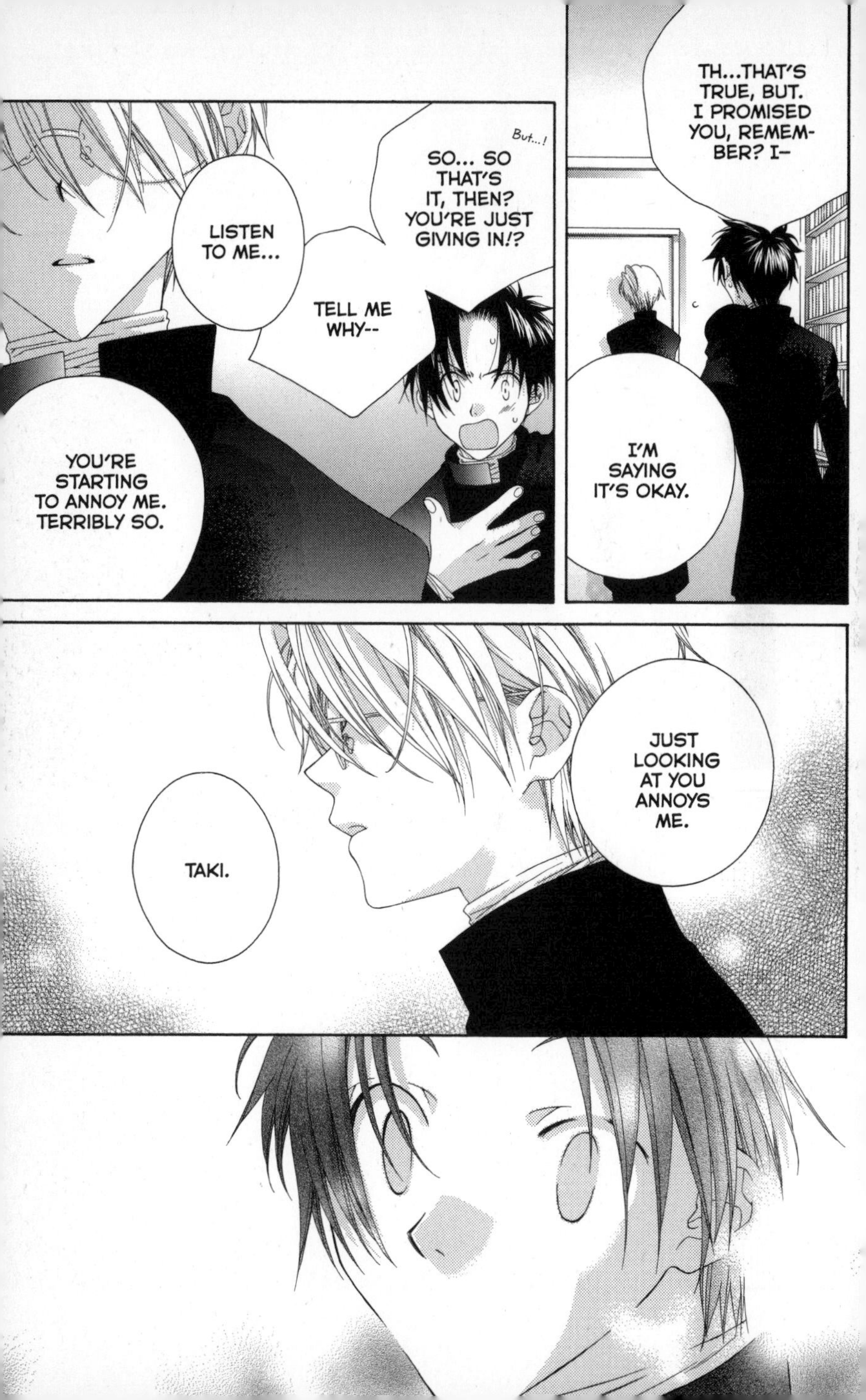
TH...THAT'S TRUE, BUT. I PROMISED YOU, REMEMBER? I–
I'M SAYING IT'S OKAY.
But...!
SO... SO THAT'S IT, THEN? YOU'RE JUST GIVING IN!?
LISTEN TO ME...
TELL ME WHY--
YOU'RE STARTING TO ANNOY ME. TERRIBLY SO.
JUST LOOKING AT YOU ANNOYS ME.
TAKI.

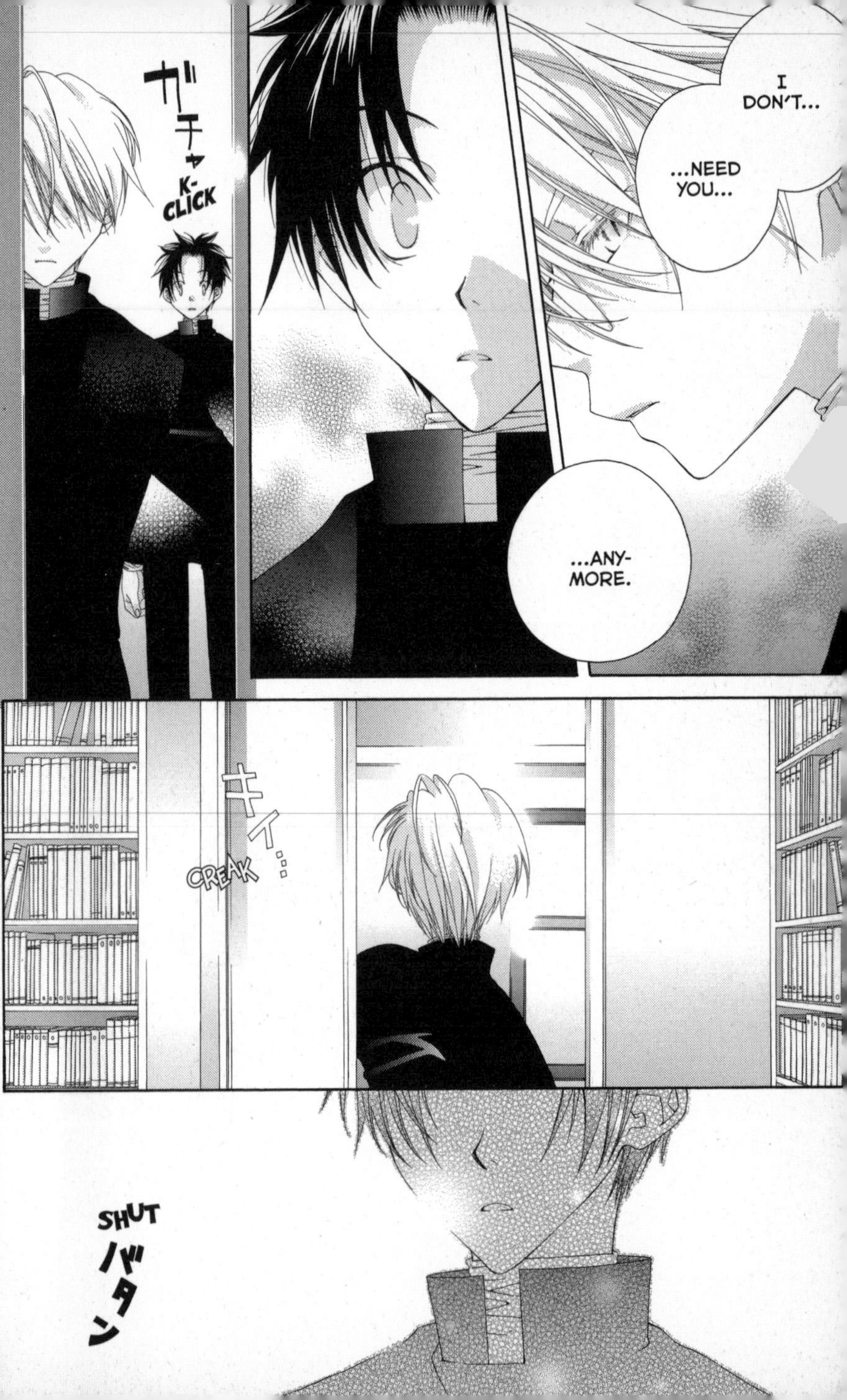
I DON'T...
...NEED YOU...
...ANY-MORE.
ガチャ
K-CLICK
キイ…
CREAK
SHUT
バタン

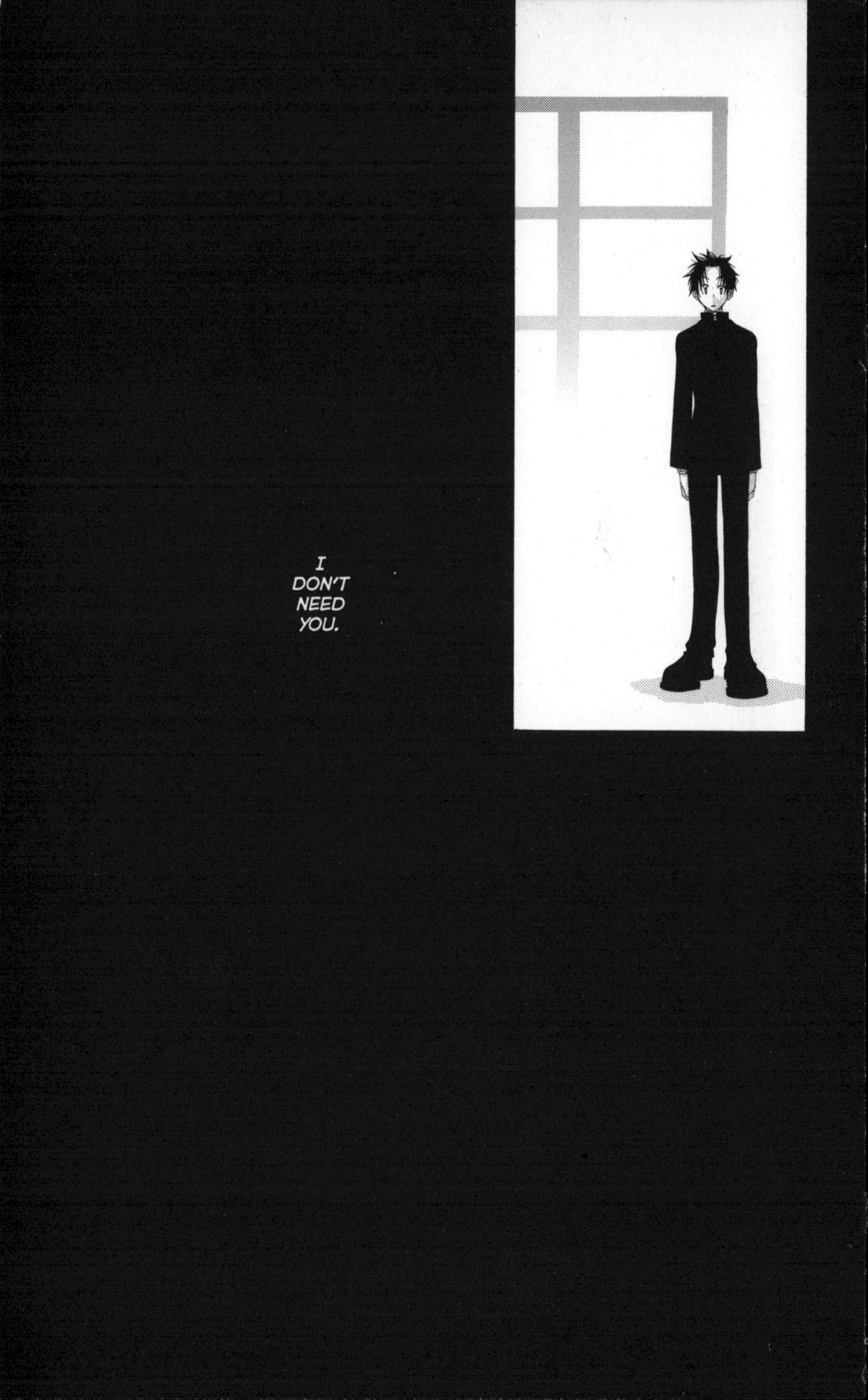
I DON'T NEED YOU.

A Puppy's Secret

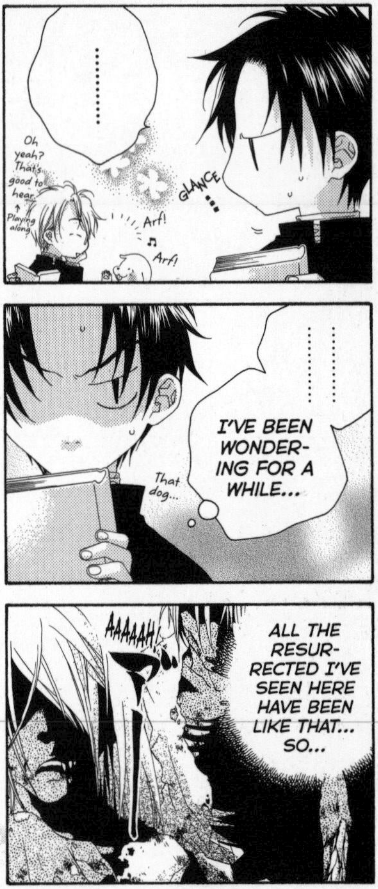

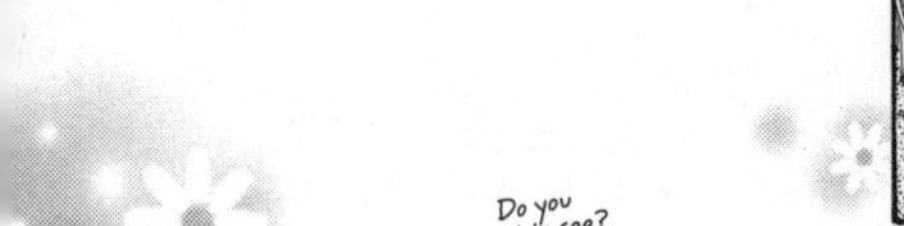

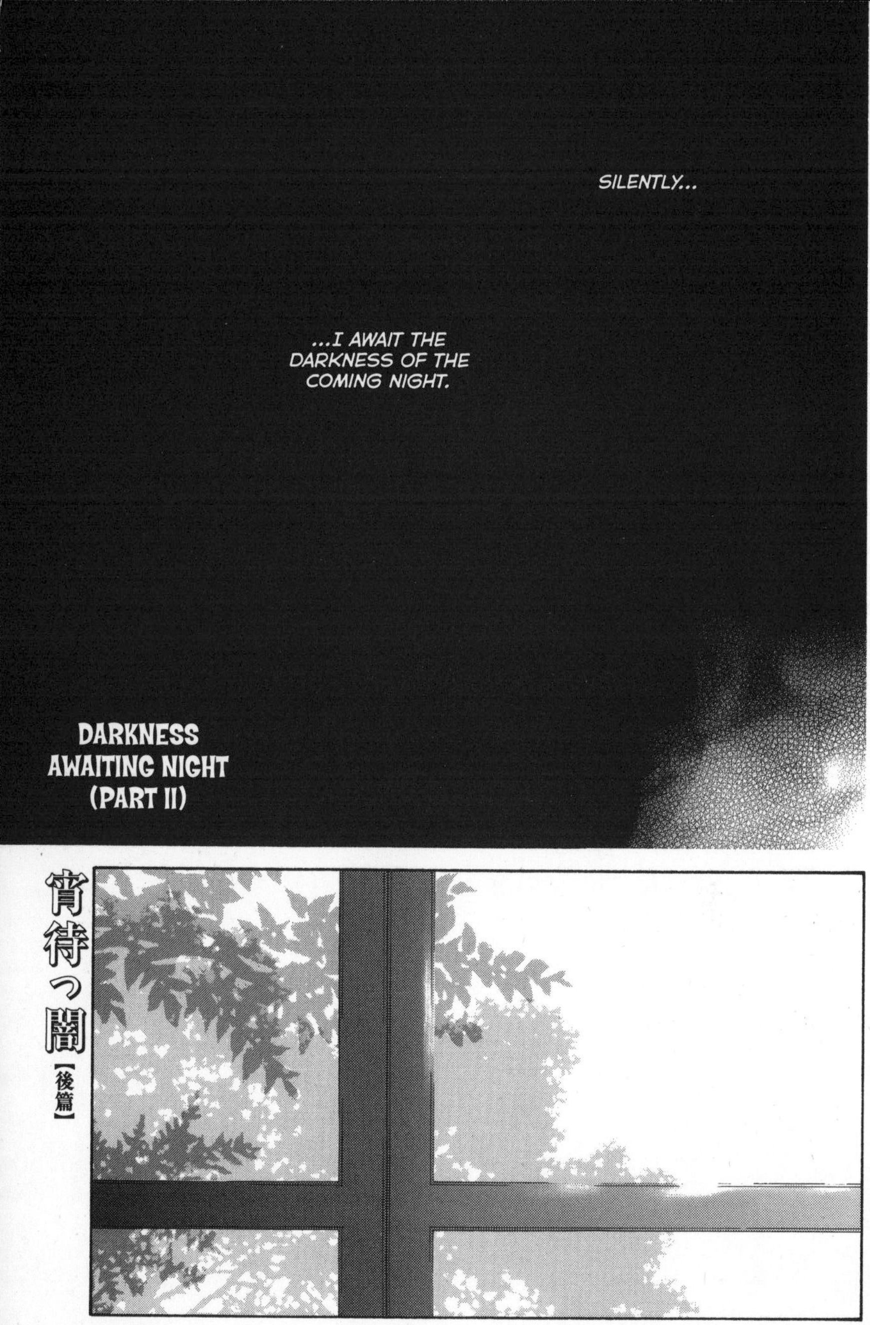
SILENTLY...
...I AWAIT THE DARKNESS OF THE COMING NIGHT.
DARKNESS AWAITING NIGHT (PART II)
宵待つ闇【後篇】

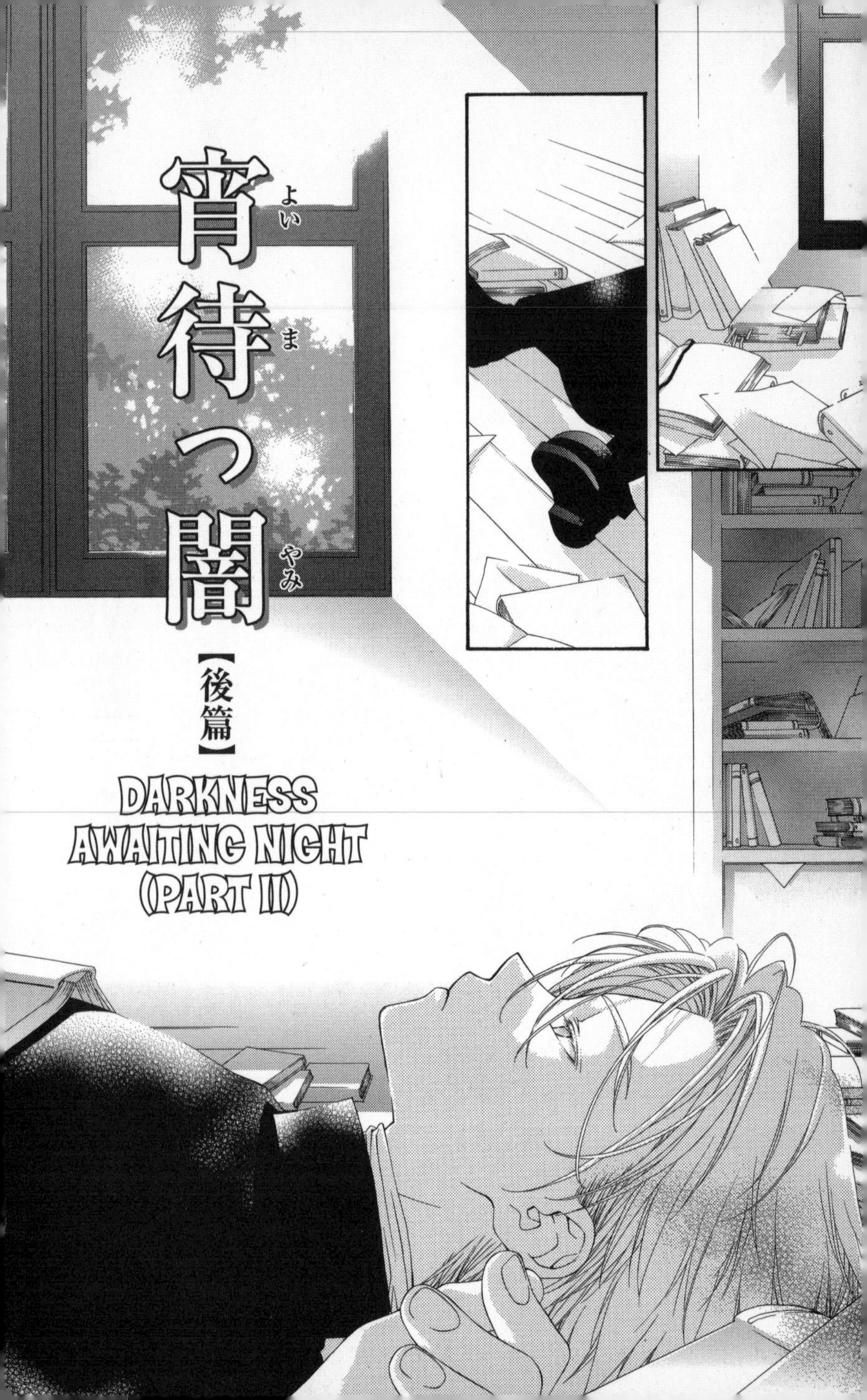
宵(よい)待(ま)つ闇(やみ)
【後篇】
DARKNESS
AWAITING NIGHT
(PART II)

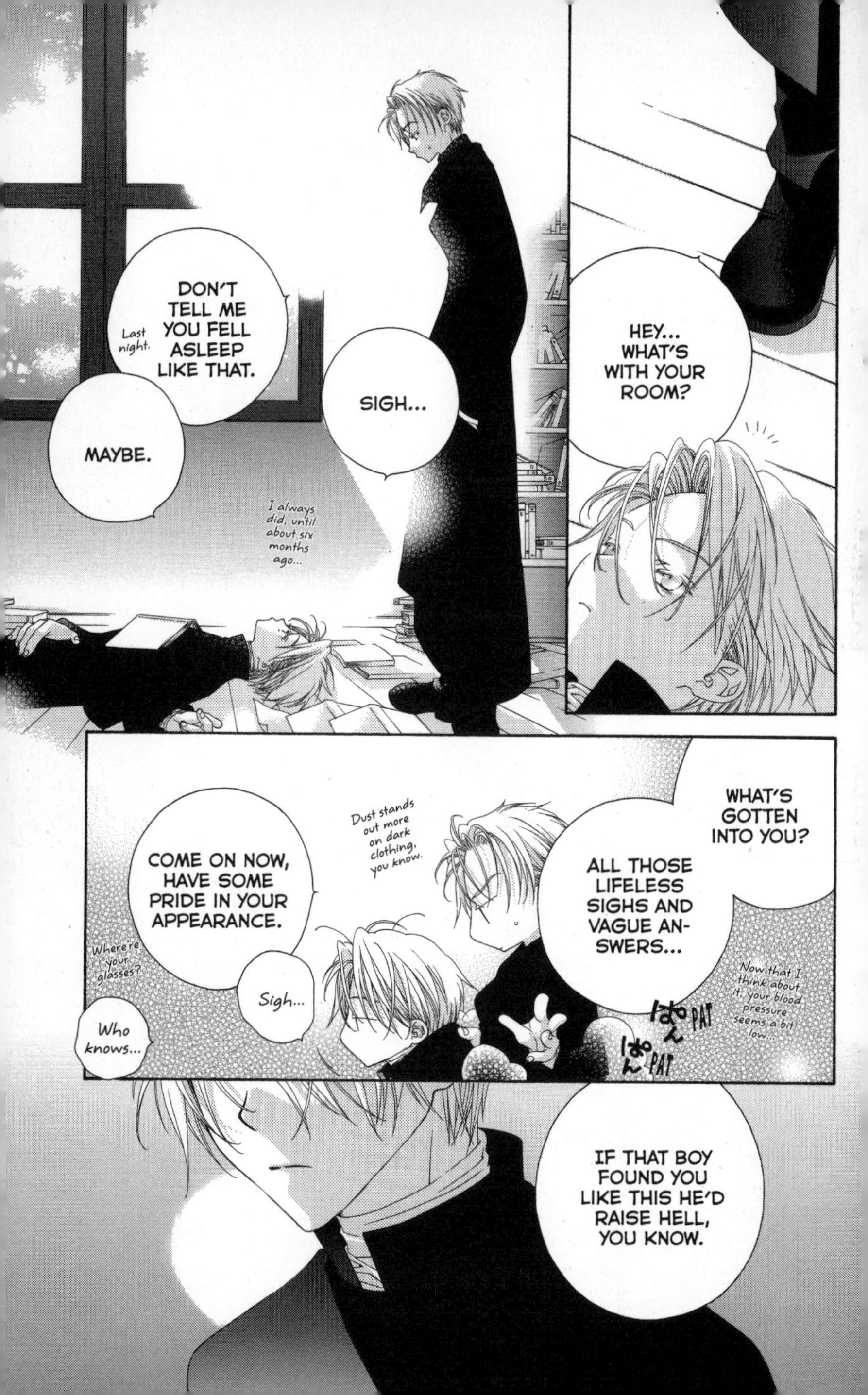
HEY... WHAT'S WITH YOUR ROOM?
SIGH...
DON'T TELL ME YOU FELL ASLEEP LIKE THAT.
Last night.
MAYBE.
I always did, until about six months ago...
WHAT'S GOTTEN INTO YOU?
ALL THOSE LIFELESS SIGHS AND VAGUE AN-SWERS...
Now that I think about it, your blood pressure seems a bit low...
ぽん PAT
ぽん PAT
Dust stands out more on dark clothing, you know.
COME ON NOW, HAVE SOME PRIDE IN YOUR APPEARANCE.
Sigh...
Where're your glasses?
Who knows...
IF THAT BOY FOUND YOU LIKE THIS HE'D RAISE HELL, YOU KNOW.

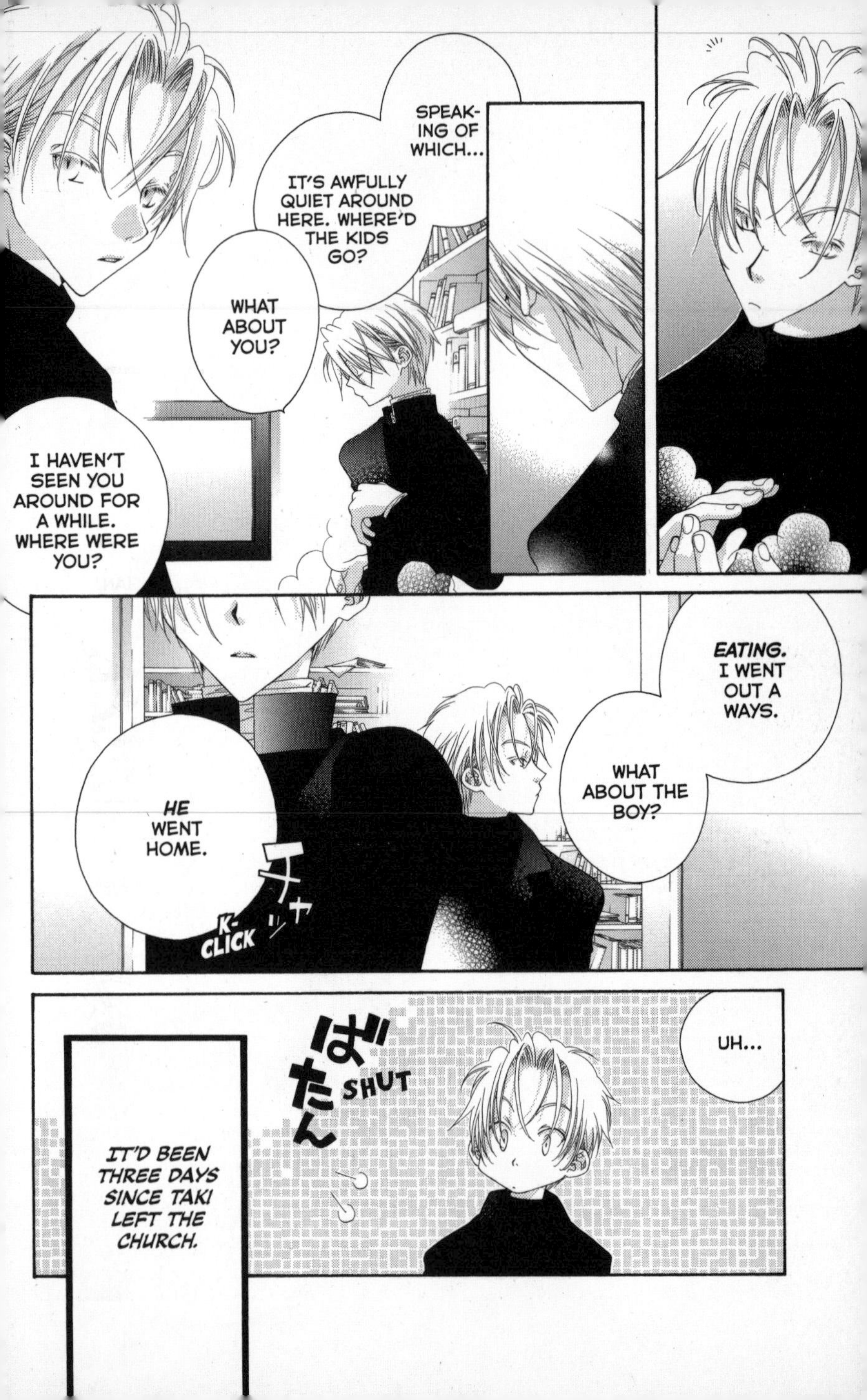
SPEAKING OF WHICH...
IT'S AWFULLY QUIET AROUND HERE. WHERE'D THE KIDS GO?
WHAT ABOUT YOU?
I HAVEN'T SEEN YOU AROUND FOR A WHILE. WHERE WERE YOU?
EATING. I WENT OUT A WAYS.
WHAT ABOUT THE BOY?
HE WENT HOME.
チャッ
K-CLICK
UH...
ばたん
SHUT
IT'D BEEN THREE DAYS SINCE TAKI LEFT THE CHURCH.

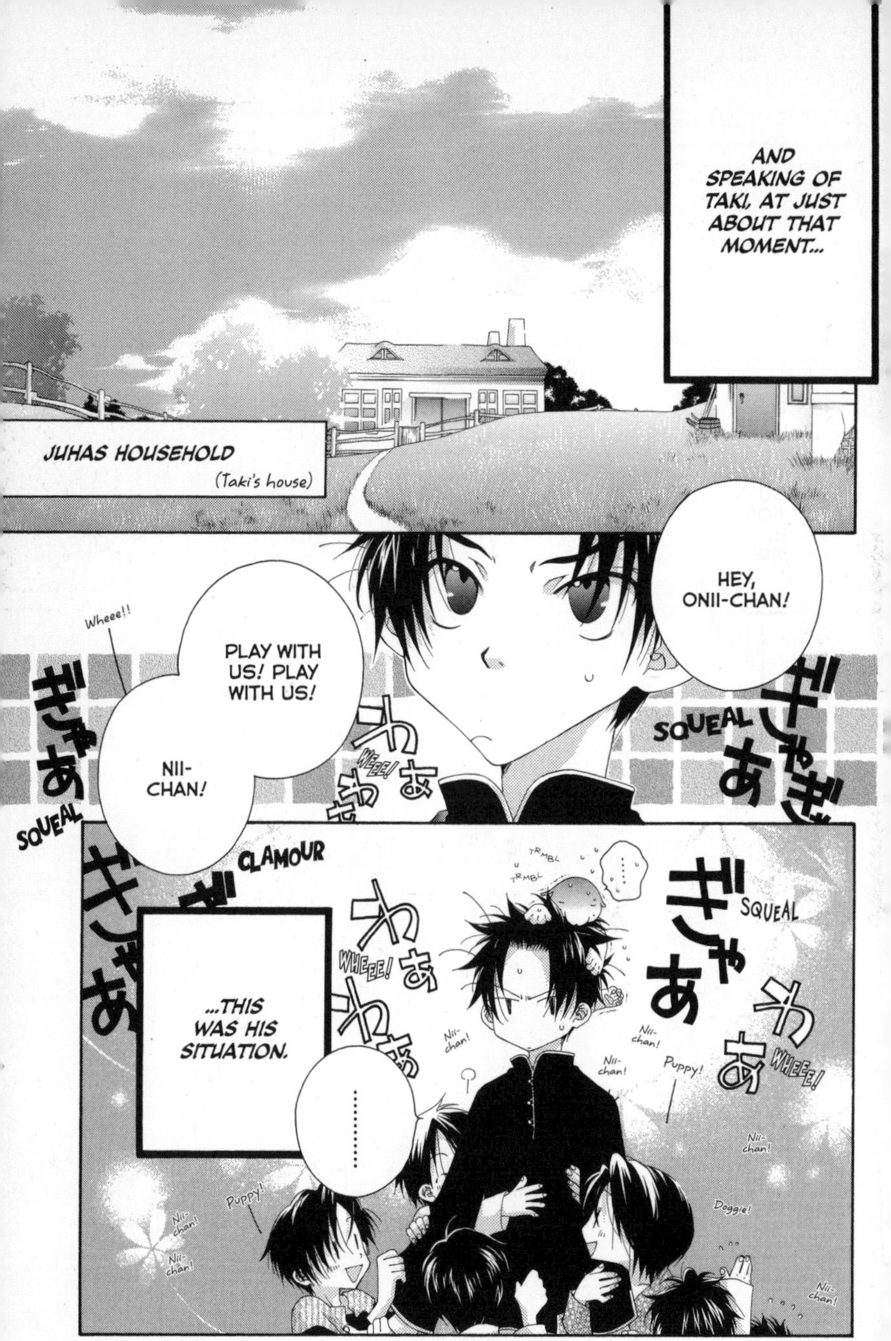
AND SPEAKING OF TAKI, AT JUST ABOUT THAT MOMENT...
JUHAS HOUSEHOLD
(Taki's house)
HEY, ONII-CHAN!
ぎゃあ
SQUEAL
わあ
WEEE!
PLAY WITH US! PLAY WITH US!
NII-CHAN!
Wheee!!
ぎゃあ
SQUEAL
CLAMOUR
ぎゃあ
SQUEAL
わあ
WHEEEE!
TRMBL
TRMBL
......
わあ
WHEEE!
...THIS WAS HIS SITUATION.
....
Nii-chan!
Nii-chan!
Nii-chan!
Puppy!
Nii-chan!
Doggie!
Puppy!
Nii-chan!
Nii-chan!
Nii-chan!

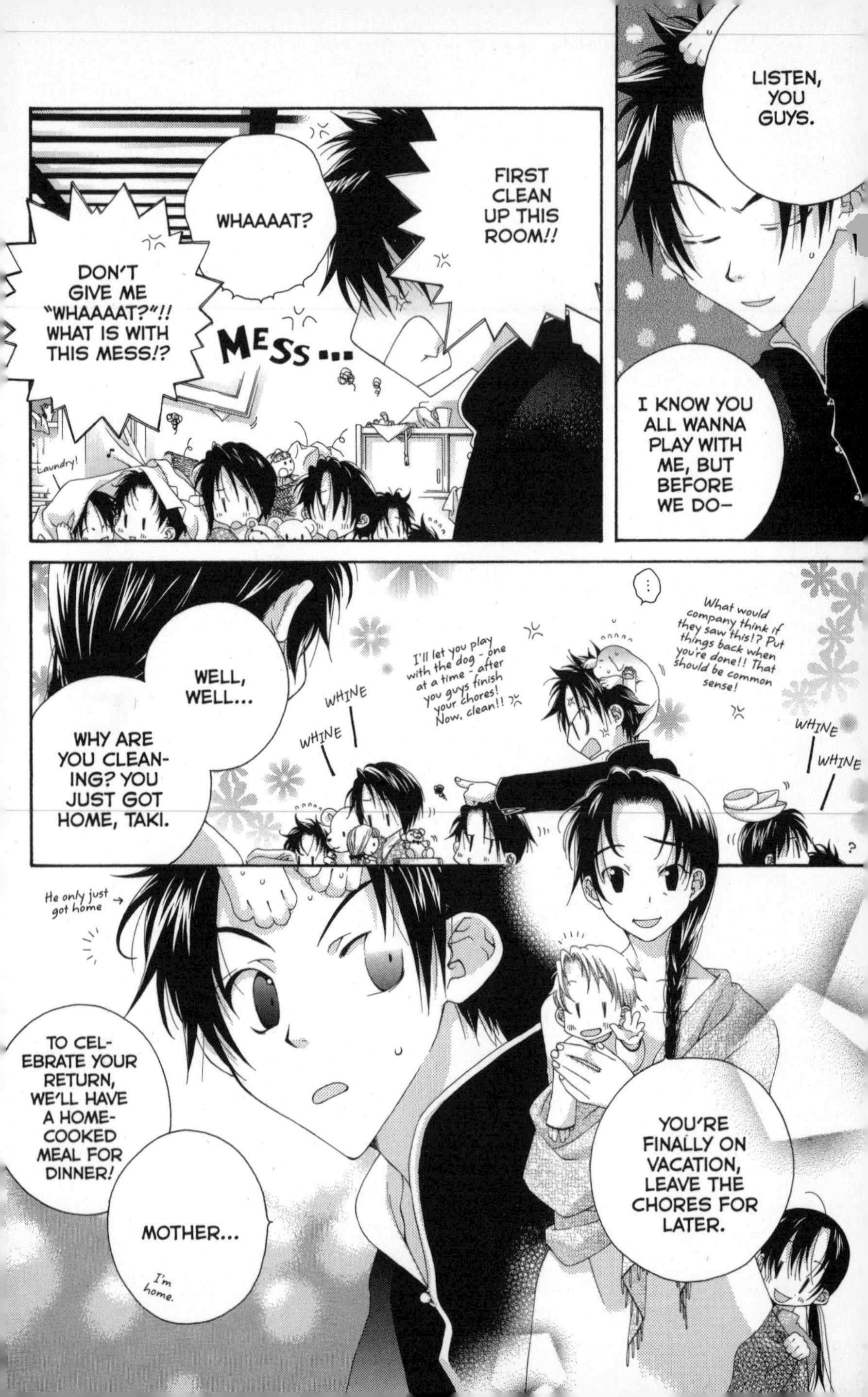
LISTEN, YOU GUYS.
I KNOW YOU ALL WANNA PLAY WITH ME, BUT BEFORE WE DO–
FIRST CLEAN UP THIS ROOM!!
WHAAAAT?
DON'T GIVE ME "WHAAAAT?"!! WHAT IS WITH THIS MESS!?
MESS...
Laundry!
...
What would company think if they saw this!? Put things back when you're done!! That should be common sense!
WHINE
WHINE
I'll let you play with the dog - one at a time - after you guys finish your chores! Now, clean!!
WHINE
WHINE
WELL, WELL...
WHY ARE YOU CLEAN-ING? YOU JUST GOT HOME, TAKI.
YOU'RE FINALLY ON VACATION, LEAVE THE CHORES FOR LATER.
TO CEL-EBRATE YOUR RETURN, WE'LL HAVE A HOME-COOKED MEAL FOR DINNER!
He only just got home
MOTHER...
I'm home.

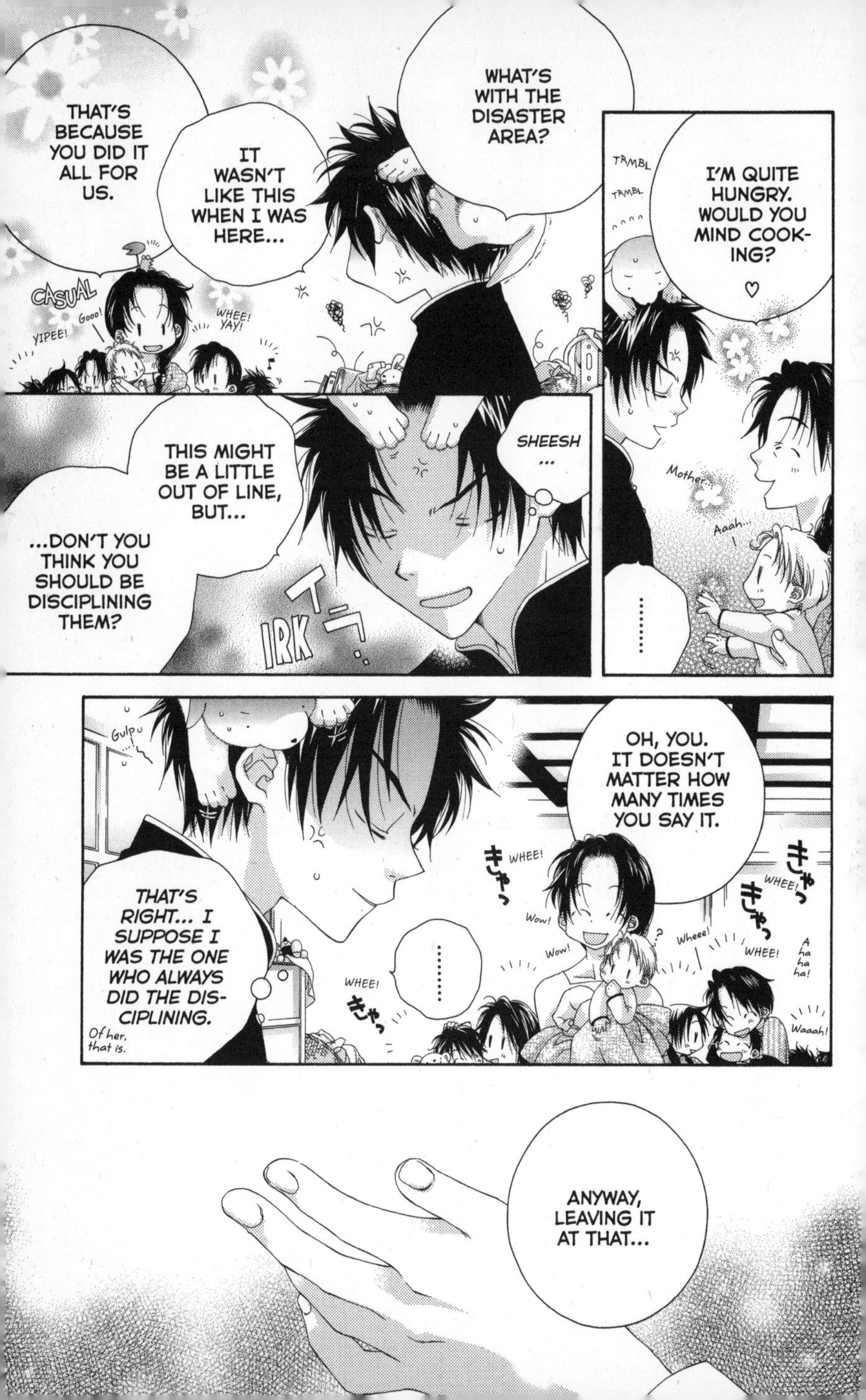
WHAT'S WITH THE DISASTER AREA?
IT WASN'T LIKE THIS WHEN I WAS HERE...
THAT'S BECAUSE YOU DID IT ALL FOR US.
CASUAL
WHEE! YAY!
Gooo!
YIPEE!
TRMBL TRMBL
I'M QUITE HUNGRY. WOULD YOU MIND COOKING? ♡
Mother...
Aaah...
......
SHEESH ...
THIS MIGHT BE A LITTLE OUT OF LINE, BUT...
...DON'T YOU THINK YOU SHOULD BE DISCIPLINING THEM?
IRK
OH, YOU. IT DOESN'T MATTER HOW MANY TIMES YOU SAY IT.
WHEE!
WHEE!
A ha ha ha!
Wheee!
WHEE!
Wow!
Wow!
Waaah!
......
WHEE!
Gulp
THAT'S RIGHT... I SUPPOSE I WAS THE ONE WHO ALWAYS DID THE DISCIPLINING.
Of her, that is.
ANYWAY, LEAVING IT AT THAT...

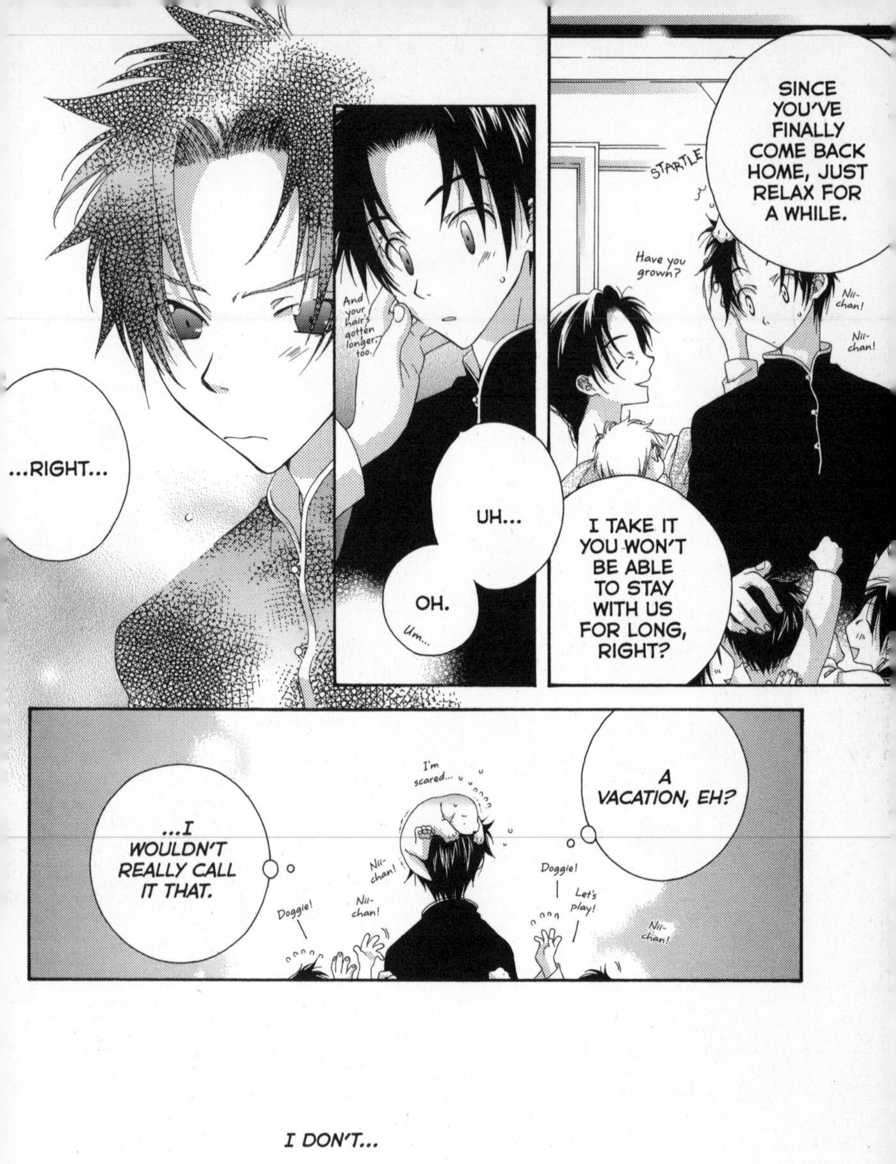
SINCE YOU'VE FINALLY COME BACK HOME, JUST RELAX FOR A WHILE.
STARTLE
Have you grown?
Nii-chan!
Nii-chan!
I TAKE IT YOU WON'T BE ABLE TO STAY WITH US FOR LONG, RIGHT?
And your hair's gotten longer, too.
UH...
OH.
Um...
...RIGHT...
A VACATION, EH?
I'm scared...
Doggie!
Let's play!
Nii-chan!
Nii-chan!
Nii-chan!
Doggie!
...I WOULDN'T REALLY CALL IT THAT.

I DON'T...

...NEED YOU.

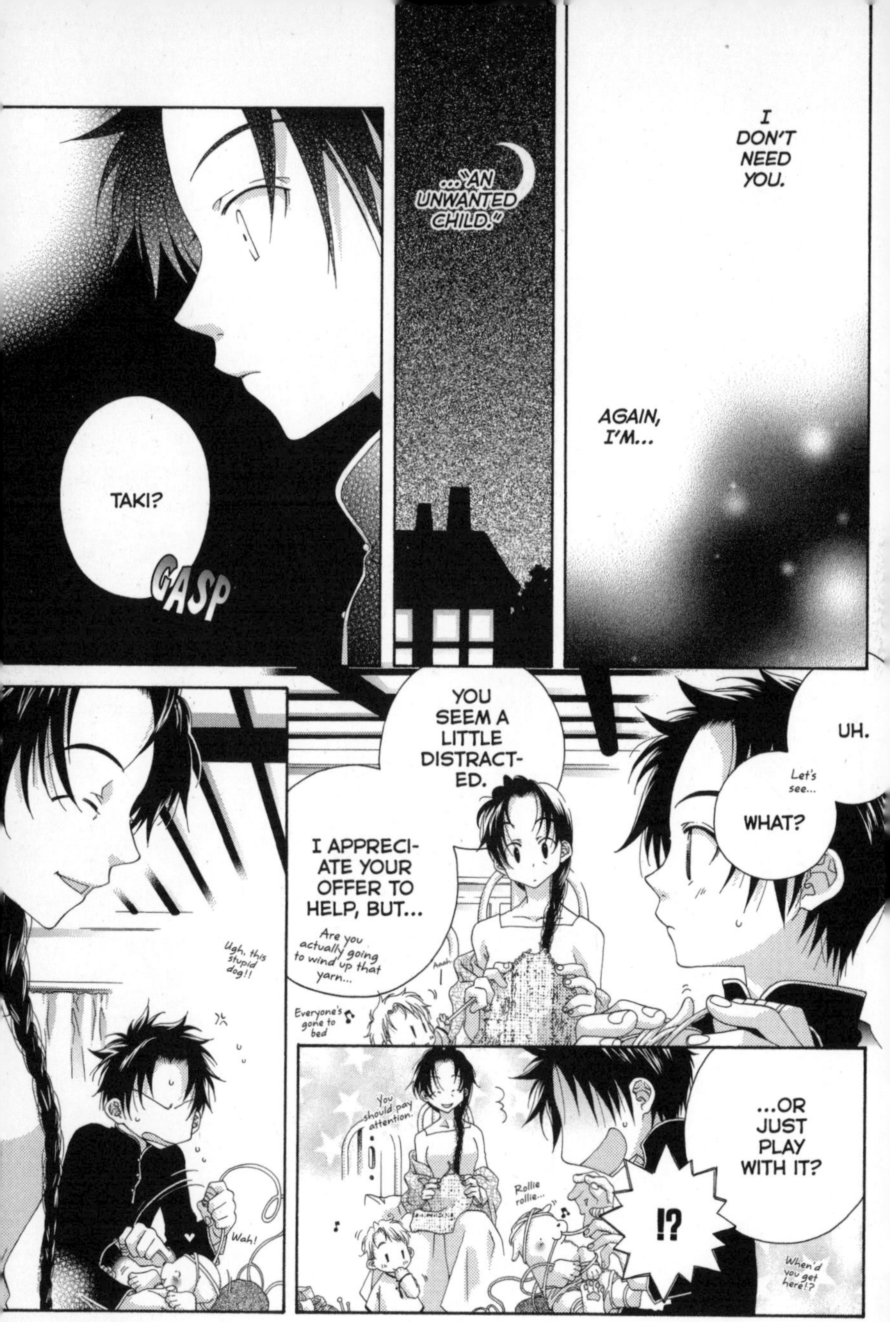
I DON'T NEED YOU.
AGAIN, I'M...
..."AN UNWANTED CHILD."
TAKI?
GASP
UH.
Let's see...
WHAT?
YOU SEEM A LITTLE DISTRACT-ED.
I APPRECI-ATE YOUR OFFER TO HELP, BUT...
Are you actually going to wind up that yarn...
Aaah
Everyone's gone to bed
...OR JUST PLAY WITH IT?
!?
When'd you get here!?
You should pay attention.
Rollie rollie...
Ugh, this stupid dog!!
Wah!

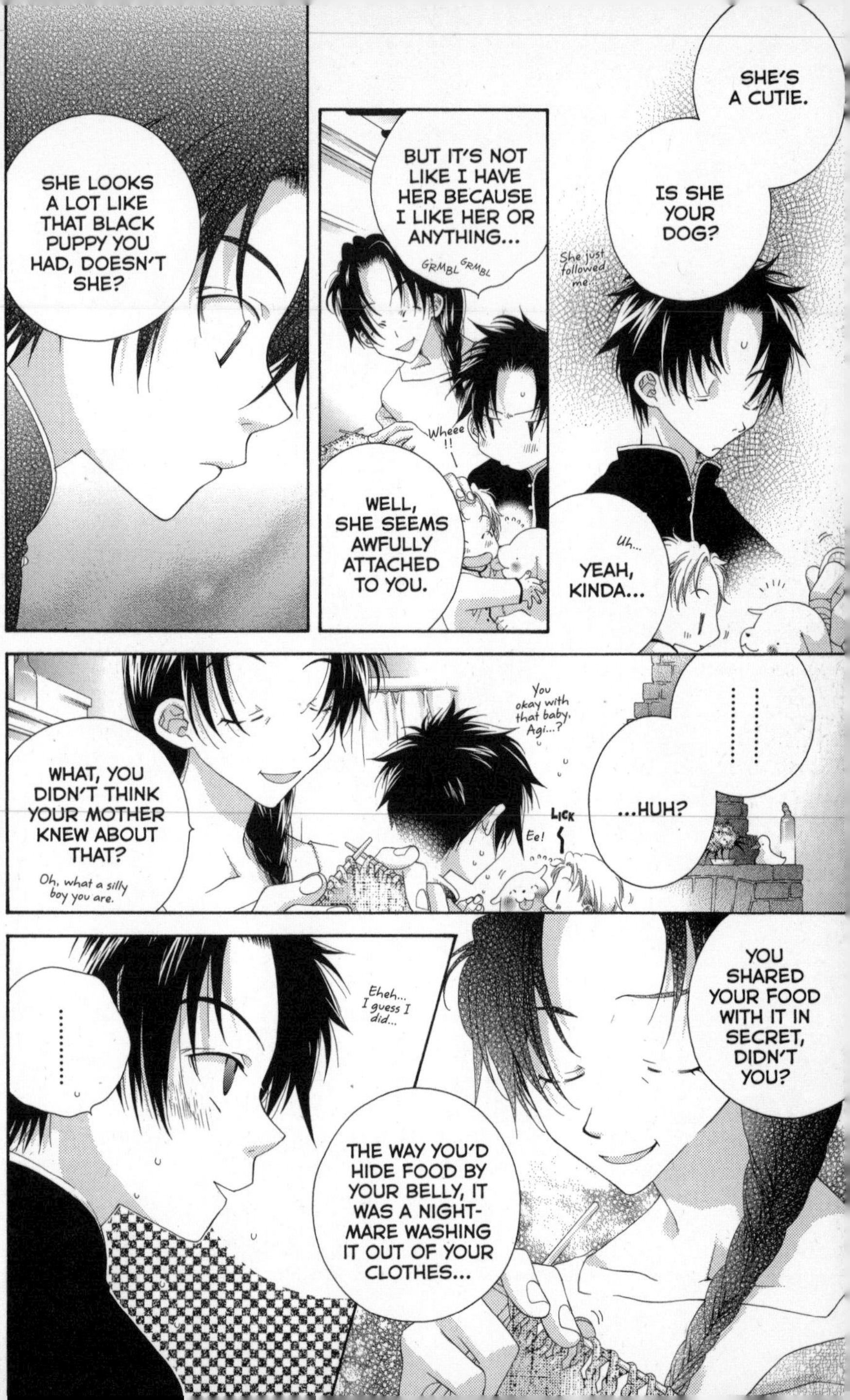
SHE'S A CUTIE.
IS SHE YOUR DOG?
She just followed me...
Uh...
YEAH, KINDA...
BUT IT'S NOT LIKE I HAVE HER BECAUSE I LIKE HER OR ANYTHING...
GRMBL GRMBL
Wheee !!
WELL, SHE SEEMS AWFULLY ATTACHED TO YOU.
SHE LOOKS A LOT LIKE THAT BLACK PUPPY YOU HAD, DOESN'T SHE?
......
...HUH?
You okay with that baby, Agi...?
LICK
Ee!
WHAT, YOU DIDN'T THINK YOUR MOTHER KNEW ABOUT THAT?
Oh, what a silly boy you are.
YOU SHARED YOUR FOOD WITH IT IN SECRET, DIDN'T YOU?
THE WAY YOU'D HIDE FOOD BY YOUR BELLY, IT WAS A NIGHT-MARE WASHING IT OUT OF YOUR CLOTHES...
Eheh... I guess I did...
......

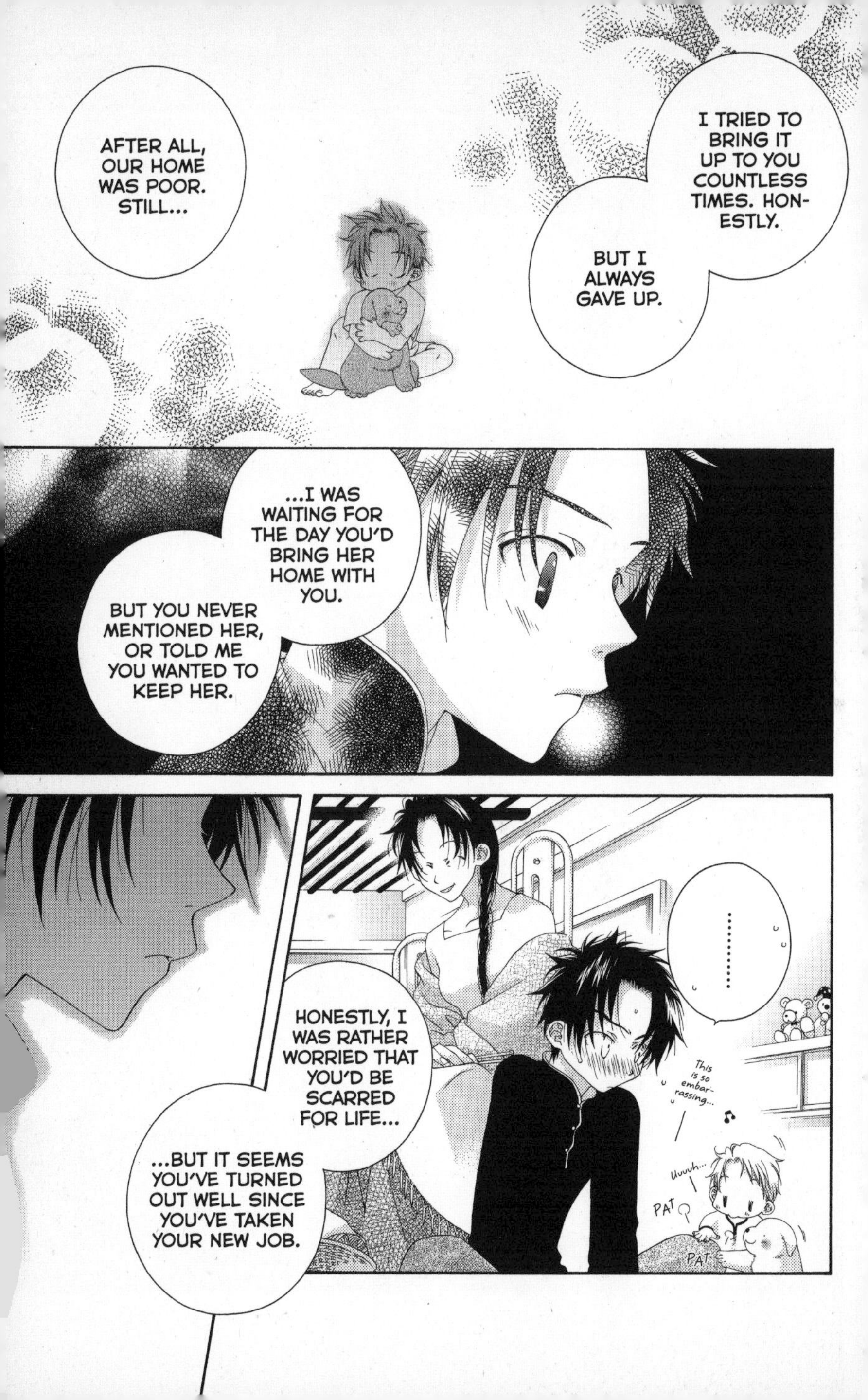
I TRIED TO BRING IT UP TO YOU COUNTLESS TIMES. HONESTLY.
BUT I ALWAYS GAVE UP.
AFTER ALL, OUR HOME WAS POOR. STILL...
...I WAS WAITING FOR THE DAY YOU'D BRING HER HOME WITH YOU.
BUT YOU NEVER MENTIONED HER, OR TOLD ME YOU WANTED TO KEEP HER.
......
This is so embarrassing...
Uuuuh...
PAT
PAT
HONESTLY, I WAS RATHER WORRIED THAT YOU'D BE SCARRED FOR LIFE...
...BUT IT SEEMS YOU'VE TURNED OUT WELL SINCE YOU'VE TAKEN YOUR NEW JOB.

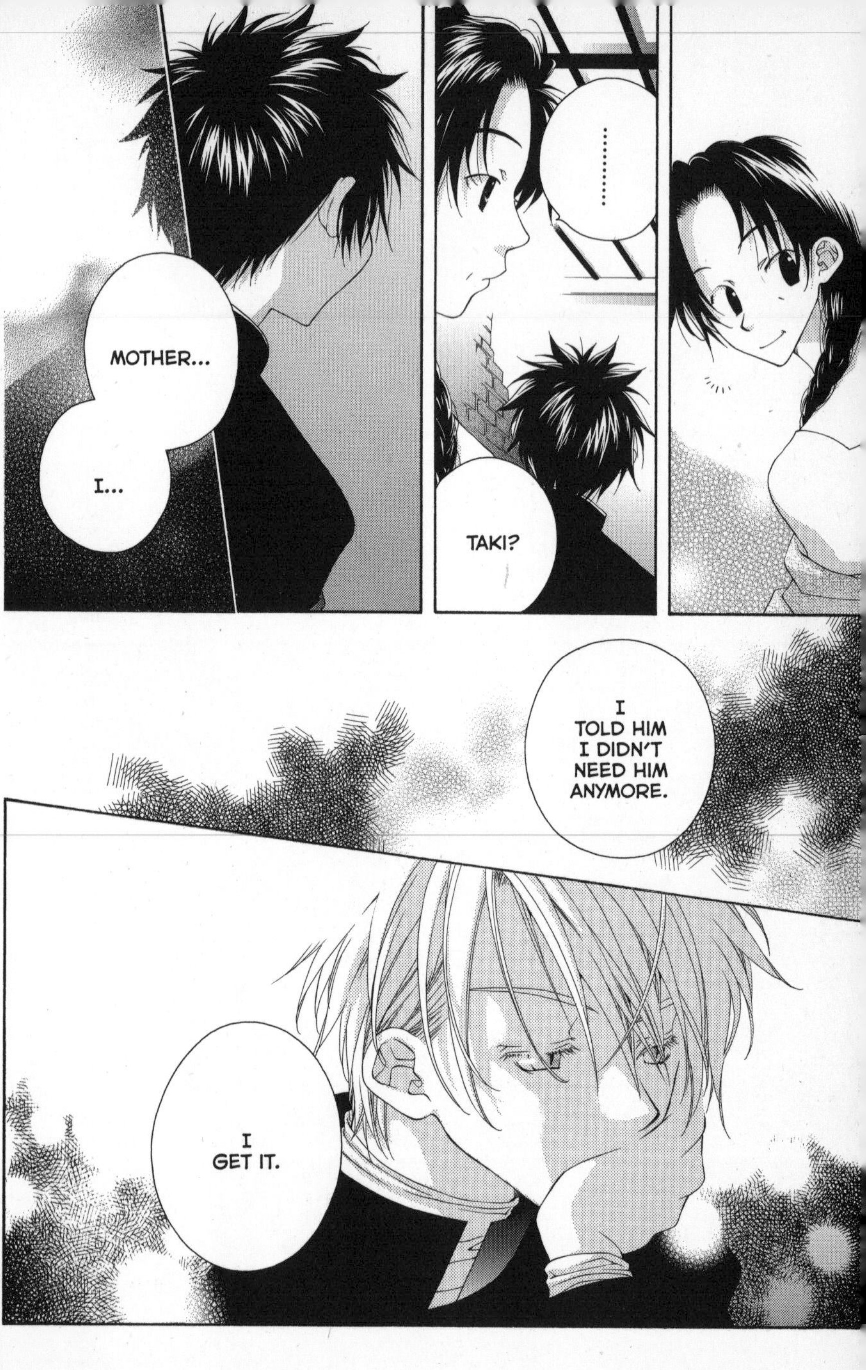
......
TAKI?
MOTHER...
I...
I TOLD HIM I DIDN'T NEED HIM ANYMORE.
I GET IT.

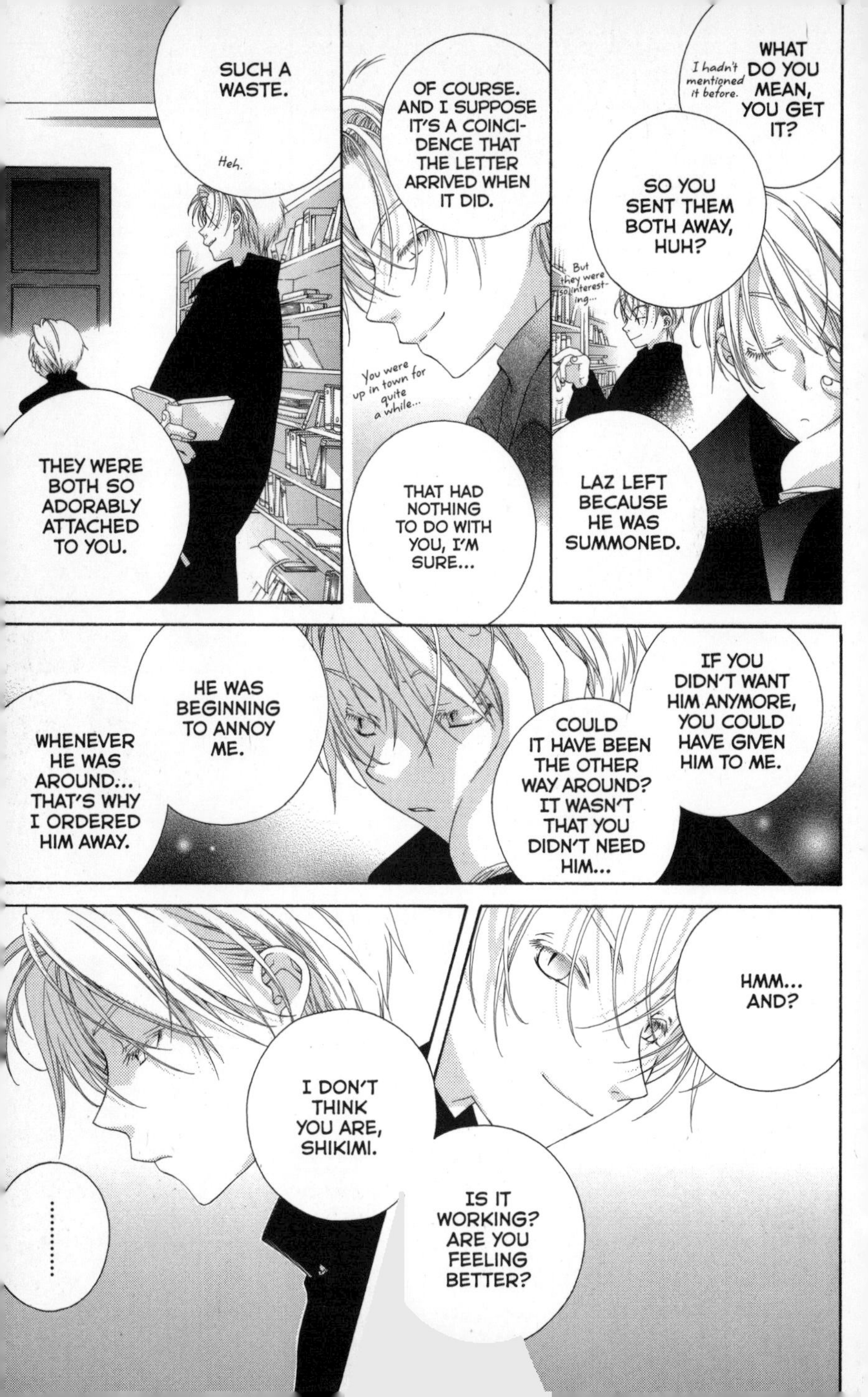
WHAT DO YOU MEAN, YOU GET IT?
I hadn't mentioned it before.
SO YOU SENT THEM BOTH AWAY, HUH?
But they were so interesting...
LAZ LEFT BECAUSE HE WAS SUMMONED.
OF COURSE. AND I SUPPOSE IT'S A COINCIDENCE THAT THE LETTER ARRIVED WHEN IT DID.
You were up in town for quite a while...
THAT HAD NOTHING TO DO WITH YOU, I'M SURE...
SUCH A WASTE.
Heh.
THEY WERE BOTH SO ADORABLY ATTACHED TO YOU.
IF YOU DIDN'T WANT HIM ANYMORE, YOU COULD HAVE GIVEN HIM TO ME.
COULD IT HAVE BEEN THE OTHER WAY AROUND? IT WASN'T THAT YOU DIDN'T NEED HIM...
HE WAS BEGINNING TO ANNOY ME.
WHENEVER HE WAS AROUND... THAT'S WHY I ORDERED HIM AWAY.
HMM... AND?
IS IT WORKING? ARE YOU FEELING BETTER?
I DON'T THINK YOU ARE, SHIKIMI.
....

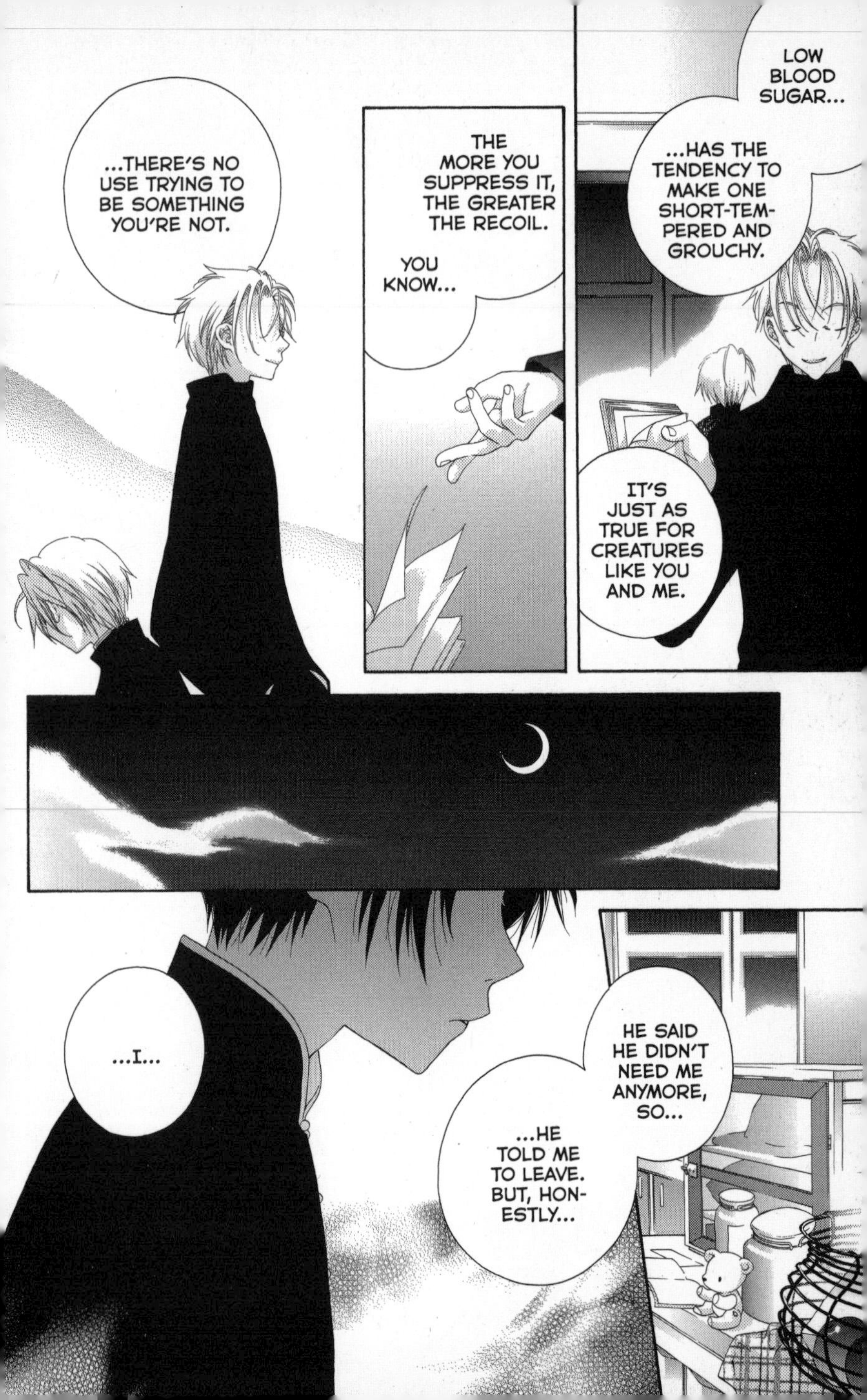
LOW BLOOD SUGAR...
...HAS THE TENDENCY TO MAKE ONE SHORT-TEMPERED AND GROUCHY.
IT'S JUST AS TRUE FOR CREATURES LIKE YOU AND ME.
THE MORE YOU SUPPRESS IT, THE GREATER THE RECOIL.
YOU KNOW...
...THERE'S NO USE TRYING TO BE SOMETHING YOU'RE NOT.
HE SAID HE DIDN'T NEED ME ANYMORE, SO...
...HE TOLD ME TO LEAVE. BUT, HONESTLY...
...I...

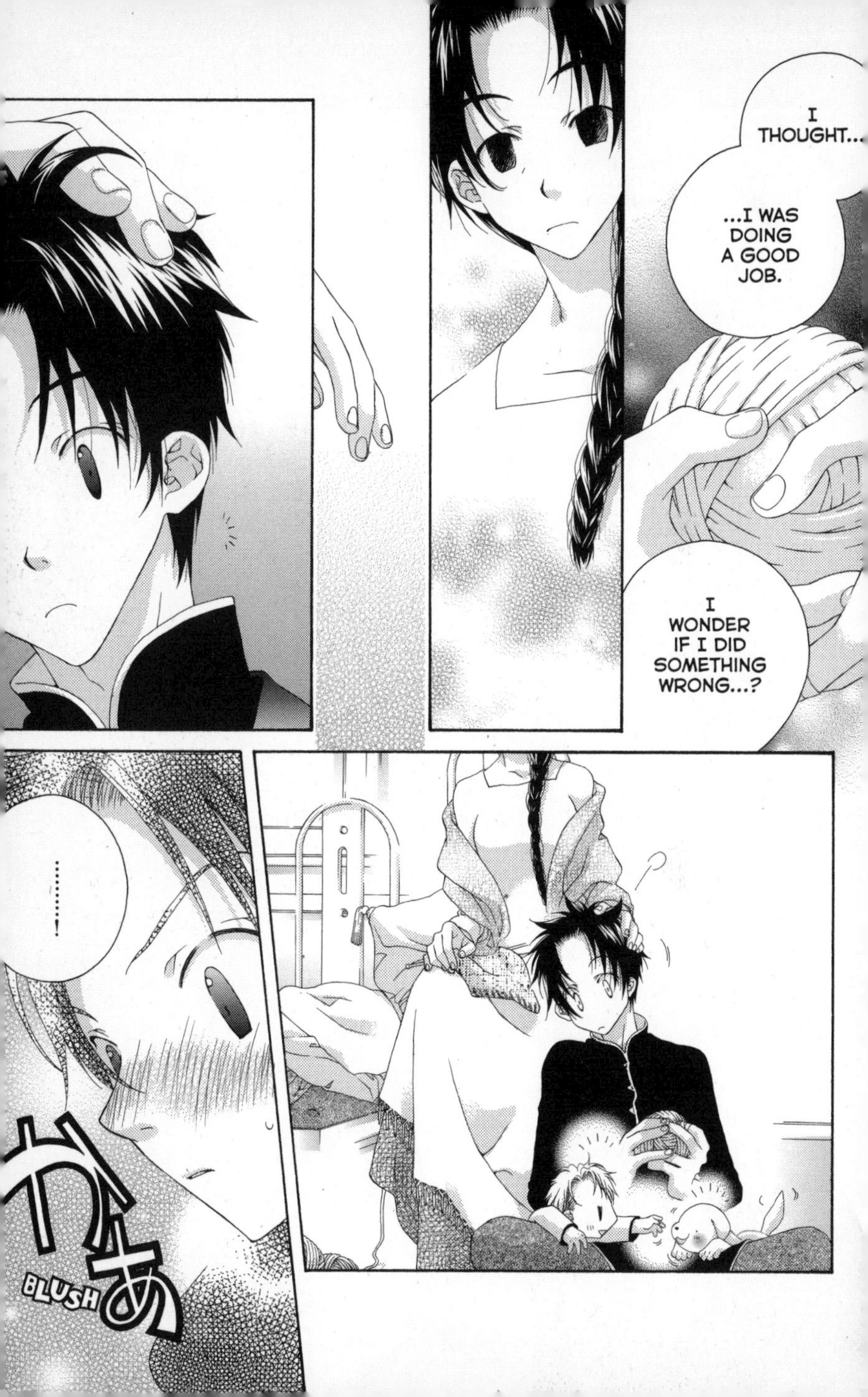
I THOUGHT...
...I WAS DOING A GOOD JOB.
I WONDER IF I DID SOMETHING WRONG...?
......!
BLUSH

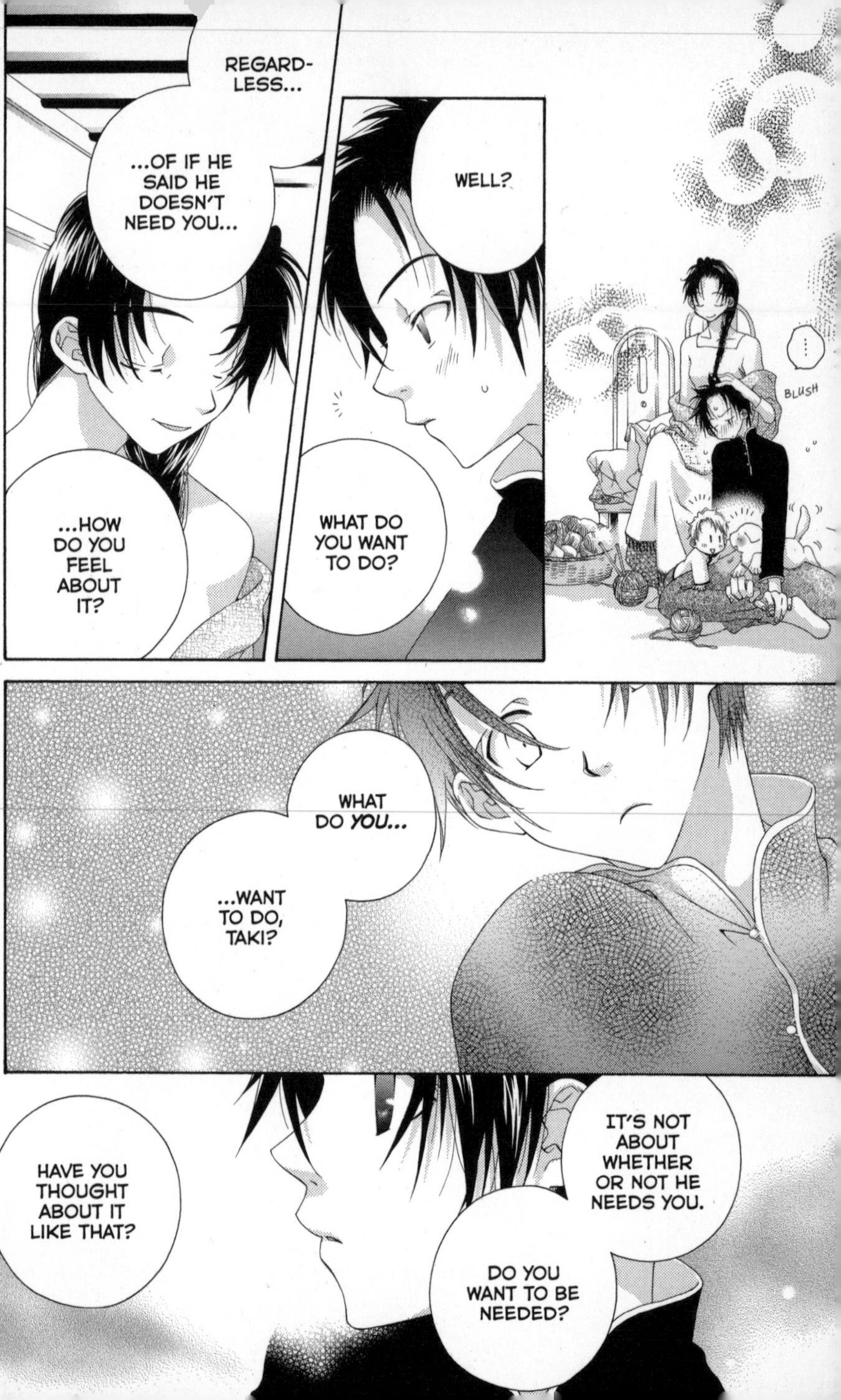
...
BLUSH
WELL?
WHAT DO YOU WANT TO DO?
REGARDLESS...
...OF IF HE SAID HE DOESN'T NEED YOU...
...HOW DO YOU FEEL ABOUT IT?
WHAT DO *YOU*...
...WANT TO DO, TAKI?
IT'S NOT ABOUT WHETHER OR NOT HE NEEDS YOU.
DO YOU WANT TO BE NEEDED?
HAVE YOU THOUGHT ABOUT IT LIKE THAT?

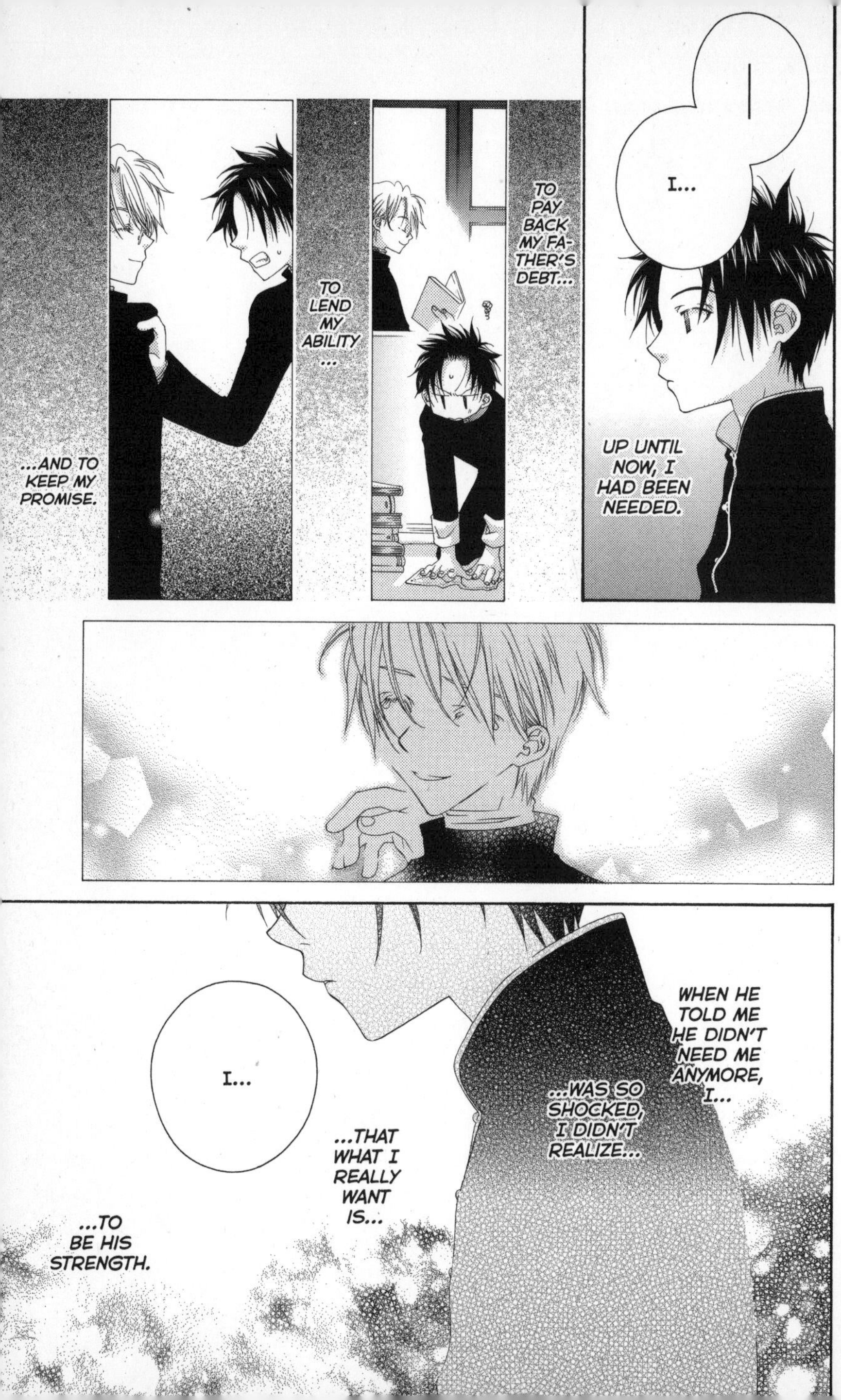
I...
UP UNTIL NOW, I HAD BEEN NEEDED.
TO PAY BACK MY FA-THER'S DEBT...
TO LEND MY ABILITY...
...AND TO KEEP MY PROMISE.
WHEN HE TOLD ME HE DIDN'T NEED ME ANYMORE, I...
...WAS SO SHOCKED, I DIDN'T REALIZE...
I...
...THAT WHAT I REALLY WANT IS...
...TO BE HIS STRENGTH.

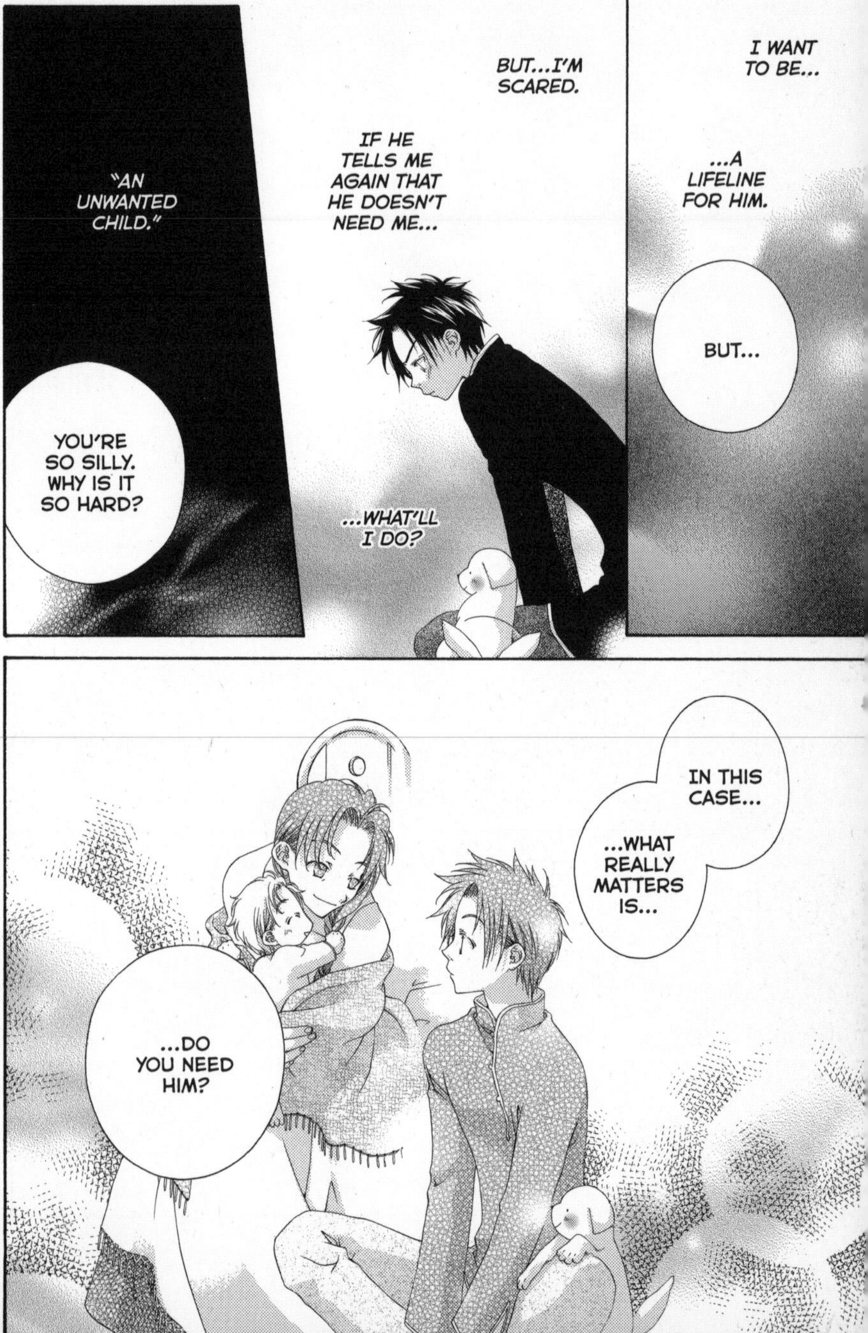
I WANT TO BE...
...A LIFELINE FOR HIM.
BUT...
BUT...I'M SCARED.
IF HE TELLS ME AGAIN THAT HE DOESN'T NEED ME...
...WHAT'LL I DO?
"AN UNWANTED CHILD."
YOU'RE SO SILLY. WHY IS IT SO HARD?
IN THIS CASE...
...WHAT REALLY MATTERS IS...
...DO YOU NEED HIM?

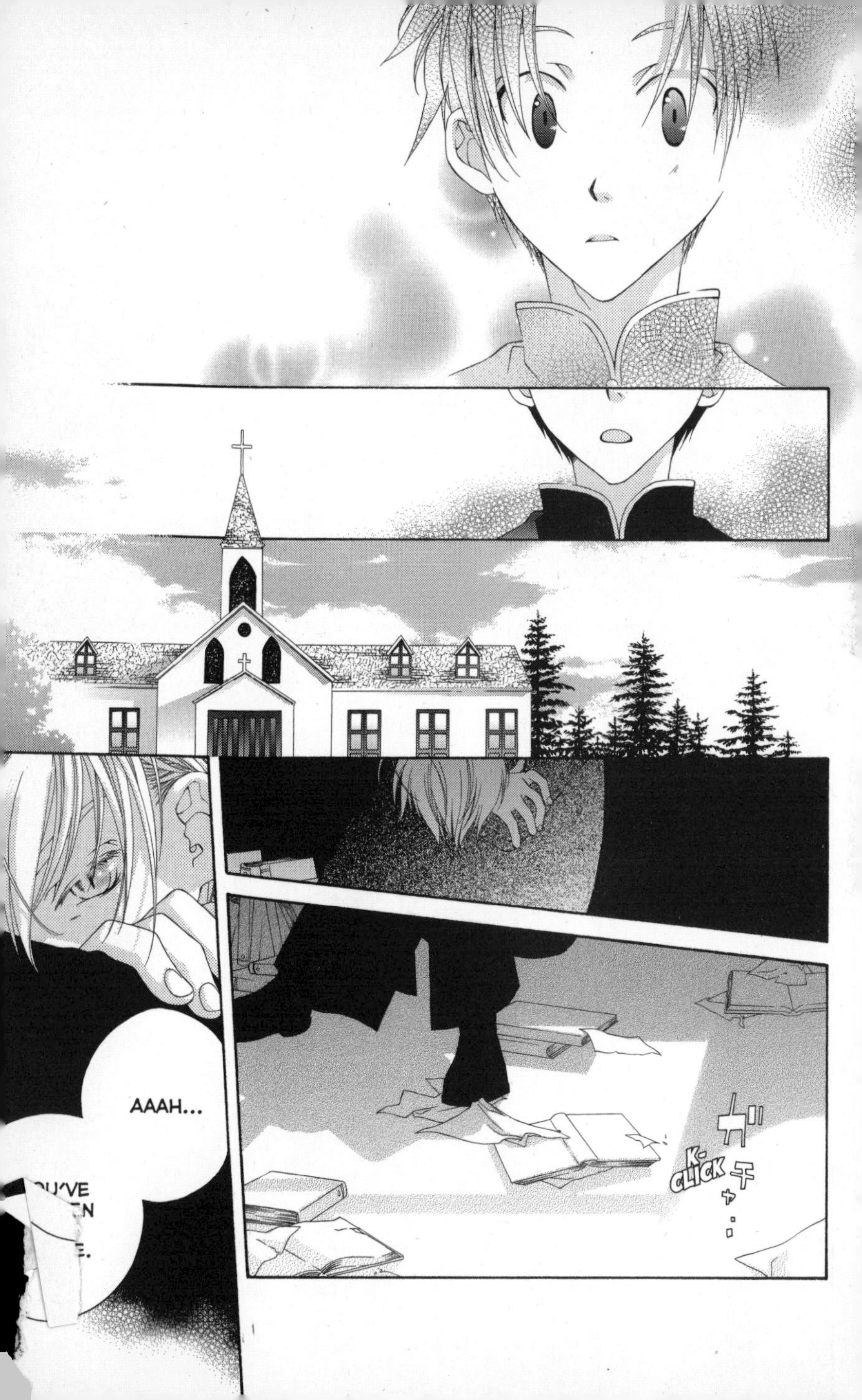

ガチャ
K-CLICK
AAAH...
OU'VE
EN
E.

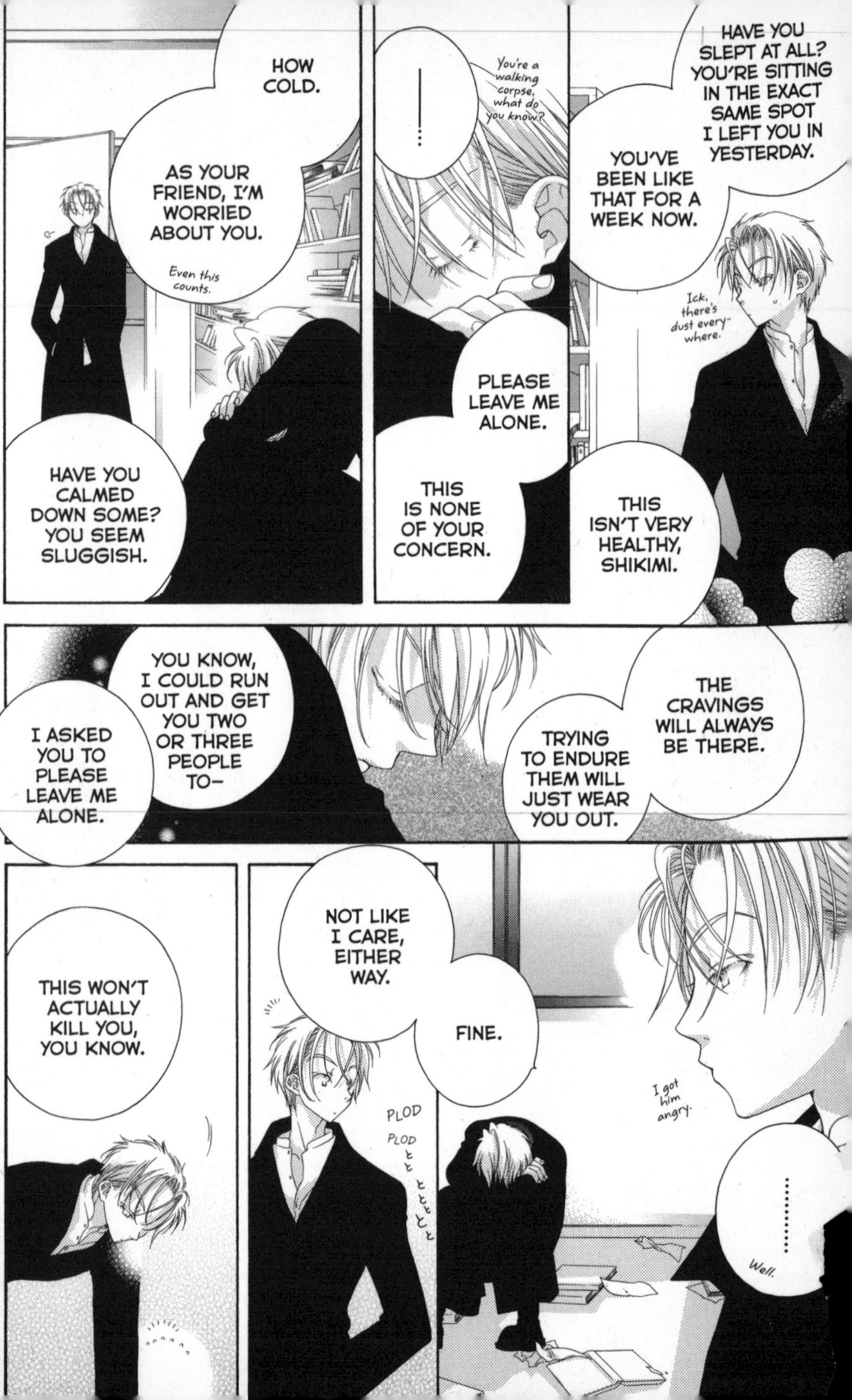
HAVE YOU SLEPT AT ALL? YOU'RE SITTING IN THE EXACT SAME SPOT I LEFT YOU IN YESTERDAY.
YOU'VE BEEN LIKE THAT FOR A WEEK NOW.
Ick, there's dust every-where.
THIS ISN'T VERY HEALTHY, SHIKIMI.
……
You're a walking corpse, what do you know?
PLEASE LEAVE ME ALONE.
THIS IS NONE OF YOUR CONCERN.
HOW COLD.
AS YOUR FRIEND, I'M WORRIED ABOUT YOU.
Even this counts.
HAVE YOU CALMED DOWN SOME? YOU SEEM SLUGGISH.
THE CRAVINGS WILL ALWAYS BE THERE.
TRYING TO ENDURE THEM WILL JUST WEAR YOU OUT.
YOU KNOW, I COULD RUN OUT AND GET YOU TWO OR THREE PEOPLE TO–
I ASKED YOU TO PLEASE LEAVE ME ALONE.
I got him angry.
……
Well.
NOT LIKE I CARE, EITHER WAY.
FINE.
PLOD
PLOD
THIS WON'T ACTUALLY KILL YOU, YOU KNOW.

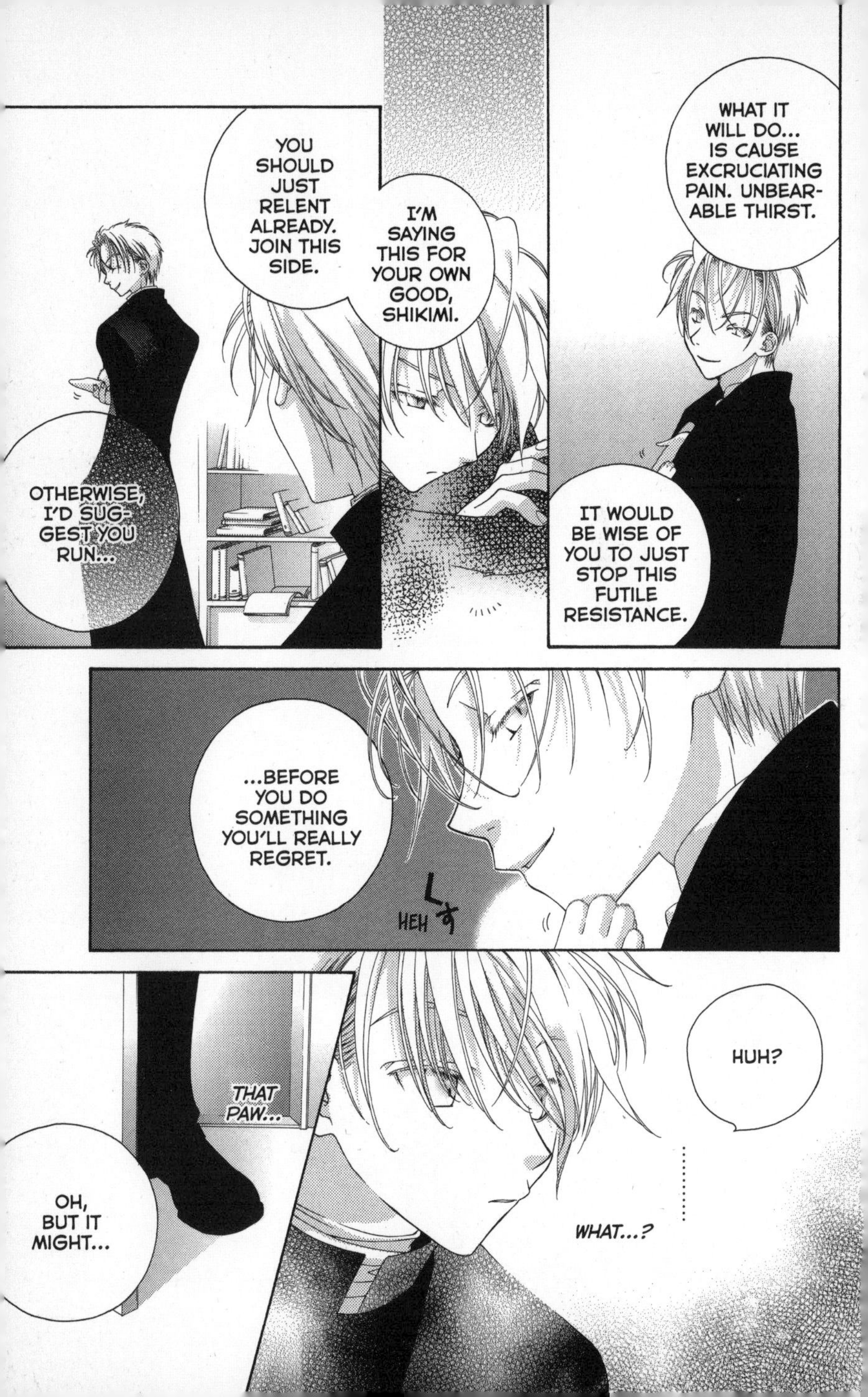
WHAT IT WILL DO... IS CAUSE EXCRUCIATING PAIN. UNBEARABLE THIRST.
IT WOULD BE WISE OF YOU TO JUST STOP THIS FUTILE RESISTANCE.
I'M SAYING THIS FOR YOUR OWN GOOD, SHIKIMI.
YOU SHOULD JUST RELENT ALREADY. JOIN THIS SIDE.
OTHERWISE, I'D SUGGEST YOU RUN...
...BEFORE YOU DO SOMETHING YOU'LL REALLY REGRET.
HEH
HUH?
......
WHAT...?
THAT PAW...
OH, BUT IT MIGHT...

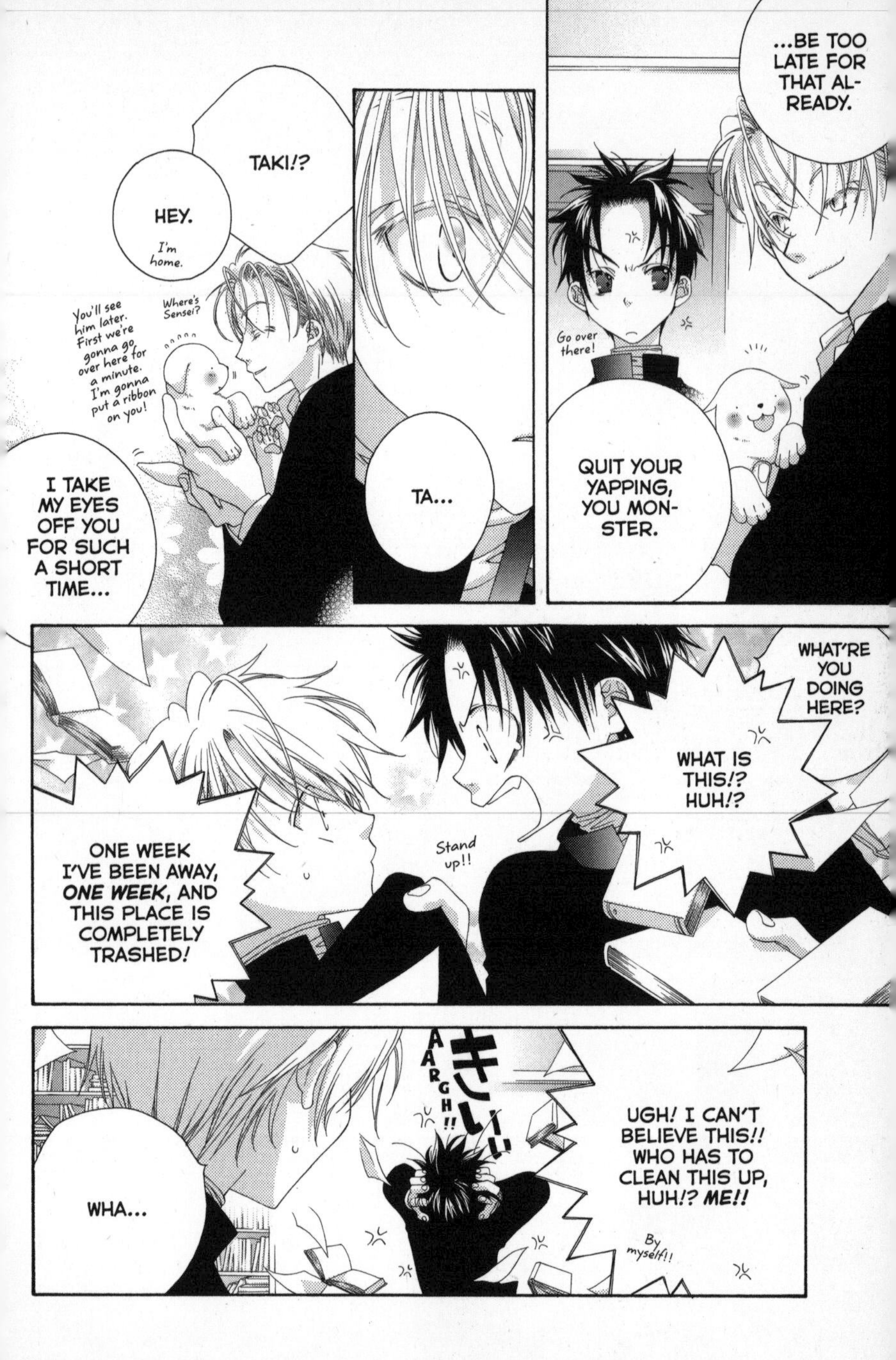
...BE TOO LATE FOR THAT AL-READY.
Go over there!
QUIT YOUR YAPPING, YOU MON-STER.
TA...
TAKI!?
HEY.
I'm home.
Where's Sensei?
You'll see him later. First we're gonna go over here for a minute. I'm gonna put a ribbon on you!
I TAKE MY EYES OFF YOU FOR SUCH A SHORT TIME...
WHAT'RE YOU DOING HERE?
WHAT IS THIS!? HUH!?
Stand up!!
ONE WEEK I'VE BEEN AWAY, ***ONE WEEK***, AND THIS PLACE IS COMPLETELY TRASHED!
UGH! I CAN'T BELIEVE THIS!! WHO HAS TO CLEAN THIS UP, HUH!? ***ME!!***
By myself!!
AARGH!!
WHA...

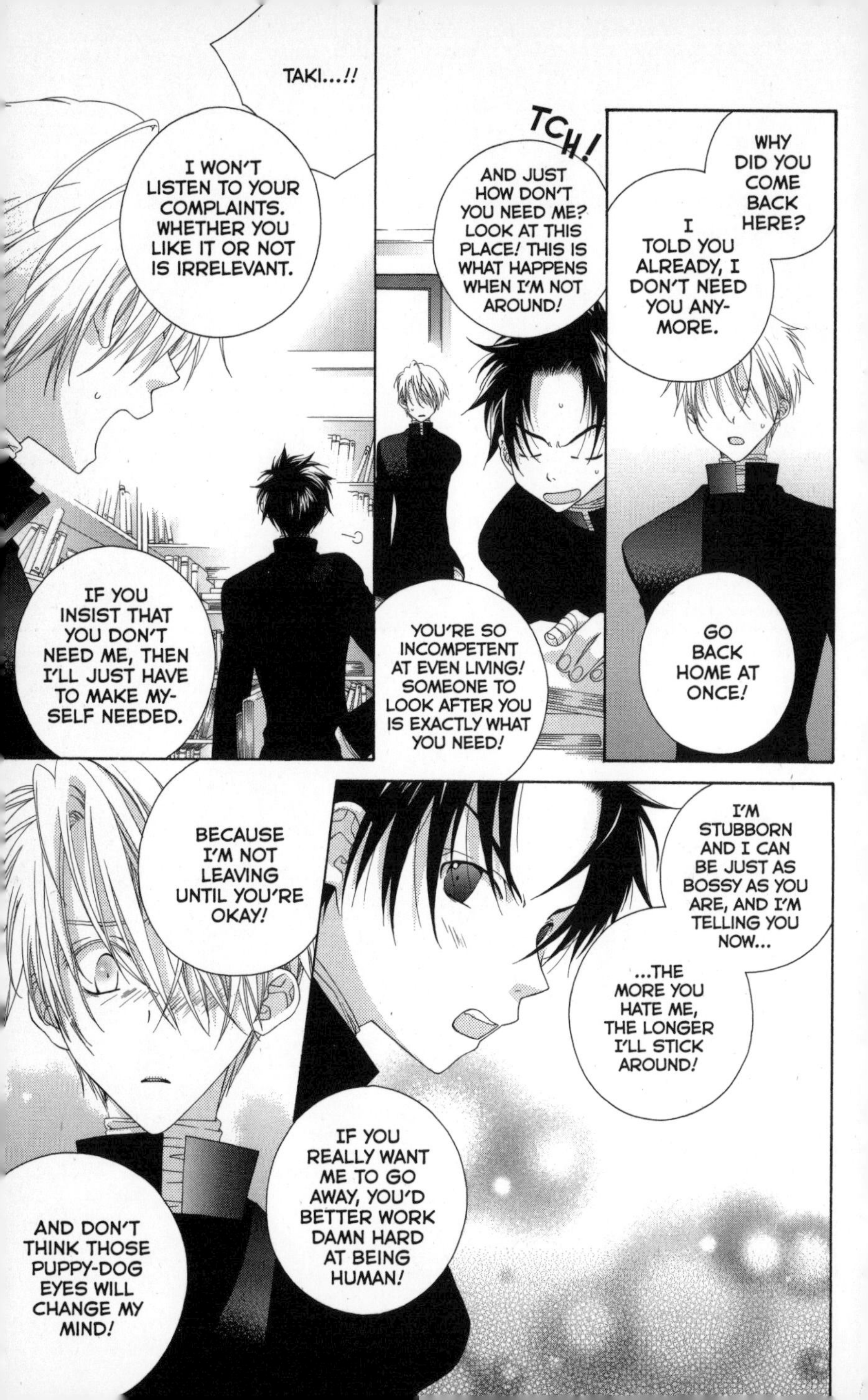
WHY DID YOU COME BACK HERE?
I TOLD YOU ALREADY, I DON'T NEED YOU ANY-MORE.
GO BACK HOME AT ONCE!
TCH!
AND JUST HOW DON'T YOU NEED ME? LOOK AT THIS PLACE! THIS IS WHAT HAPPENS WHEN I'M NOT AROUND!
YOU'RE SO INCOMPETENT AT EVEN LIVING! SOMEONE TO LOOK AFTER YOU IS EXACTLY WHAT YOU NEED!
TAKI...!!
I WON'T LISTEN TO YOUR COMPLAINTS. WHETHER YOU LIKE IT OR NOT IS IRRELEVANT.
IF YOU INSIST THAT YOU DON'T NEED ME, THEN I'LL JUST HAVE TO MAKE MY-SELF NEEDED.
I'M STUBBORN AND I CAN BE JUST AS BOSSY AS YOU ARE, AND I'M TELLING YOU NOW...
...THE MORE YOU HATE ME, THE LONGER I'LL STICK AROUND!
BECAUSE I'M NOT LEAVING UNTIL YOU'RE OKAY!
IF YOU REALLY WANT ME TO GO AWAY, YOU'D BETTER WORK DAMN HARD AT BEING HUMAN!
AND DON'T THINK THOSE PUPPY-DOG EYES WILL CHANGE MY MIND!

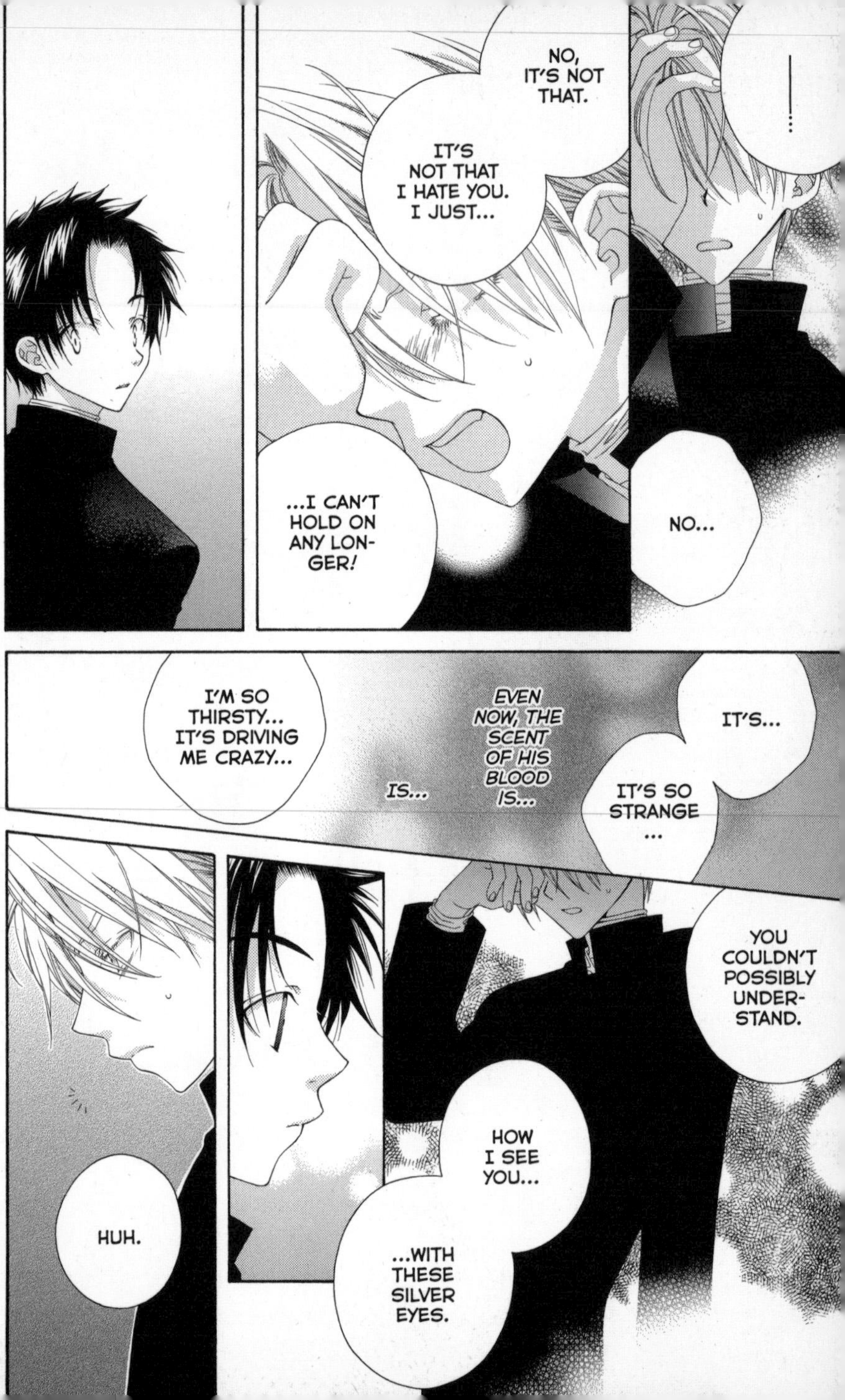
......
NO...
NO, IT'S NOT THAT.
IT'S NOT THAT I HATE YOU. I JUST...
...I CAN'T HOLD ON ANY LONGER!
IT'S...
IT'S SO STRANGE...
EVEN NOW, THE SCENT OF HIS BLOOD IS...
IS...
I'M SO THIRSTY... IT'S DRIVING ME CRAZY...
YOU COULDN'T POSSIBLY UNDERSTAND.
HOW I SEE YOU...
...WITH THESE SILVER EYES.
HUH.

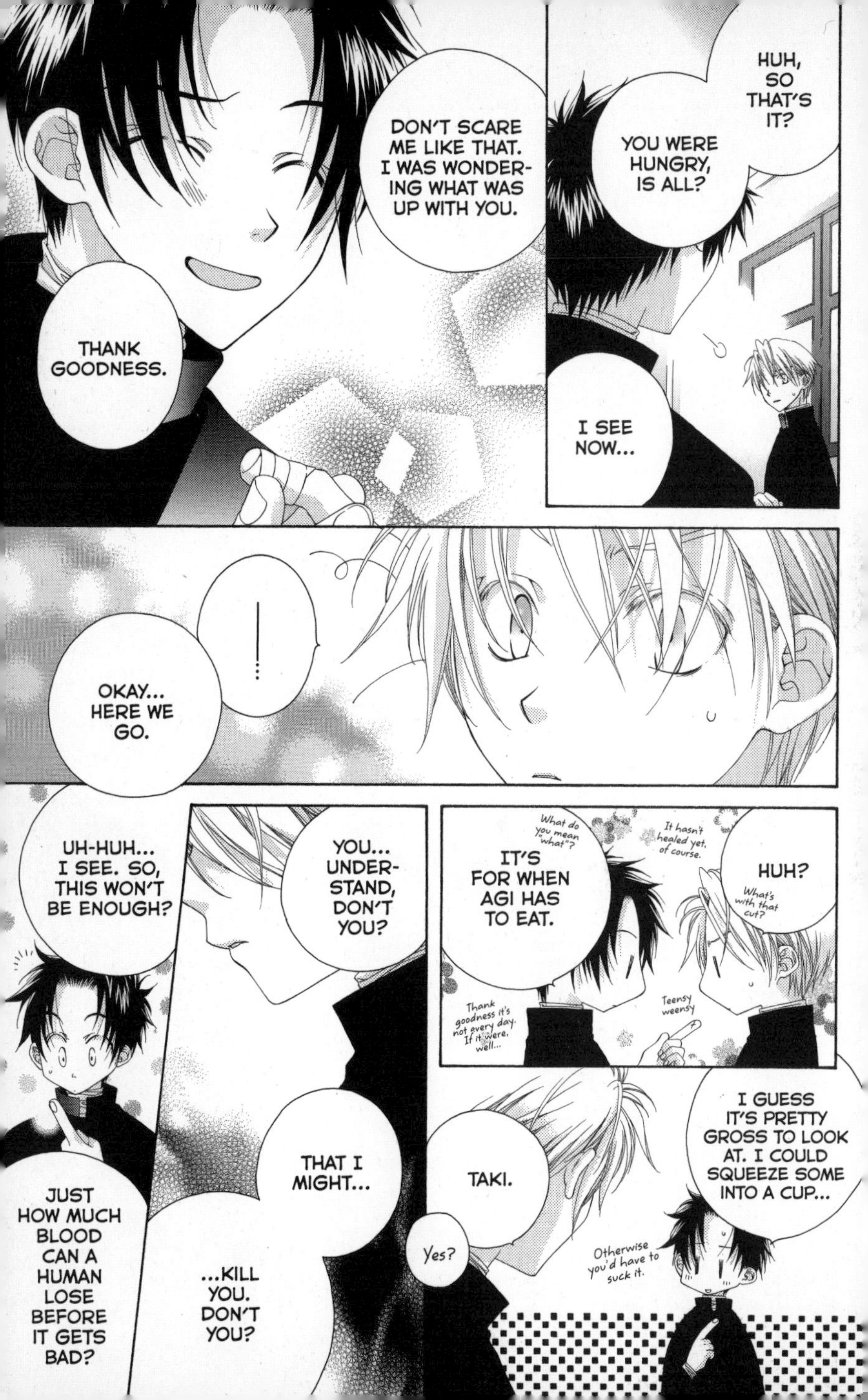
HUH, SO THAT'S IT?
YOU WERE HUNGRY, IS ALL?
I SEE NOW...
DON'T SCARE ME LIKE THAT. I WAS WONDERING WHAT WAS UP WITH YOU.
THANK GOODNESS.
...!
OKAY... HERE WE GO.
HUH?
What's with that cut?
It hasn't healed yet, of course.
IT'S FOR WHEN AGI HAS TO EAT.
What do you mean "what"?
Teensy weensy
Thank goodness it's not every day. If it were, well...
I GUESS IT'S PRETTY GROSS TO LOOK AT. I COULD SQUEEZE SOME INTO A CUP...
Otherwise you'd have to suck it.
TAKI.
Yes?
YOU... UNDERSTAND, DON'T YOU?
THAT I MIGHT...
...KILL YOU. DON'T YOU?
UH-HUH... I SEE. SO, THIS WON'T BE ENOUGH?
JUST HOW MUCH BLOOD CAN A HUMAN LOSE BEFORE IT GETS BAD?

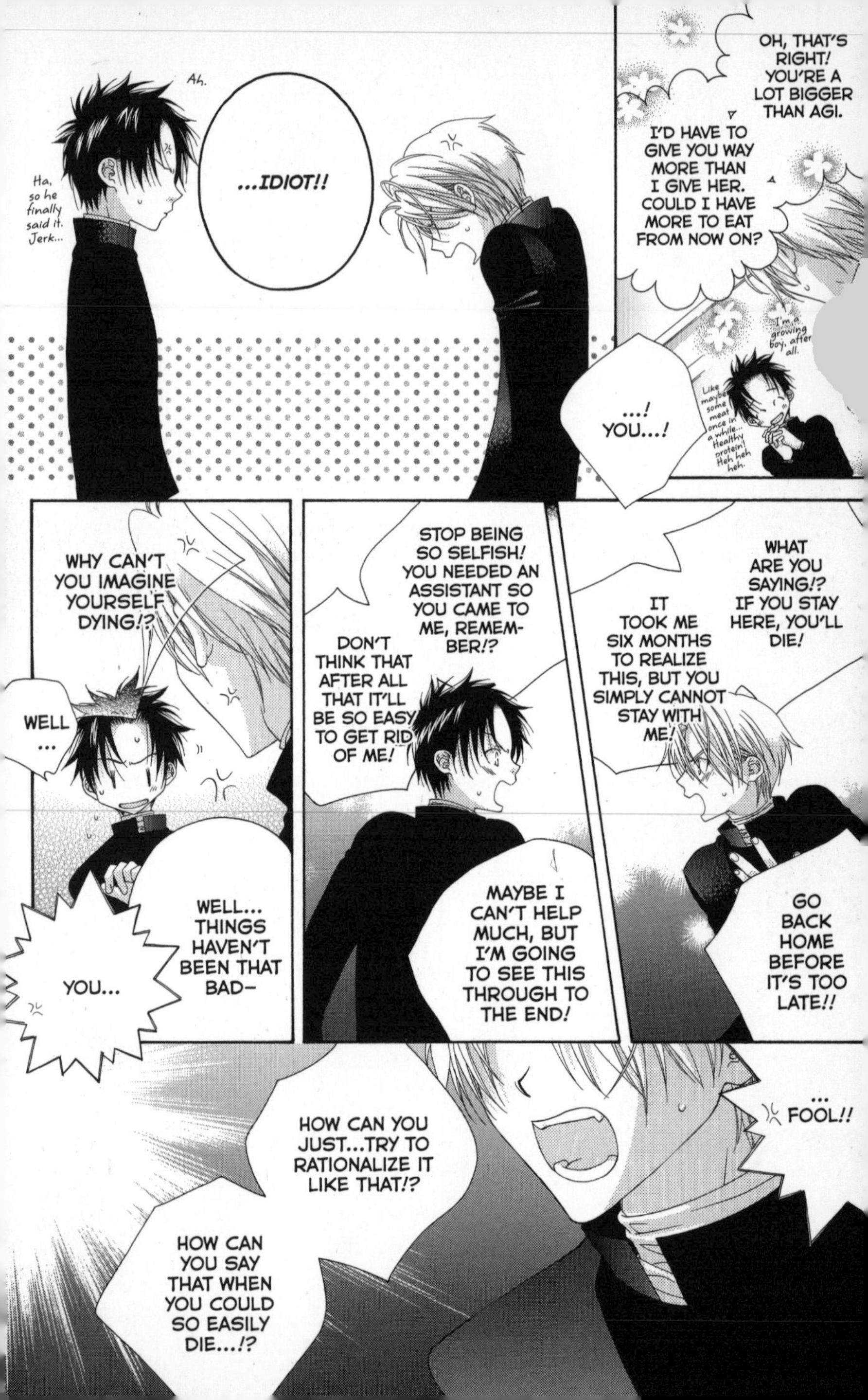
OH, THAT'S RIGHT! YOU'RE A LOT BIGGER THAN AGI.
I'D HAVE TO GIVE YOU WAY MORE THAN I GIVE HER. COULD I HAVE MORE TO EAT FROM NOW ON?
I'm a growing boy, after all.
Like maybe some meat once in a while... Healthy protein! Heh heh heh.
...! YOU...!
Ah.
...IDIOT!!
Ha, so he finally said it. Jerk...
WHAT ARE YOU SAYING!? IF YOU STAY HERE, YOU'LL DIE!
IT TOOK ME SIX MONTHS TO REALIZE THIS, BUT YOU SIMPLY CANNOT STAY WITH ME!
GO BACK HOME BEFORE IT'S TOO LATE!!
STOP BEING SO SELFISH! YOU NEEDED AN ASSISTANT SO YOU CAME TO ME, REMEMBER!?
DON'T THINK THAT AFTER ALL THAT IT'LL BE SO EASY TO GET RID OF ME!
MAYBE I CAN'T HELP MUCH, BUT I'M GOING TO SEE THIS THROUGH TO THE END!
WHY CAN'T YOU IMAGINE YOURSELF DYING!?
WELL...
WELL... THINGS HAVEN'T BEEN THAT BAD—
YOU...
...FOOL!!
HOW CAN YOU JUST...TRY TO RATIONALIZE IT LIKE THAT!?
HOW CAN YOU SAY THAT WHEN YOU COULD SO EASILY DIE...!?

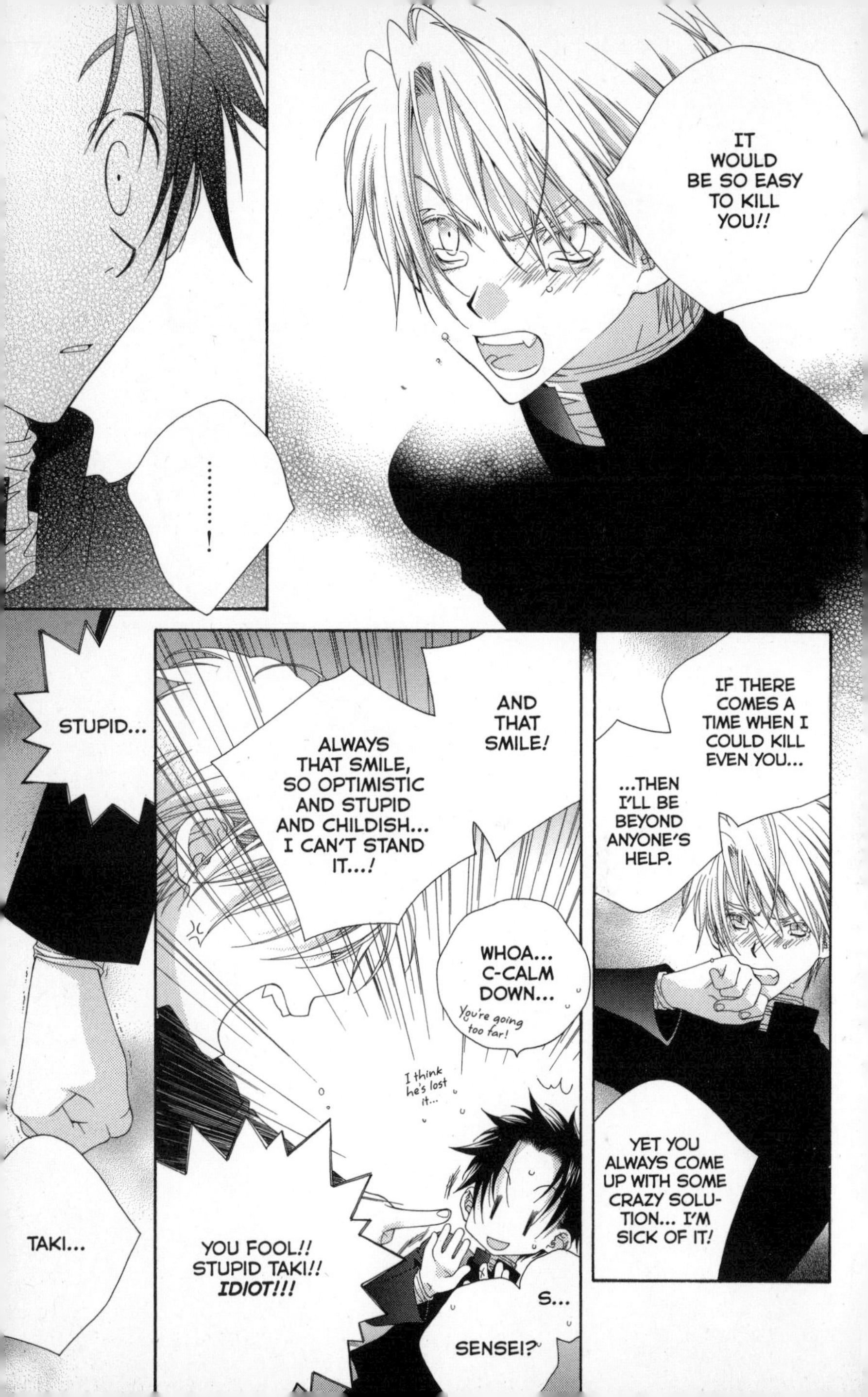
IT WOULD BE SO EASY TO KILL YOU!!
......!
IF THERE COMES A TIME WHEN I COULD KILL EVEN YOU...
...THEN I'LL BE BEYOND ANYONE'S HELP.
YET YOU ALWAYS COME UP WITH SOME CRAZY SOLU-TION... I'M SICK OF IT!
AND THAT SMILE!
ALWAYS THAT SMILE, SO OPTIMISTIC AND STUPID AND CHILDISH... I CAN'T STAND IT...!
WHOA... C-CALM DOWN...
You're going too far!
I think he's lost it...
YOU FOOL!! STUPID TAKI!! *IDIOT!!!*
S...
SENSEI!?
STUPID...
TAKI...

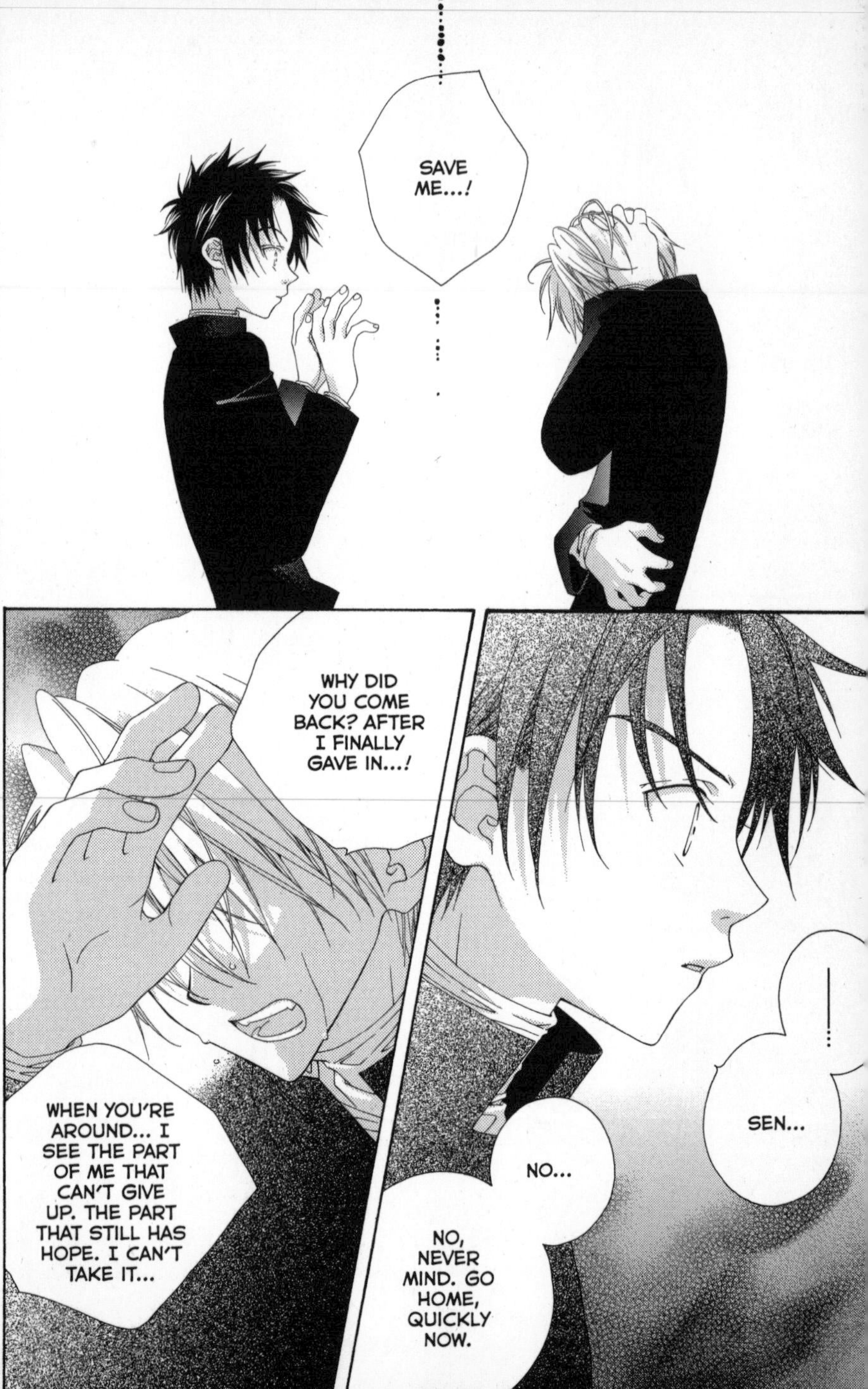
SAVE ME...!
......
SEN...
NO...
NO, NEVER MIND. GO HOME, QUICKLY NOW.
WHY DID YOU COME BACK? AFTER I FINALLY GAVE IN...!
WHEN YOU'RE AROUND... I SEE THE PART OF ME THAT CAN'T GIVE UP. THE PART THAT STILL HAS HOPE. I CAN'T TAKE IT...

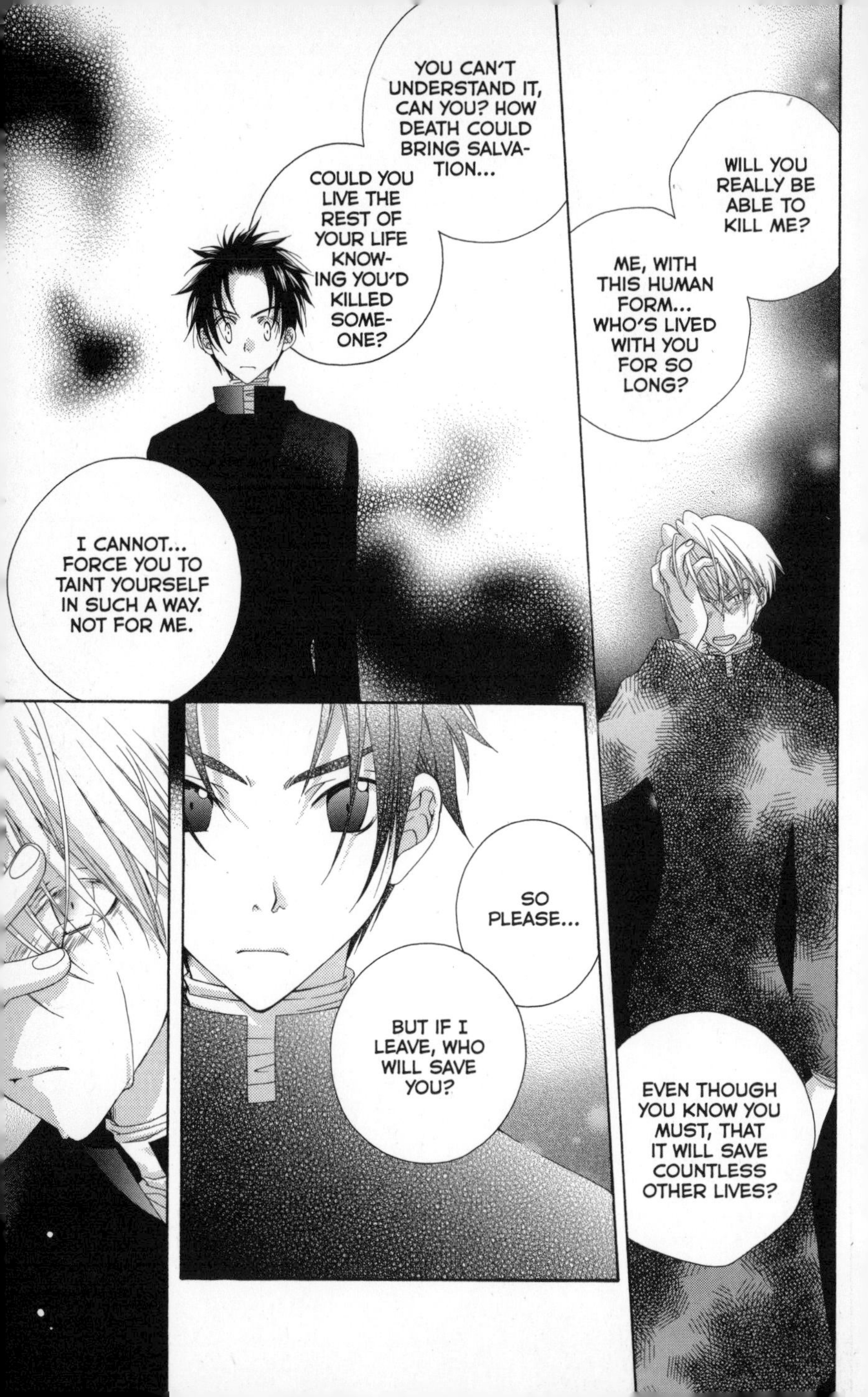
WILL YOU REALLY BE ABLE TO KILL ME?
ME, WITH THIS HUMAN FORM... WHO'S LIVED WITH YOU FOR SO LONG?
EVEN THOUGH YOU KNOW YOU MUST, THAT IT WILL SAVE COUNTLESS OTHER LIVES?
YOU CAN'T UNDERSTAND IT, CAN YOU? HOW DEATH COULD BRING SALVA-TION...
COULD YOU LIVE THE REST OF YOUR LIFE KNOW-ING YOU'D KILLED SOME-ONE?
I CANNOT... FORCE YOU TO TAINT YOURSELF IN SUCH A WAY. NOT FOR ME.
SO PLEASE...
BUT IF I LEAVE, WHO WILL SAVE YOU?

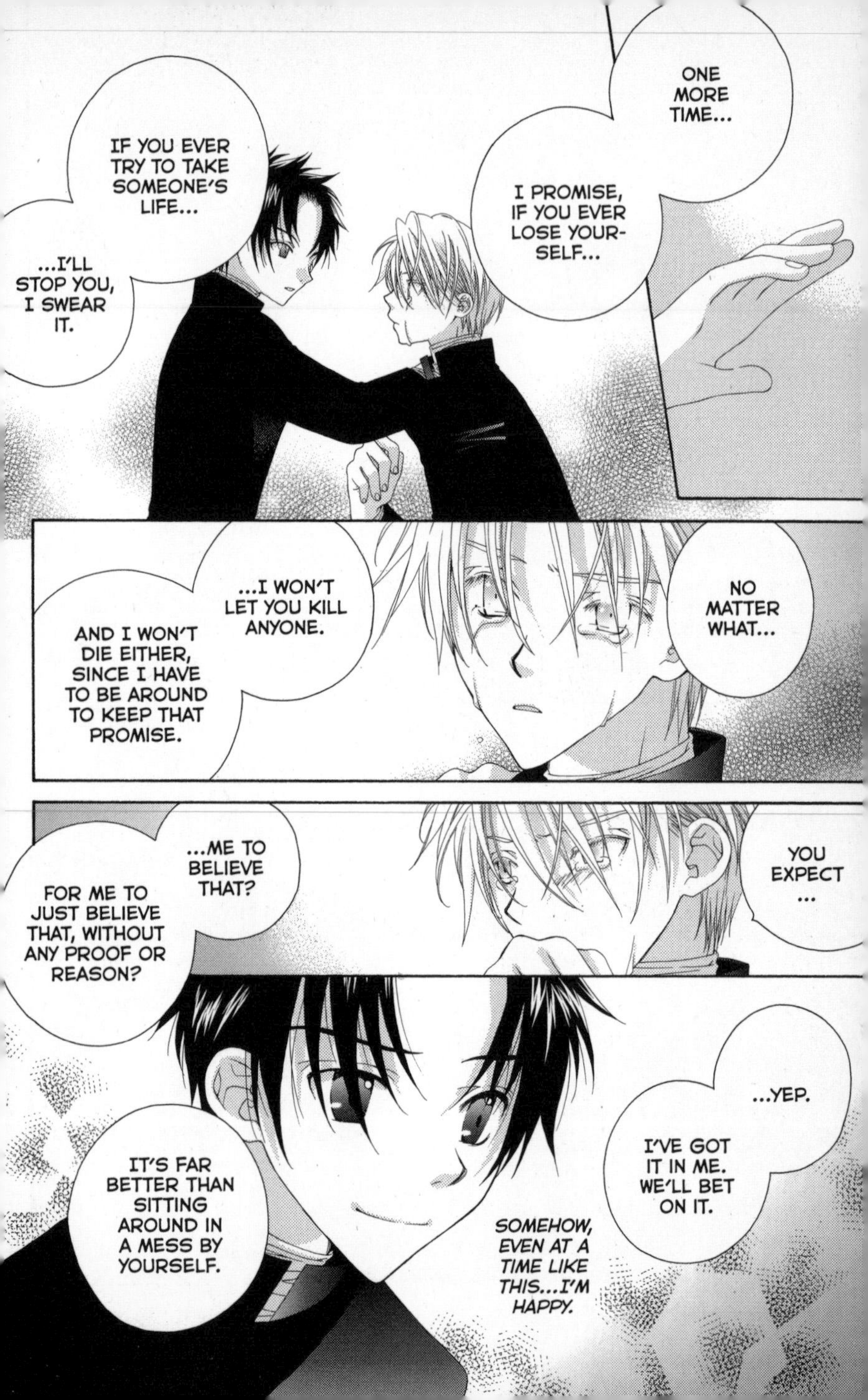
ONE MORE TIME...
I PROMISE, IF YOU EVER LOSE YOURSELF...
IF YOU EVER TRY TO TAKE SOMEONE'S LIFE...
...I'LL STOP YOU, I SWEAR IT.
NO MATTER WHAT...
...I WON'T LET YOU KILL ANYONE.
AND I WON'T DIE EITHER, SINCE I HAVE TO BE AROUND TO KEEP THAT PROMISE.
YOU EXPECT ...
...ME TO BELIEVE THAT?
FOR ME TO JUST BELIEVE THAT, WITHOUT ANY PROOF OR REASON?
...YEP.
I'VE GOT IT IN ME. WE'LL BET ON IT.
SOMEHOW, EVEN AT A TIME LIKE THIS...I'M HAPPY.
IT'S FAR BETTER THAN SITTING AROUND IN A MESS BY YOURSELF.

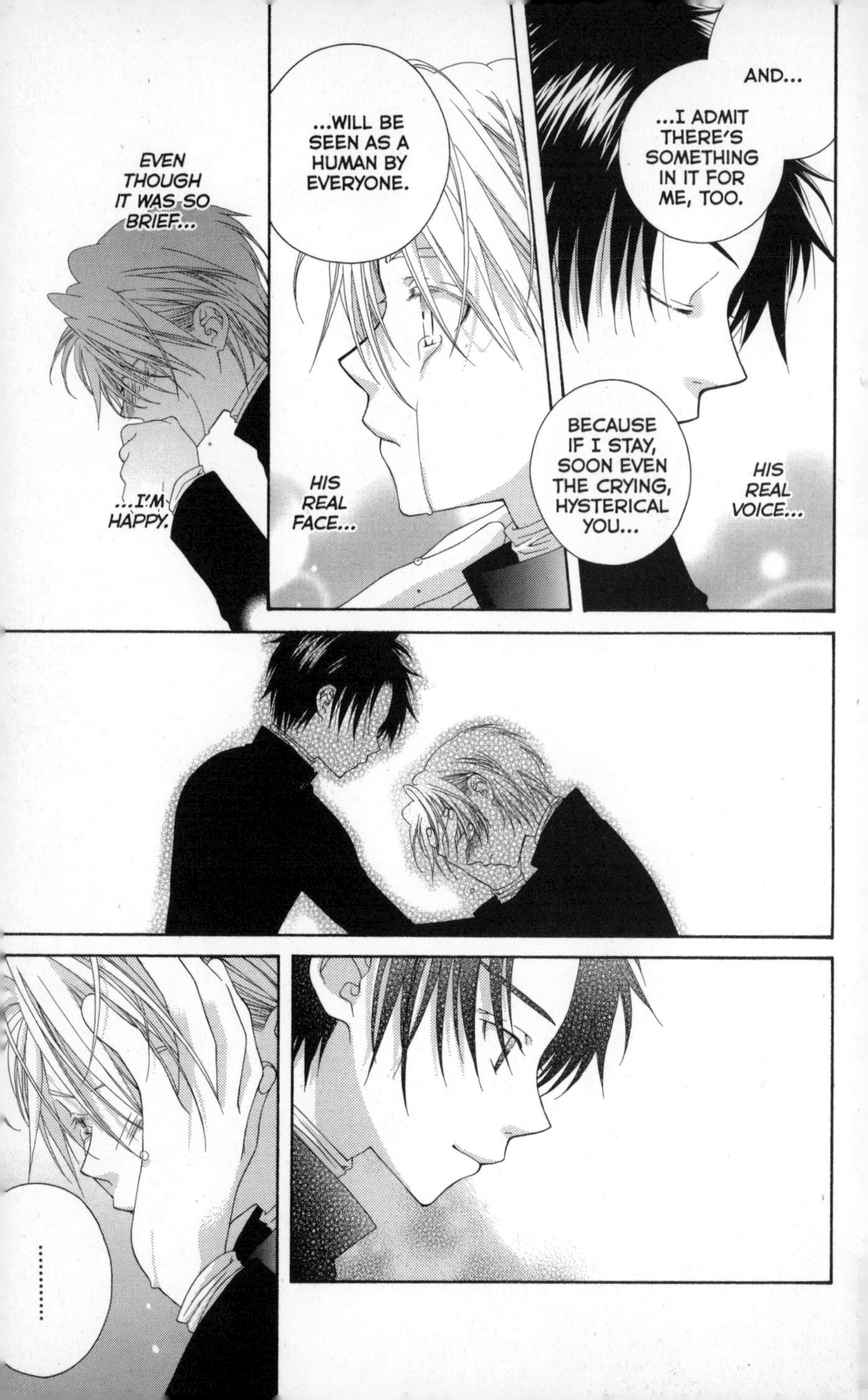
AND...
...I ADMIT THERE'S SOMETHING IN IT FOR ME, TOO.
BECAUSE IF I STAY, SOON EVEN THE CRYING, HYSTERICAL YOU...
HIS REAL VOICE...
...WILL BE SEEN AS A HUMAN BY EVERYONE.
HIS REAL FACE...
EVEN THOUGH IT WAS SO BRIEF...
...I'M HAPPY.
....

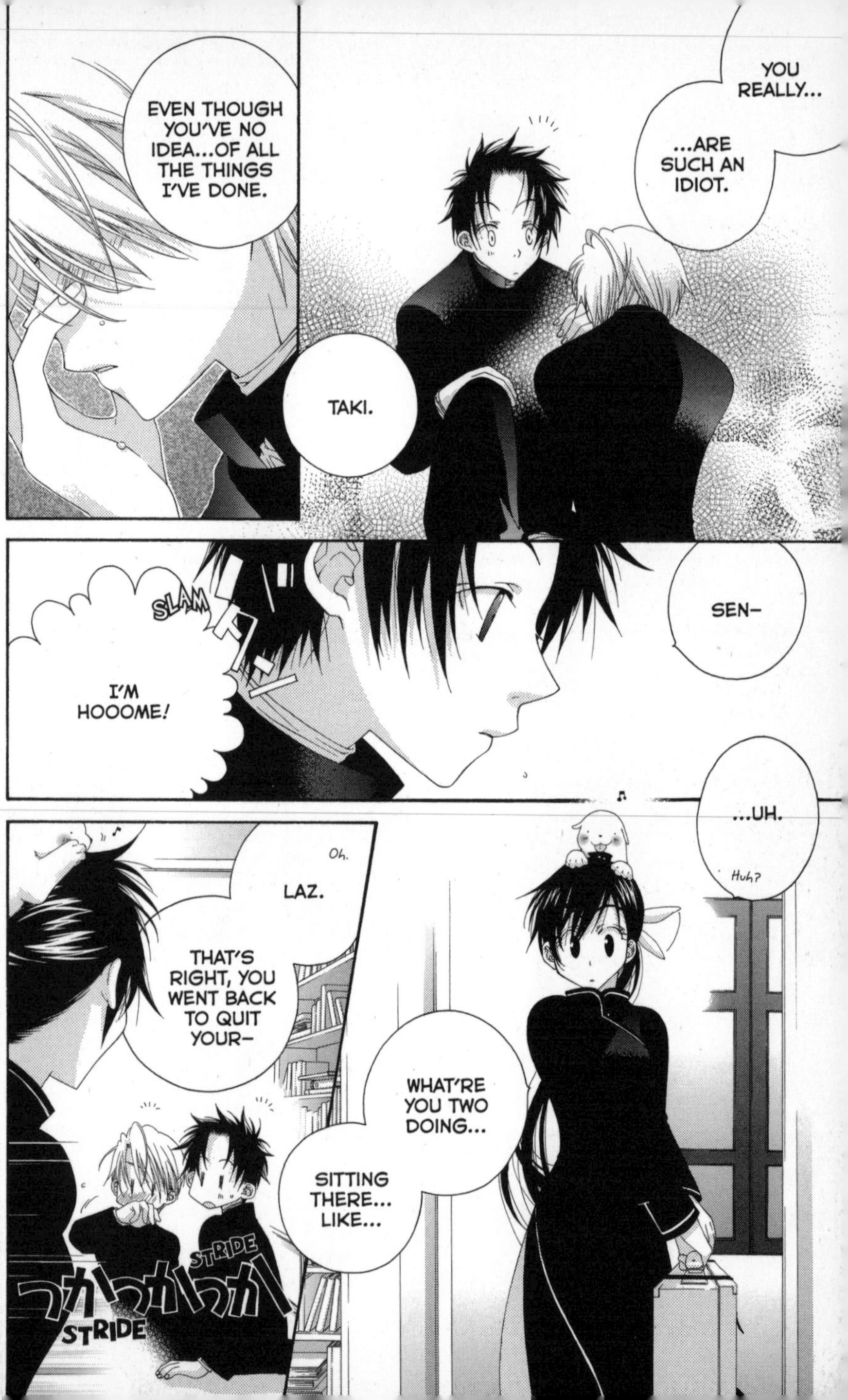
YOU REALLY...
...ARE SUCH AN IDIOT.
TAKI.
EVEN THOUGH YOU'VE NO IDEA...OF ALL THE THINGS I'VE DONE.
SEN-
SLAM
I'M HOOOME!
...UH.
Huh?
WHAT'RE YOU TWO DOING...
SITTING THERE... LIKE...
Oh.
LAZ.
THAT'S RIGHT, YOU WENT BACK TO QUIT YOUR-
STRIDE
つかつかつか
STRIDE

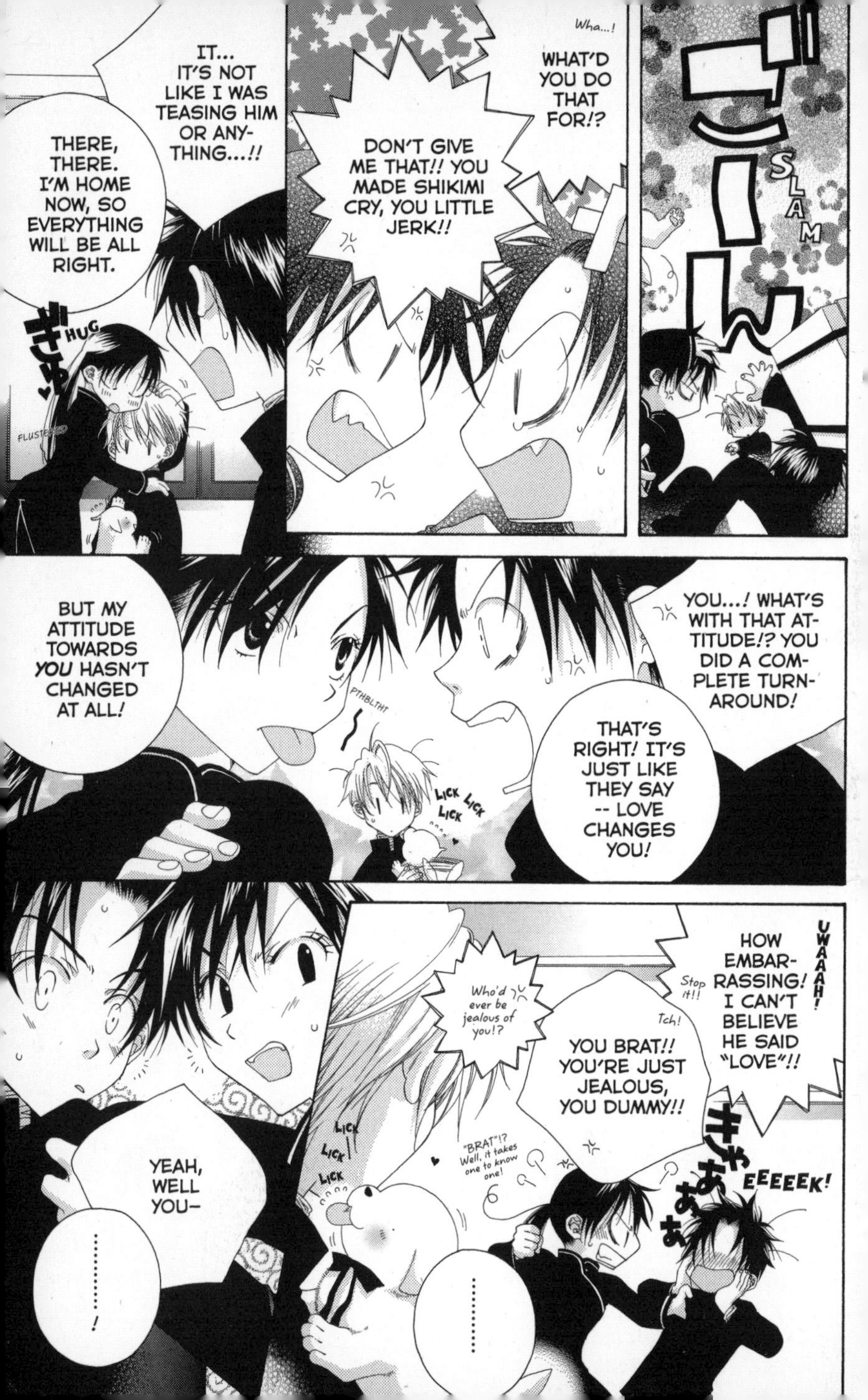
SLAM
Wha...!
WHAT'D YOU DO THAT FOR!?
DON'T GIVE ME THAT!! YOU MADE SHIKIMI CRY, YOU LITTLE JERK!!
IT... IT'S NOT LIKE I WAS TEASING HIM OR ANY-THING...!!
THERE, THERE. I'M HOME NOW, SO EVERYTHING WILL BE ALL RIGHT.
HUG
FLUSTERED
YOU...! WHAT'S WITH THAT AT-TITUDE!? YOU DID A COM-PLETE TURN-AROUND!
THAT'S RIGHT! IT'S JUST LIKE THEY SAY -- LOVE CHANGES YOU!
LICK LICK LICK
PTHBLTHT
BUT MY ATTITUDE TOWARDS YOU HASN'T CHANGED AT ALL!
UWAAAH!
HOW EMBAR-RASSING! I CAN'T BELIEVE HE SAID "LOVE"!!
Stop it!!
Tch!
YOU BRAT!! YOU'RE JUST JEALOUS, YOU DUMMY!!
Who'd ever be jealous of you!?
EEEEEK!
"BRAT"!? Well, it takes one to know one!
LICK LICK LICK
......
YEAH, WELL YOU–
......!

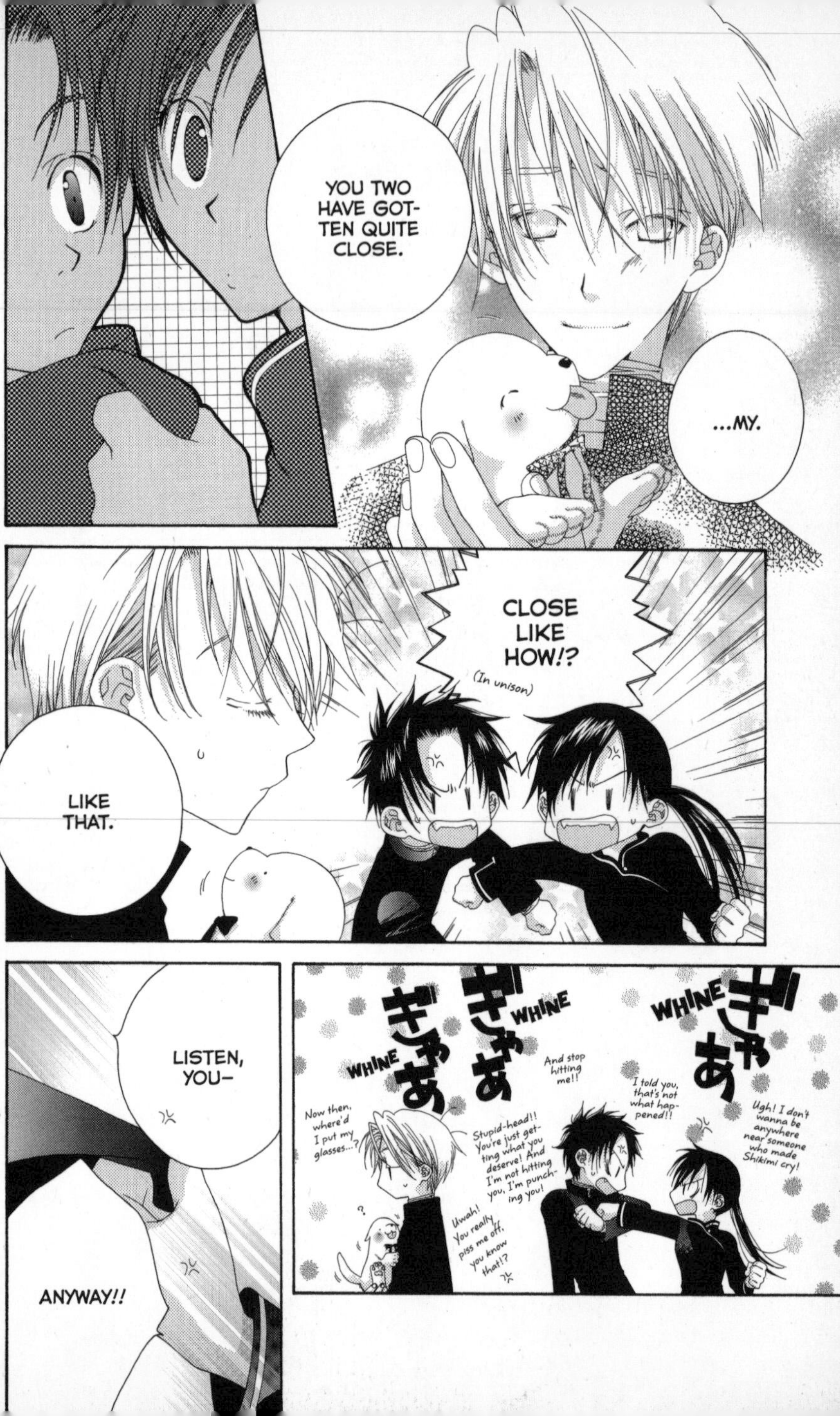

YOU TWO HAVE GOT-TEN QUITE CLOSE.
...MY.
CLOSE LIKE HOW!?
(In unison)
LIKE THAT.
WHINE
ぎゃあ
WHINE
ぎゃあ
WHINE
ぎゃあ
Ugh! I don't wanna be anywhere near someone who made Shikimi cry!
I told you, that's not what hap-pened!!
And stop hitting me!!
Stupid-head!! You're just get-ting what you deserve! And I'm not hitting you, I'm punch-ing you!
Uwah! You really piss me off, you know that!?
Now then, where'd I put my glasses...?
LISTEN, YOU–
ANYWAY!!

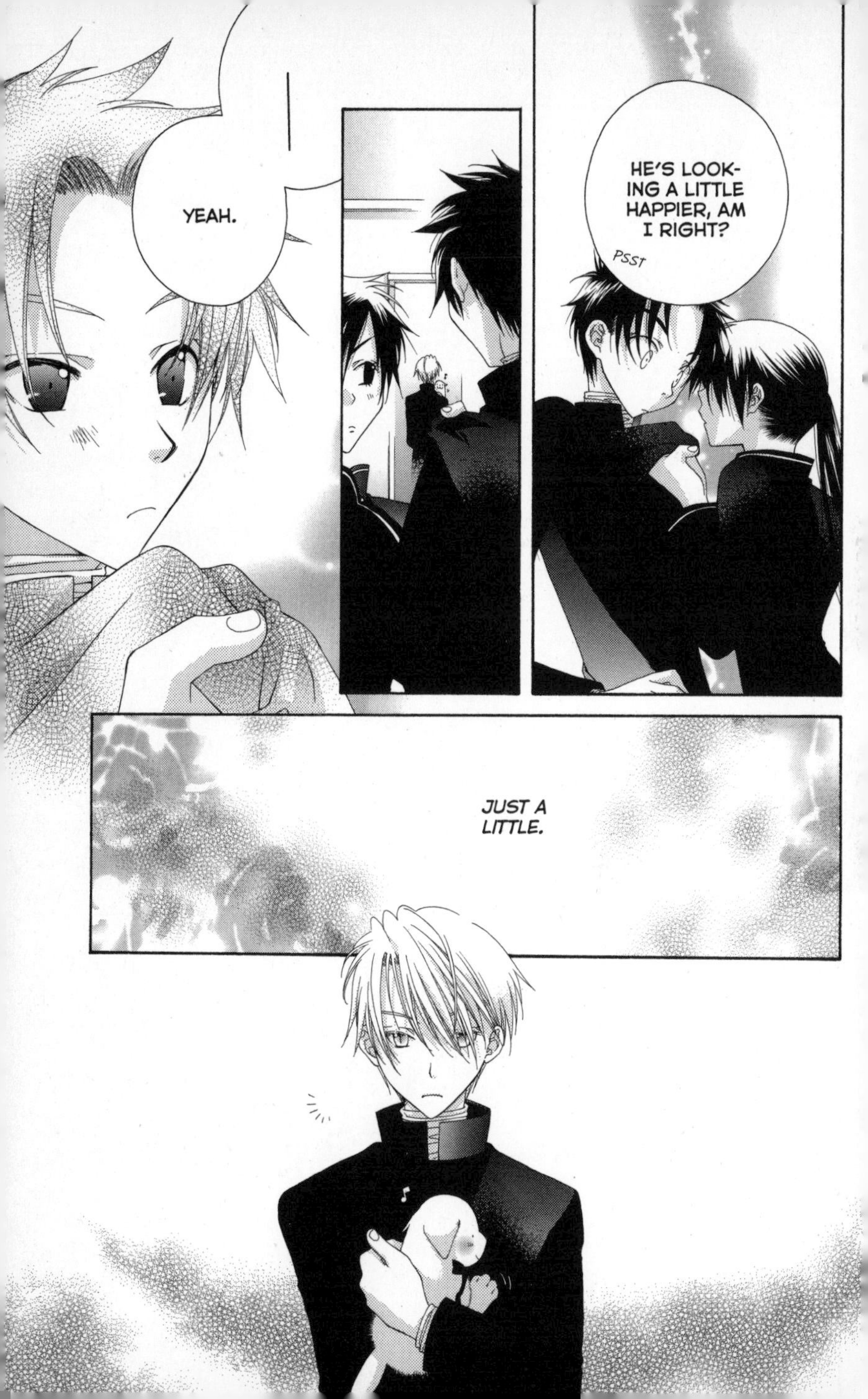
HE'S LOOKING A LITTLE HAPPIER, AM I RIGHT?
PSST
YEAH.
JUST A LITTLE.

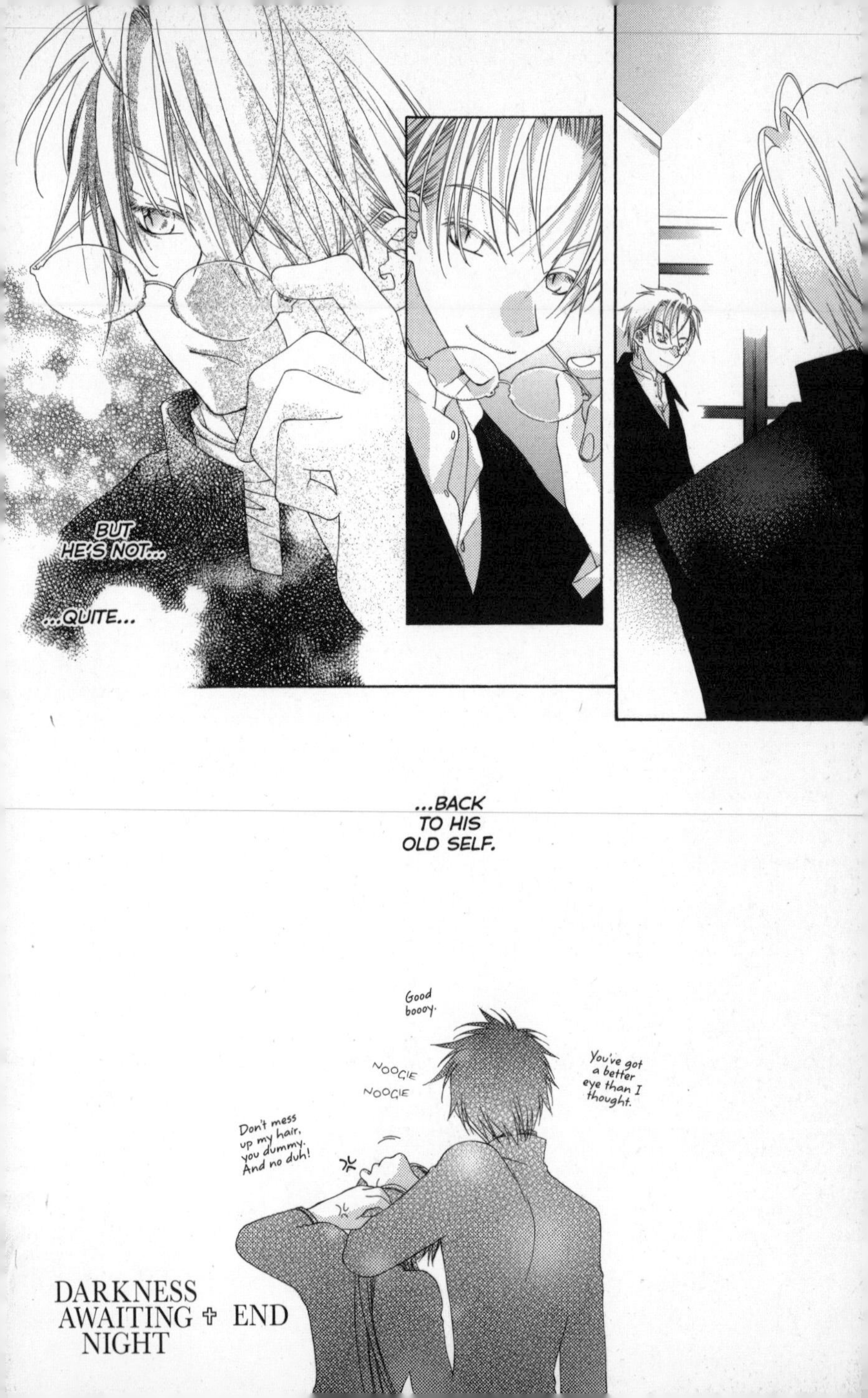

BUT HE'S NOT...
...QUITE...
...BACK TO HIS OLD SELF.
You've got a better eye than I thought.
Good boooy.
NOOGIE NOOGIE
Don't mess up my hair, you dummy. And no duh!
DARKNESS AWAITING NIGHT ✝ END

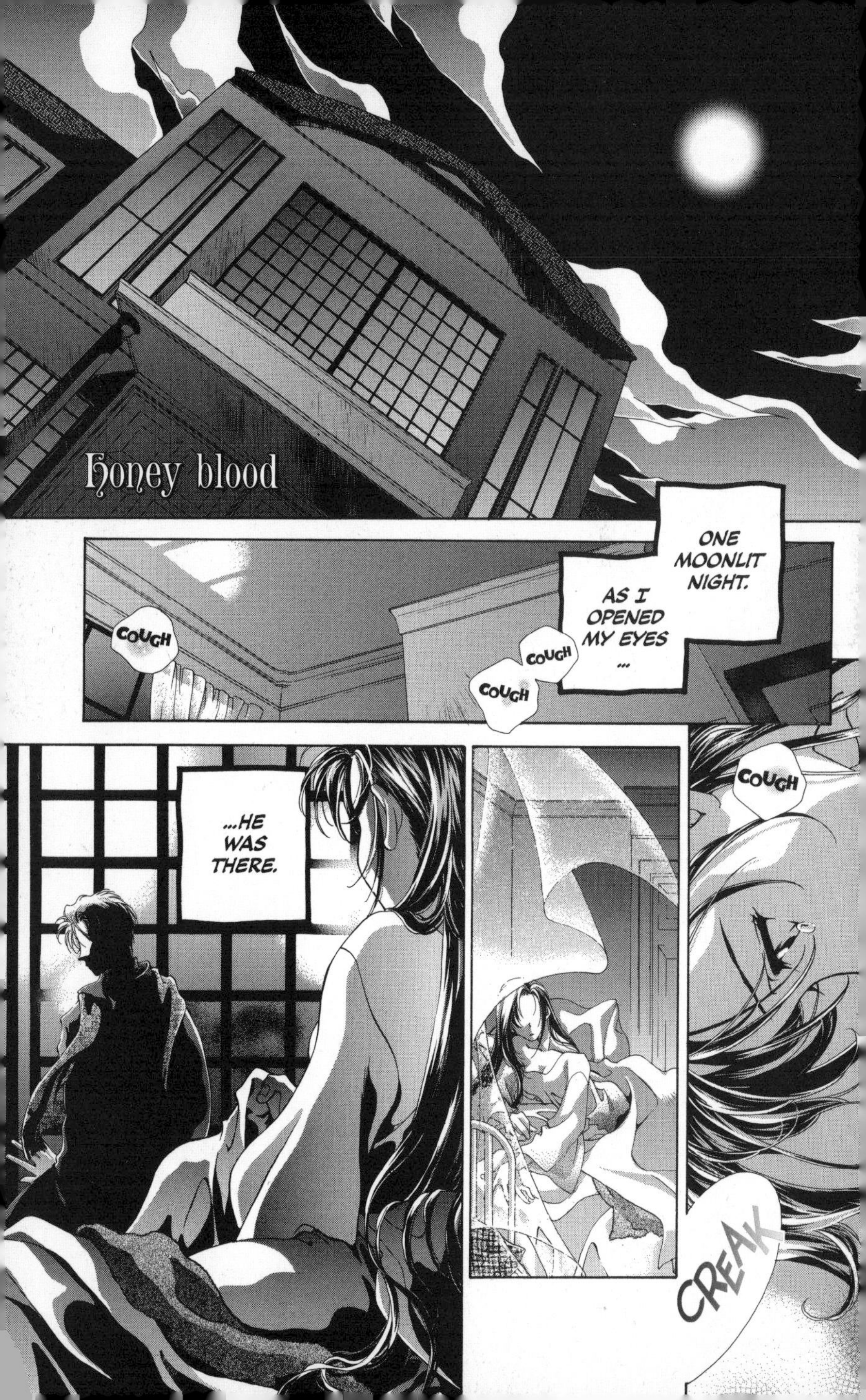
Honey blood
ONE MOONLIT NIGHT.
AS I OPENED MY EYES ...
COUGH
COUGH
COUGH
COUGH
CREAK
...HE WAS THERE.

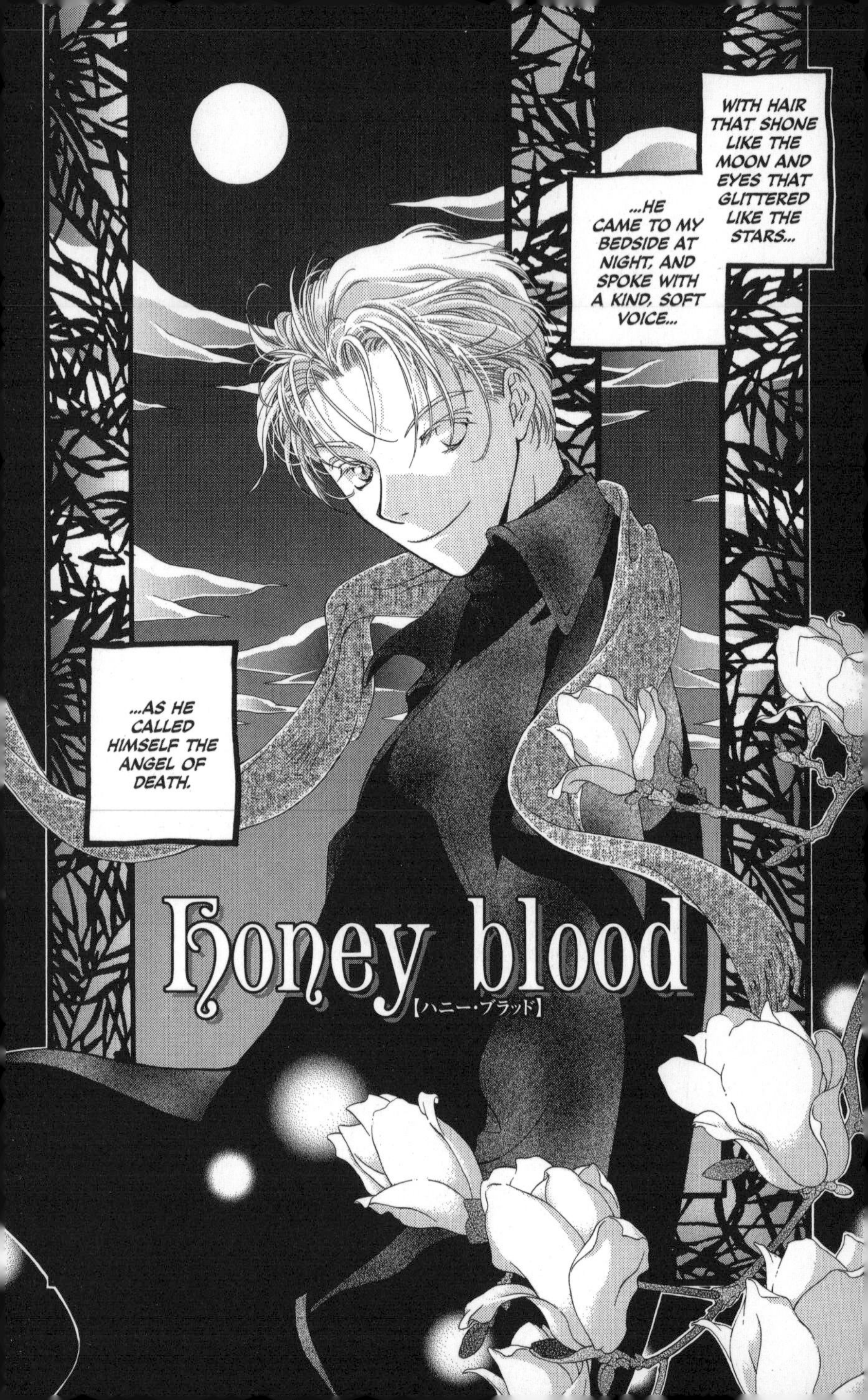
WITH HAIR THAT SHONE LIKE THE MOON AND EYES THAT GLITTERED LIKE THE STARS...
...HE CAME TO MY BEDSIDE AT NIGHT, AND SPOKE WITH A KIND, SOFT VOICE...
...AS HE CALLED HIMSELF THE ANGEL OF DEATH.
Honey blood
【ハニー・ブラッド】

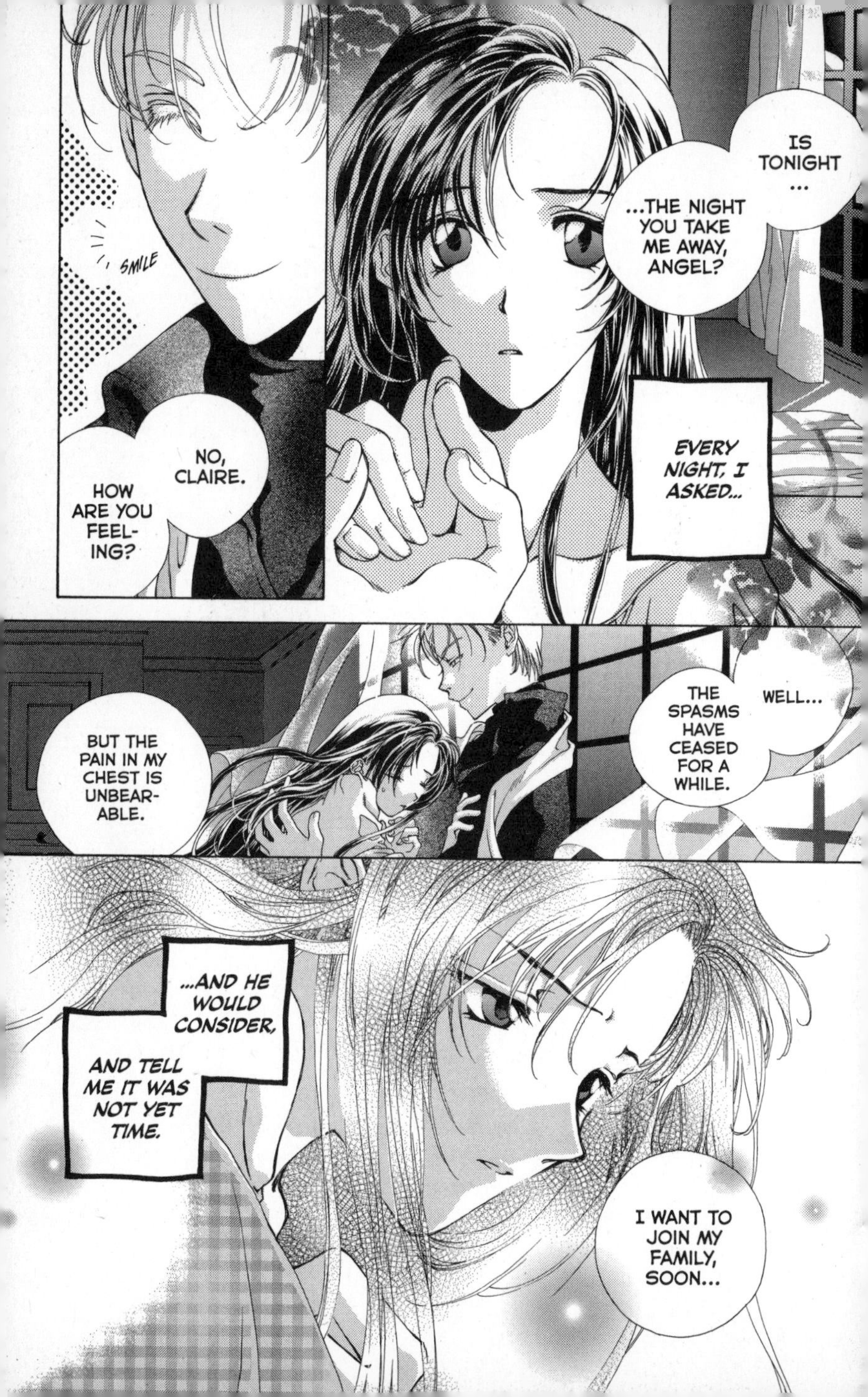
IS TONIGHT ...
...THE NIGHT YOU TAKE ME AWAY, ANGEL?
EVERY NIGHT, I ASKED...
SMILE
NO, CLAIRE.
HOW ARE YOU FEEL-ING?
WELL...
THE SPASMS HAVE CEASED FOR A WHILE.
BUT THE PAIN IN MY CHEST IS UNBEARABLE.
...AND HE WOULD CONSIDER,
AND TELL ME IT WAS NOT YET TIME.
I WANT TO JOIN MY FAMILY, SOON...

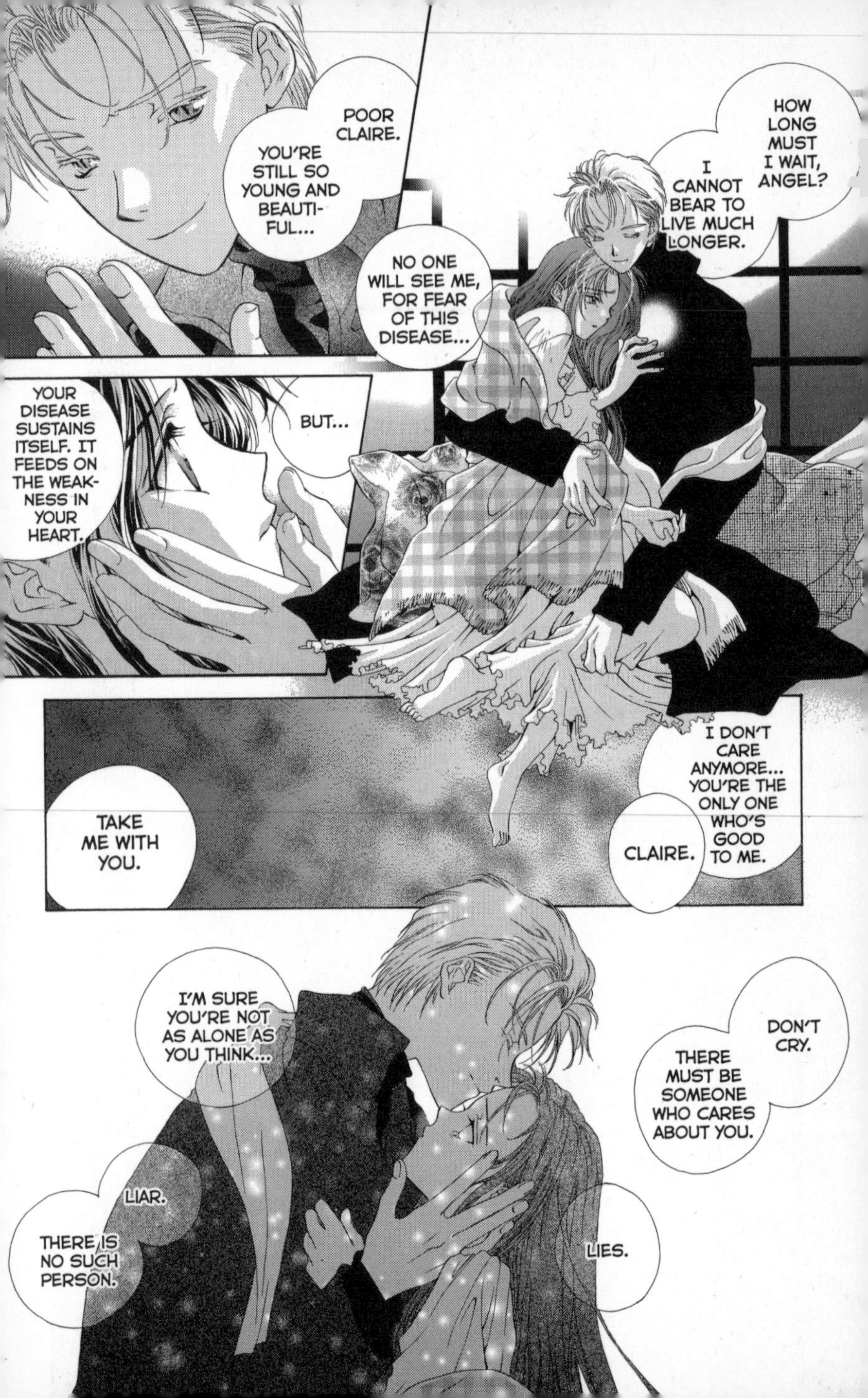
HOW LONG MUST I WAIT, ANGEL?
I CANNOT BEAR TO LIVE MUCH LONGER.
NO ONE WILL SEE ME, FOR FEAR OF THIS DISEASE...
POOR CLAIRE.
YOU'RE STILL SO YOUNG AND BEAUTI-FUL...
BUT...
YOUR DISEASE SUSTAINS ITSELF. IT FEEDS ON THE WEAK-NESS IN YOUR HEART.
I DON'T CARE ANYMORE... YOU'RE THE ONLY ONE WHO'S GOOD TO ME.
CLAIRE.
TAKE ME WITH YOU.
DON'T CRY.
THERE MUST BE SOMEONE WHO CARES ABOUT YOU.
I'M SURE YOU'RE NOT AS ALONE AS YOU THINK...
LIES.
LIAR.
THERE IS NO SUCH PERSON.

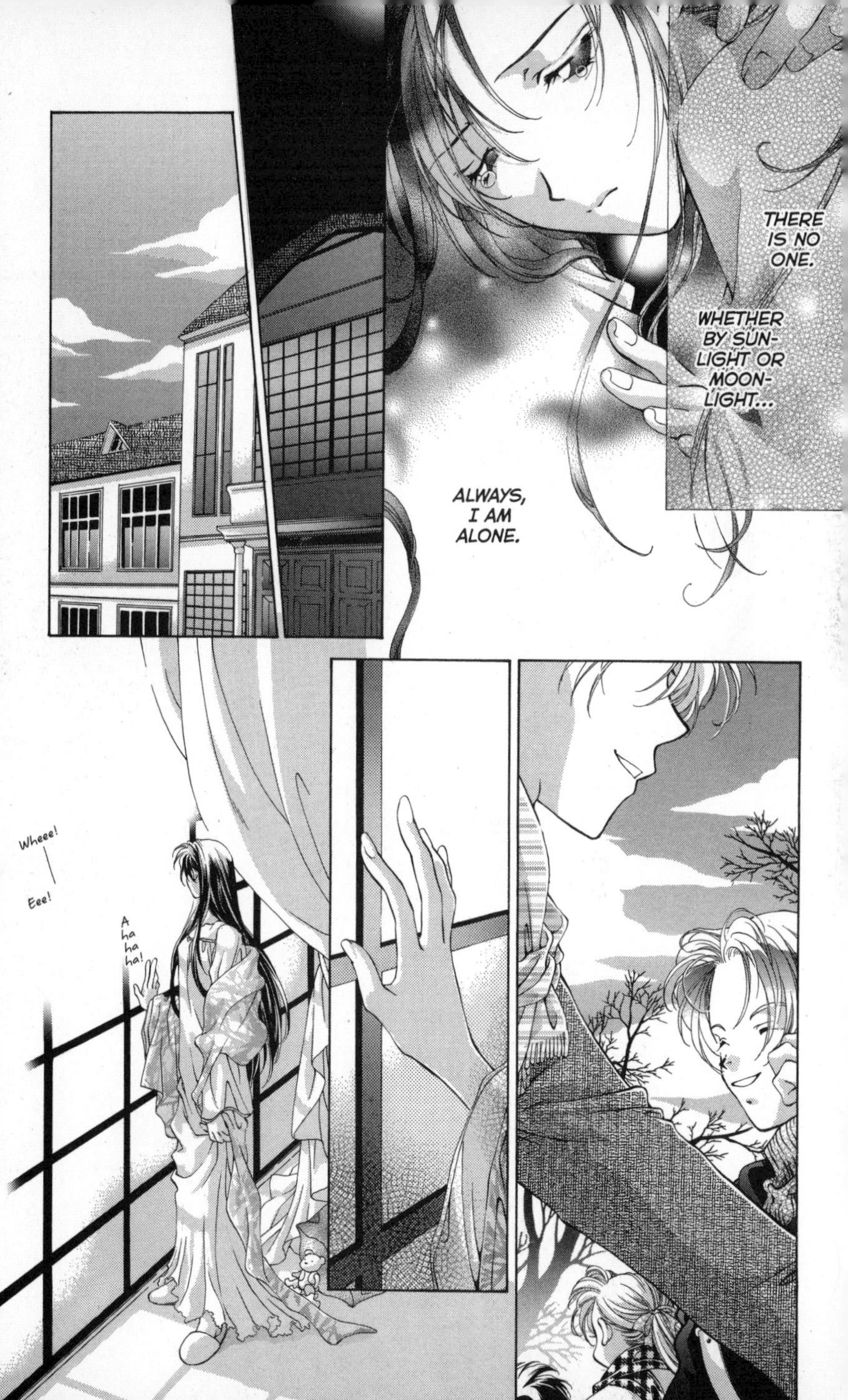
THERE IS NO ONE.
WHETHER BY SUN-LIGHT OR MOON-LIGHT...
ALWAYS, I AM ALONE.
A ha ha ha!
Wheee!
Eee!

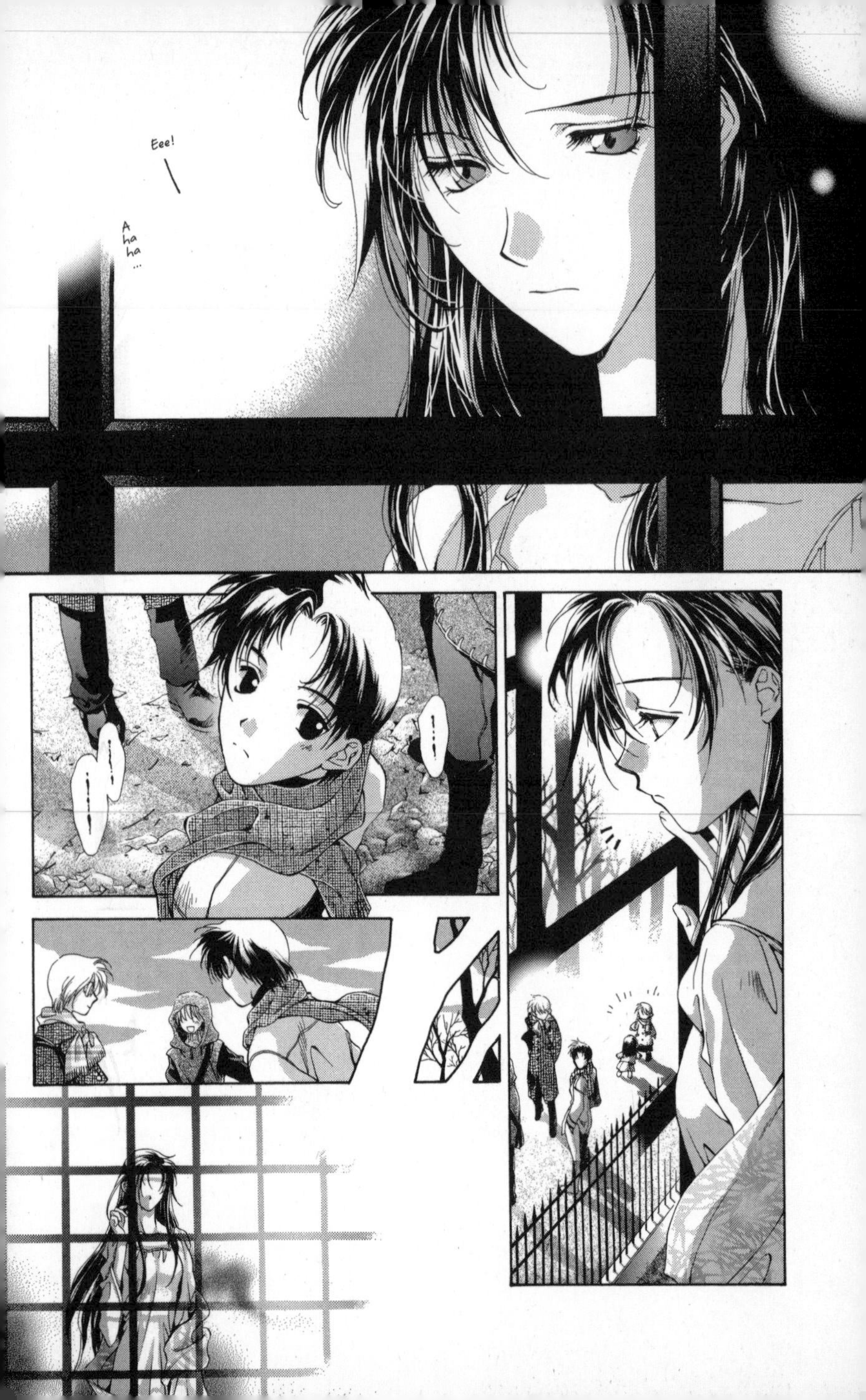

Eee!
Aha ha...
...!
...!
......!

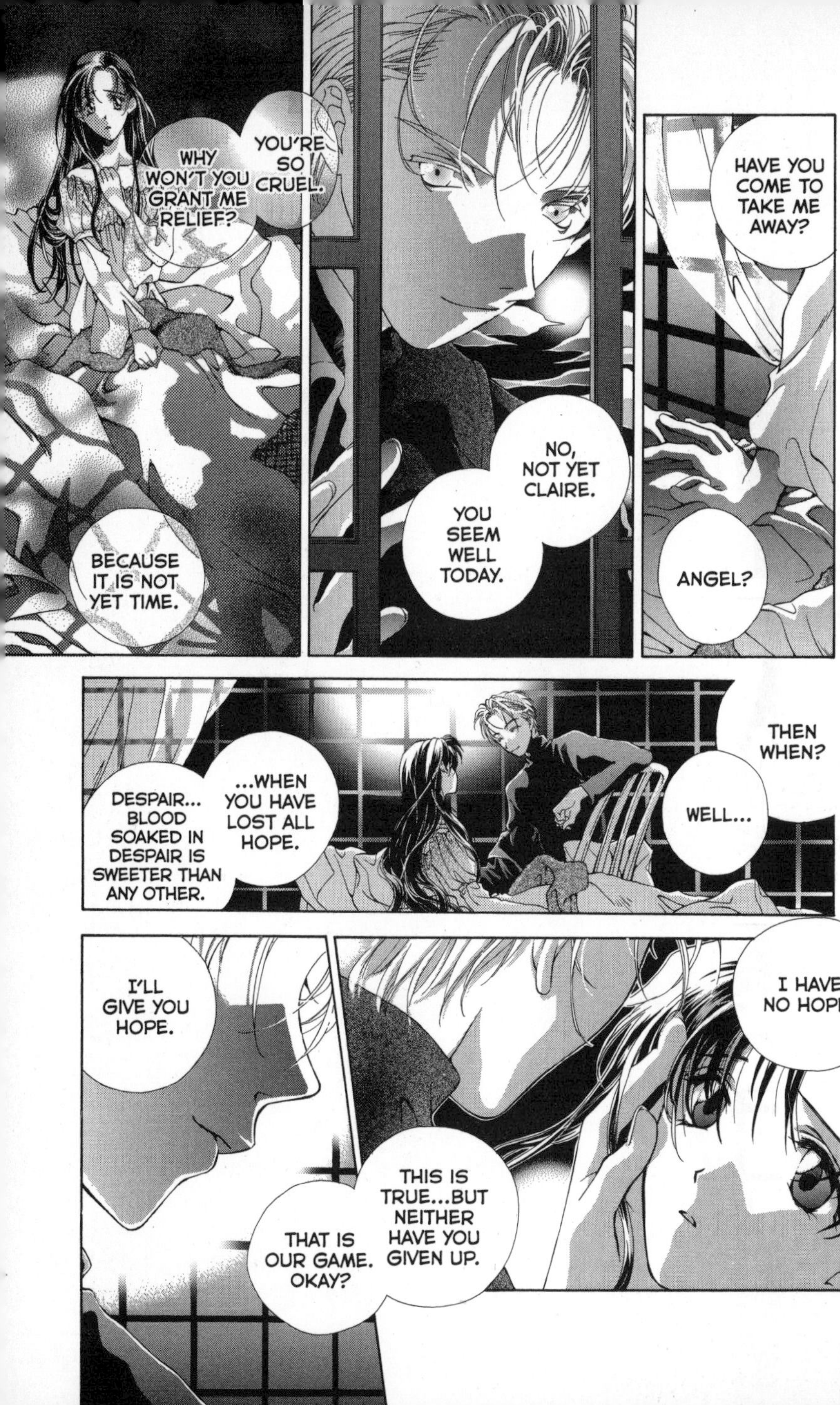

HAVE YOU COME TO TAKE ME AWAY?
ANGEL?
NO, NOT YET CLAIRE.
YOU SEEM WELL TODAY.
YOU'RE SO CRUEL.
WHY WON'T YOU GRANT ME RELIEF?
BECAUSE IT IS NOT YET TIME.
THEN WHEN?
WELL...
...WHEN YOU HAVE LOST ALL HOPE.
DESPAIR... BLOOD SOAKED IN DESPAIR IS SWEETER THAN ANY OTHER.
I HAVE NO HOPE.
THIS IS TRUE...BUT NEITHER HAVE YOU GIVEN UP.
THAT IS OUR GAME. OKAY?
I'LL GIVE YOU HOPE.

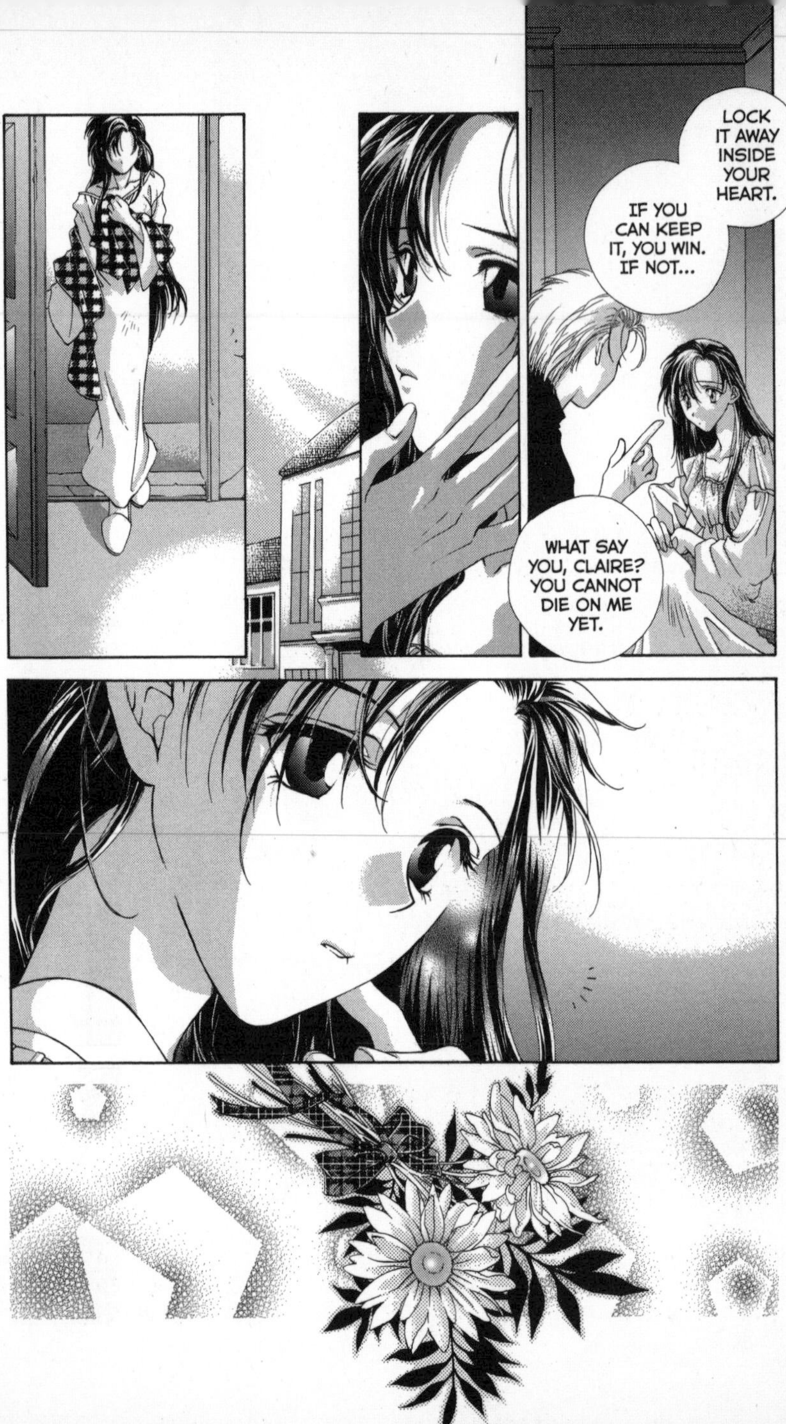
LOCK IT AWAY INSIDE YOUR HEART.
IF YOU CAN KEEP IT, YOU WIN. IF NOT...
WHAT SAY YOU, CLAIRE? YOU CANNOT DIE ON ME YET.

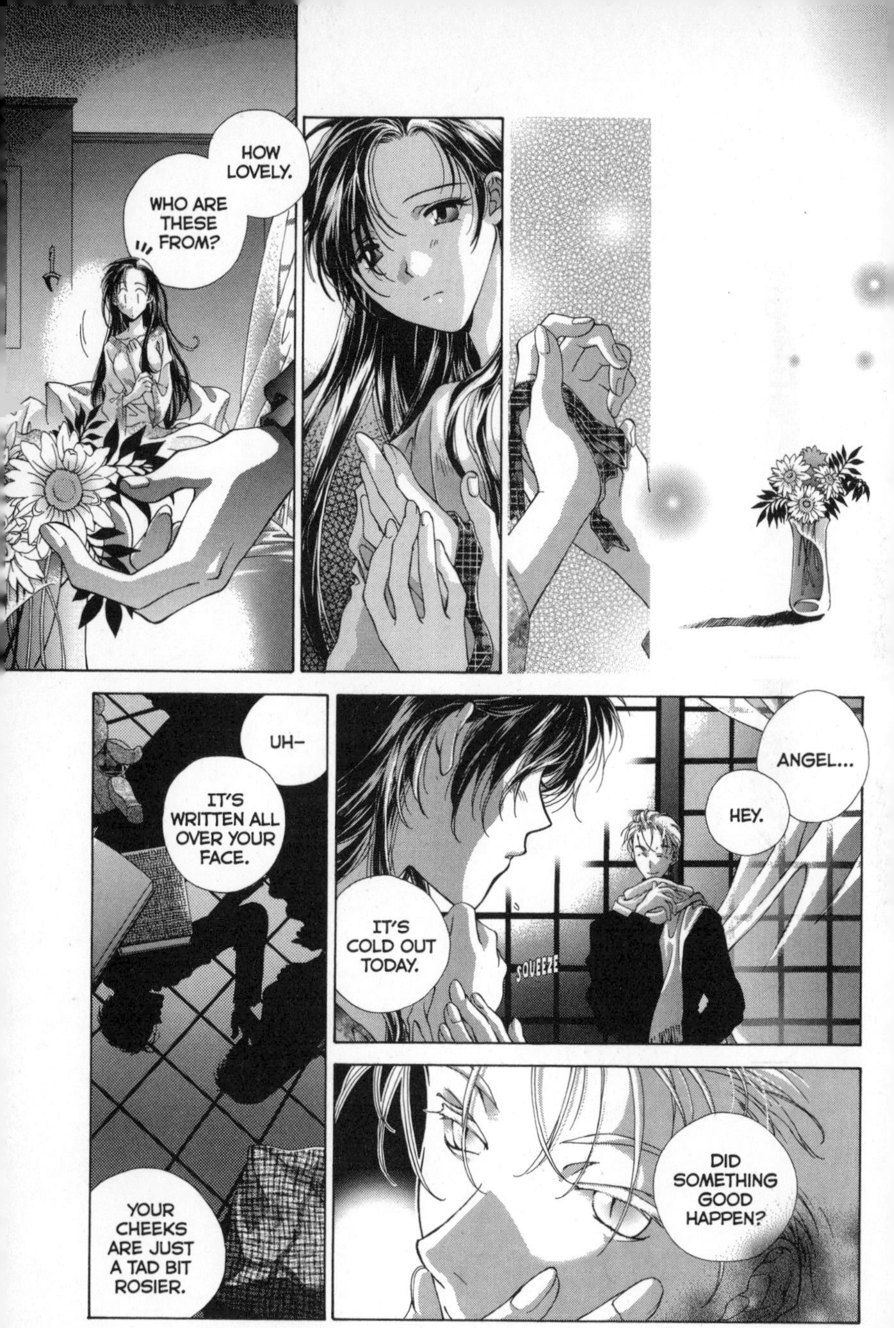
HOW LOVELY.
WHO ARE THESE FROM?
ANGEL...
HEY.
IT'S COLD OUT TODAY.
SQUEEZE
DID SOMETHING GOOD HAPPEN?
UH–
IT'S WRITTEN ALL OVER YOUR FACE.
YOUR CHEEKS ARE JUST A TAD BIT ROSIER.

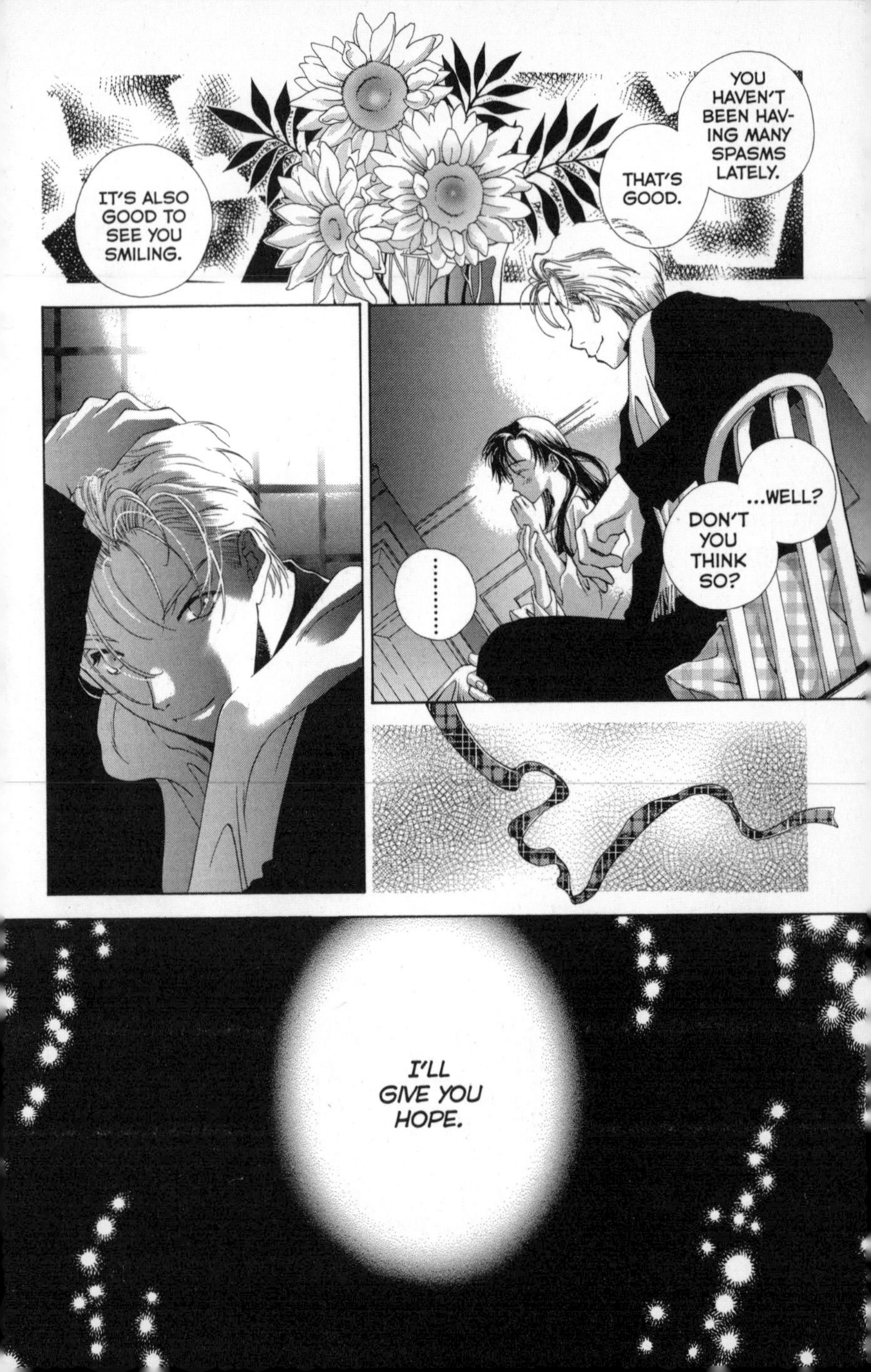
YOU HAVEN'T BEEN HAV-ING MANY SPASMS LATELY.
THAT'S GOOD.
IT'S ALSO GOOD TO SEE YOU SMILING.
...WELL? DON'T YOU THINK SO?
......
I'LL GIVE YOU HOPE.

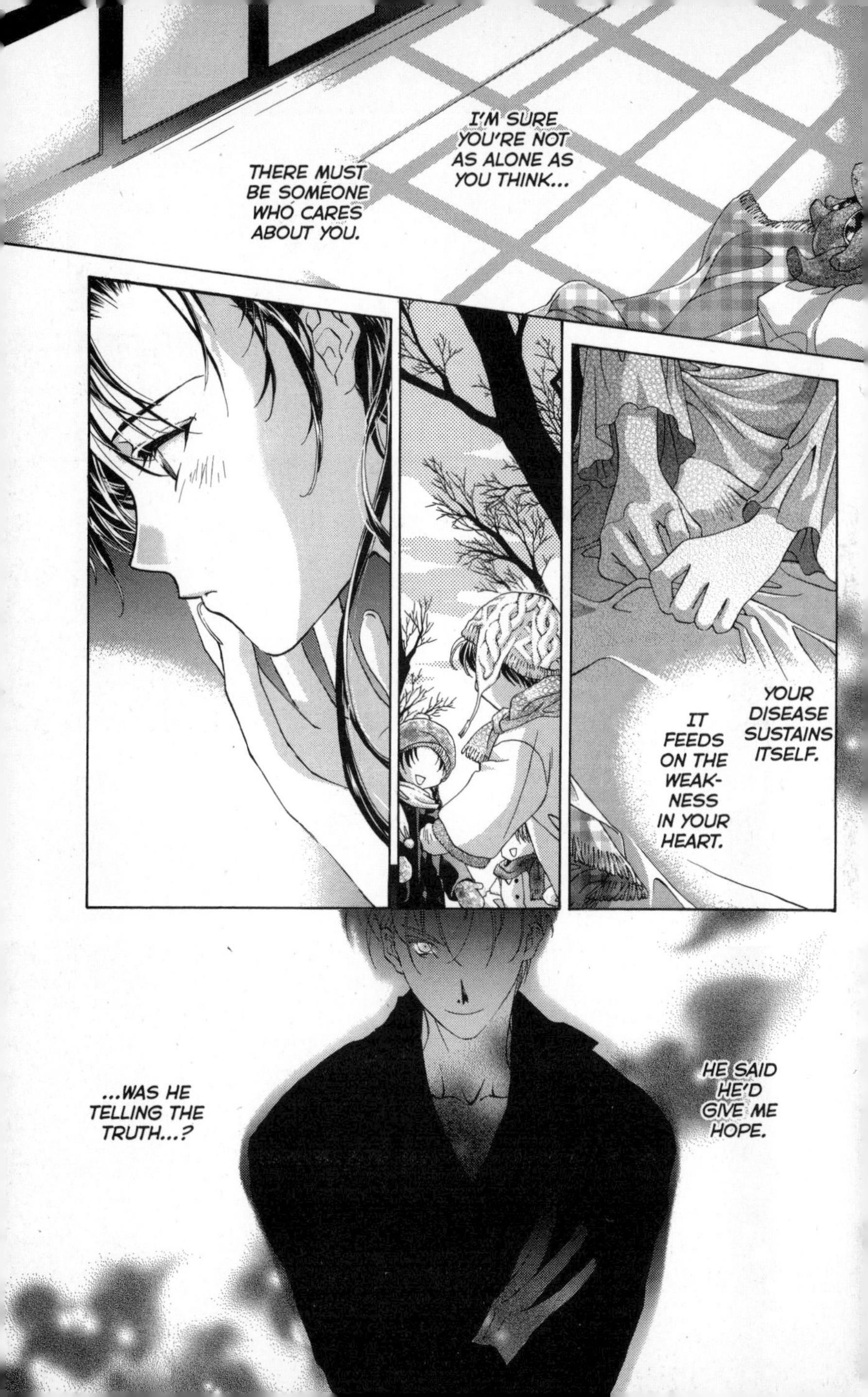
I'M SURE YOU'RE NOT AS ALONE AS YOU THINK...
THERE MUST BE SOMEONE WHO CARES ABOUT YOU.
YOUR DISEASE SUSTAINS ITSELF.
IT FEEDS ON THE WEAK-NESS IN YOUR HEART.
HE SAID HE'D GIVE ME HOPE.
...WAS HE TELLING THE TRUTH...?

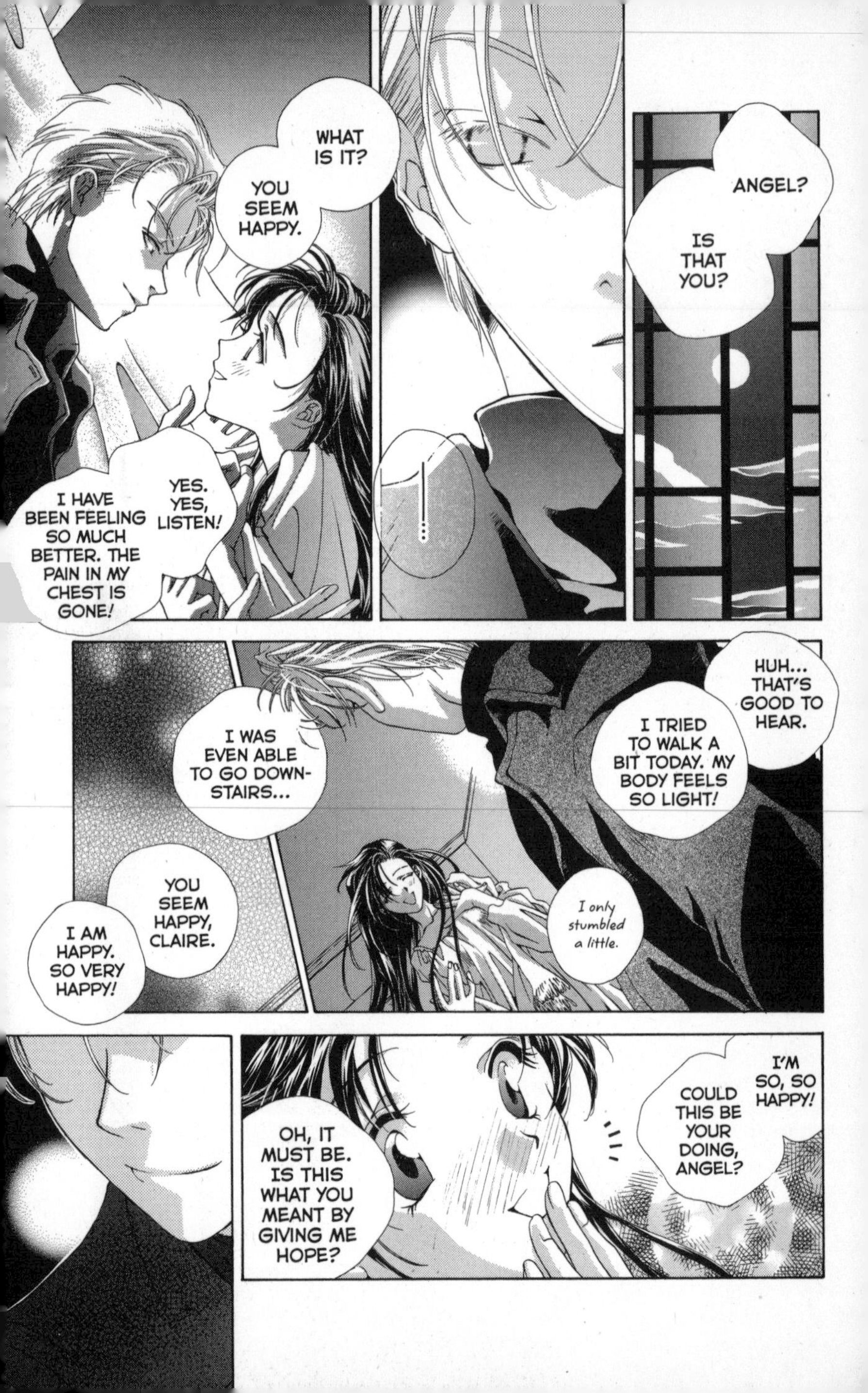
ANGEL?
IS THAT YOU?
!...
WHAT IS IT?
YOU SEEM HAPPY.
YES. YES, LISTEN!
I HAVE BEEN FEELING SO MUCH BETTER. THE PAIN IN MY CHEST IS GONE!
HUH... THAT'S GOOD TO HEAR.
I TRIED TO WALK A BIT TODAY. MY BODY FEELS SO LIGHT!
I WAS EVEN ABLE TO GO DOWN-STAIRS...
I only stumbled a little.
YOU SEEM HAPPY, CLAIRE.
I AM HAPPY. SO VERY HAPPY!
I'M SO, SO HAPPY!
COULD THIS BE YOUR DOING, ANGEL?
OH, IT MUST BE. IS THIS WHAT YOU MEANT BY GIVING ME HOPE?

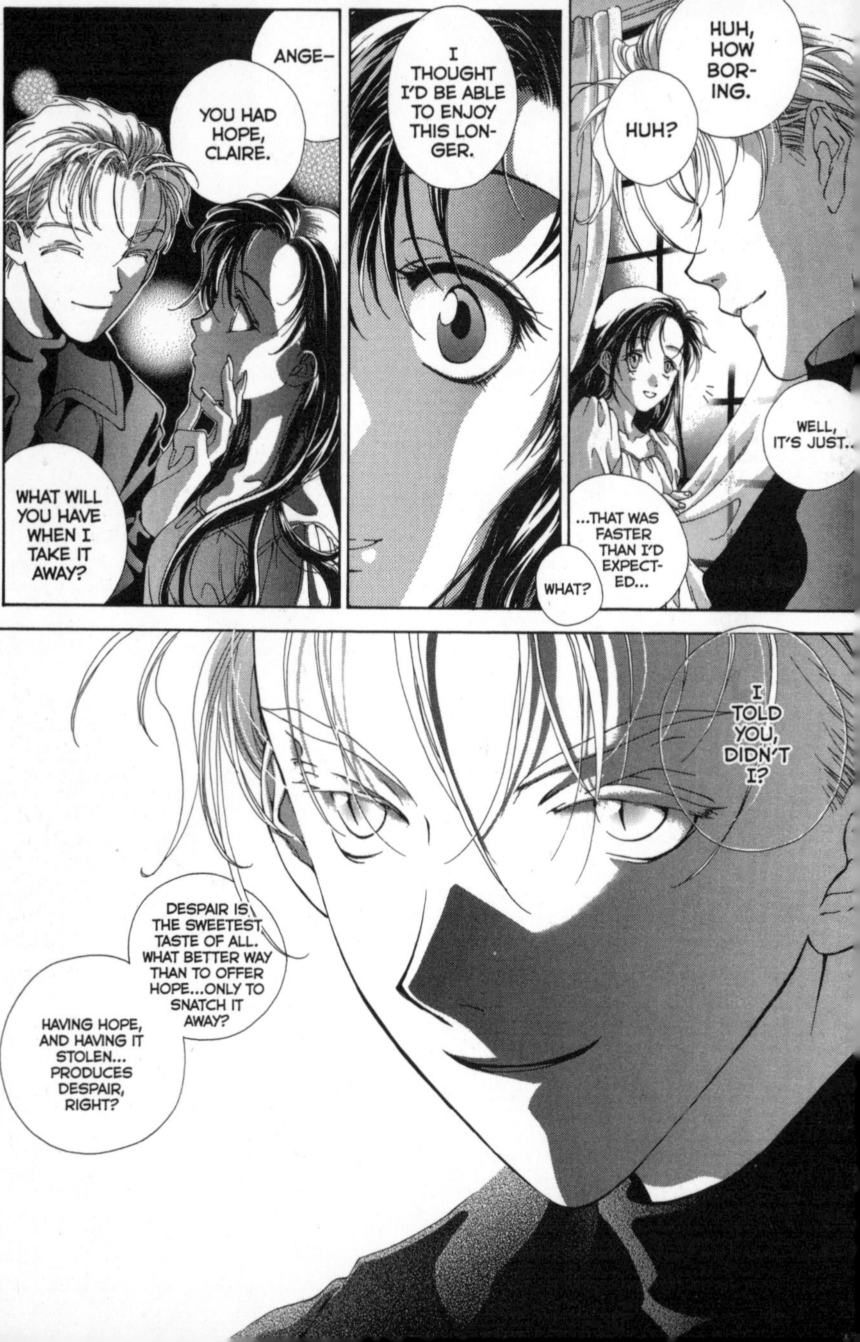
HUH, HOW BOR-ING.
HUH?
WELL, IT'S JUST...
...THAT WAS FASTER THAN I'D EXPECT-ED...
WHAT?
I THOUGHT I'D BE ABLE TO ENJOY THIS LON-GER.
ANGE—
YOU HAD HOPE, CLAIRE.
WHAT WILL YOU HAVE WHEN I TAKE IT AWAY?
I TOLD YOU, DIDN'T I?
DESPAIR IS THE SWEETEST TASTE OF ALL. WHAT BETTER WAY THAN TO OFFER HOPE...ONLY TO SNATCH IT AWAY?
HAVING HOPE, AND HAVING IT STOLEN... PRODUCES DESPAIR, RIGHT?

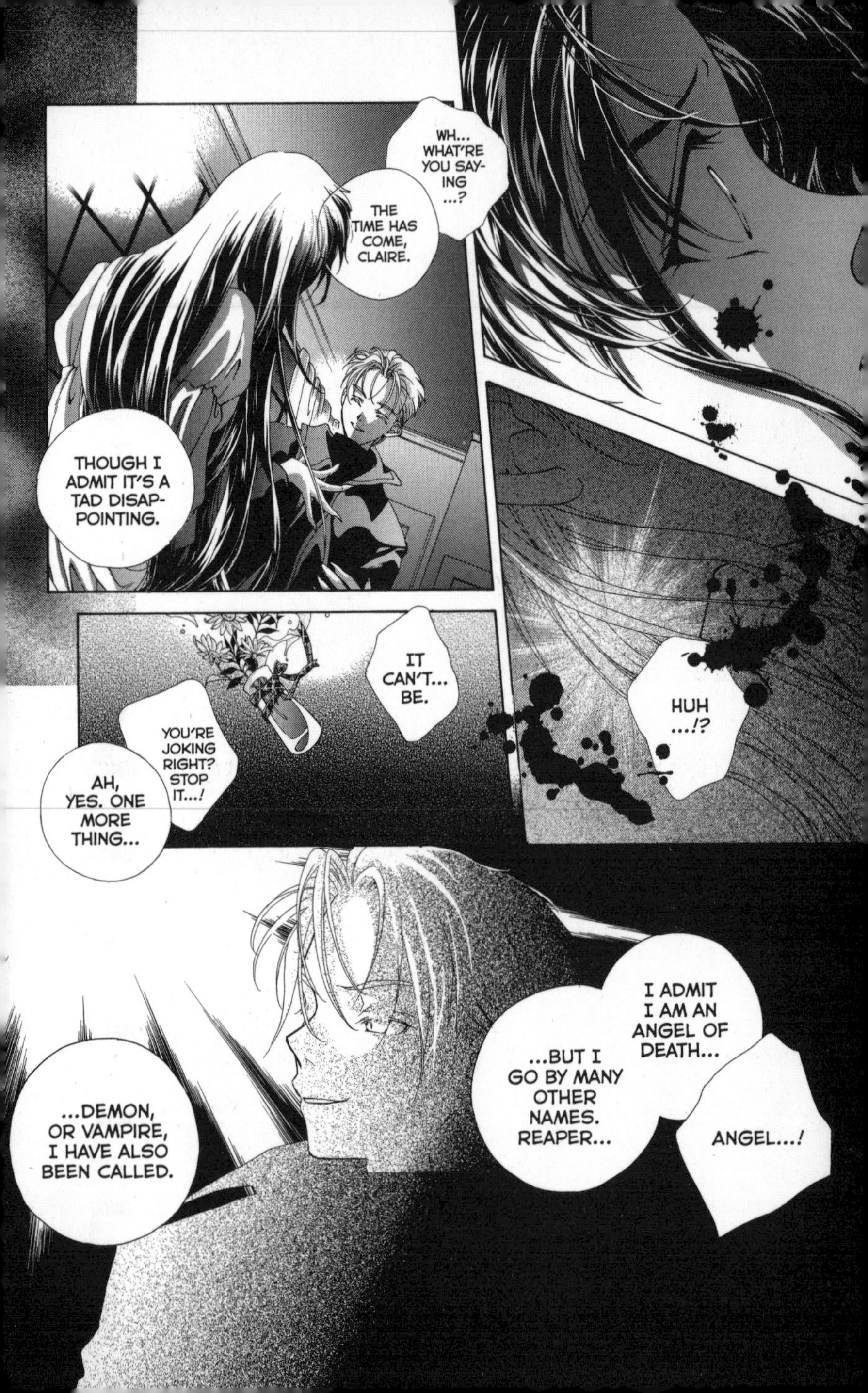
THE TIME HAS COME, CLAIRE.
WH... WHAT'RE YOU SAYING...?
THOUGH I ADMIT IT'S A TAD DISAPPOINTING.
HUH ...!?
IT CAN'T... BE.
YOU'RE JOKING RIGHT? STOP IT...!
AH, YES. ONE MORE THING...
ANGEL...!
I ADMIT I AM AN ANGEL OF DEATH...
...BUT I GO BY MANY OTHER NAMES. REAPER...
...DEMON, OR VAMPIRE, I HAVE ALSO BEEN CALLED.

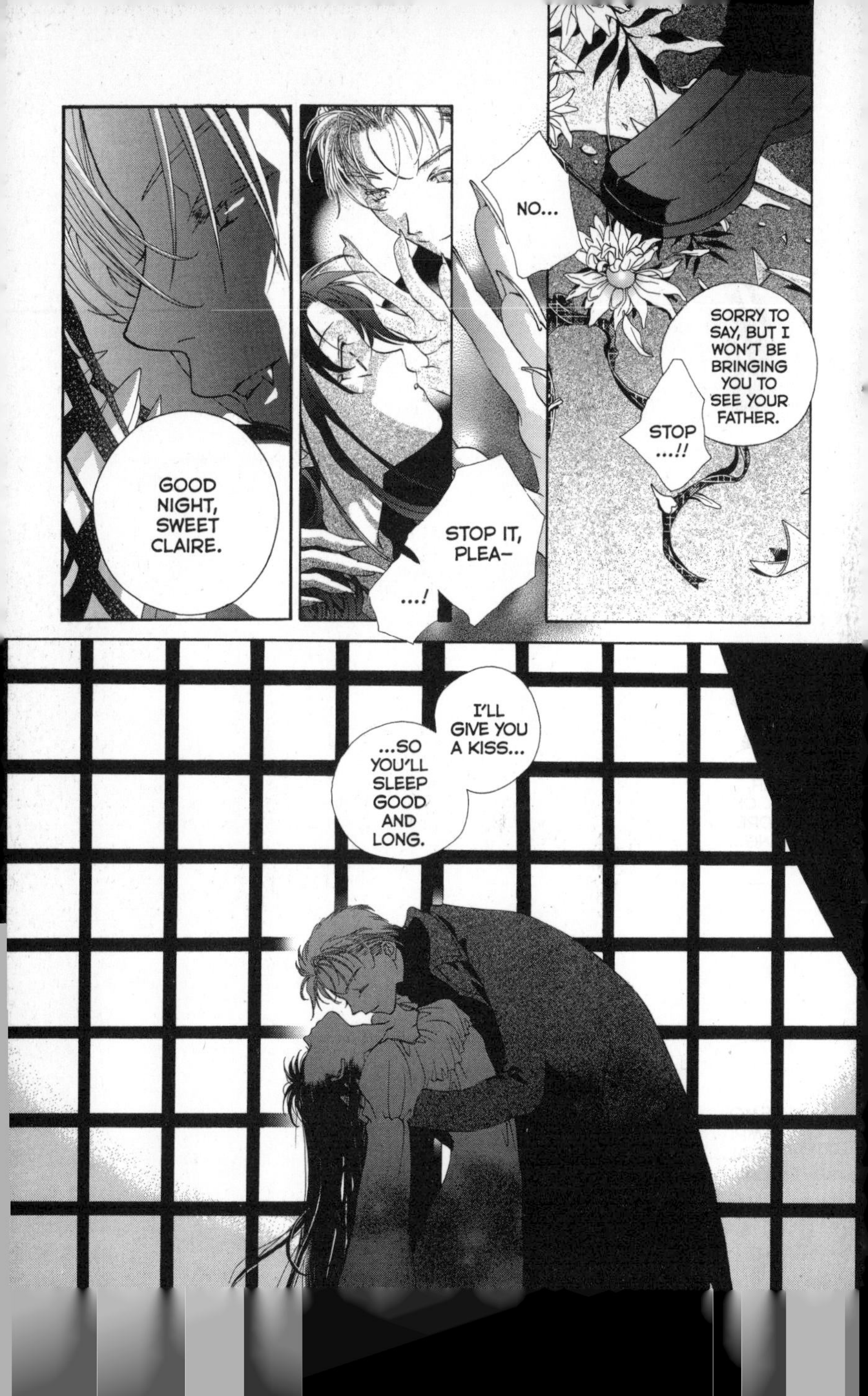
NO...
SORRY TO SAY, BUT I WON'T BE BRINGING YOU TO SEE YOUR FATHER.
STOP ...!!
STOP IT, PLEA–
...!
GOOD NIGHT, SWEET CLAIRE.
I'LL GIVE YOU A KISS...
...SO YOU'LL SLEEP GOOD AND LONG.

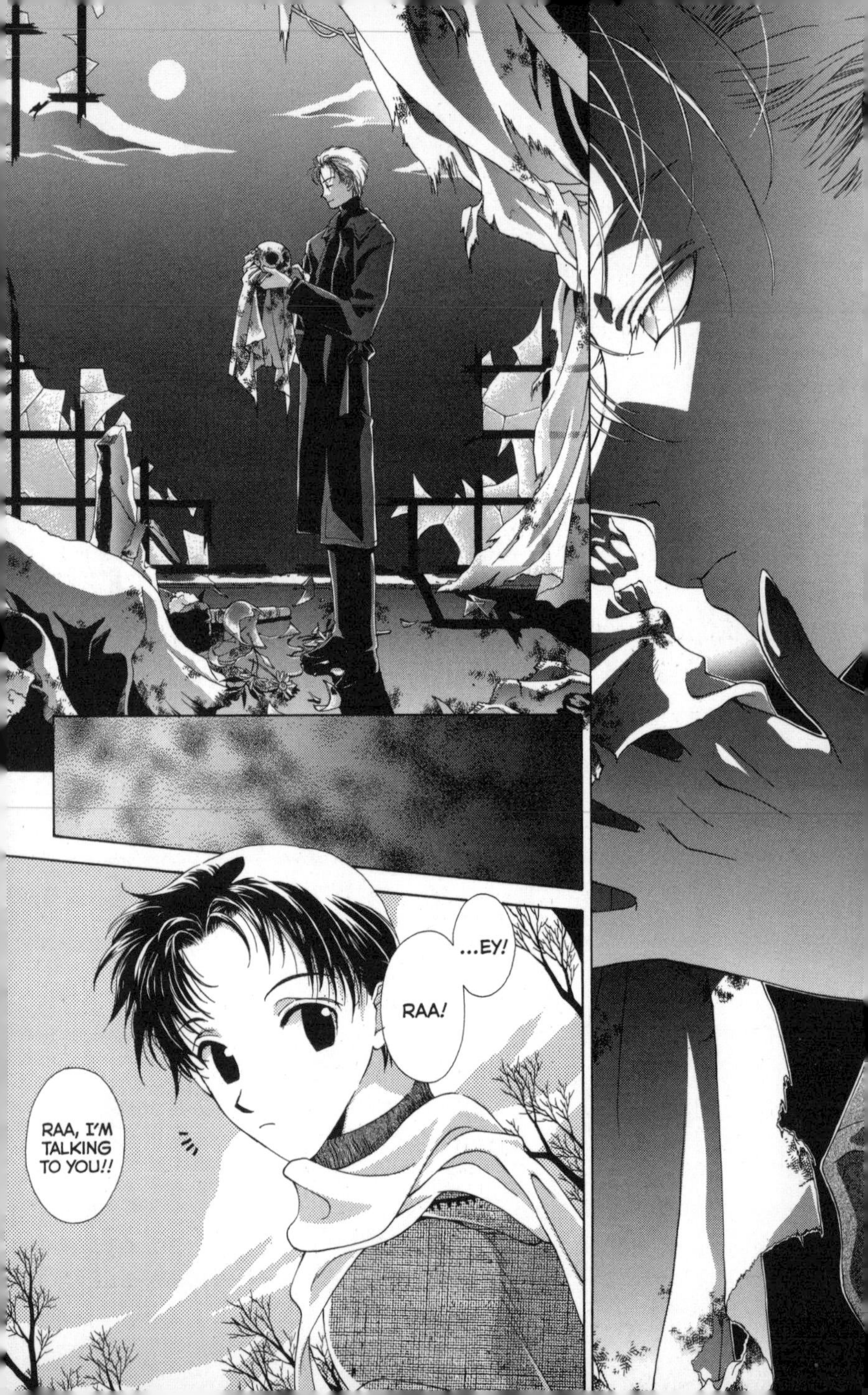
...EY!
RAA!
RAA, I'M TALKING TO YOU!!

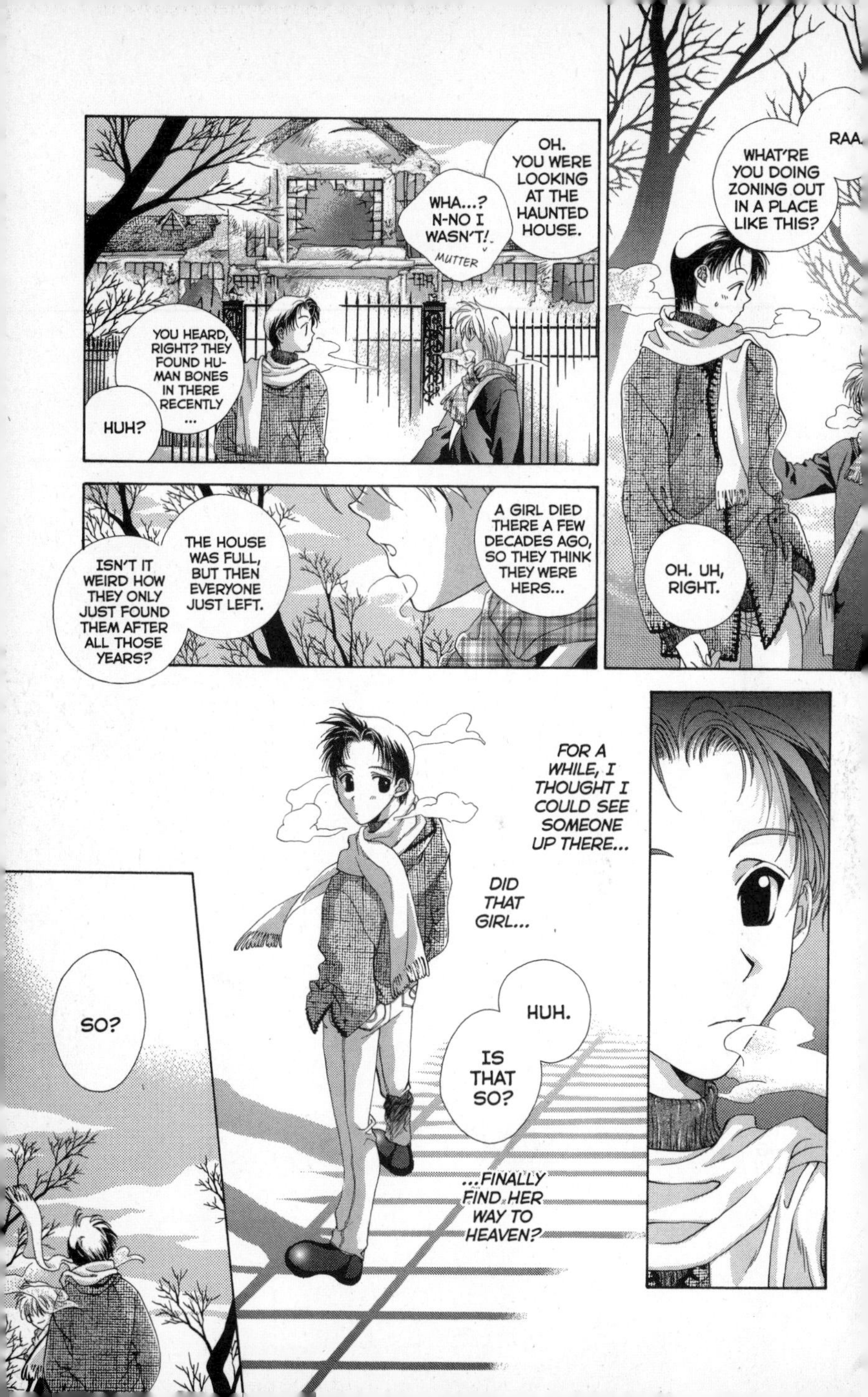
RAA.
WHAT'RE YOU DOING ZONING OUT IN A PLACE LIKE THIS?
OH. UH, RIGHT.
OH. YOU WERE LOOKING AT THE HAUNTED HOUSE.
WHA...? N-NO I WASN'T!
MUTTER
YOU HEARD, RIGHT? THEY FOUND HU-MAN BONES IN THERE RECENTLY...
HUH?
A GIRL DIED THERE A FEW DECADES AGO, SO THEY THINK THEY WERE HERS...
THE HOUSE WAS FULL, BUT THEN EVERYONE JUST LEFT.
ISN'T IT WEIRD HOW THEY ONLY JUST FOUND THEM AFTER ALL THOSE YEARS?
FOR A WHILE, I THOUGHT I COULD SEE SOMEONE UP THERE...
DID THAT GIRL...
...FINALLY FIND HER WAY TO HEAVEN?
HUH.
IS THAT SO?
SO?

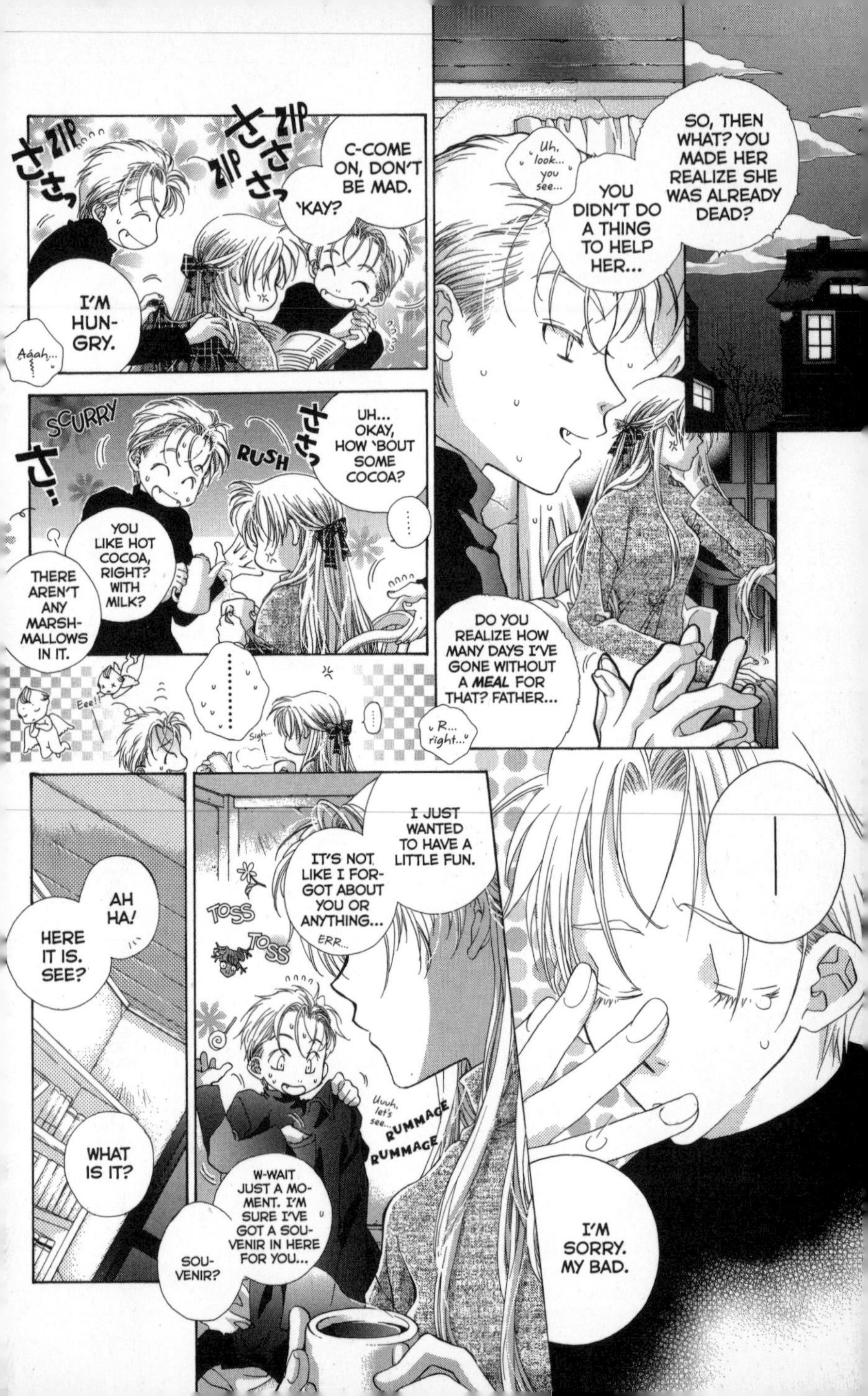
SO, THEN WHAT? YOU MADE HER REALIZE SHE WAS ALREADY DEAD?
YOU DIDN'T DO A THING TO HELP HER...
Uh, look... you see...
DO YOU REALIZE HOW MANY DAYS I'VE GONE WITHOUT A *MEAL* FOR THAT? FATHER...
R... right...
C-COME ON, DON'T BE MAD. 'KAY?
ZIP
ZIP
ZIP
I'M HUNGRY.
Aáah...
UH... OKAY, HOW 'BOUT SOME COCOA?
RUSH
SCURRY
......
YOU LIKE HOT COCOA, RIGHT? WITH MILK?
THERE AREN'T ANY MARSHMALLOWS IN IT.
....
....
Sigh...
Eee!!
I'M SORRY. MY BAD.
I JUST WANTED TO HAVE A LITTLE FUN.
IT'S NOT LIKE I FORGOT ABOUT YOU OR ANYTHING...
ERR...
TOSS
TOSS
Uuuh, let's see...
RUMMAGE
RUMMAGE
W-WAIT JUST A MOMENT. I'M SURE I'VE GOT A SOUVENIR IN HERE FOR YOU...
SOUVENIR?
AH HA! HERE IT IS. SEE?
WHAT IS IT?

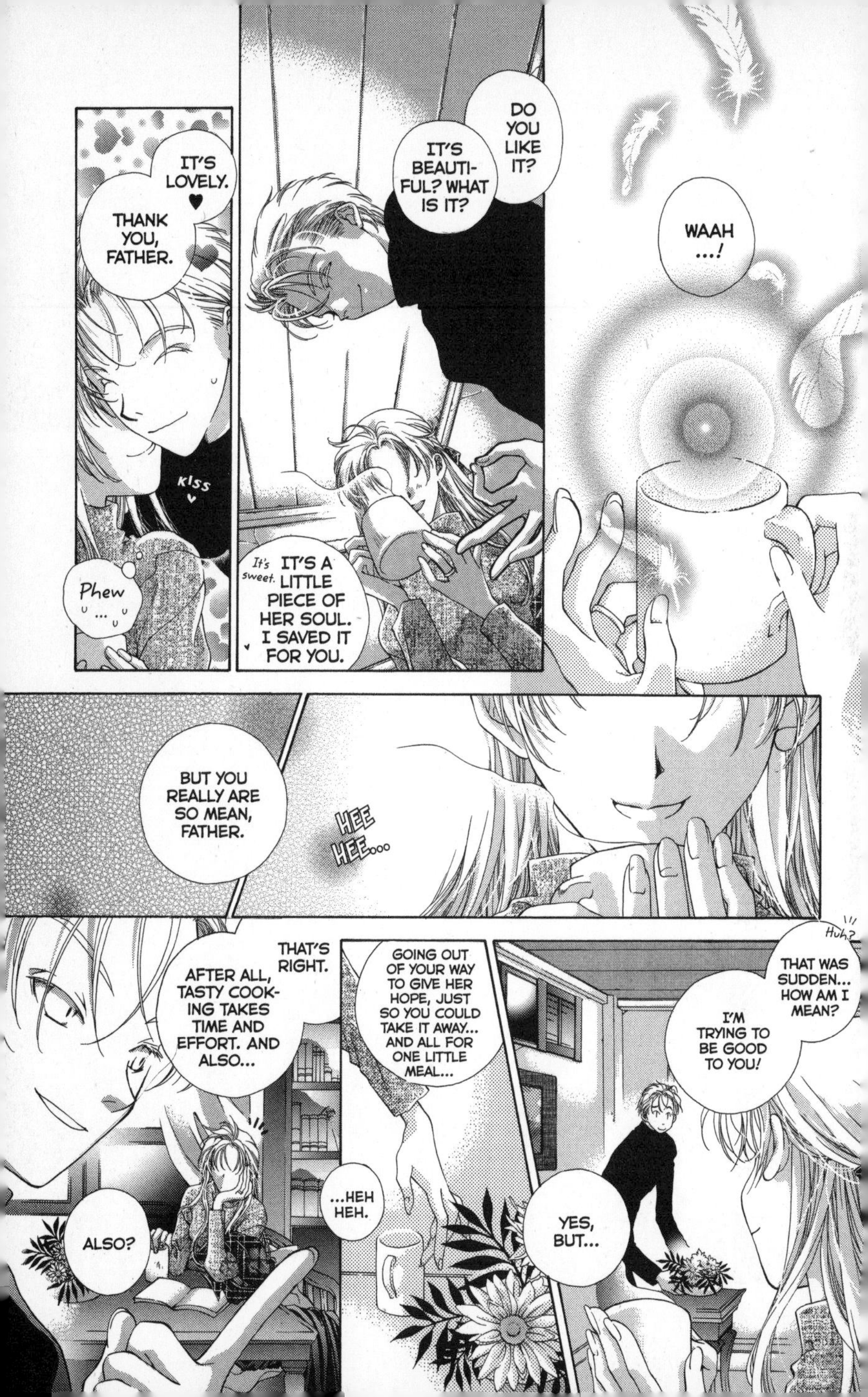
WAAH ...!
DO YOU LIKE IT?
IT'S BEAUTI-FUL? WHAT IS IT?
IT'S A LITTLE PIECE OF HER SOUL. I SAVED IT FOR YOU.
It's sweet.
IT'S LOVELY.
THANK YOU, FATHER.
KISS
Phew ...
HEE HEE...
BUT YOU REALLY ARE SO MEAN, FATHER.
Huh?
THAT WAS SUDDEN... HOW AM I MEAN?
I'M TRYING TO BE GOOD TO YOU!
YES, BUT...
GOING OUT OF YOUR WAY TO GIVE HER HOPE, JUST SO YOU COULD TAKE IT AWAY... AND ALL FOR ONE LITTLE MEAL...
...HEH HEH.
THAT'S RIGHT.
AFTER ALL, TASTY COOK-ING TAKES TIME AND EFFORT. AND ALSO...
ALSO?

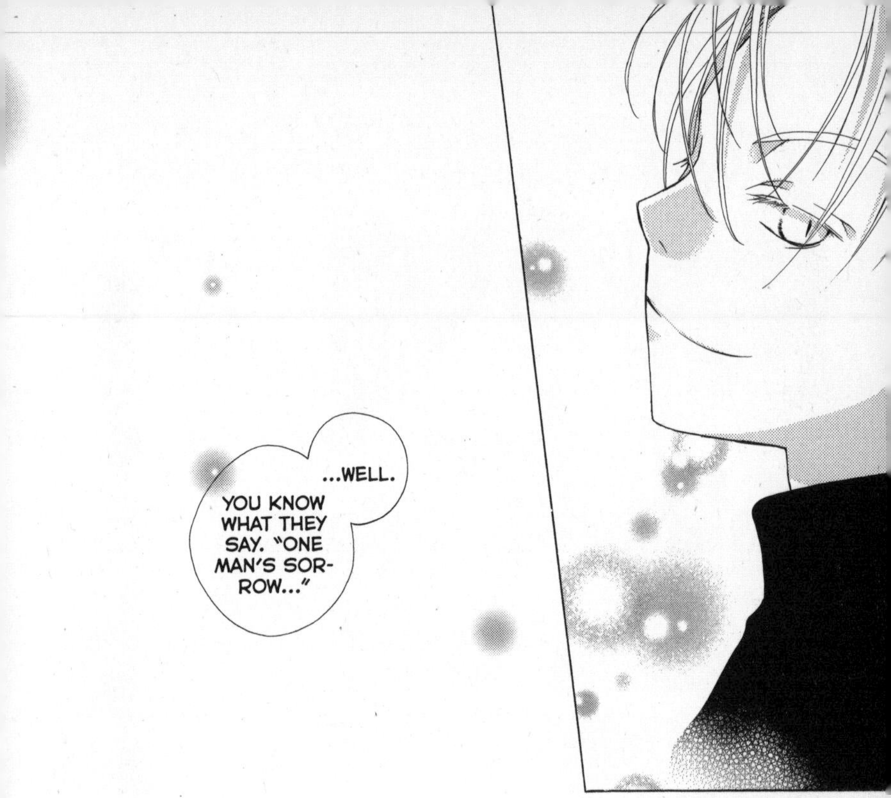
...WELL.
YOU KNOW WHAT THEY SAY. "ONE MAN'S SOR-ROW..."

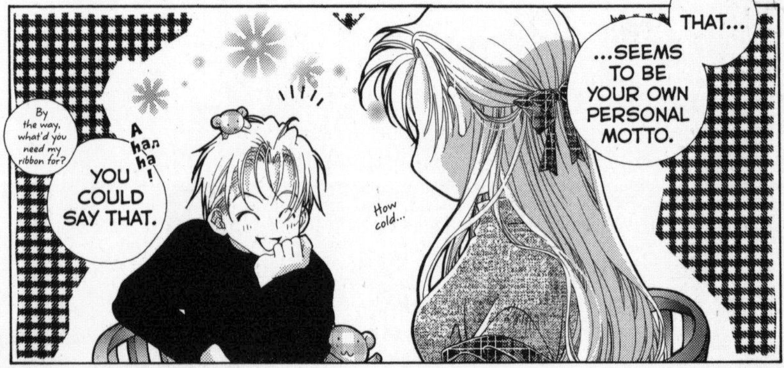
THAT...
...SEEMS TO BE YOUR OWN PERSONAL MOTTO.
How cold...
A ha♪ ha!
YOU COULD SAY THAT.
By the way, what'd you need my ribbon for?

Honey blood ✝ END

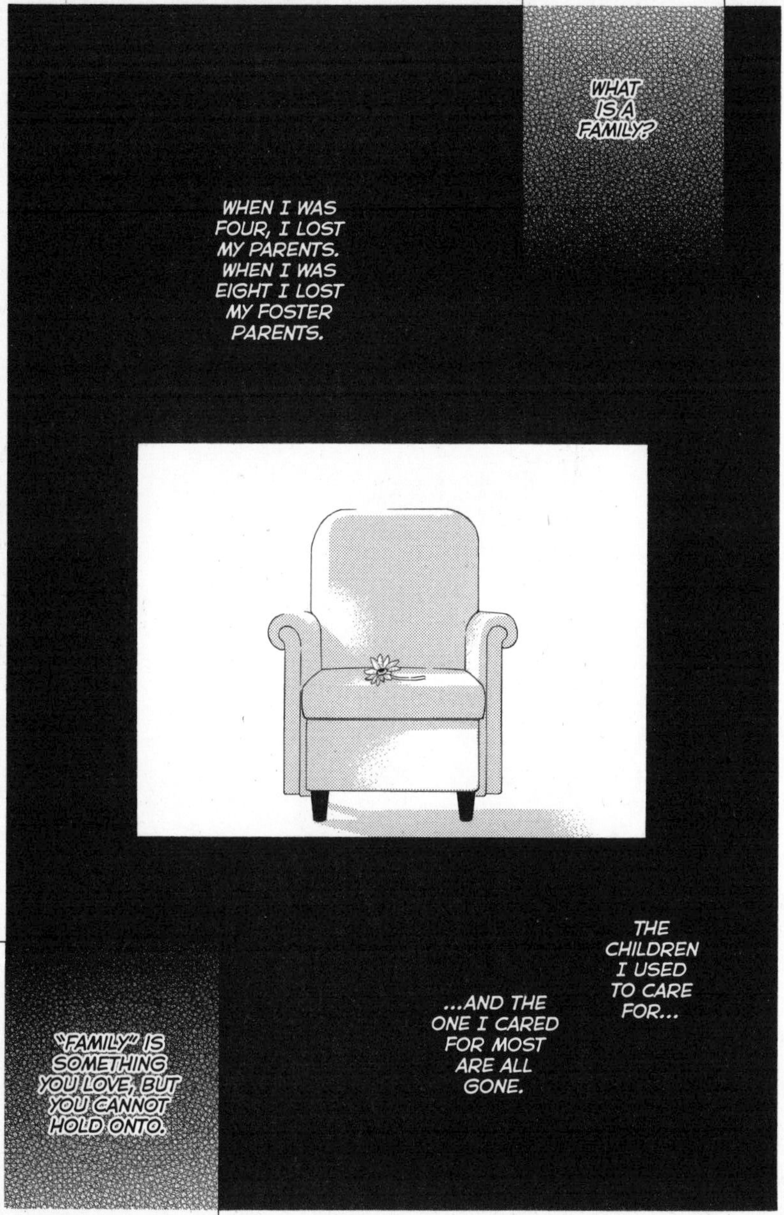
WHAT IS A FAMILY?
WHEN I WAS FOUR, I LOST MY PARENTS. WHEN I WAS EIGHT I LOST MY FOSTER PARENTS.
THE CHILDREN I USED TO CARE FOR...
...AND THE ONE I CARED FOR MOST ARE ALL GONE.
"FAMILY" IS SOMETHING YOU LOVE, BUT YOU CANNOT HOLD ONTO.

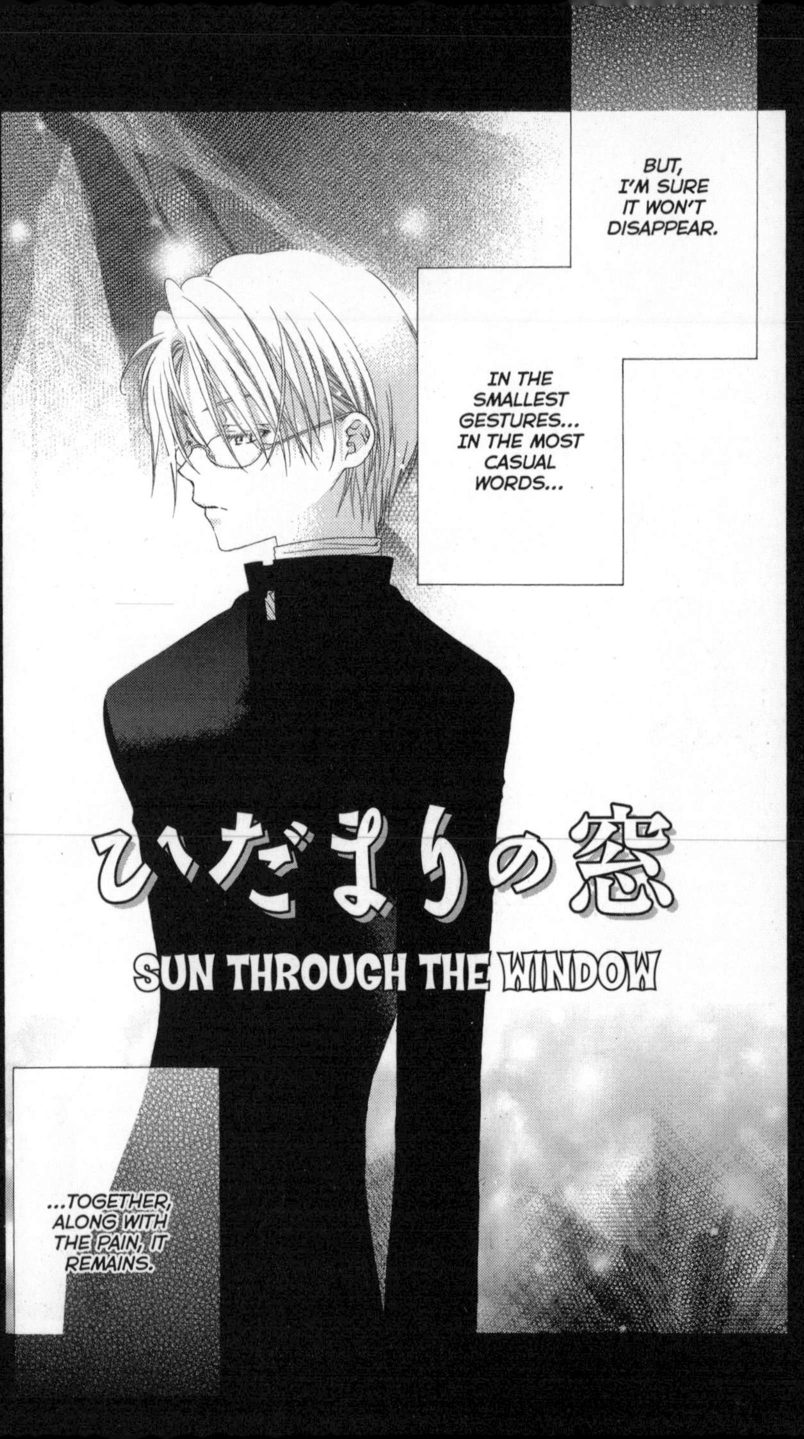
BUT, I'M SURE IT WON'T DISAPPEAR.
IN THE SMALLEST GESTURES... IN THE MOST CASUAL WORDS...
ひだまりの窓
SUN THROUGH THE WINDOW
...TOGETHER, ALONG WITH THE PAIN, IT REMAINS.

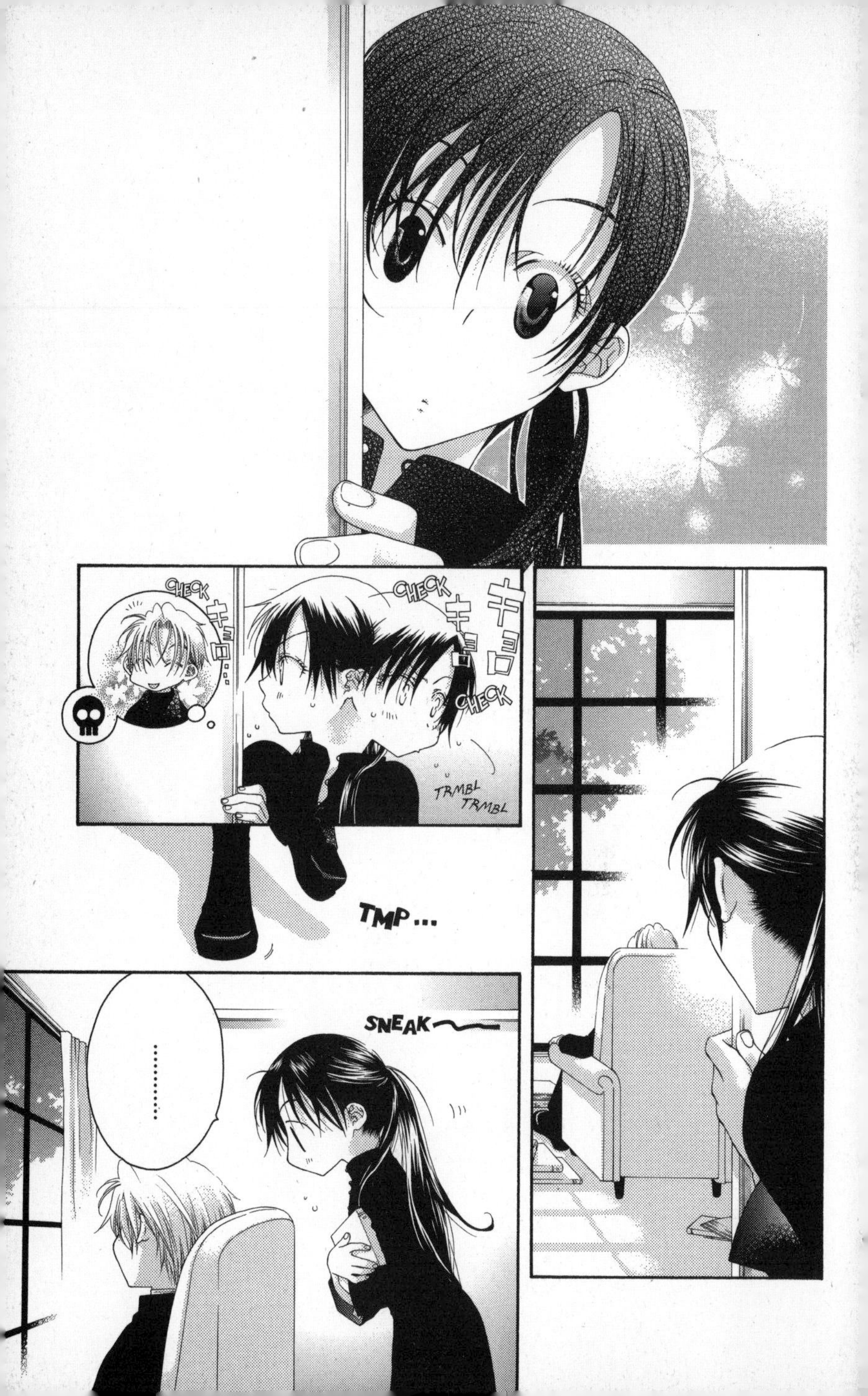
CHECK
キョロ
キョロ
CHECK
CHECK
キョロ...
TRMBL TRMBL
TMP...
SNEAK~
......

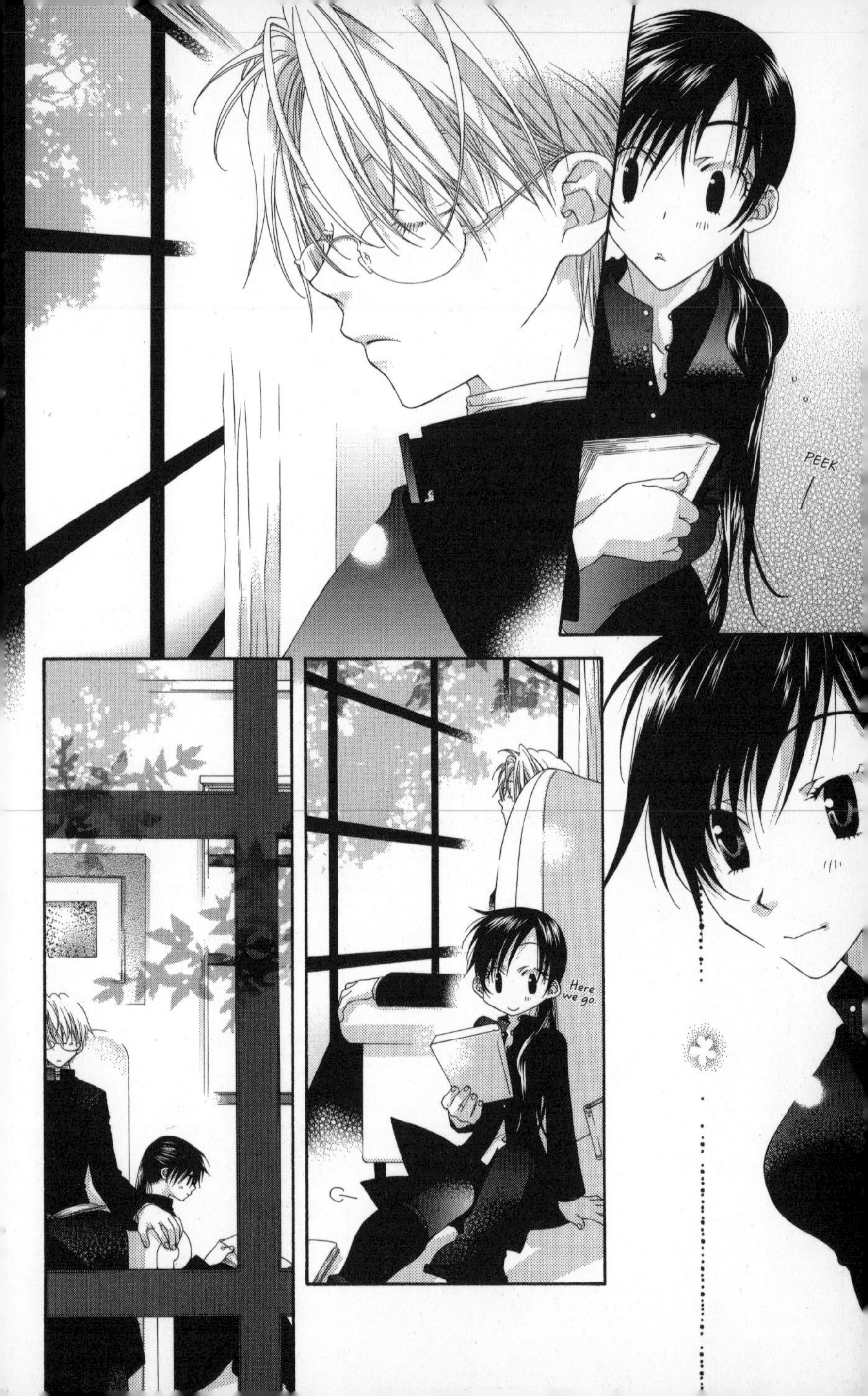
PEEK
Here we go.

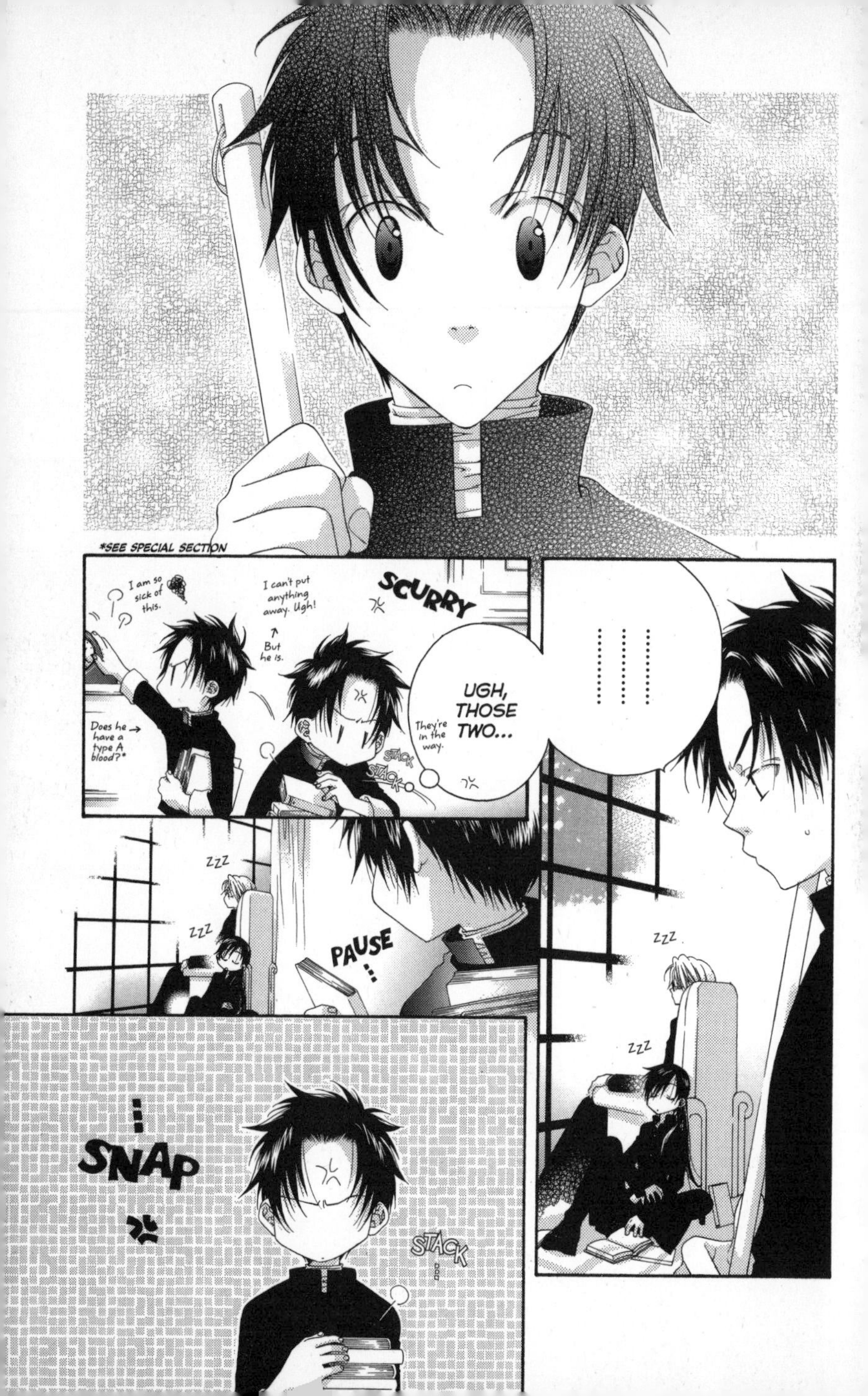
......
ZZZ
ZZZ
UGH, THOSE TWO...
They're in the way.
SCURRY
I can't put anything away. Ugh!
But he is.
I am so sick of this.
Does he have a type A blood?*
STACK
STACK
PAUSE...
ZZZ
ZZZ
...SNAP
STACK

*SEE SPECIAL SECTION

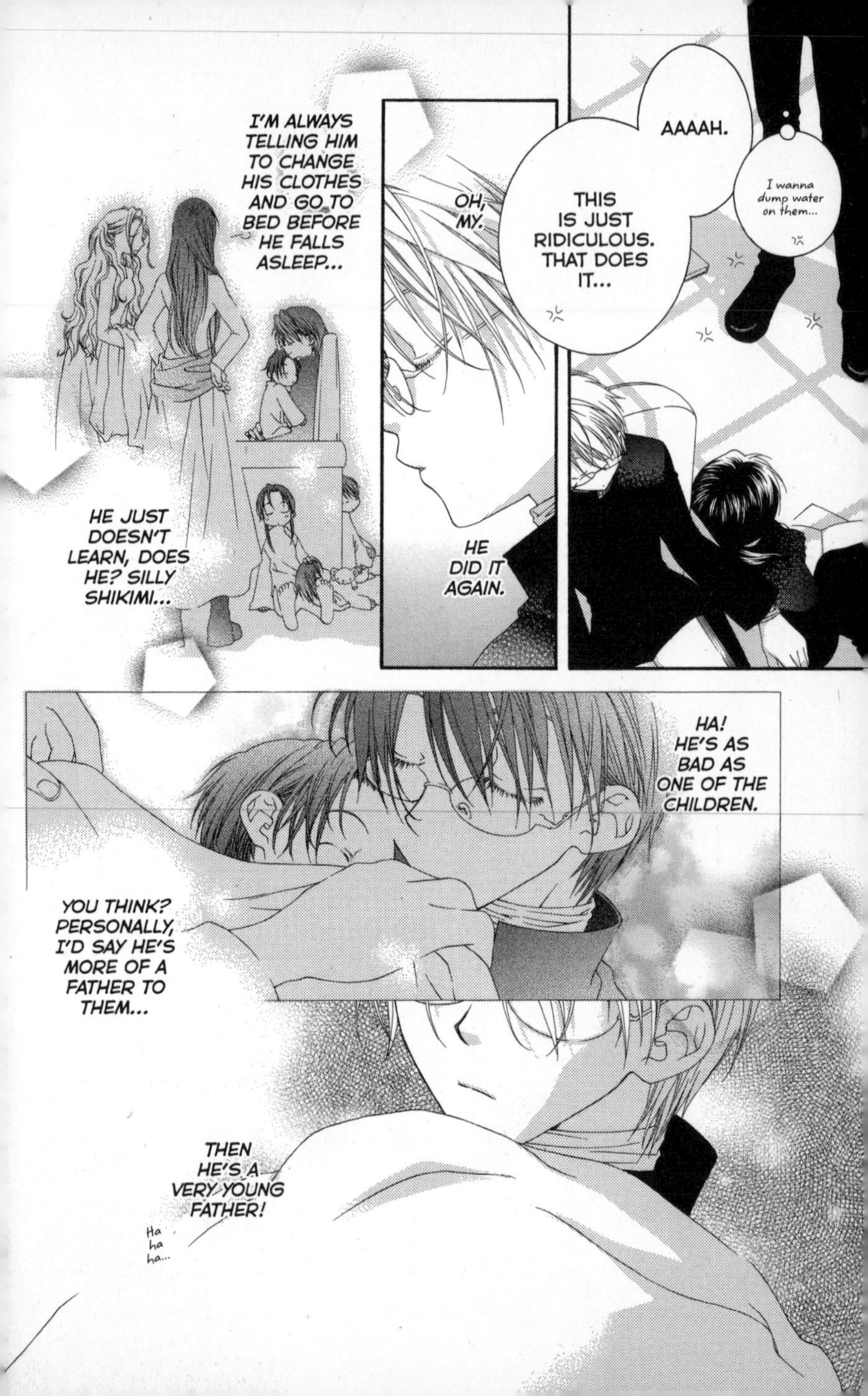
AAAAH.
THIS IS JUST RIDICULOUS. THAT DOES IT...
I wanna dump water on them...
OH, MY.
HE DID IT AGAIN.
I'M ALWAYS TELLING HIM TO CHANGE HIS CLOTHES AND GO TO BED BEFORE HE FALLS ASLEEP...
HE JUST DOESN'T LEARN, DOES HE? SILLY SHIKIMI...
HA! HE'S AS BAD AS ONE OF THE CHILDREN.
YOU THINK? PERSONALLY, I'D SAY HE'S MORE OF A FATHER TO THEM...
THEN HE'S A VERY YOUNG FATHER!
Ha ha ha...

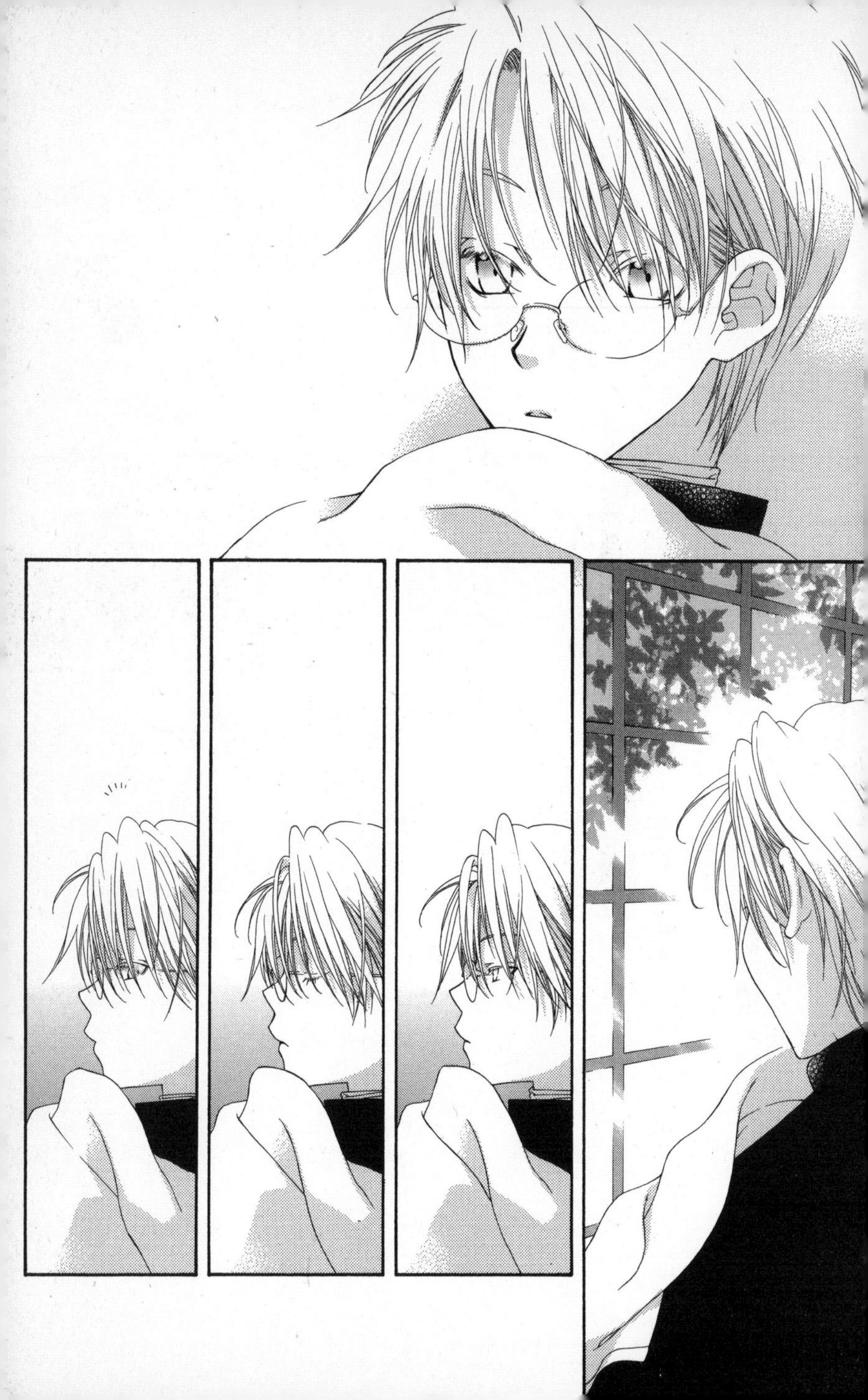

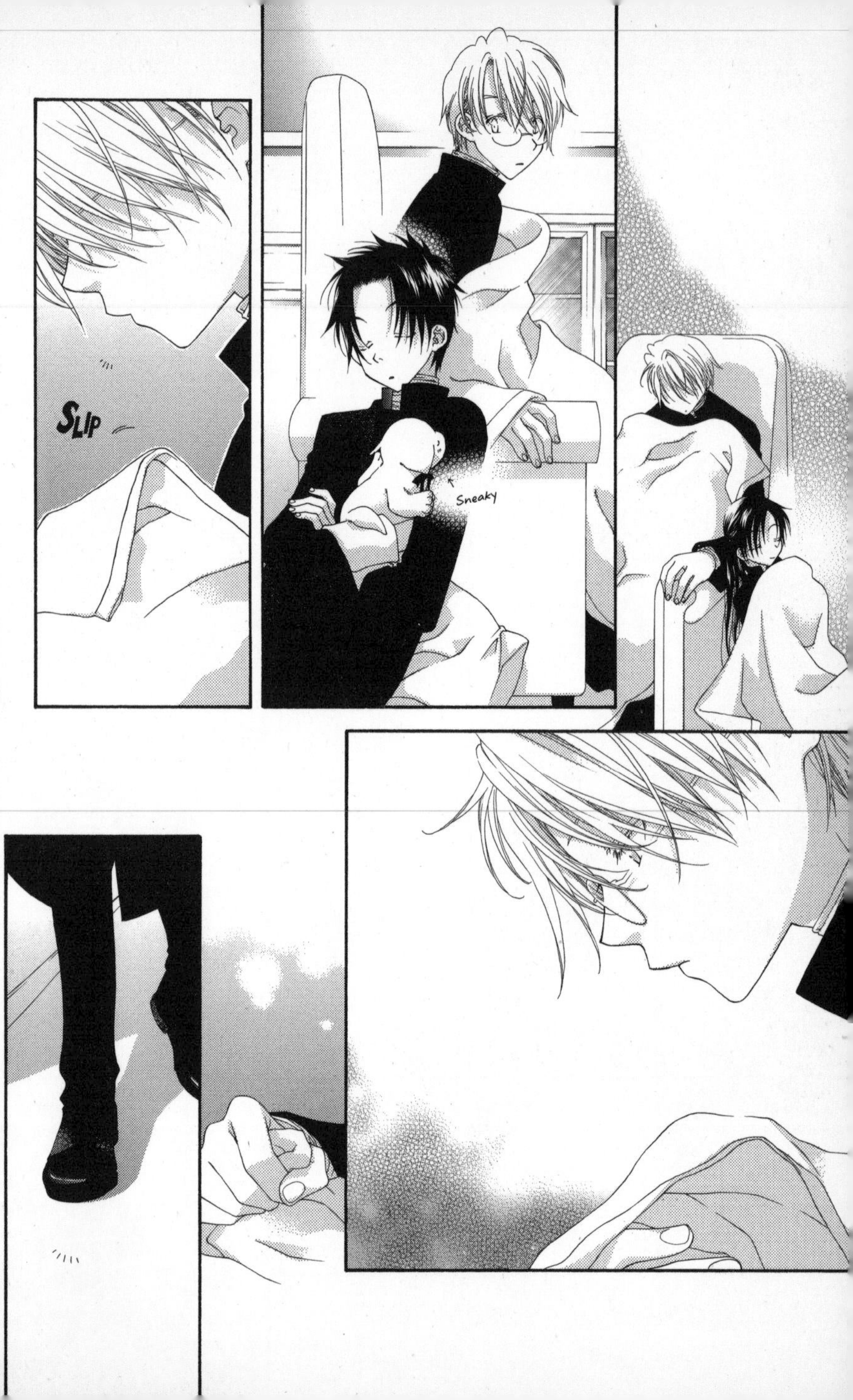
Sneaky
SLIP

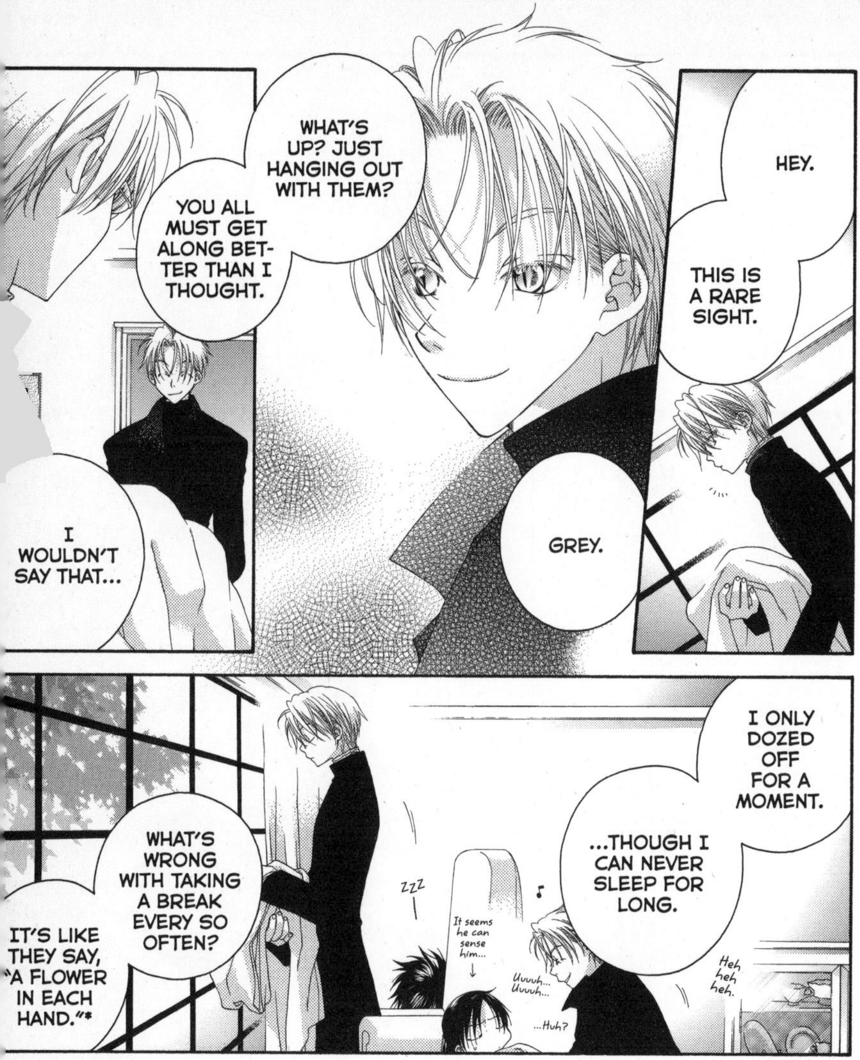
HEY.
THIS IS A RARE SIGHT.
GREY.
WHAT'S UP? JUST HANGING OUT WITH THEM?
YOU ALL MUST GET ALONG BET-TER THAN I THOUGHT.
I WOULDN'T SAY THAT...
I ONLY DOZED OFF FOR A MOMENT.
...THOUGH I CAN NEVER SLEEP FOR LONG.
Heh heh heh.
...Huh?
Uuuuh... Uuuuh...
It seems he can sense him...
ZZZ
WHAT'S WRONG WITH TAKING A BREAK EVERY SO OFTEN?
IT'S LIKE THEY SAY, "A FLOWER IN EACH HAND."*

*SEE TRANSLATOR'S NOTES

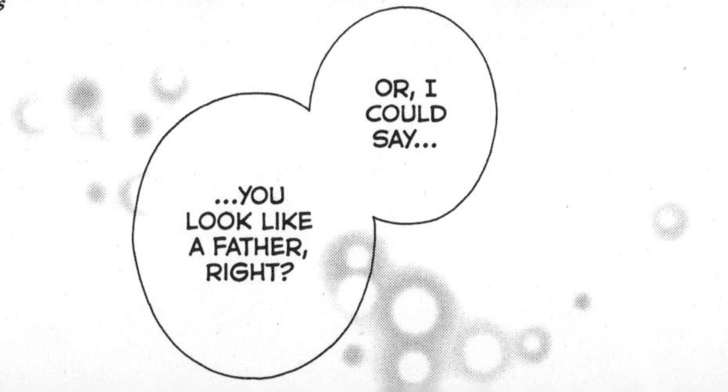
OR, I COULD SAY...
...YOU LOOK LIKE A FATHER, RIGHT?

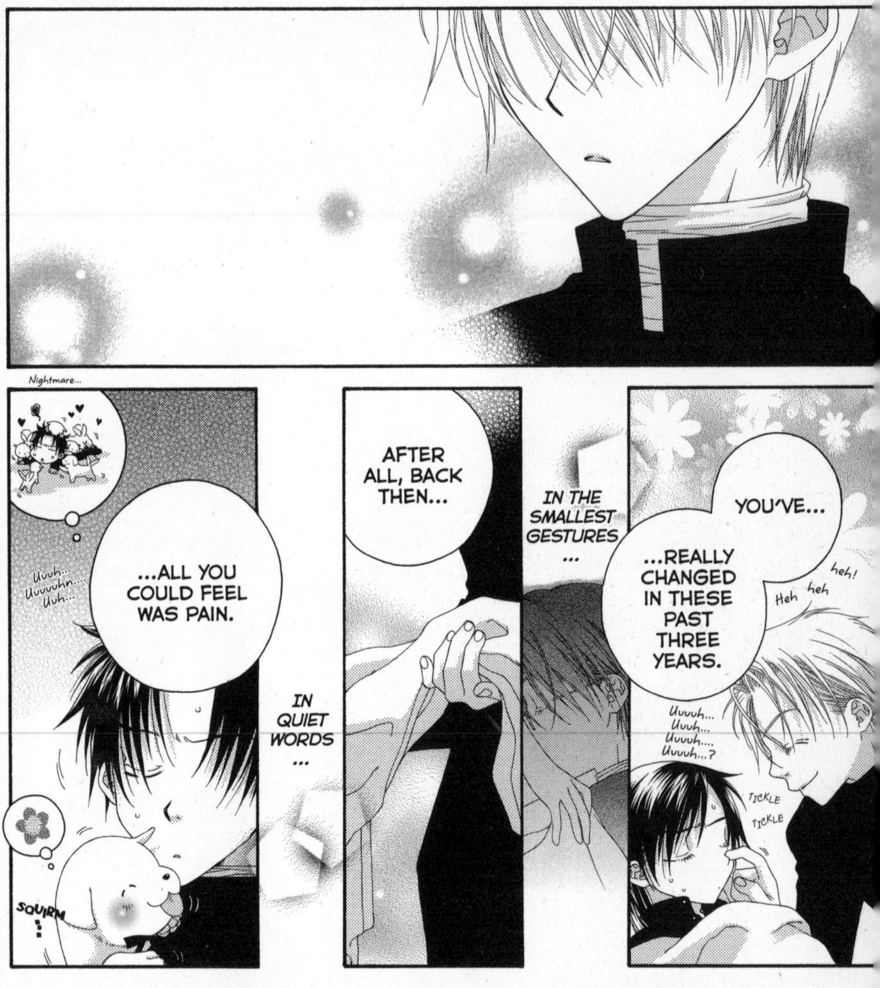
YOU'VE...
...REALLY CHANGED IN THESE PAST THREE YEARS.
Heh heh heh!
IN THE SMALLEST GESTURES...
Uuuuh... Uuuh... Uuuuh.... Uuuuh...?
TICKLE TICKLE
AFTER ALL, BACK THEN...
IN QUIET WORDS...
...ALL YOU COULD FEEL WAS PAIN.
Nightmare...
Uuuh... Uuuuuhn.... Uuh...
SQUIRM

...IT WON'T FADE AWAY.

I KNOW IT.

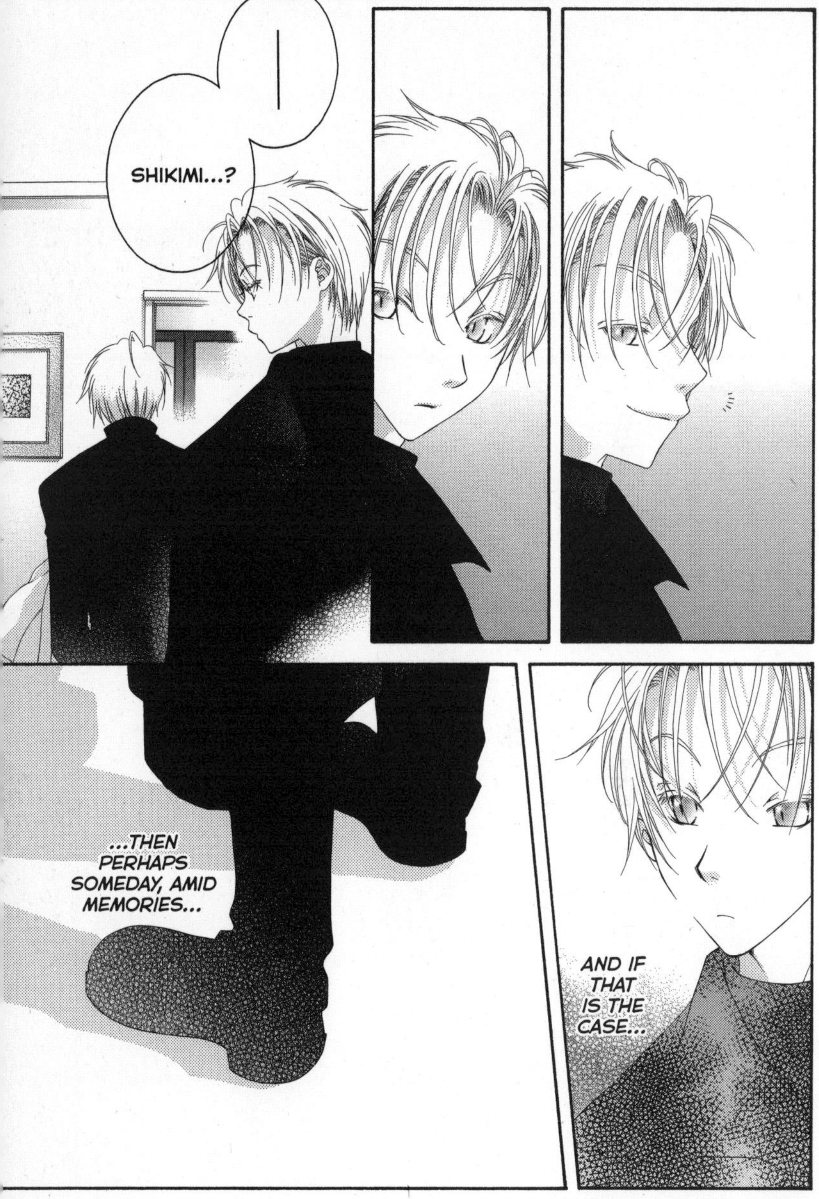
SHIKIMI...?
AND IF THAT IS THE CASE...
...THEN PERHAPS SOMEDAY, AMID MEMORIES...

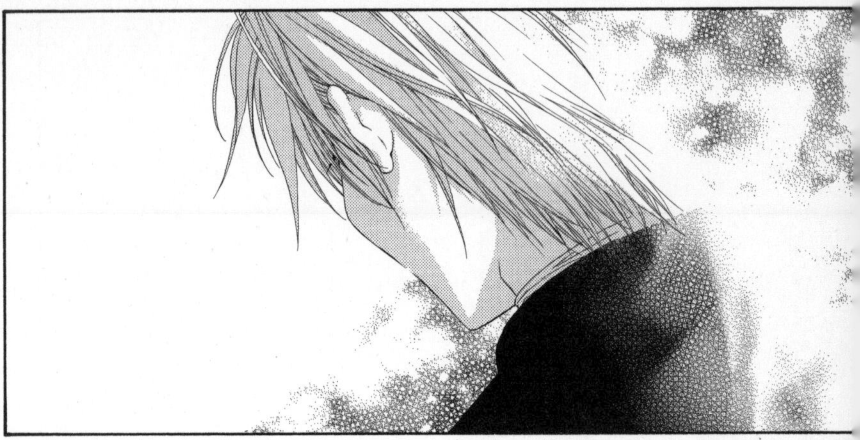
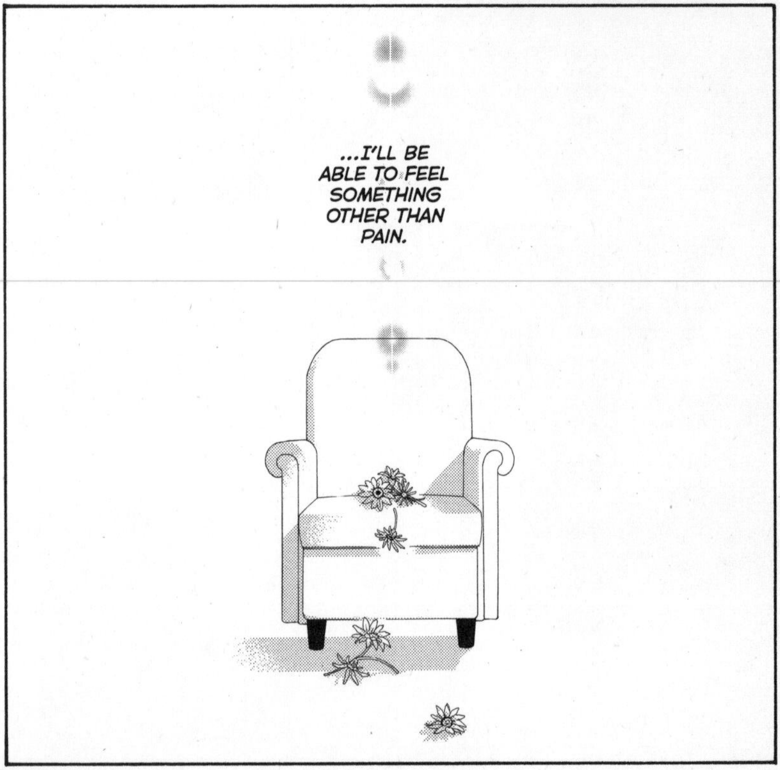
...I'LL BE ABLE TO FEEL SOMETHING OTHER THAN PAIN.

SUN THROUGH THE WINDOW ✢ END

BLACK SUN SILVER MOON

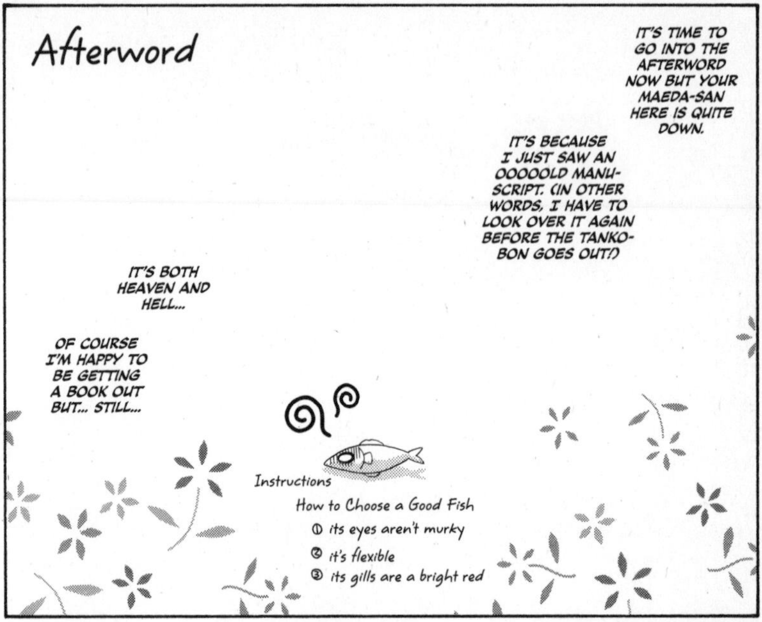
Afterword
IT'S TIME TO GO INTO THE AFTERWORD NOW BUT YOUR MAEDA-SAN HERE IS QUITE DOWN.
IT'S BECAUSE I JUST SAW AN OOOOOLD MANU-SCRIPT. (IN OTHER WORDS, I HAVE TO LOOK OVER IT AGAIN BEFORE THE TANKO-BON GOES OUT!)
IT'S BOTH HEAVEN AND HELL...
OF COURSE I'M HAPPY TO BE GETTING A BOOK OUT BUT... STILL...
Instructions
How to Choose a Good Fish
① its eyes aren't murky
② it's flexible
③ its gills are a bright red

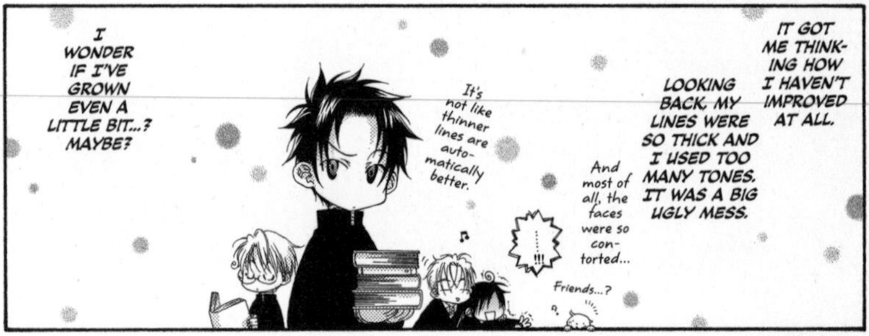
IT GOT ME THINK-ING HOW I HAVEN'T IMPROVED AT ALL.
LOOKING BACK, MY LINES WERE SO THICK AND I USED TOO MANY TONES. IT WAS A BIG UGLY MESS.
And most of all, the faces were so con-torted...
...!!!
Friends...?
It's not like thinner lines are auto-matically better.
I WONDER IF I'VE GROWN EVEN A LITTLE BIT...? MAYBE?

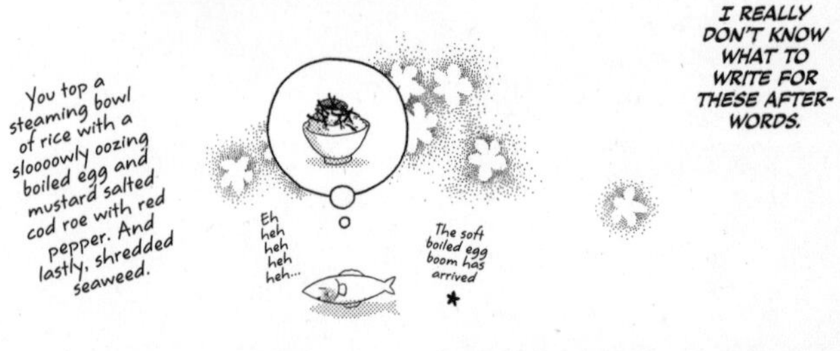
I REALLY DON'T KNOW WHAT TO WRITE FOR THESE AFTER-WORDS.
The soft boiled egg boom has arrived ★
Eh heh heh heh heh...
You top a steaming bowl of rice with a sloooowly oozing boiled egg and mustard salted cod roe with red pepper. And lastly, shredded seaweed.

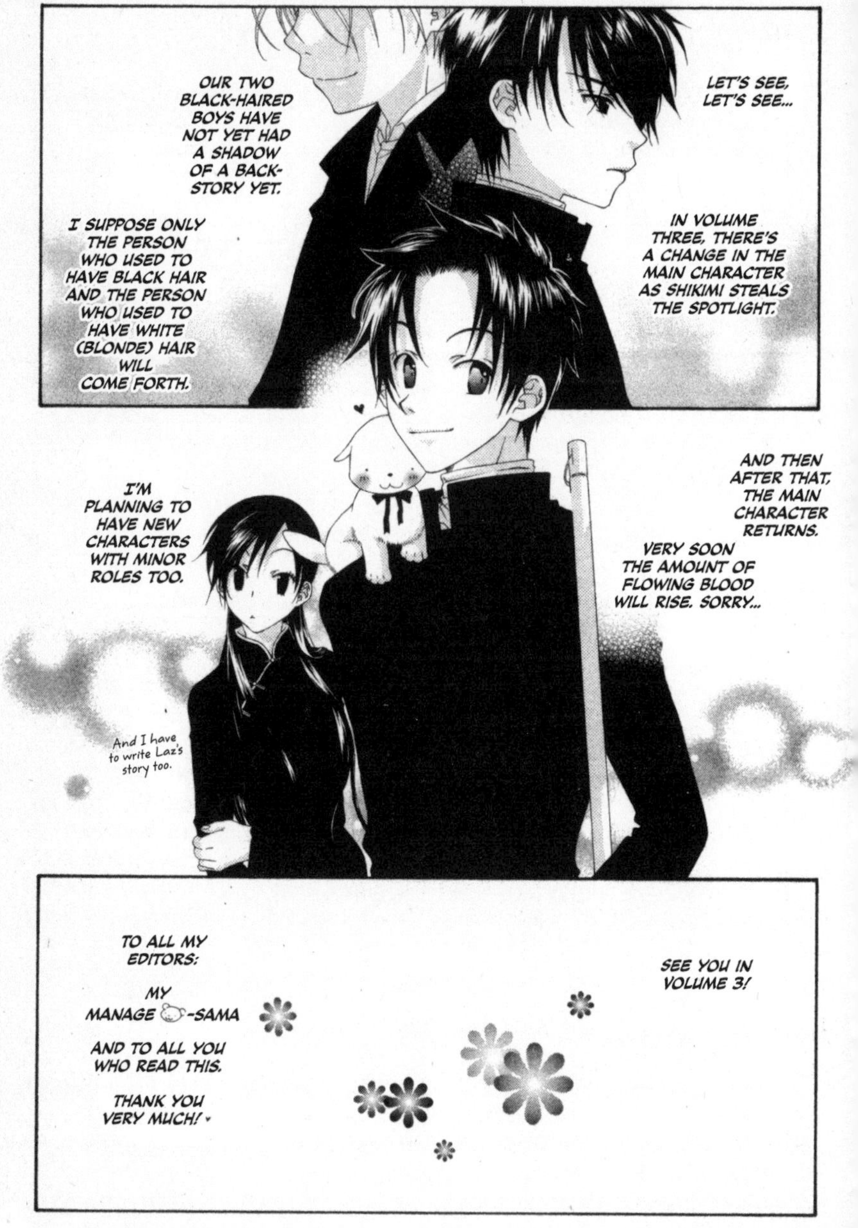
LET'S SEE, LET'S SEE...
IN VOLUME THREE, THERE'S A CHANGE IN THE MAIN CHARACTER AS SHIKIMI STEALS THE SPOTLIGHT.
OUR TWO BLACK-HAIRED BOYS HAVE NOT YET HAD A SHADOW OF A BACK-STORY YET.
I SUPPOSE ONLY THE PERSON WHO USED TO HAVE BLACK HAIR AND THE PERSON WHO USED TO HAVE WHITE (BLONDE) HAIR WILL COME FORTH.
AND THEN AFTER THAT, THE MAIN CHARACTER RETURNS.
VERY SOON THE AMOUNT OF FLOWING BLOOD WILL RISE. SORRY...
I'M PLANNING TO HAVE NEW CHARACTERS WITH MINOR ROLES TOO.
And I have to write Laz's story too.
SEE YOU IN VOLUME 3!
TO ALL MY EDITORS:
MY MANAGE -SAMA
AND TO ALL YOU WHO READ THIS.
THANK YOU VERY MUCH!

Blood Types
& Personality

Blood types are the same to Japanese as Horoscopes are to Westerners. They are believed to predict a person's personality and character, and to play a role in compatibility between partners.

The Traits

- Type A people are said to be hyper-organized and perfectionists. Taki fulfills his blood type's expectations with his perfectionism and tidiness.

- Type B people are called "The Hunters" as they are strong and a little unpredictable. This can make them a little incompatible with others...especially Type A's. That's why it's little surprise that Laz is a Type B with her individualist attitude and antagonistic relationship with Taki.

- Type O people are supposedly loyal and passionate. We will see a character down the road who is the embodiment of this quite a bit.

- Type AB people are cool and rational. No characters thus far have been revealed to be this blood type.

Fact vs. Fiction

Since the discovery of blood types at the turn of the 20th century, people have tried to find a connection between blood type and our value as humans. Some have justified race superiority through blood type frequencies and most Asian cultures swear by its association with personality. To this day, however, the only scientifically founded evidence that blood type has an effect on the body is that there is some correlation between race and dominant blood type, and specific blood types are susceptible to certain illnesses.

The Buzz

Almost everybody in Japan knows his or her blood type and there are plenty of venues willing to capitalize on this. Dating services use it as an indicator of good matches, and some companies have even been known to split up their work force according to blood type to group certain personalities together in an effort to increase productivity. For many, however, it's merely a source of entertainment and spice.

Translators Notes

Pg. 19 – Indou

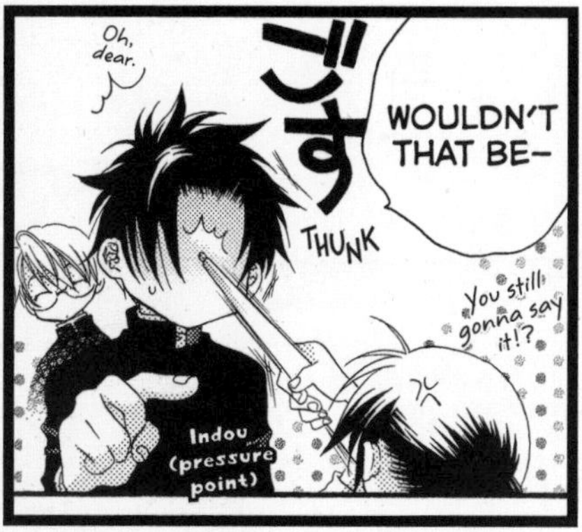
WOULDN'T THAT BE–
ずす
THUNK
Oh, dear.
You still gonna say it!?
Indou (pressure point)

The location of "indou" is right between the eyebrows. When pressure is applied to it, such ailments as hay fever, emphysema, nosebleeds, and vertigo can be cured. It is one of the many locations on the body believed to benefit the body's systems by the use of acupressure.

Pg. 171 – "A flower in each hand"

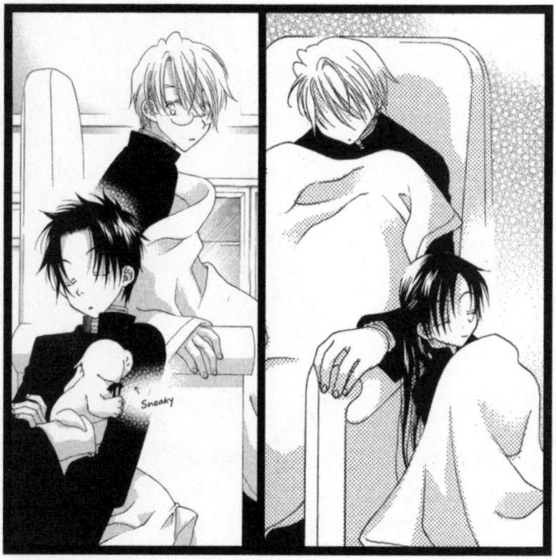
Sneaky

The Japanese phrase "to have a flower in each hand" means that a young man is being escorted by two lovely ladies. In this case, Sensei is apparently with two such lovely youths, Taki and Laz.

BONUS TALK

FLOWERS, TOYS, AND THE FROZEN MOON

That was a two-parter. The giant Agi (that was the cover illustration for the second half and then made into an extra image for this volume) was popular when it first came out. Regarding Laz, I'm often asked "So is it a guy or a girl?" to which I answer...it's what you see. At first I was a little unsure who I should have him fall for between Taki and Shikimi, but my editors helped me decide on Shikimi. "Taki already has Agi" is what they said. And so I am writing Taki and Laz to have a sort-of sibling relationship. It's a real help having those two, and then the one dog, offer comic relief.

DOOR OF LIGHT

What an appropriate title... After that I thought of a better one, but by then it was too late...
Even for ever-optimistic Taki there are plenty of things that scare him. I tried to draw just one of them here. Then there's Grey...I wanted to depict him in a creepier grooosss kind away but...he came out surprisingly clean.

LAZLO VARGA

15 years old.
Probably has Type B blood.

The type who thinks himself very strong and walks to the beat of his own drum.
I want to give him clothes that are easy to move around in. It doesn't look it at all but he really is a powerful Demon Slayer. He has tons of older siblings.
His height is 160cm more or less...

GREY

Age Unknown.
Given age is 26-27.

He may look like he's sturdy and strong but since he died of an illness, he might be rather meager when he takes off his clothes.
The reason he always keeps his coat on is because he'll burn in the sun... Which gets people asking me "but doesn't he move about during the day?"...heh heh.
He's the youngest of seven children.
He's probably a little over 180cm tall.

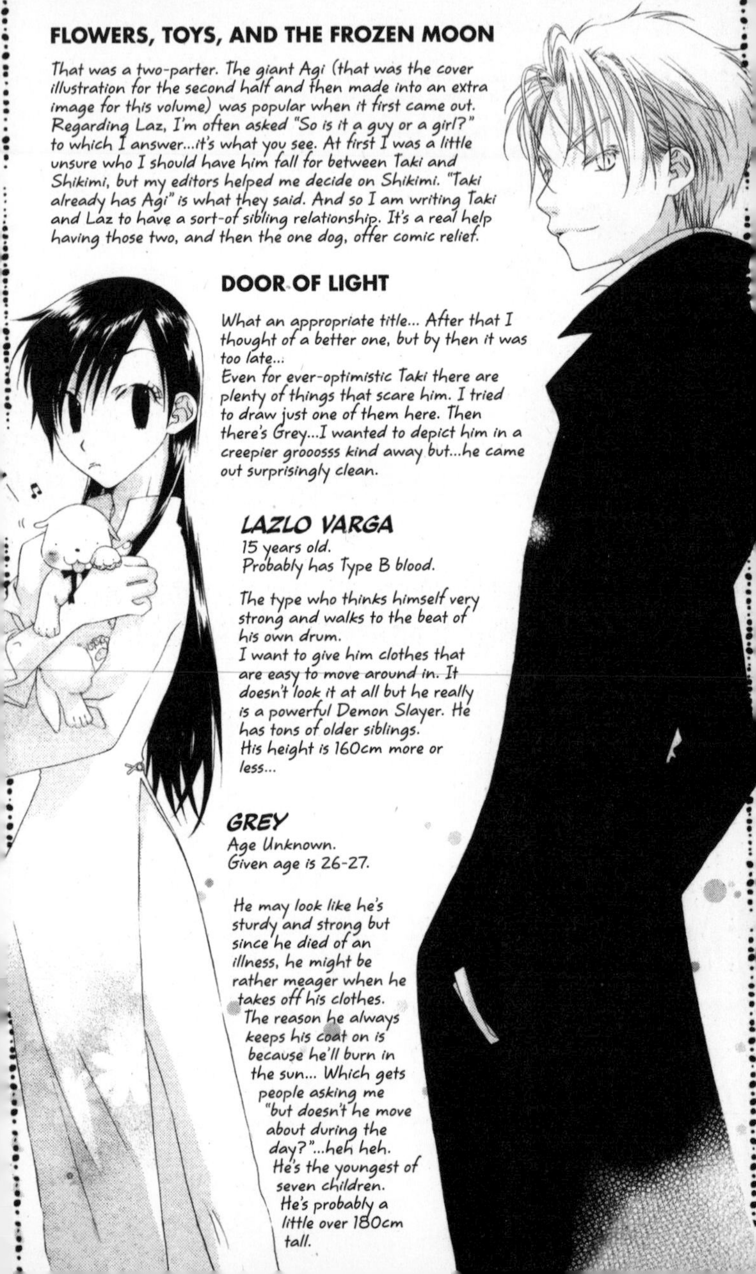

DARKNESS AWAITING NIGHT

This was another two-parter. The second part was just jam-packed, wasn't it? It might be that I should have taken it a little slower but when Shikimi started to lose it I just couldn't stop. Though actually I'd wanted to make that a far later chapter...
Getting angry, carrying on, and crying... it was a busy chapter for Shikimi. It was funny even for me to hear him saying "Stupid! Fool!" like that.

But I digress... When I'd be told by my friends that while Taki was at home, it didn't look like Shikimi had bathed once, I used to get so mad! (ha). Nah, but really since it doesn't last very long, it's okay.

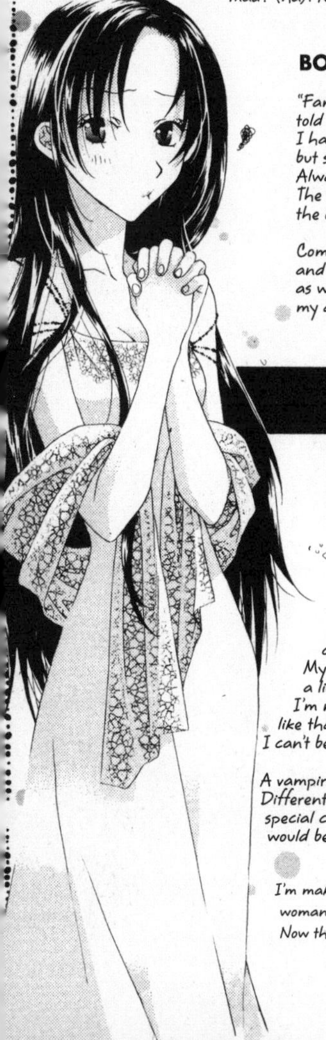

BONUS: SUN THROUGH THE WINDOW

"Family" and "Heartwarming" were the rare themes I was told to draw but...somehow it went in a different direction.... I had a choice between making a 12-pager and a 28-pager but since I was short on time I went with the short one. Always so slow at drawing...
The longer story I had to give up on was between Taki and the oldest of his little sisters.

Compared to volume 1, the story feels much more different and has grown far darker... And it only gets more like that as we go on. For those of you who like heartwarming stories, my apologies...

Honey blood

"Um...Do you think I could completely redo it...?"

"That's impossible."

...Is what we discussed but after looking over it, I couldn't **not** meddle with it. I did it and scrammed. My words of "I'll go along with it and not fix it" became a lie... I'm sorry.
I'm not very forgiving when it comes to the small things like that. I can't take it... Even so, I do the minimum. I can't believe I debuted with such a piece...

A vampire is, in other words, a corpse that's returned to life. Different regions have different terms for it and ignoring that special characteristic and looking at his origin, I suppose Grey would best be called a "strigoi"...I think?

I'm making it so that he's not related to the young woman in the story but he's the type to be sweet to his relatives. Now that I think about it, I didn't give her a name.

In Volume 3 of

BLACK SUN SILVER MOON

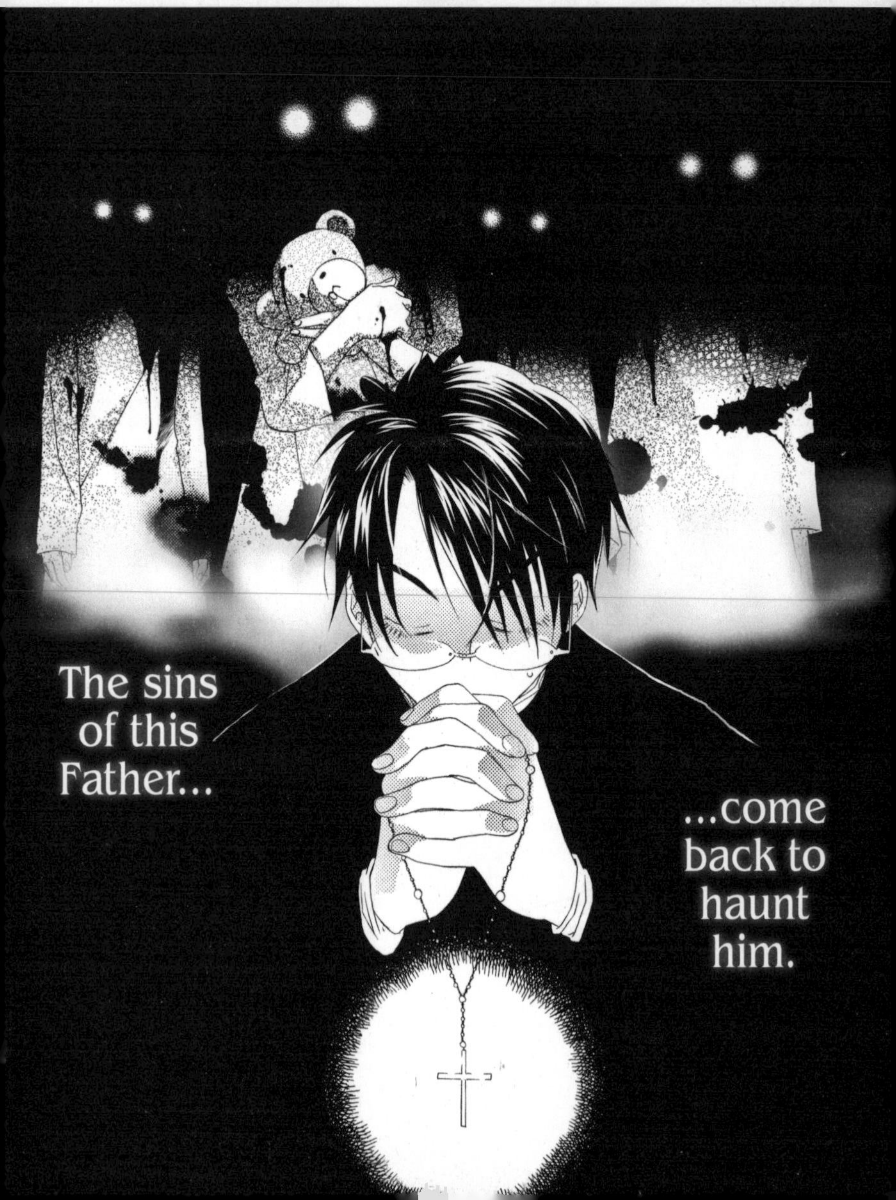

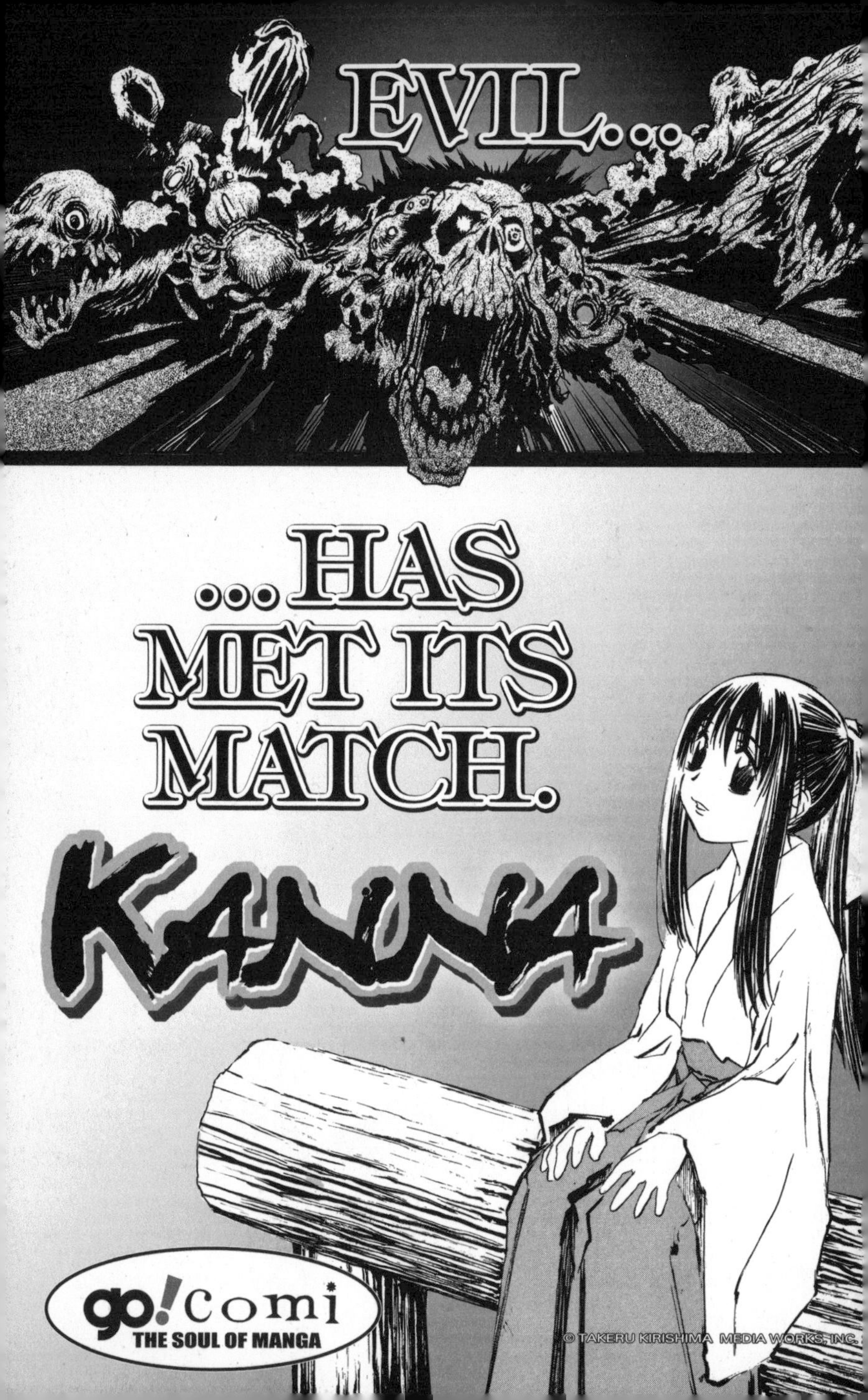
EVIL...
...HAS MET ITS MATCH.
KANNA
go!comi
THE SOUL OF MANGA
© TAKERU KIRISHIMA MEDIA WORKS, INC.

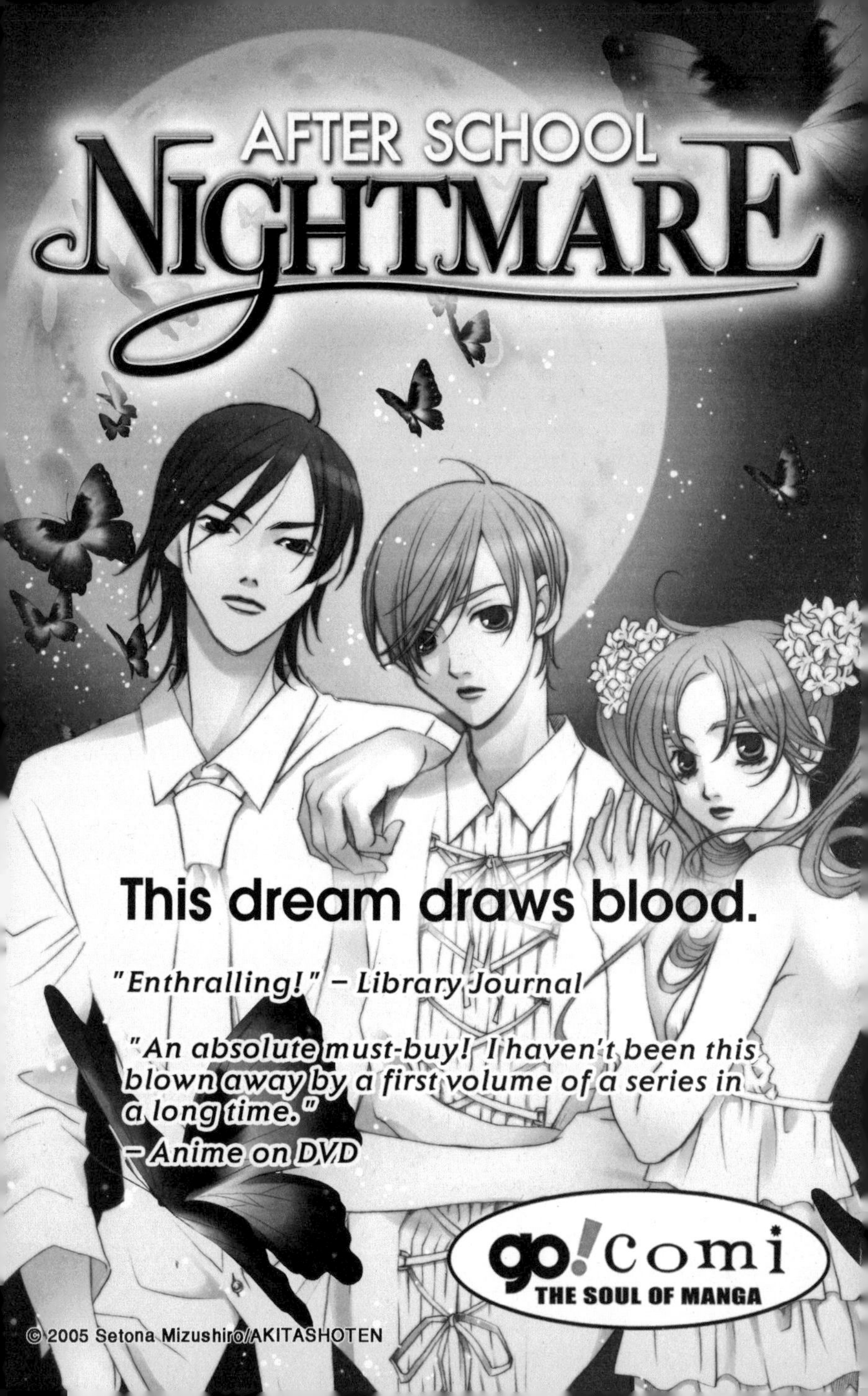
AFTER SCHOOL NIGHTMARE
This dream draws blood.
"Enthralling!" – Library Journal
"An absolute must-buy! I haven't been this blown away by a first volume of a series in a long time."
– Anime on DVD
go!comi
THE SOUL OF MANGA
© 2005 Setona Mizushiro/AKITASHOTEN

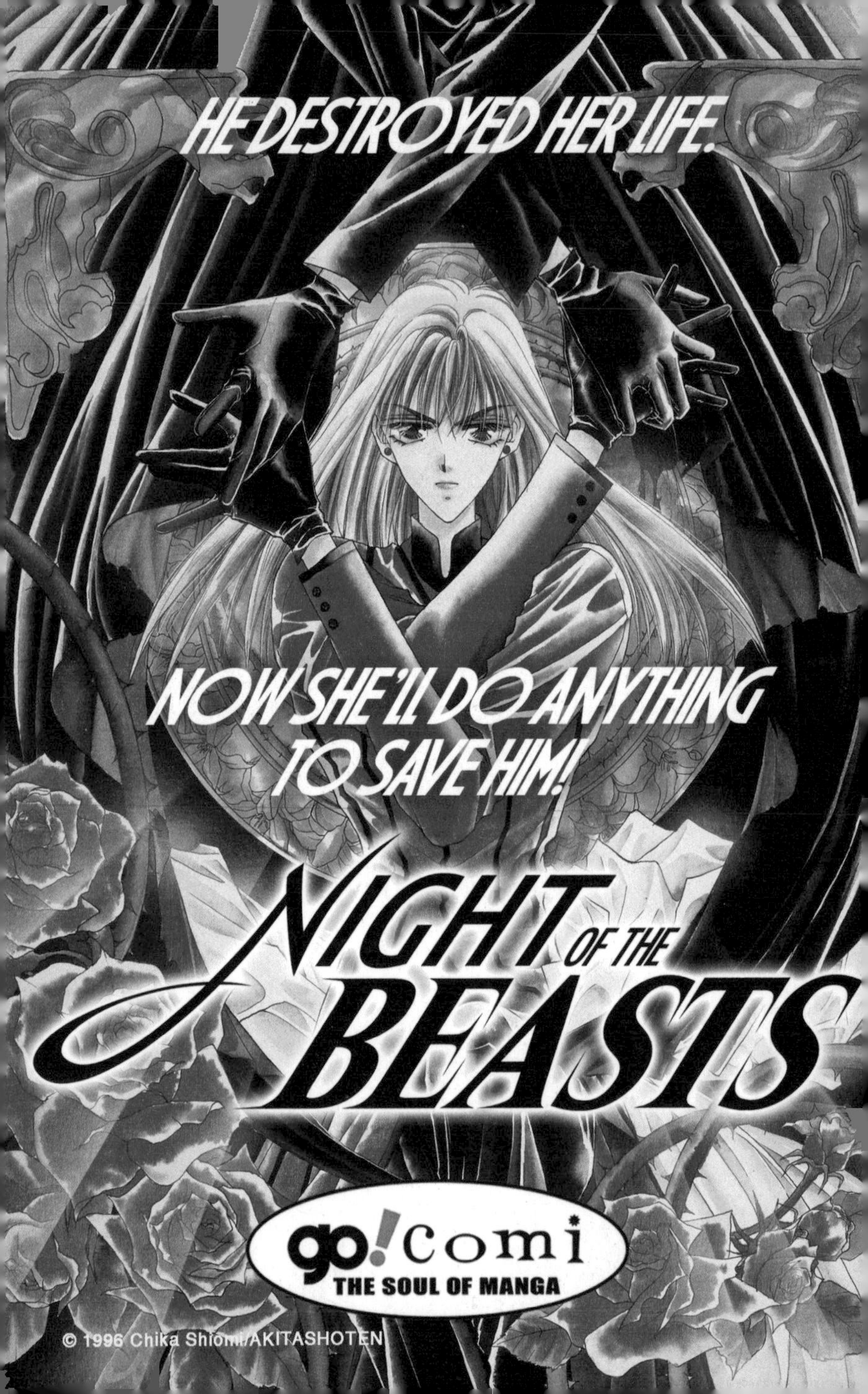
HE DESTROYED HER LIFE.
NOW SHE'LL DO ANYTHING TO SAVE HIM!
NIGHT OF THE BEASTS
go!comi
THE SOUL OF MANGA
© 1996 Chika Shiomi/AKITASHOTEN

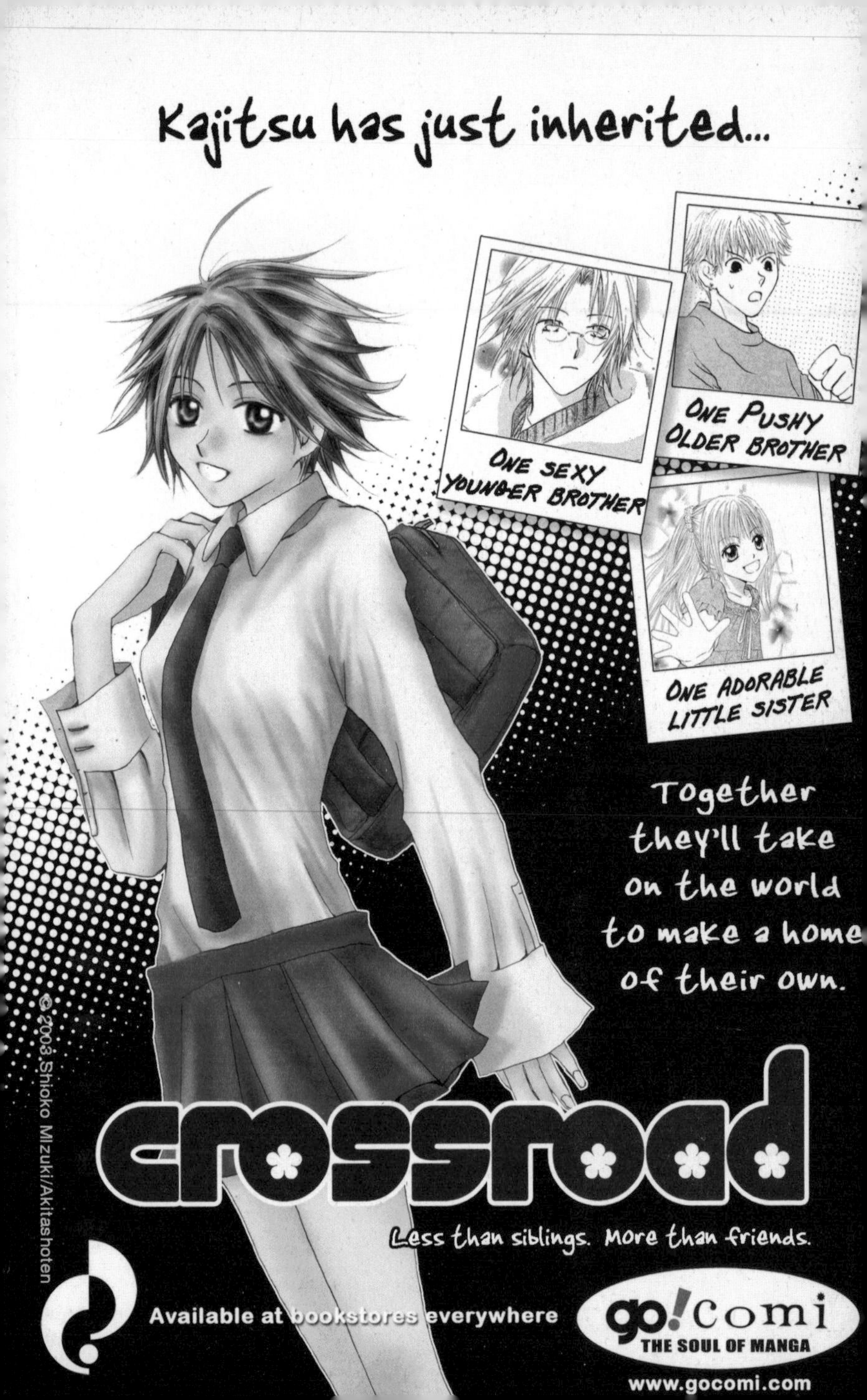

Kajitsu has just inherited...
One sexy younger brother
One pushy older brother
One adorable little sister
Together they'll take on the world to make a home of their own.
© 2003 Shioko Mizuki/Akitashoten
crossroad
Less than siblings. More than friends.
Available at bookstores everywhere
go!comi
THE SOUL OF MANGA
www.gocomi.com

DISCARD